Designing Integrated Industrial Policies Volume II

Very little has been written on industrialization and deindustrialization in Asia and Africa. This reference work sheds illuminating light upon the industrial development in Asia and Africa. It also provides an in-depth look at China's engagement and migrant labor in Africa. The book also addresses the roles of public-private partnership (PPP) and international development cooperation and how they are fundamental to industrialization in Asia and Africa.

Designing Integrated Industrial Policies will be a very useful reference, particularly as a how-to guide on industrial promotion and designing integrated industrial policies not only for economic growth and job creation but also for "inclusive" development. It offers country cases and illustrates useful tools for industrial policy simulation and for evidence-based policymaking through these concrete examples.

Shigeru Thomas Otsubo is Professor of Development Economics/International Development and the Director of the Economic Development Policy & Management Program at the Graduate School of International Development (GSID), Nagoya University, Japan.

Christian Samen Otchia is Associate Professor of Development Economics at the Graduate School of International Development (GSID), Nagoya University, Japan. He is also an affiliate member of the African Growth and Development Policy modeling consortium.

Routledge Studies in the Modern World Economy

International Trade and Sustainable Development
Economic, historical and moral arguments for asymmetric global trade
Bob Milward

Ageing, Long-term Care Insurance and Healthcare Finance in Asia
Sabrina Ching Yuen Luk

What Made Korea's Rapid Growth Possible?
Jungho Yoo

Economic Growth, Inequality and Crony Capitalism
The case of Brazil
Danilo Rocha Limoeiro

Emerging Bond Markets
Shedding light on trends and patterns
Tamara Teplova, Tatiana V. Sokolova and Qaiser Munir

Designing Integrated Industrial Policies
For inclusive development in Asia Volume I
Edited by Shigeru Thomas Otsubo and Christian Samen Otchia

Designing Integrated Industrial Policies
For inclusive development in Africa and Asia Volume II
Edited by Shigeru Thomas Otsubo and Christian Samen Otchia

The Economic Development of Bangladesh in the Asian Century
Prospects and perspectives
Edited by Quamrul Alam, Atiur Rahman and Shibli Rubayat Ul Islam

For more information about this series, please visit: www.routledge.com/Routledge-Studies-in-the-Modern-World-Economy/book-series/SE0432

Designing Integrated Industrial Policies Volume II

For Inclusive Development in Africa and Asia

Edited by Shigeru Thomas Otsubo and Christian Samen Otchia

Routledge
Taylor & Francis Group
LONDON AND NEW YORK

First published 2021
by Routledge
2 Park Square, Milton Park, Abingdon, Oxon OX14 4RN

and by Routledge
605 Third Avenue, New York, NY 10017

First issued in paperback 2022

Routledge is an imprint of the Taylor & Francis Group, an informa business

Publisher's Note
The publisher has gone to great lengths to ensure the quality of this reprint but points out that some imperfections in the original copies may be apparent.

British Library Cataloguing-in-Publication Data
A catalogue record for this book is available from the British Library

Library of Congress Cataloging-in-Publication Data
Names: Otsubo, Shigeru, editor. | Otchia, Christian Samen, editor.
Title: Designing integrated industrial policies / edited by
Shigeru Thomas Otsubo and Christian Samen Otchia.
Description: Abingdon, Oxon ; New York, NY : Routledge, 2021. |
Series: Routledge studies in the modern world economy |
Includes bibliographical references and index. |
Contents: Volume I. For inclusive development in Asia –
Volume II. For inclusive development in Africa and Asia.
Identifiers: LCCN 2020023099 (print) | LCCN 2020023100 (ebook) |
ISBN 9780367896355 (hardback : vol. 1) | ISBN 9780367896379 (hardback : vol. 2) |
ISBN 9781003020233 (ebook) | ISBN 9781003020240 (ebook)
Subjects: LCSH: Industrial policy–Developing countries. |
Industrial promotion–Developing countries. |
Economic development–Developing countries.
Classification: LCC HD3616.D443 D47 2021 (print) |
LCC HD3616.D443 (ebook) | DDC 338.9009172/4–dc23
LC record available at https://lccn.loc.gov/2020023099
LC ebook record available at https://lccn.loc.gov/2020023100

ISBN 13: 978-0-367-61176-7 (pbk)
ISBN 13: 978-0-367-89637-9 (hbk)
ISBN 13: 978-1-00-302024-0 (ebk)

DOI: 10.4324/9781003020240

Typeset in Galliard
by Newgen Publishing UK

Contents

List of figures ix
List of tables xii
List of contributors xiii
Preface xv
Acknowledgments xix
List of abbreviations xx

PART I
Industrial promotion in retrospect and prospect 1

1 Introduction: Leading issues in industrial promotion in today's globalized world 3
SHIGERU THOMAS OTSUBO AND CHRISTIAN SAMEN OTCHIA

2 The state of global manufacturing and risks of deindustrialization in the developing world 46
CHRISTIAN SAMEN OTCHIA AND SHIGERU THOMAS OTSUBO

3 The importance of manufacturing development and structural change for pro-poor growth 95
NOBUYA HARAGUCHI AND JUERGEN AMANN

PART III
Designing integrated industrial policies in Africa 133

13 Mechanisms and impacts of innovation on firm survival: Evidence from Sub-Saharan Africa 135
CHRISTIAN SAMEN OTCHIA

14 Local and foreign-owned SMEs' contribution to industrial development through knowledge spillovers in Africa: The case of Tanzania 161
JEAN-CLAUDE MASWANA AND HAWA MUNISI

15 Is China's growing interest in Africa a blessing or a curse for the continent's industrialization drive? 183
ERIC OSEI-ASSIBEY

16 A new partnership between business and development: A case study of Ethiopia's industrial development 203
IZUMI OHNO AND SAYOKO UESU

PART IV
Designing integrated industrial policies in sub- and super-national regions 237

17 Taking part in RCEP: CGE analysis focusing on industrial impact 239
KEN ITAKURA

18 Promoting both industrial development and regional convergence: Toward a regionally inclusive industrial policy 256
CARLOS MENDEZ

Name index 277
Subject index 282

Contents in Volume I

List of figures ix
List of tables xiii
List of contributors xvi
Preface xix
Acknowledgments xxiii
List of abbreviations xxiv

PART I
Industrial promotion in retrospect and prospect 1

1 Introduction: Leading issues in industrial promotion in today's globalized world 3
SHIGERU THOMAS OTSUBO AND CHRISTIAN SAMEN OTCHIA

2 The state of global manufacturing and risks of deindustrialization in the developing world 46
CHRISTIAN SAMEN OTCHIA AND SHIGERU THOMAS OTSUBO

3 The importance of manufacturing development and structural change for pro-poor growth 95
NOBUYA HARAGUCHI AND JUERGEN AMANN

PART II
Designing integrated industrial policies in Asia and the Pacific 133

4 A *de facto* industrial policy and its effects on the least developed countries 135
NOBUAKI MATSUNAGA AND KANA HARAGUCHI

5 Towards pro-poor industrial policies in Indonesia: Progress, challenges, and future directions 155
ANANG GUNAWAN, RULYUSA PRATIKTO, AND TEGUH DARTANTO

6 Industrial policy and development in Laos: Trade, industrial estates, and enterprise development 186
SOUKSAVANH VIXATHEP AND ALAY PHONVISAY

7 Promoting local SMEs through GVCs: A framework and case study of Laotian SMEs 217
CHANHPHASOUK VIDAVONG AND SHIGERU THOMAS OTSUBO

8 The role of Thailand's industrial promotion policies in ASEAN 244
CHALAIPORN AMONVATANA

9 Thailand's industrial policy: Its history and recent development 270
NALITRA THAIPRASERT AND PHANIDA ROIDOUNG

10 The process of change in the economic development model of the Pacific Island Countries under the influence of globalization 298
TETSUO UMEMURA

11 "Made in China 2025" and the recent industrial policy in China 337
KUCUK ALI AKKEMIK AND MURAT YÜLEK

12 Promoting exports by the ASEAN SMEs: Impediments, drivers, and conducive policies 365
UTUMPORN JITSUTTHIPHAKORN AND SHIGERU THOMAS OTSUBO

Name index 396
Subject index 401

Figures

1.1	Sustainable Development Goals for 2015–2030	5
1.2	Poverty-growth-inequality triangle under globalization	7
1.3	Share of employment in industry vs. GDP per capita	18
1.4	Share of value-added in industry vs. GDP per capita	18
1.5	Share of value-added in manufacturing vs. GDP per capita	19
1.6	Share of employment in service sector vs. GDP per capita	19
1.7	Share of value-added in service sector vs. GDP per capita	19
2.1	World manufacturing employment and real value-added	47
2.2	Log of per capita manufacturing value-added	50
2.3	Manufactures exports	53
2.4	G7, China, and 3 Risers' share of world manufacturing and real value-added	54
2.5	Convergence by income group	55
2.6	Convergence by time period	56
2.7	Manufacturing employment, growth index, and shares	57
2.8	Unconditional convergence in manufacturing labor productivity	58
2.9	Medium and high-tech manufacturing value-added and exports	60
2.10	Medium and high-tech manufacturing value-added and exports by income groups and regions	61
2.11	Correlation of per capita manufacturing value-added growth in consecutive decades	62
2.12	Correlation of employment share and manufacturing value-added share	64
2.13	Industrialization: estimated period share in early industrialized countries	66
2.14	Deindustrialization: estimated period share, post-1960	66
2.15	Deindustrialization: estimated period share by income group	67
2.16	Deindustrialization: estimated period share by geographical region	68
2.17	Deindustrialization: estimated period share by geographical sub-regions	69
2.18	Structural change for developed countries	71
2.19	Structural change: within Asia comparisons	72
2.20	Structural change: within Latin America comparisons	73

2.21 Structural change: within Sub-Saharan Africa comparisons 73
2.22 Structural change of the Big Three 75
2.23 Structural change: comparing the Big Three and East Asia 75
2.24 Structural change: comparing the Big Three and Southeast Asia 76
2.25 Structural change: comparing the Big Three and South Asia 77
2.26 Structural change: comparing the Big Three and India and China 78
2.27 Reduction in the share of manufacturing employment since the peak year of manufacturing employment 80
2.28 Changing landscape of the service sector 81
2.29 Sectoral growth rates of labor productivity 82
2.30 Manufacturing labor productivity versus manufacturing employment shares over time 83
2.31 Global value chains linkages by income group and region 85
2.32 Impact of global value chains on manufacturing 85
2.33 Special Economic Zones and manufacturing value-added 87
2.34 Special Economic Zones and manufacturing employment 88
3.1 GDP composition by income and sector 96
3.2 Manufacturing value-added contribution to GDP, 1950–2017 98
3.3 Pro-poor growth over time 102
3.4 Quintile distribution of per capita GDP, 1965–2017; individual country series by group 103
3.5 Value-added and employment share by income for selected manufacturing industry 105
3.6 Value-added by income for selected manufacturing industry 107
3.7 Employment-to-population by income for selected manufacturing industry 108
3.8 Accumulated value-added by income for selected manufacturing industry 110
3.9 Accumulated employment by income for selected manufacturing industry 110
3.10 Growth elasticities of value-added and employment/population by income for selected manufacturing industry 112
3.11 Changes in value-added over time by income for selected manufacturing industry 113
3.12 Changes in employment over time by income for selected manufacturing industry 114
3.13 Changes in accumulated value-added by income for selected manufacturing industry 115
3.14 Changes in accumulated employment by income for selected manufacturing industry 116
3.15 Domestic employment linkages over time by selected manufacturing industry 118
3.16 Domestic employment linkages: textiles, wearing apparel and leather industry over time for selected countries 119

3.17 Domestic employment linkages: shares over time by economic development and selected manufacturing industry 120
3.18 Manufacturing environmental sustainability 121
3.19 Manufacturing industry-level CO_2 emission per unit of real value-added 122
13.1 Firm survival by real GDP per capita (ln) 136
13.2 Firm survival by year 137
13.3 Firm survival by sector and by year 137
14.1 Annual employment growth (%) 169
14.2 Ranking of the top business obstacles for firms 169
14.3 Proportion of inputs of foreign origin 170
14.4 Inadequately educated workforce as a major constraint 171
14.5 Formal training 171
14.6 Use of foreign technology 172
14.7 Internationally recognized quality certification 172
15.1 Chinese trade and loans to Africa, 2000–2017 187
15.2 Chinese FDI flows to Africa 188
15.3 Gross revenues of Chinese construction projects in Africa 188
15.4 Chinese workers in Africa, 2009–2016 189
16.1 Financial flows from OECD-DAC countries to developing countries 204
16.2 Evolution of MDGs to SDGs 207
16.3 The case of SDG business in Senegal 213
16.4 GDP growth and forecasts, 2000–2024 (%) 217
16.5 External financial flows to Ethiopia (US$ million) 218
16.6 FDI inflows to Ethiopia, 2000–2018 (US$ million) 218
16.7 Trade-related ODA to Ethiopia (2006/2008–2017) 225
16.8 Major components of industrial support (2006/2008–2017) 225
17.1 Exports of value-added and GDP for 2005–2015 245
17.2 Viet Nam's exports of value-added for 2005–2015 245
17.3 Viet Nam's participation in global value chains for 2005–2015 246
17.4 GVC participation rates for 2005–2015 247
17.5 Import sourcing by agent 248
18.1 Productivity gaps across sectors in developing and developed countries 258
18.2 Structural change enhances growth only in Asia 259
18.3 Premature deindustrialization of developing countries 260
18.4 Regional incomes gaps in developing and developed countries 261
18.5 Spatial distribution of regional income gaps 262
18.6 Regional income convergence and divergence across countries 263
18.7 Structural change patterns of Japan 267
18.8 Regional convergence process of Japan 268
18.9 The role of structural change and within-sector growth on regional convergence 269

Tables

1.1	Poverty reduction under the MDGs, 1990–2015	4
1.2	Definitions of industrial policies	10
1.3	Classification of policy interventions	12
1.4	Summary of policy options under the WTO	28
2.1	Recent trends in global manufacturing output	49
3.1	Manufacturing industry classification based on ISIC Revision 3	127
3.2	Input-output table structure of n-sector economy	129
3.3	Employment contribution table structure of n-sector economy	131
13.1	Sample description	141
13.2	Transition matrix	142
13.3	Export patterns	143
13.4	Distribution of innovation by country	144
13.5	Descriptive statistics	145
13.6	Correlation matrix	147
13.7	Determinant of ICT adoption	150
13.8	Determinant of technological innovation	153
13.9	Determinant of firm survival	154
13.10	Mechanism	157
15.1	Definition and description of variables	194
15.2	Summary statistics	196
15.3	Effect of Chinese exports on manufacturing and industry GDP growth	197
15.4	Chinese FDI and manufacturing and industry GDP growth of African economies	198
15.5	Chinese contracts and manufacturing and industry GDP	199
16.1	Status of selected industrial parks in Ethiopia	220
17.1	Input-output table for Viet Nam	241
17.2	Multiregional input-output table for three regions in 2015	243
17.3	Impact of RCEP on bilateral trade volume, 2035	251
17.4	Decomposition of the export volume from Viet Nam to Japan, 2035	252
17.5	Impact of RCEP on real GDP, 2035	253
18.1	The role of structural change and within-sector growth on regional convergence	268

Contributors

Kucuk Ali Akkemik, Professor, Faculty of Economics, Yamaguchi University, Japan.

Juergen Amann, PhD Fellow, School of Economics, University of Nottingham, the United Kingdom.

Chalaiporn Amonvatana, Associate Professor, Faculty of Economics, Chulalongkorn University, Thailand.

Teguh Dartanto, Vice Dean of Academic Affairs, Faculty of Economics and Business, University of Indonesia, Indonesia.

Anang Gunawan, Regional Development Planner, Ministry of National Development Planning (BAPPENAS), Republic of Indonesia, Indonesia.

Kana Haraguchi, PhD student, Graduate School of International Cooperation Studies (GSICS), Kobe University, Japan.

Nobuya Haraguchi, Chief, Research and Industrial Policy Advice Division, Department of Policy Research and Statistics, United Nations Industrial Development Organization (UNIDO), Austria.

Ken Itakura, Professor, Graduate School of Economics, Nagoya City University, Japan.

Utumporn Jitsutthiphakorn, Senior Economist, Central Bank of Thailand, Thailand.

Jean-Claude Maswana, Professor, School of Economics, Ritsumeikan University, Japan.

Nobuaki Matsunaga, Professor, Graduate School of International Cooperation Studies (GSICS), Kobe University, Japan.

Carlos Mendez, Associate Professor, Economic Development Policy and Management Program, Graduate School of International Development (GSID), Nagoya University, Japan.

Hawa Munisi, Lecturer, Institute of Finance Management (IFM), Dar es Salaam, Tanzania.

Izumi Ohno, Professor, National Graduate Institute for Policy Studies (GRIPS), Japan.

Eric Osei-Assibey, Associate Professor, Department of Economics, University of Ghana, Ghana.

Christian Samen Otchia, Associate Professor, Economic Development Policy and Management Program, Graduate School of International Development (GSID), Nagoya University, Japan.

Shigeru Thomas Otsubo, Professor, Economic Development Policy and Management Program, Graduate School of International Development (GSID), Nagoya University, Japan.

Alay Phonvisay, Assistant Professor, Faculty of Economics and Business Management, National University of Laos, Laos.

Rulyusa Pratikto, Head of Graduate School of Social Science, Parahyangan Catholic University, Indonesia.

Phanida Roidoung, Economist, Public Debt Management Office, Ministry of Finance, Kingdom of Thailand, Thailand.

Nalitra Thaiprasert, Assistant Professor, Faculty of Economics, Chiang Mai University, Thailand.

Sayoko Uesu, Research Associate, National Graduate Institute for Policy Studies (GRIPS), Japan.

Tetsuo Umemura, Professor, Economic Development Policy and Management Program, Graduate School of International Development (GSID), Nagoya University, Japan.

Chanhphasouk Vidavong, Deputy Director, Trade Policy Research Division, Economic Research Institute for Industry and Trade, Ministry of Industry and Commerce, Lao People's Democratic Republic, Laos.

Souksavanh Vixathep, Associate Professor, School of Economics and Management, University of Hyogo, Japan.

Murat Yülek, Professor and President, OSTIM Technical University, Ankara, Turkey.

Preface

Rationale for this book

Promotion of sustained development of domestic industry is essential to boost economic growth and employment creation that will bring about poverty reduction in developing countries. Under a system of international economic institutions that allowed a relatively broad policy space, Japan and the other East Asian countries that have achieved rapid economic growth have succeeded in developing their infant and key industries under a diverse set of industrial policies. They have also achieved higher productivity, advanced their industries, and promoted exports by making use of foreign capital and imported technology; thus, all these countries have realized "catch-up" industrialization through the traditional follower-country strategy. However, developing countries in the 1980s and onward have had to promote their industries under economic globalization and international economic systems that were oriented toward free trade and overseas investment. They also had to face competitive pressure from China and India, and were forced to develop their own industries within a limited policy space, attributed to the expanded global production network of multinational corporations (MNCs), while under stricter international economic governance. In addition, global manufacturing activities have considerably shifted into higher value-added products that embody innovations in the forms of product upgrading and branding, leaving little room for most manufacturers in developing countries unless they are content with lower value-added activities. However, this share of lower value-added manufacturing has been declining on top of the declining share of manufacturing itself in the global economy. As a result, the world has come to witness the process of deindustrialization, often at a premature stage of economic development, in many developing countries.

Taking into consideration that those economies of developing countries have been caught in low-income and middle-income traps, and that today the term "industrial policy" is considered in a rather broader sense as a collective development policy which is being applied more widely, this book, which is an outcome of international joint research projects financed by the Japan Society for the Promotion of Science (JSPS), intends to focus on the design of an "integrated industrial policy." The central aim of this book is to promote inclusive and sustainable industrialization (Sustainable Development Goal [SDG] 9) and to promote sustained, inclusive, and sustainable economic growth, as well as full and productive employment (SDG 8) in order to end poverty (SDG 1).

This book will do the following: (1) present the history and current state of industrialization and deindustrialization in developing countries; (2) introduce typologies of industrial policies and surrounding arguments; (3) discuss the importance of the manufacturing sector and the reasons for deindustrialization; (4) account for the roles of SMEs and global value chains (GVCs); (5) use both macro-econometric and firm-based micro-econometric analyses of (de)industrialization; (6) present country cases as concrete examples; (7) discuss and analyze topical issues such as the role of China in Africa's industrialization; (8) present tools for industrial policy simulation for evidence-based policymaking; and (9) address the roles of public-private partnership (PPP) and international development cooperation in promoting industrial development in developing countries. All in all, this book intends to serve as an integrated and balanced reference work which offers policymakers, researchers, and students in the international development cooperation community guidance in designing integrated industrial policies for inclusive development in today's globalized world.

Uniqueness of this book

The salient features of this book are the following:

1. It is compiled as the result of a well-coordinated four-year international joint research project participated in by 16 academic and research institutions with researchers from 11 countries (Austria, Bolivia, the Democratic Republic of Congo, Ghana, Indonesia, Japan, Laos, Tanzania, Thailand, Turkey, and the UK), with support from the Japan Society for Promotion of Science (JSPS).
2. It contains conceptual/typological discussions, rigorous empirical studies both at the macro- and micro-economic (firm) levels, with an interesting set of country case studies, and a collection of cross-cutting thematic issues and analyses.
3. It does not rehash the success stories of Japan and the Asian Tigers (Hong Kong, Singapore, South Korea, and Taiwan) as they have already been well documented and the global economic environment today is very different from when the "East Asian miracle" was created.
4. Instead, it focuses on ordinary developing countries in Asia and Africa, including countries such as Indonesia and Thailand, where governments have tended not to subscribe to industrial promotion by so-called industrial policies.
5. It includes analyses on "China in Africa" and an analysis on the future of China's industrial development "Made in China 2025" and its impact on developing countries.
6. It is produced as a joint venture between academic researchers and policymakers.

7. The contributors include those with working experiences in trend-setting international organizations, such as the UN, UNIDO, and the World Bank, as well as those working for national institutions in developing countries which deal with policymaking and its execution in industrial promotion, such as the National Developing Planning Agency of Indonesia (BAPPENAS), the Ministry of Industry and Commerce of the Laotian government, and the Ministry of Finance, and the Central Bank of Thailand.
8. It is also a contribution to the worldwide discussion of SDGs, as this book intends to present discussions/analyses of industrial promotion and industrial policies not only for the sake of economic growth and job creation but also for "inclusive" development. To this end, the book addresses impacts on income and spatial (geographical) inequalities, thereby capturing industrial promotion in the context of the poverty-growth-inequality (PGI) triangle.

At present, there is no single reference book that intends to serve as a well-balanced guide for those in the international development community on the subjects of inclusive industrial promotion in the PGI context in order to provide integrated policy packages that bridge interrelated Sustainable Development Goals (including SDGs 1, 8, and 9).

Readership of this book

The book's intended readership includes the following:

1. Policymakers (including their bureaucratic brains) and practitioners in the international development community, such as the governments (and aid-related agencies) of developed and developing countries, international organizations, NGOs, and so forth.
2. Academics, students, and other researchers seeking well-balanced and rather comprehensive references regarding the role of industrialization in development, the impacts of globalization on industrialization and deindustrialization, and the integrated strategies for industrial promotion of inclusive development.
3. International and local business leaders who wish to understand key trends in the ongoing process of (de)industrialization and the surrounding policy frameworks, including new public-private partnerships (PPPs).

Structure of this book

Having reconfirmed the importance of proactive industrial promotion policies for sustained economic growth and poverty reduction in developing countries, recent discussions focus more on design, implementation, and evaluation for evidence-based policymaking. It is also widely recognized today that policy coordination and integration are highly desired for industrial policies to take on the challenges of producing "inclusive" development under the SDGs framework. In order for us to deal with these issues and challenges in industrial promotion, this book consists of the following four parts in two volumes (Volume I and Volume II).

Part I Industrial Promotion in Retrospect and Prospect
Part II Designing Integrated Industrial Policies in Asia and the Pacific
Part III Designing Integrated Industrial Policies in Africa
Part IV Designing Integrated Industrial Policies in Sub- and Super-National Regions

Part I consists of three introductory chapters. Chapter 1 presents industrial promotion and industrial policies in retrospect and prospect. It provides concepts, definitions, and issues to be discussed in this volume while stressing the need for modern and integrated strategies. It also captures industrial promotion in the poverty-growth-inequality (PGI) triangle in order for us to discuss "inclusive" strategies. Chapter 2 presents data and descriptive statistics that constitute a common background. What do we really know about the changing state of global manufacturing? How and why has the trend of premature deindustrialization emerged in many parts of the developing world? Chapter 3 revisits the importance of manufacturing and the risks associated with premature deindustrialization in pursuing pro-poor growth and inclusive development. Chapters 2 and 3, together, present a holistic picture of the past and present state of industrialization, structural change, and their impact on increases in value-added and employment.

As most of the chapters in this book deal with issues/topics of industrial promotion not only by applying theories and conceptual frameworks but also in relation to existing problems and policies within a specific country context, the next two parts of the book present chapters by countries used as cases or targets of rigorous economic/econometric analyses. Part II (Chapters 4–12 in Volume I) is for countries in Asia and the Pacific region. Part III (Chapters 13–16) presents chapters that take countries in Africa as their cases. However, this does not mean that any particular topic is only relevant to a particular set of countries or a region. Instead, it means that realistic industrial policy discussion needs cases and targets on the ground.

Part IV contains two chapters that deal with regional issues/topics of industrial promotion. Chapter 17 discusses the impact of super-national regional economic cooperation such as the Regional Trading Agreement (RTA) and the Regional Comprehensive Economic Partnership (RCEP) for industrial promotion at the regional level. Chapter 18 discusses regional parity and regional "inclusiveness" in the context of sub-national regions as a country pursues industrial development in a balanced or unbalanced manner. Chapter 17 introduces policy simulations using Computable General Equilibrium (CGE) models. Chapter 18 introduces the analyses of regional convergence/divergence to investigate the interaction between industrial development and regional convergence.

Acknowledgments

Ms Lam Yong Ling, Commissioning Editor, Taylor & Francis Asia Pacific (Routledge, Singapore) and her assistants, Ms Phua Samantha and Mr Tan Sheng Bin, have been dedicated to this work in cooperating with us from planning, creating, and including up to publication of this book. On behalf of our team, we would like to express our deepest gratitude to them.

Our special thanks go to our Research Assistants for this phase of the project, Dr Sai Seng Sai, Dr Ibrahim Issifu, Dr Chanhphasouk Vidavong, Mr Anang Budi Gunawan, and Ms Utumporn Jitsutthiphakorn, who helped in processing data, conducting econometric analyses, and editing the work. Chanhphasouk, Anang, and Utumporn also contributed chapters to this book as development policymakers in the government ministries in their home countries. Our thanks also go to others who served as Research Assistants during the past phases of this research project, and who also participated as contributors to this book: Dr Nalitra Thaiprasert, Dr Eric Osei-Assibey, Dr Teguh Dartanto, Dr Phanida Roidoung, and Dr Carlos Mendez. They contributed chapters to this book as professors or development practitioners in their countries in Asia and Africa.

We would also like to express our sincere appreciation to Dr Adam Smith (yes, Adam Smith) for proofreading the English manuscripts. Last but not the least, we, the editors of this book, wish to extend our sincere gratitude to all the contributors/writers for their participation.

On a personal note, I, Shigeru Thomas Otsubo, wish to express my gratitude to my wife Mikako. Her devoted support keeps me hopeful, depite being a researcher in the process of losing the ability to see. Christian Samen Otchia also wishes to express his gratitude to his wife Hiroko for her inspiring assistance and constant understanding and patience.

March 2020
Shigeru Thomas Otsubo
Christian Samen Otchia

Abbreviations

2SLS	Two-stage Least Squares regression
3 Risers	India, Korea, and Indonesia
3SLS	Three-stage Least Squares regression
ADB	Asian Development Bank
ADLI	Agricultural Development Led Industrialization
AEC	ASEAN Economic Community
AFAS	ASEAN Framework Agreement on Services
AFC	Asian financial crisis
AFTA	ASEAN Free Trade Agreement
AGOA	African Growth and Opportunity Act
AI	Artificial Intelligence
AIA	ASEAN Investment Area
AKP	The Justice and Development Party (in Turkish: Adaletve Kalkınma Partisi)
AOTS	Association for Overseas Technical Cooperation for Sustainable Partnership, Japan
ARDL	autoregressive distributed lag
ASEAN	Association of Southeast Asian Nations
ATC	Agreement on Textiles and Clothing
ATT	assisted technology transfer
AU	African Union
B.E.	Buddhist Era
BAPPENAS	National Development Planning Agency of Indonesia
BB	Bureau of the Budget
BCtA	Business Call to Action
BGMEA	Bangladesh Garment Manufacturers and Exporters Association
Big Three	Japan, Korea, and Taiwan
BMZ	Federal Ministry for Economic Development and Cooperation, Germany
BOI	Board of Investment
BoP	balance of payment
BOP	base of the pyramid
BOT	Bank of Thailand

BRI	Belt and Road Initiative
BSS	business supporting survey
CAE	Chinese Academy of Engineering
CAIT	Climate Analysis Indicators Tool
CAMARTEC	Center for Agricultural Mechanization and Rural Technology
CARI	China-Africa Research Initiative
CC	Central Committee (China)
CCP	Chinese Communist Party
CCTV	closed-circuit television
CDE	constant difference of elasticities
CDM	Crepon, Duguet, and Mairesse
CEP	comprehensive economic partnership
CEPT	common effective preferential tariff
CES	constant elasticity of substitution
CGE	computable general equilibrium
CIP	competitive industrial performance
CLMV	Cambodia, Laos, Myanmar, and Vietnam
CO_2	carbon dioxide
COMECON	Council for Mutual Economic Assistance
COMESA	Common Market for Eastern and Southern Africa
COSTECH	Commission for Science and Technology, Tanzania
CSC	China State Council
CSOs	civil society organizations
CSR	corporate social responsibility
CTI	Confederation of Tanzanian Industries
DAC	Development Assistance Committee
DANIDA	Danish International Development Agency
DFAT	Department of Foreign Affairs and Trade, Australia
DFID	Department for International Development, UK
DIV	Development Innovation Ventures
DOSMEP	Department of Small and Medium-Sized Enterprise Promotion
DRC	Democratic Republic of the Congo
EAP	East Asia and Pacific
EBA	Everything-But-Arms
ECA	Europe and Central Asia
ECCSA	Ethiopian Chamber of Commerce and Sectoral Association (ECCSA)
EEC	Eastern Economic Corridor
EECO	Eastern Economic Corridor Office
EIC	Ethiopian Investment Commission
EKI	Ethiopia Kaizen Institute
EOI	Export-Oriented Industrialization
EPPCF	Ethiopia Public Private Consultative Forum
EPRDF	Ethiopian People's Revolutionary Democratic Front
EPZs	export processing zones

ERIA	Economic Research Institute for ASEAN and East Asia
ERMs	Extended Regression Models
ESCAP	Economic and Social Commission for Asia and the Pacific (in Thailand)
ETIDI	Ethiopian Textile Industry Development Institute
EU	European Union
FDI	foreign direct investment
FDRE	Federal Democratic Republic of Ethiopia
FOCAC	Forum on China-Africa Cooperation
FPO	Fiscal Policy Office
FSM	Federated States of Micronesia
FTAAP	free trade area of the Asia-Pacific
FYP	Five-Year Plan
G7	Group of Seven (Canada, France, Germany, Italy, Japan, the United Kingdom, and the United States)
GATS	General Agreement on Trade in Services
GATT	General Agreement on Tariffs and Trade
GCI	Global Competitiveness Index
GDA	Global Development Alliance
GDP	Gross Domestic Product
GGDC	Groningen Growth and Development Center
GIZ	Deutsche Gesellschaft für Internationale Zusammenarbeit
GMM	generalized method of moments
GNP	gross national product
GOI	Government of Indonesia
GOI-IMF	Government of Indonesia-International Monetary Fund
GOL	Government of Laos
GRIPS	National Graduate Institute for Policy Studies, Japan
GSID	Graduate School of International Development, Nagoya University, Japan
GSP	generalized system of preferences
GTAP	Global Trade Analysis Project
GTP	Growth and Transformation Plan, Ethiopia
GTZ	Deutsche Gesellschaft für Technische Zusammenarbeit
GVCs	global value chains
H&M	Hennes and Mauritz
HCI	Human Capital Index
HICs	high-income countries
HIP	Hawassa Industrial Park, Ethiopia
ICOR	incremental capital-output ratio
ICT	information and communication technology
IDE-JETRO	Institute of Developing Economies, Japan External Trade Organization
IDN	Indonesia
IDR	Industrial Development Report

IEA	International Energy Agency
IFC	International Financial Corporation
IFCT	Industrial Finance Corporation of Thailand
IFR	International Federation of Robotics
ILO	International Labour Organization
IMF	International Monetary Fund
INDSTAT	Industrial Statistics Database of the UNIDO
I-O	input-output
IoT	Internet of Things
IPD	Initiative for Policy Dialogue
IPDC	Industrial Park Development Corporation, Ethiopia
IPRs	Intellectual Property Rights
IPs	industrial parks
IR	Industrial Revolution
IR1	First Industrial Revolution
IR2	Second Industrial Revolution
IR3	Third Industrial Revolution
IR4	Fourth Industrial Revolution
ISI	import-substitution industrialization
ISIC	International Standard Industrial Classification
ISO	International Organization for Standardization
IT	information and technology
JETRO	Japan External Trade Organization
JICA	Japan International Cooperation Agency
KHM	Cambodia
KI	key indicators
LAC	Latin America and Caribbean
Lao PDR	Lao Peoples' Democratic Republic
LCR	local content requirement
LDCs	least developed countries
LICs	low-income countries
LIP	Law on Investment Promotion
LMICs	lower middle-income countries
LNCCI	Lao National Chamber of Commerce and Industry
LSB	Lao Statistic Bureau
LTA	Long-Term Arrangement on International Trade in Cotton Textiles
M&E	monitoring and evaluation
MDGs	Millennium Development Goals
MEDA	Mennonite Economic Development Associates
MENA	Middle East and North Africa
METI	Ministry of Economy, Trade and Industry, Japan
MFA	Multi-Fiber Arrangement
MFN	most-favored-nation
MHT	medium and high-tech

MIC 2025	Made in China 2025
MIDA	Malaysian Investment Development Authority
MIIT	Ministry of Industry and Information Technology, China
MIRAB	Migration (MI), Remittance (R), Foreign Aid (A), and Public Bureaucracy (B)
MITI	Ministry of International Trade and Industry, Japan
MJTD	Myanmar Japan Thilawa Development, Limited
MMR	Myanmar
MNC	multinational corporation
MOFA	Ministry of Foreign Affairs, Japan
MOFCOM	Ministry of Commerce of the People's Republic of China
MOI	Ministry of Industry
MOIC	Ministry of Industry and Commerce
MOU	memorandum of understanding
MP3EI	Master Plan for Acceleration and Expansion of Indonesia Economic Development
MPI	Ministry of Planning and Investment
MRIO	Multi-Regional Input-Output
MRTA	mega regional trade agreement
MVA	manufacturing value-added
MWP	Minimum Wage Province
MYS	Malaysia
NA	National Assembly
NAAMA	National Accounts – Analysis of Main Aggregates
NDRC	National Development and Reform Commission, China
NEDB	National Economic Development Board
NEDCO	National Estates & Designing Consultancy
NEM	New Economic Mechanism (*Chintanakan Mai*)
NEPAD	New Partnership for Africa's Development
NESDB	National Economic and Social Development Board
NGOs	non-governmental organizations
NIES	newly industrializing economies
NIFT	National Institute of Fashion Technology, India
NIGP	National Income Generation Program
NPC	National People's Congress, China
NPOs	non-profit organizations
NSEDP	National Socio-Economic Development Plan
ODA	Official Development Assistance
ODI	outward direct investment
OECD	Organization for Economic Co-operation and Development
OECF	Overseas Economic Cooperation Fund, Japan
OJT	on-the-job training
OOF	other official flows
OPM	Office of the Prime Minister

PASDEP	Plan for Accelerated and Sustained Development to End Poverty, Ethiopia
P-G-I	poverty-growth-inequality
PGI triangle	poverty-growth-inequality triangle
PHL	the Philippines
PISU	Private Investment in State Undertaking Act
PM	Prime Minister
PMG	pooled mean group
PPP	public-private partnership
PPP	purchasing power parity
PPSU	Public-Private in State Undertaking Act
PVH	Phillips-Van Heusen Corporation
QCD	quality, cost, delivery
R&D	research and development
RCA	revealed comparative advantage
RCEP	regional comprehensive economic partnership
RCT	randomized controlled trial
REER	real effective exchange rate
RFI	resource for infrastructure
RIIP	regionally inclusive industrial policy
RMG	ready-made garment
RoO	rules of origin
ROW	rest of the world
RTA	Regional Trade Agreement
(r)VA	(real, i.e. deflated) value-added
S&T	science and technology
SAM	social accounting matrix
SC	smiling curve
SCMs	subsidies and countervailing measures
SDGs	Sustainable Development Goals
SDPRP	Sustainable Development and Poverty Reduction Program, Ethiopia
SEC	State Economic Commission, China
SEI	strategic emerging industries
SEPO	State Enterprise Policy Office
SETC	State Economic and Trade Commission, China
SEZ	Special Economic Zone
SIDA	Swedish International Development Cooperation Agency
SIDO	Small Industries Development Organization
SIDS	Small Islands Developing States
SITES	small island tourists economies
SMEPDC	Small and Medium-Sized Enterprise Promotion and Development Committee
SMEs	small and medium-sized enterprises

SMRJ	Organization for Small and Medium Enterprises and Regional Innovation, Japan
SOE	state-owned enterprise
SPC	State Planning Commission, China
SRC	Structural Reform Commission, China
SSA	Sub-Saharan Africa
STA	Short-Term Arrangement Regarding International Trade in Cotton Textiles
STI	science, technology and innovation
TAFSIO	Tanzanian Federation of Small Industries Organizations
TEMDO	Tanzania Engineering and Manufacturing Design Organization
THA	Thailand
TICAD	Tokyo International Conference on African Development
TIKA	Turkish International Cooperation and Development Agency
TIRDO	Tanzania Industrial Research Development Organization
TMB	Thai Military Bank
TOURAB	Tourism (TOU), Remittance (R), Foreign Aid (A), and the Public Bureaucracy (B)
TPI	tourism penetration ratio
TPP	Trans-Pacific Partnership
TRIMS	trade-related investment measures
TRIPS	trade-related aspects of intellectual property rights
TTIP	Transatlantic Trade and Investment Partnership
TUSKON	Turkish Confederation of Businessmen and Industrialists
TVET	Technical and Vocational Education and Training
UK	United Kingdom
UMICs	upper middle-income countries
UN	United Nations
UN/CEFACT	United Nations Centre for Trade Facilitation and Electronic Business
UNCTAD	United Nations Conference on Trade and Development
UNDP	United Nations Development Programme
UNECA	United Nations Economic Commission for Africa
UNICEF	United Nations Children's Fund
UNIDO	United Nations Industrial Development Organization
UNSTAT	United Nations Statistics Division
UNU-MERIT	United Nations University – Maastricht Economic and Social Research Institute on Innovation and Technology
URT	United Republic of Tanzania
US	United States of America
USAID	United States Agency for International Development
USD	US dollar
VETA	Vocational Educational and Training Authority
VNM	Vietnam

WB	World Bank
WBES	World Bank Enterprise Survey
WDI	World Development Indicators
WEF	World Economic Forum
WGI	world governance indicators
WIOD	world input-output database
WIOT	world input-output tables
WTO	World Trade Organization
WWII	World War II

Part I

Industrial promotion in retrospect and prospect

1 Introduction

Leading issues in industrial promotion in today's globalized world

Shigeru Thomas Otsubo and Christian Samen Otchia

1.1 Prologue

Following the UN Millennium Development Goals (MDGs) era that ended in 2015 with mixed results, the world development community has set about the new era with the UN Sustainable Development Goals (SDGs) as the post-2015 global goals.[1] In search of a sustainable society and a sustainable planet, the SDGs include 17 goals expanded from the 8 goals under the MDGs. Aside from the major changes made from the MDGs to the SDGs such as (1) an application of the goals not only to the developing world but also to the developed world (the global agenda); (2) diversifying areas where "sustainability" should apply; and (3) collaborative efforts to cope with factors that impede sustainability in each country (internal affairs), goals that explicitly deal with "growth engine(s)" and inequality are now included in this new set of global goals.

The number one goal of this global agenda continues to be poverty reduction. Under the MDGs, the following Goal 1 and Targets were set.

Goal 1: Eradicate extreme poverty and hunger.

- Target 1. Halve, between 1990 and 2015, the proportion of people whose income is less than $1 a day.
- Target 2. Achieve full and productive employment and decent work for all, including women and young people.
- Target 3. Halve, between 1990 and 2015, the proportion of people who suffer from hunger.

These are the only economic (growth-related) goal/targets in the MDGs. Inequality issues were not explicitly dealt with.

Table 1.1 summarizes the changing poverty profile under the MDGs. As the UN community declared in 2013, at an aggregate level, the poverty headcount ratio in the developing world was halved by 2010 as compared to the level that prevailed in the reference year of 1990.[2] However, a careful review of Table 1.1 reveals the following facts: (1) most of the poverty reduction was produced in China, the "factory of the world," up to 2005; (2) India, the "back office of the world," joined this successful club after 2005; and (3) Sub-Saharan Africa, due to its relatively high population growth, saw increasing numbers of poor, even though the poverty headcount ratio has been declining.

Table 1.1 Poverty reduction under the MDGs, 1990–2015

	(a) Changes in Regional Poverty HCR (%)						(b) Changes in Poor Population (million)					
Developing Regions	1990	1999	2005	2011	2013	2015	1990	1999	2005	2011	2013	2015
East Asia & Pacific	61.3	38.5	18.9	8.6	3.6	2.3	1117	781	403	191	81	53
China	66.2	40.2	18.5	7.9	1.9	0.7	751	504	241	106	26	10
Europe & Central Asia	5.2 (1993)	7.9	4.9	2.1	1.6	1.5	44 (1993)	68	43	19	14	14
Latin America & Caribbean	14.8	13.5	9.9	5.7	4.6	3.9	66	70	56	34	28	25
Middle East & North Africa	6.2	3.8	3.1	2.7	2.6	4.2	16	12	11	11	11	18
South Asia	47.3	..	33.7	19.8	16.1	..	536	..	510	327	274	..
India	45.9 (1993)	..	38.2 (2004)	21.2	..	..	..	424 (1993)	430 (2004)	264	..	..
Sub-Saharan Africa	54.7	58.3	50.8	45.0	42.4	41.0	280	381	389	..	..	..
Low & middle income	44.4	34.8	25.0	16.4	13.3	11.8	1887	1717	1342	953	793	722

Given these mixed accomplishments during the MDGs era and the resurgence of arguments for sustained economic growth as a necessary (but not sufficient) condition for employment generation, poverty reduction, and political stability in various corners of the world,[3] the post-2015 development agenda presented in Figure 1.1 as SDGs encompasses goals of inclusive economic growth, industrial development, and reduced inequalities.

Goal 1: End poverty in all its forms everywhere.
Goal 8: Promote inclusive and sustainable economic growth, employment, and decent work for all.
Goal 9: Build resilient infrastructure, promote sustainable industrialization, and foster innovation.
Goal 10: Reduce inequality within and among countries.

In the socioeconomic progress of a developing country, sustainable development of domestic industries is essential to boost economic growth and employment creation that brings about poverty reduction. Under a system of international economic institutions that allowed a relatively broad policy space, Japan and the Asian Tigers that achieved rapid economic growth succeeded in developing their infant and key industries under a diverse set of industrial policies.[4] They also achieved higher productivity, increased their industry, and promoted exports by making use of foreign capital and imported technology; thus, all these have realized the "catch-up" industrialization (through the traditional follower-country strategy). However, developing countries in the 1980s and later had to promote their industries under economic globalization and an international economic system that was oriented toward freer trade and overseas investment. They also had to face competitive pressure from China and India, and were forced to develop their own industries within a limited policy space, attributed to the expanded global production network of multinational corporations (global value chains; GVCs), and in a stricter international economic environment.

Taking into consideration that the economies of developing countries had been polarized, and that today the term "industrial policy" is considered in a rather broad sense as a collective development policy and is being applied more widely, this book (published in two volumes in order to disseminate the findings from an international joint research project) intends to focus on the design of an "integrated industrial policy" that tries to promote "inclusive" industrial development by using the various forces of globalization. It will (1) analyze

Figure 1.1 Sustainable Development Goals for 2015–2030

Source: Downloaded from www.un.org/sustainabledevelopment/news/communications-material/(2017.02.23)

comparatively the cases of industrial policies and institutions of selected countries in Asia and Africa: and (2) combine a wide range of empirical analyses such as macro (economy-wide) and micro (firm-level) econometric analyses, and indicative integrated industrial policy simulations with the use of Computable General Equilibrium models. The ultimate goal of this research is to advocate an integrated set of effective policies that will promote the survival of industries in developing countries, under global competition and integration, which includes domestic policies, policies that should be coordinated within a framework of regional economic cooperation, and present initiatives to be taken under the scheme of international development cooperation. This book pays extra attention to the potential of various public-private partnership (PPP) initiatives, and explicitly deals with business enterprises and entrepreneurs as key target actors of industrial policies.

Throughout these studies, the "poverty triangle" of economic growth, inequality, and poverty reduction under globalization presented in Figure 1.2 will be used as a common framework. In this context, the success in industrial promotion, corporate development, and employment generation are considered to be the keys to poverty reduction, while each country's development governance, institutions, and policies (and the levels of policy integration/coordination) will be dealt with as control factors.

1.2 Industrial policy debates in retrospect

Industrial policies were treated in a rather neutral manner (including discussions on their positive and negative sides) in the *East Asian Miracle: Economic Growth and Public Policy* (World Bank, 1993) under the propagated development strategy that stressed public-private partnership and "functionalism." Later on, with the expansion of neoliberalism, those industrial policies were considered in a negative light. Krueger (1997) and others pointed out the risk facing policymakers in selecting the right industries to be promoted. While the growth performance of the developing countries under globalization has become polarized, Chang (2003) argued that these developing nations should be given the same "policy space" in industrial policies as the industrialized countries had previously been. Rodrik (2008b) subscribed to the same view, even being joined by the OECD in the late 2000s. In the OECD, opinions such as "industrial policies are not dirty words" and "industrial policy is back" emerged. Following the policy recommendations made by Cimoli, Dosi, and Stiglitz (2009) in the Initiative for Policy Dialogue (IPD), based at Columbia University, Lin and Chang (2009), Lin and Monga (2010), and Lin (2012) and others discussed whether industrial policies ought to focus on industries with comparative advantage following the tradition, or whether new industries should be strategically created. These debates are often referred to now as new "competitive advantage" versus traditional "comparative advantage" of industries to be selected for promotion. Following this debate, industrial policies in a broader sense are argued, in the recent years, as being an integrated strategy for economic development. It is interesting to note that both Krueger and Lin served as chief economists at the World Bank, and during this time the policy stance of the Bretton Woods institutions was transformed into a more realistic one. It is now widely known that "integrated" industrial policies and supporting policy studies are essential for the proactive and dynamic promotion of surviving industries that can achieve international competitiveness in this globalized world.

Thus, industrial policy is once again at the top of the policy agenda. To a significant extent, economists demonstrate a broad consensus that "coordinated" measures to promote and facilitate industrial upgrading and diversification are determining factors to accelerate structural transformation, sustain growth, and create better jobs.[5] Unlike the success stories of Japan and the Asian Tigers in the past, the history of industrial policy in Africa and Latin America is filled with failure and cautionary tales. However, the new consensus is empirically supported by the wide variation of the pattern and process of structural transformation among countries; that is, it is growth-enhancing in countries that successfully implemented industrial policies and growth-reducing in countries that neglected investment in agriculture, infrastructure, and human skills. For instance, Salazar-Xirinachs et al. (2014) argued that East Asian countries used targeted measures to help them absorb know-how, technology, and knowledge from the rest of the world, assimilating these factors at a tremendous pace and diversifying into new and more sophisticated industrial powerhouses.

The reason for this intense use of industrial policies is that product diversification and sophistication are found to be the keys to translate high economic growth into good quality employment and poverty reduction (Felipe et al., 2012; Hausmann, Hwang, & Rodrik, 2007; Hausmann & Klinger, 2006; Mishra,

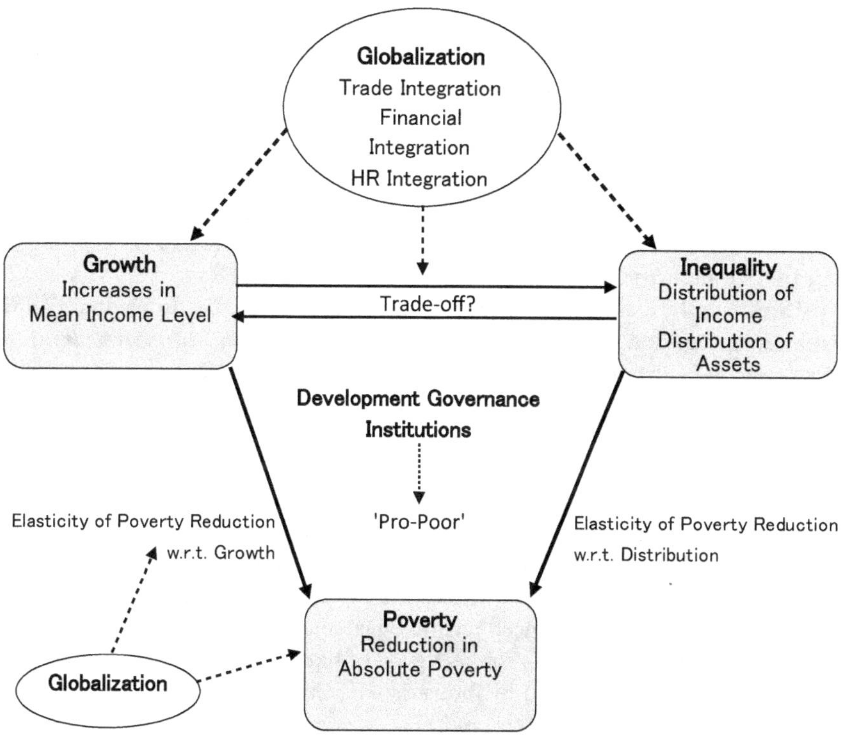

Figure 1.2 Poverty-growth-inequality triangle under globalization
Source: Adapted from Otsubo (2009, Figure 1.2) and Otsubo (2016, Figure 2.1).

Lundstrom, & Anand, 2011). According to Hausmann and Klinger (2006), countries that export goods associated with higher productivity levels grow more rapidly, even after controlling for initial income per head, human capital levels, and time-invariant country characteristics. Along the same lines, countries that export the greatest number of categories of products and those which have more products at different prices within those categories tend to have higher levels of gross domestic product (GDP) (ESCAP, 2011). Therefore, diversification toward higher-value products is crucial for developing countries to boost and sustain economic growth. To diversify, countries need to upgrade the technology in their production and upskill their existing labor (ACET, 2014).

It is, however, worth noting that industrial policies are country-specific, depending on the existing capabilities and institutional capacities (Chang, 2010; Crespi, Fernández-Arias, & Stein, 2014; Ferraz, Kupfer, & Marques, 2014; Hausmann & Hidalgo, 2011). Gabriele (2010), for example, pointed out that the role of the state in China, far from withering away, is massive, dominant, and crucial to China's industrial development. This role has been recently reflected by the position of China as the world's largest manufacturer and it is often called "the factory of the world." In China, the role of the state in economic development has taken the form of both creating the enabling environment and direct intervention, in terms of promoting structural change and thereby growth in productivity and employment (Lo & Wu, 2014). Felipe et al. (2013) further claimed that the key factor underlying China's rapid development during the last 50 years was its intrinsic ability to master and accumulate new and more complex capabilities, which was augmented in 1979 with the implementation of the Equity Joint Venture Law that paved the way for foreign direct investment (FDI) induction and the establishment of export processing zones (EPZs) as an integral part of their industrial policy.

More recently, Hallward-Driemeier and Nayyar published an influential World Bank report entitled *Trouble in the Making? The Future of Manufacturing-Led Development* (Hallward-Driemeier & Nayyar, 2018). This report issued a warning for today's developing countries about relying on the traditional manufacturing-led growth strategy where cross-border investments in low-skill labor-intensive manufacturing sectors were promoted for the sake of job creation in unskilled labor-abundant societies. While these lower-value-added manufacturing sectors have been under constant competitive pressure from producers in China and then India, this World Bank report pointed out that successful drivers for productivity and economic growth had already shifted to higher-value-added manufacturing, supported by newer and advanced technologies, such as robotics, design and factory automation, that in turn require a pool of highly skilled human capital and positive externalities produced by industrial clustering. Given this sea change in the global manufacturing system and GVCs, creation of locational advantages within developing countries, other than inexpensive labor, has become an even tougher challenge that calls for proper policy interventions and facilitations. In this context, this World Bank report suggested policy actions on competitiveness (higher productivity and a better business environment, improved institutions, and infrastructure), capabilities (new skills and better management), and connectedness (freer trade in goods and services) (Hallward-Driemeier & Nayyar, 2018). While the points and modalities of policy interventions are still debatable, the need for smart and coordinated industrial policies in a broader sense is clear and present.

1.3 Defining industrial policies

In general, the literature on industrial policy can be divided into three streams of research: (1) studies discussing the definition, the instruments, and the rationale/justification, and country experiences with industrial policy; (2) studies that discuss new and emerging issues related to industrial development/promotion, such as the changing role of "manufacturing" in the "industries" to be promoted and "policy space" for the developing world in their industrialization; and (3) studies that take on industrial policy evaluations, both in terms of methodologies and their applications. The literature on definition, instruments, and rationale of industrial policy has been the core in the past, joined by country case studies.

However, most of the recent discussions on industrial policy have gone beyond the issues of how to define industrial policies to how to design and implement them in today's context. With the heightened need for evidence-based policymaking (both design and implementation) in our development community, advances in industrial policy evaluation are called for. The issue has grown in importance also in the light of recent developments in evaluation methodologies and identification techniques in health, education, and labor market studies. Despite this, very few studies have discussed the quantitative methods for high quality evaluation of industrial policies.

Nonetheless, the first step is reviewing the discussions on the definitions and instruments of industrial policies since any analyses in this area of research can lead to significantly different conclusions if different definitions and instruments are presumed.

The definition of industrial policy has been the most controversial issue in the debate related to industrial policy. Because industrial policy is complex and holistic, its definition has implications in terms of the degree of government intervention, coverage of industry, choice of policy instruments, and the methods of evaluating the impact, and so forth. Therefore, most of the studies in the field start with a definition of industrial policy. Simply put, industrial policy means any policy that affects the evolution and advance of industry. However, there are several definitions of industrial policy.[6] We argue that, broadly, industrial policy is a large set of strategic and proactive government interventions to address market failures that prevail in the economy and to promote/develop new industrial capabilities and institutional capacities to accelerate the structural transformation necessary for growth and sustainable development. As a good example, Chapter 4 of this book introduces the discussion of international arrangements and public policies of developed countries potentially playing the role of *de facto* industrial policies for developing countries, using the case of the Multi-Fiber Arrangement (MFA) and the Generalized System of Preferences (GSP), which eventually promoted the garment industry in Bangladesh, one of the least developed countries.

Before going any further, we would like to present an indicative summary of definitions/types of industrial policies. Table 1.2 is constructed, partially drawing on the discussions presented in various studies including Di Maio (2014), in order to inform the readers of the kinds of traditional and new criteria that we normally use to classify industrial policies into categories.

Specific objectives of industrial policies may differ across countries, across time, and across stages of development. For most developing countries, the goal of industrial policy is to address market failures and create conditions for investment, productivity growth, and economic transformation, resulting in economic growth and job creation. In their efforts to replicate the success stories of the Asian Tigers and Asian newly industrializing economies (NIES), the latecomers to the Association of Southeast Asian Nations (ASEAN) (Cambodia, Myanmar, Laos, and Vietnam) and many African countries today align themselves in the general definition of industrial policy, where the goal is set to address market failures as a step toward economic transformation and productive job generation.

The United Nations Economic Commission for Africa (UNECA) and the African Union (AU), in championing the active mobilization of industrial policies in Africa, subscribe to a more holistic view. They focus on building strong and inclusive institutions, and on addressing gaps in infrastructure, energy supply, skills, and financing as identified by the industrial stakeholders (UNECA & AU, 2014). With the limitations caused by these identified gaps, African countries today are formulating and implementing new industrial policies centered on developing special economic zones (SEZs).[7]

With regard to the instruments of industrial policies, there is a wide range of policy tools/interventions used by governments to induce structural transformation from lower productive activities to more productive ones. In addition, readers will be exposed to different sets of narrowly or broadly defined industrial policy instruments both in the micro- and macro-economic dimensions, and in the geographical dimensions from domestic regional, national, and super-national regional to global economies. As a good example of categorizing industrial policy instruments, we would like to introduce one indicative 2x2 table created by Weiss (2016) for the classification of interventions (i.e., policy instruments) by adopting vertical vs. horizontal and public-input-based vs. market-based types/definitions shown in Table 1.2. It is replicated here, as Table 1.3, as one excellent example of how to summarize/categorize some of the key measures in industrial policymaking. By choosing and combining a particular set of types/definitions presented in Table 1.2, one can create a similar 2x2 table of policy instruments depending on the needs of policy design.

Table 1.2 Types/definitions of industrial policies

Selective/vertical/narrow vs. general/horizontal/broad (coverage)	Industrial policy is selective when it uses vertical measures that target specific industries, firms, sectors, or factors of production. Winners, key industries, and beneficiaries are picked. Industrial policies in a narrow sense.	On the other hand, general industrial policies are comprised of functional and horizontal measures that benefit all industries by producing investment-conducive environment. Industrial policies in a broader sense.
Small vs. large (scope)	Small scope refers to public inputs to improve productivity of existing activities.	Large scope refers to efforts to establish new industries.
Public-input-based vs. market-based (modality)	Public inputs refer to provisions of public goods/funds and organizational changes (legislation, accreditation, R&D, transport and other infrastructure specific to an industry) that private sector does not supply adequately.	Market-based incentives operate through price regulations and taxation.

Table 1.2 Cont.

Rising industries vs. sunset industries (facilitation)	Industrial policies that aim to promote dynamic/ rising sectors of the economy or to create new industries.	Industrial policies that facilitate the "death" of sunset industries in order to free up resources for new activities. They may also provide social safety net for those who suffer in the transition. This facilitation should also minimize damage to accumulated capabilities that still may have relevance for the performance of new activities.
Competitiveness-GDP vs. beyond-GDP (goals)	Industrial policy has traditionally been targeted to increase productivity and competitiveness of a targeted sector or the economy as a whole.	Industrial policy could specifically target beyond-GDP goals such as environmental sustainability, subjective well-being, pro-poorness/ inclusiveness, etc.
Piecewise vs. integrated (integration)	Industrial policies are designed and implemented in a piecewise manner without much coordination among policies, policymakers (ministries), or stakeholders such as businesses and communities.	Industrial policies are designed and implemented in an integrated manner with active coordination among policies, policymakers (ministries), and stakeholders such as businesses and communities.
National vs. sub-national vs. super-national (policy unit)	Industrial polices have been often discussed in the context of policy design and implementation at a national level. Central governments are the key players.	Industrial policies today should also be discussed at sub-national and super-national levels. At a sub-national level, regional/ spatial distribution of industries is discussed in the context of equitable regional development. As a super-national level, new regional cooperation arrangements such as the AEC and the strengthened AU emerged as the key players in design and coordinated implementation of industrial strategies for the region as a whole.

(*continued*)

Table 1.2 Cont.

Old vs. modern (vintage)	In the old view, the term industrial policy referred to state intervention to reallocate resources in favor of the manufacturing sector and within manufacturing toward high productivity, dynamic sub-sectors (Weiss, 2016, p. 136). Industrial policy was solely in the hands of the state. Two key policies were particularly implemented, namely, infant industry protection and export promotion policies. Trade was used strategically to provide market opportunities for competitive sectors.	The modern industrial policy emphasizes the role of public-private partnership/ dialogue in the design and implementation of industrial policies. It involves active coordination among government agencies, between public and private entities, among entrepreneurs and local communities, etc. Dimensions of integration for integrated policy making and execution should be explored. It is a learning process, where the policy mix is continuously adjusted and adapted.

Source: Authors' construction.

Table 1.3 Classification of policy interventions

Policy intervention	*Horizontal*	*Vertical*
Public inputs	Broad-based skills training Infrastructure regulatory reform Banking sector regulatory reform Standard setting bodies	Sector-specific skills training Targeted infrastructure investment Business plans for selected sectors Public-private research consortia
Market-based provision	Corporation tax reform General labor subsidy Export promotion – credit availability, duty-drawbacks, tax treatment Export processing zones General venture capital funding General credit guarantees for SMEs Subsidized credit to all SMEs Tax incentives for R&D	Specific tax holidays Sector-specific labor subsidy Sector-specific export promotion Selective import protection Sector-specific venture capital funding Selective credit guarantees Directed credit Selective R&D incentives Price support schemes

Source: Weiss (2016, 138, Table 8.1). Reproduced by permission of Taylor and Francis, a division of Informa plc.

1.4 Arguments and theoretical underpinnings for industrial policies

In this section, we review typical arguments for and against industrial policies. The debate on the rationale of industrial policy has also evolved over time. There is a justification to use functional, horizontal, and general industrial policies as opposed to selective, vertical, and narrow industrial policies.[8] The need to combine horizontal industrial policy with sector-specific policy is advocated in Latin America (Alvarez, 2013). For Stiglitz and Monga (2013), the question is not whether any government should use industrial policy, but rather how best to apply it.

The common objection to industrial policies is built on two main arguments: asymmetric information and corruption. Having identified the active roles of government in pursuing industrial development in East Asia, it has often been argued that industrial policy might not work in Africa because of deficiencies in governance. Deficiencies in governance include corruption and rent-seeking activities. In contrast, Greenwald and Stiglitz (2013) argued that effective industrial policies can be implemented in countries with significant deficiencies in governance. An important reason for this is that industrial policies have succeeded in some instances in which they were designed to correct market failures or even have corrected government failures. The set of countries of South Korea, China, and Taiwan prioritized policies to address market imperfections before improving their respective institutions (Rodrik, 1995, 1996).

There is, in fact, a great deal of agreement on the theoretical and logical underpinnings for industrial policies. First of all, it is widely accepted that markets and economies are generally characterized by the existence of negative externalities, and under these circumstances, a competitive market system may not lead to a Pareto-efficient outcome (Greenwald & Stiglitz, 1986; Pack & Saggi, 2006).[9] According to Lall (2004), economic theory justifies selectivity where market failures affect some activities more than others, and restoring equilibrium calls for more intervention in specific activities. Therefore, industrial policy is called for in order to address market failure.[10] Theoretically speaking, there are two possible roles for industrial policies.[11] Industrial policies can be designed to address externalities and solve coordination problems (imperfect competition, pollution, coordination failure, capital market imperfection, and so on). They should also provide an enabling environment for innovation by promoting creation and dissemination of knowledge.

Government interventions to promote structural transformation were justified to variable degrees in countries such as Japan, the Asian Tigers, Indonesia, Malaysia, Thailand, China, Vietnam, and India, in order to protect infant industries (Lall, 2004) and foster industrial development. More recently, the case of infant industry protection is supported by the existence and persistence of information externality (Hausmann & Rodrik, 2003; Lin, 2012; Rodrik, 2004, 2008a). Tax incentives and subsidies can be used to build capabilities for industrial development, such as the capacity to acquire necessary imports (e.g., expensive machinery) and to provide workforce training.

Industrial policy is also important to fix market failures (Rodrik, 2004, 2008a). This argument has been supported both by those who view industrial policy as tools to shape sectoral allocation of economic activities and by those who advocate the general/horizontal type of industrial policies. Another justification stems from the fact that latecomer countries face more severe market failures than those faced by mature market economies. According to Altenburg (2013), industrial policy is needed to encourage entrepreneurship and an entrepreneurial class, promote skills development at all levels, and set up regulatory institutions and quality assurance. For instance, for a primary commodity producer/exporter to diversify into higher-value-added products, it takes numerous capabilities that can only be promoted with country-specific policies. The most often advocated generic policies in the literature (Felipe et al., 2010; Page, 2012) have highlighted policy interventions to address market failures by developing skills and an infrastructure as the basis to manufacture and export high-value products. For example, Felipe et al. (2010), in their study on how rich countries became rich, in which they categorized 779 products based on their sophistication and connectivity to other products, found that 75 out of 154 countries sampled belong to the "low product" trap as they mostly export unsophisticated and unconnected products.[12] They conclude that countries in the "low product" trap need to acquire skills, technology, and knowledge, and improve their organizational capabilities to escape from this trap. Similarly, Page (2012) discussed policies for African economies to reallocate resources to higher productivity activities in the agro-industry, manufacturing, or tradable services. He argued that Africa should focus on pushing exports, building capabilities, and supporting agglomeration in addition to investment climate reforms that aim to reduce the skill and infrastructure gaps. In the same vein, Lin and Treichel (2012) argued that technological innovation, industrial diversification, and industrial upgrading are typically accompanied by changes in capital and skills requirements for firms as well as by changes in their market scope and infrastructure needs due to the evolving nature of production that is embodied in the process of innovation. Put differently, diversification is typically accompanied by changes in hard and soft infrastructure requirements.

1.5 Structure of the book and the questions to be addressed

Having reconfirmed the importance of proactive industrial promotion policies for sustained economic growth and poverty reduction in developing countries, recent discussions focus more on design, implementation, and evaluation for evidence-based policymaking. It is also widely recognized today that policy coordination and integration are necessary requirements for industrial policies to take on the challenges of producing "inclusive" development under the SDGs' framework. In order for us to deal with these issues and challenges in industrial promotion, this book consists of the following four parts in two volumes:

Part I Industrial promotion in retrospect and prospect
Part II Designing integrated industrial policies in Asia and the Pacific
Part III Designing integrated industrial policies in Africa
Part IV Designing integrated industrial policies in sub- and super-national regions

Part I consists of three introductory chapters, contained in both Vol. I and Vol. II. Chapter 1 presents industrial promotion and industrial policies in retrospect and prospect. It provides concepts, definitions, and issues to be discussed in this book while stressing the need for modern and integrated strategies. It also captures industrial promotion in the Poverty-Growth-Inequality (PGI) triangle in order for us to discuss "inclusive" strategies. Chapter 2 presents data and descriptive statistics that constitute a common background. What do we really know about the changing state of global manufacturing? How and why has the trend of premature deindustrialization emerged in many parts of the developing world? Chapter 3 revisits the importance of manufacturing and the risks associated with premature deindustrialization in pursuing pro-poor growth and inclusive development. Chapters 2 and 3, together, present a holistic picture of the past and present state of industrialization, structural change, and their impact on increases in value-added and employment.

As most of the chapters in this book deal with issues/topics of industrial promotion not only in theories and conceptual frameworks but also in relation to existing problems and policies within a specific country context, the next two Parts of the book present chapters by countries used as cases or targets of rigorous economic/econometric analyses. Part II (Chapters 4–12) discusses countries in Asia and the Pacific region. Part III (Chapters 13–16) presents chapters that use countries in Africa as their cases. However, this does not mean that any particular topic is only relevant to a particular set of countries or a region. Instead, it means that realistic industrial policy discussion needs cases and targets on the ground.

Part IV contains two chapters that deal with regional issues/topics of industrial promotion. Chapter 17 discusses the impact of super-national regional economic cooperation such as the Regional Trading Agreement (RTA) and the Regional Comprehensive Economic Partnership (RCEP) for industrial promotion at the regional level. Chapter 18 discusses regional parity and regional "inclusiveness" in the context of sub-national regions as a country pursues industrial development in a balanced or unbalanced manner. Chapter 17 introduces policy simulations using computable general equilibrium (CGE) models. Chapter 18 introduces the analyses of regional convergence/divergence to investigate the interaction between industrial development and regional convergence.

This book does not rehash the success stories of Japan, South Korea, and Taiwan as they have already been well documented and the global economic environment today is very different from when the "East Asian miracle" was created. Instead, this book focuses on ordinary developing countries in Asia and Africa, including countries such as Indonesia and Thailand, where governments have tended not to subscribe to industrial promotion by so-called "industrial policies." The book includes analyses on "China in Africa" and an analysis on the future of China's industrial development initiative "Made in China 2025" and its impact on developing countries. This book also intends to contribute to the worldwide discussion of SDGs as discussions/analyses on industrial promotion and industrial policies not only for the sake of economic growth and job creation but also for "inclusive" development are presented. To this end, the book addresses impacts on income and spatial (geographical) inequalities, thereby capturing industrial promotion in the context of the Poverty-Growth-Inequality (PGI) triangle, as shown in Figure 1.2.

Another unique feature of this book comes from the fact that this book is produced as a joint venture between academic researchers and policymakers. Contributors include those with working experiences in trend-setting international organizations, such as the United Nations (UN), the United Nations Industrial Development Organization (UNIDO), and the World Bank, as well as those working for national institutions in the developing countries which deal with policymaking and the execution of industrial promotion, such as the National Development Planning Agency of Indonesia (BAPPENAS), the Ministry of Industry and Commerce of the Laotian government, and the Ministry of Finance and the Central Bank of Thailand.

The issues/questions and specific industrial policy options that each chapter tries to address are partly previewed in the next subsection in conjunction with the key questions, related to industrial promotion in today's globalized world economy, to be addressed in this book.

1.6 Leading issues in industrial promotion in today's globalized world

1.6.1 What is the present state of industrialization and deindustrialization?

Does manufacturing still matter?
Can manufacturing still be the engine of growth?

The classic and dominant view relates industry to the manufacturing sector for its role as the engine of economic growth (Chenery, Robinson, & Syrquin, 1986; Kaldor, 1966). Historically, rapid and sustained economic growth is highly correlated with an expansion of manufacturing and reallocation of resources to more productive activities (Hausmann, Hwang, & Rodrik, 2007; Hausmann & Klinger, 2006; Hausmann & Rodrik, 2003; McMillan & Rodrik, 2011; McMillan, Rodrik, & Verduzco-Gallo, 2014). Manufacturing has the fastest productivity growth, faster than services and agriculture, pays higher wages (ILO, 2014), and has strong spillover effects (backward and forward linkages) to other sectors (Hirschman, 1958). This means that a rapidly growing manufacturing sector enhances productivity growth in other sectors of the economy, and therefore, leads to higher economic growth.[13] For natural resource-based economies whose exports depend on a primary commodity, diversifying the export structure away from primary products to manufacturing has been a key policy in order to build resilience to external shocks (Amin Guitierrez de Pineres & Ferrantino, 2000) and sustain growth (McMillan & Harttgen, 2014). The other main argument in favor of diversifying into manufacturing lies in the fact that diversification is needed to sustain growth and significantly reduce poverty. This argument is supported by the fact that export diversification toward manufacturing is linked to increased employment, exports, and GDP growth (Agosin, 2007; Herzer & Nowak-Lehmann, 2006; Lederman & Maloney, 2007).

A more recent view argues that industrial policy should target all economic activities that have similar characteristics to manufacturing, such as tradable and high productive services and agro-processing. For example, Ohno (2013) includes manufacturing, agriculture, services, and logistics as a set of production sectors for industrial policy to focus on. The sector should be precisely targeted, for example, on non-traditional and high-yielding varieties of agricultural products or high-value service activities, such as software development and tourism (Altenburg, 2011; Rodrik, 2008a).

There are several reasons for this, the most important is that recent evidence shows that manufacturing is a necessary but not sufficient condition for eventual prosperity (Dadush, 2015; Felipe et al., 2014). For example, Felipe et al. (2014) related manufacturing employment and output shares to the GDP per capita of 52 economies to study whether it is currently possible to become rich without building large manufacturing sectors. The authors find that higher manufacturing employment shares are strongly related to a subsequent rise in income per capita. However, the findings also suggest that it is becoming more difficult for actual developing countries to achieve higher manufacturing shares and therefore this limits their potential to industrialize through manufacturing. Dadush (2015) conducted similar, but less robust, cross-country regression of GDP per capita growth for 107 countries over the period 2000–2012. The estimated effect of manufacturing share of value-added is significant and varies between 0.44 and 0.51 for developing countries. His findings corroborate those of Felipe et al. (2014) in that developing countries would have to achieve a very large increase in their manufacturing share to see an appreciable acceleration in their growth rate. Felipe et al. (2009) find that services had a larger effect than manufacturing on growth in developing Asia. The main reason for this finding is that, in recent decades, rapid productivity growth has occurred outside manufacturing, in large part due to the application of computer-based technologies. Another reason for targeting all economic sectors stems from the fact that the world has entered a post-industrial era where the service and other non-manufacturing sectors have come to dominate the economic structure of many economies, both in terms of output and employment.

The observed relationships between income levels and manufacturing (or industry) shares in total value-added and total employment in cross-country data for the three most recent decades (1994–1996, 2004–2006, and 2014–2016) are presented in Figures 1.3, 1.4, and 1.5.[14] In Figure 1.3, although the

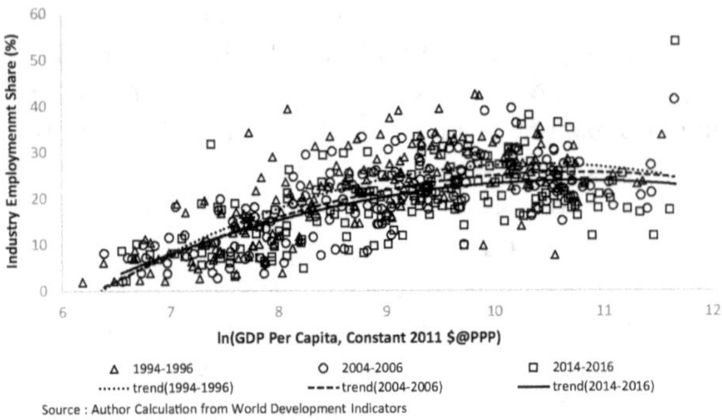

Figure 1.3 Share of employment in industry vs. GDP per capita
Source: Authors' compilation based on World Development Indicators, 2019.

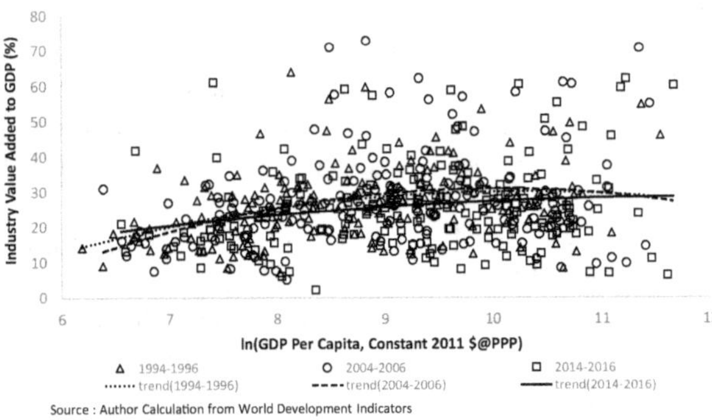

Figure 1.4 Share of value-added in industry vs. GDP per capita
Source: Authors' compilation based on World Development Indicators, 2019.

inverted U-shape relationship between the income levels and industry employment shares in a cross-country comparison have been preserved, throughout three decades, the curve has been shifting down, implicating a secular decline in the importance of industry in explaining/generating employment.[15] In terms of the relationships between income levels and value-added shares, Figure 1.4 (industry) and Figure 1.5 (manufacturing) again show that fitted curves have been shifting down, pointing to the declines in the peak shares at the middle range of per capita income. This pattern is more prominent when manufacturing is singled out of the industry group.[16]

Figure 1.6 (employment) and Figure 1.7 (value-added) present the relationships between income levels and service shares in total employment and total value-added in cross-country data for the same time points. Unlike the case for industry (or manufacturing), the shares of service continue to rise both in

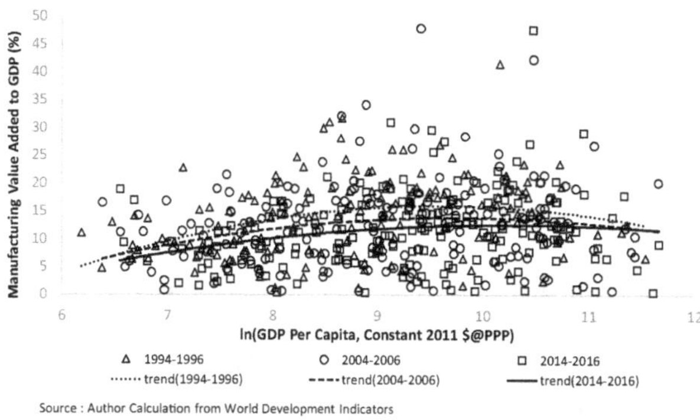

Figure 1.5 Share of value-added in manufacturing vs. GDP per capita
Source: Authors' compilation based on World Development Indicators, 2019.

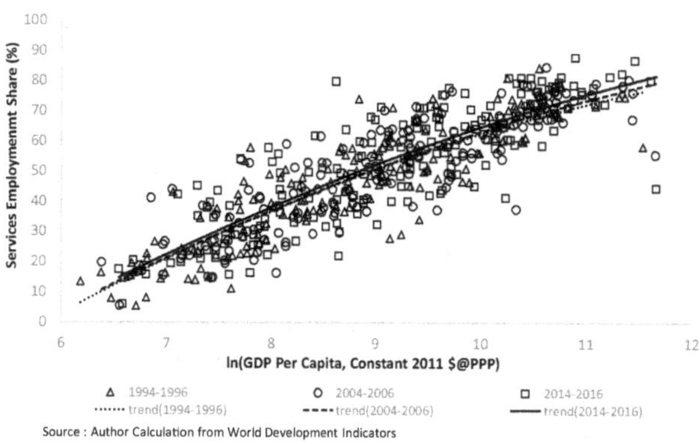

Figure 1.6 Share of employment in service sector vs. GDP per capita
Source: Authors' compilation based on World Development Indicators, 2019.

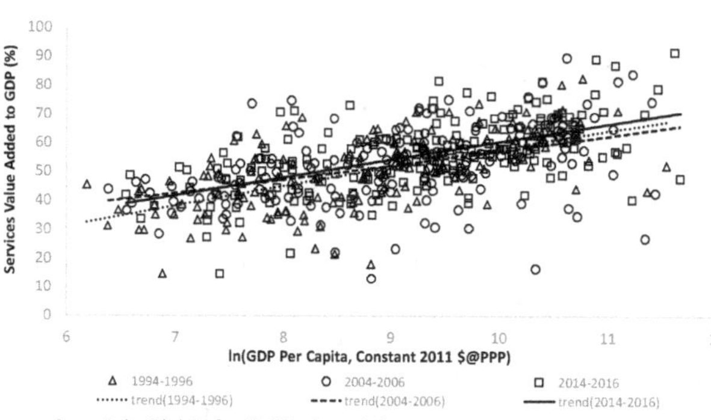

Figure 1.7 Share of value-added in service sector vs. GDP per capita
Source: Authors' compilation based on World Development Indicators, 2019.

employment and value-added as per capita income increases. Fitted curves have been shifting up over these three decades pointing to the increasing importance of the service sector in the global economy. Interestingly, the differences in the curvatures of fitted curves between employment and value-added shares seem to indicate higher productivity in the service sector in higher-income countries. The possibility of the service sector yielding higher productivities and real wages seem to have been supported by advances in technologies such as ICT and the Internet of Things (IoT).

Exports of commercial services, for example, have nearly tripled in the last decade and have surpassed agriculture and industry as the leading income-generating sector across Africa (UNECA & AU, 2014). This was made possible due to the revolution of ICT and transport technologies, and the growing importance of trade and value chains. Despite the fact that growth in the manufacturing sector has been partially responsible for the boom of high productive public utilities and construction, recent evidence also showed the contribution of coordinated measures to promote and accelerate growth in the non-manufacturing sectors, such as tourism and food production. For example Chang, Andreoni, and Kuan (2014) demonstrate how Brazil and Chile have successfully used policies to expand natural resource-processing industries and food production. In the context of African countries, even the relatively successful recent growth has been jobless. While services have surpassed agriculture and industry as the leading income-generating sectors across Africa, this has not created the quantity or quality of jobs normally expected from expanding manufacturing and labor-intensive production (UNECA, 2014).[17]

As a good case study from Asia, Chapter 5 discusses Indonesia's efforts towards pro-poor industrial policies. Indonesia, with its young and expanding population, and with a rising middle class, has observed a strong expansion of its service sector, but without shifting employment out of manufacturing. The government of Indonesia recently started its march toward manufacturing upgrading and promoting high-yielding manufacturing-related services with its Indonesian Industrial Revolution Version 4.0.

From a policy perspective, does this imply that industrial policy should target only high productive activities in service and agro-processing? As one of the key service sector-based industrialization trends, tourism development and international trade in tourism will be dealt with in Chapter 10 drawing on cases of development models from the Pacific Island Countries.

Chapter 2 looks further into these trends in industrialization and deindustrialization.

In Chapter 3, "The importance of manufacturing development and structural change for pro-poor growth," Haraguchi and Amann elaborate on the importance of industrial structural change by investigating development patterns within manufacturing. Their aim is to highlight the relevance of manufacturing and to promote pro-poor growth pathways of industrial development. The authors revisit the current debate on whether the importance of manufacturing for economic development has changed by reviewing the latest advances in the field linked to their own empirical analyses.

1.6.2 Have developing countries been marginalized to low value-added manufacturing?

Is there a space for the manufacturing industry in developing countries to grow?

Are there any opportunities for higher-value-added manufacturing and manufacturing-related services left for the majority of developing countries?

Related to the first set of questions, policymakers in developing countries and scholars have started to assess the existence of spaces that manufacturing industries in developing countries can grow into.

Discussed above, an influential World Bank report *Trouble in the Making? The Future of Manufacturing-Led Development* (Hallward-Driemeier & Nayyar, 2018) was introduced. This report issued a warning for today's developing countries about their continued reliance on the traditional manufacturing-led growth strategy where cross-border investments in low-skill labor-intensive manufacturing sectors were promoted for the sake of job creation in unskilled labor-abundant societies. Successful drivers for productivity and economic growth had already shifted to higher-value-added manufacturing supported by newer and advanced technologies, that in turn requires a pool of highly skilled human capital that is not readily available in most developing countries. The same report also pointed out that success in this higher-value-added manufacturing is limited to only a handful of economies. Some 55 percent of the world's manufactured goods were produced in developed/industrialized countries, and China, the world's largest manufacturing producer accounted for another 25 percent in 2015, leaving only one-fifth of the total pie for the other developing countries (Hallward-Driemeier & Nayyar, 2018).

Latecomers need specific and proactive industrial policy to accelerate the process of development and diversify into higher-value-added products. The reason often raised by economists is that the new initial conditions for Asia's latecomers and African economies to create manufacturing growth are different from those faced by the Asian Tigers. The difference stems from the fact that successful Asian economies followed highly unusual and distinctive paths of growth. In the initial stage of the (East) Asian industrial development, global trade was characterized by a rapidly growing manufacturing sector, whereas the nature of global trade today is characterized by highly-productive service (manufacturing-related service) sectors. In recent years, "Factory Asia" has become the new key player in global manufacturing and service trade, with China at the center due to its successful creation of "competitive" or "dynamic" comparative advantage, with India growing into a "back office of the world." The world economy is now driven by shifts in demand and innovations in products/services, processes/operations, materials, and information technology. It contrasts with China's initial condition, which was characterized by the shifts in the cost and the availability of factor inputs (Manyika et al., 2012). That is, the initial conditions that China and other East Asian economies faced created an opportunity for them to industrialize with labor-intensive, export-oriented manufacturing. According to the projection by Anderson and Strutt (2014), China will become the world's top producing country not only of primary products but also of manufacturing products. In fact, China had already become the world's top manufacturing producer by 2015 (with 25 percent of the world's total manufacturing value-added in 2015). Global manufacturing is characterized by high specialization in small tasks due to the fragmentation of production processes and the extension of GVCs. This may not be beneficial for Asia's latecomers or African economies who contribute a small portion of low value-added labor-intensive activities to the global manufacturing value chains. The Asian Tigers benefitted from a rapidly expanding manufacturing sector. The Asian latecomers are trying to capitalize on the last extensions of the global production networks. The African Lions are benefitting from increases in productivity in selective service sectors, while the agricultural sector remains unproductive.[18] The food processing industry can be considered a groundbreaking sector for its path to manufacturing growth.

In recent years, China and Factory Asia started to move up the quality ladder by manufacturing more goods with high-skilled content. The production system has become very fragmented with an increasing role of trade in tasks (trade in intermediate goods) and efficient logistics (manufacturing-related services).[19] As a consequence, economies are becoming more and more integrated through supply/value chains. According to Manyika et al. (2012), high R&D and trade-intensive industries, such as automotives, the chemical sector, and pharmaceuticals, represent the largest share (34 percent) of global manufacturing value-added while labor-intensive goods represent only 7 percent. Regional processing of rubber, plastic, metal, and food products represents 28 percent of total manufacturing value-added and is labor- and trade-intensive. In 2012, China manufactured half of the industrialized countries' products (UNIDO, 2013). The projection by Anderson and Strutt (2014) indicates that China will remain the world's top manufacturer in 2030 with a share of 28.9 percent of global value-added.

Nonetheless, the new initial conditions for industrial development, with Factory Asia as the new player in the global manufacturing and service trade, offer exploitable possibilities for Africa and other developing regions to industrialize. For example, Page (2012) has argued that rising costs and demand in Asia can serve as an opportunity for Africa to industrialize. Similarly, UNIDO (2013) pointed out that Africa faces openings in low-tech labor-intensive industries such as agro-industry, textiles, and clothing and apparel. The same should be true for Asia's latecomers.

Many chapters in Part II (Asia) and Part III (Africa) of this book try to deal with this issue at least partially. In Chapter 5, "Toward pro-poor industrial policies in Indonesia: progress, challenges, and future directions," Gunawan, Pratikto, and Dartanto touch upon Indonesia's most recent industrial promotion strategy of Indonesia 4.0. In Chapter 9, "Thailand's industrial policy: its history and recent development," Thaiprasert and Roidoung introduce Thailand's most recent strategy of Thailand 4.0. Both of these master plans for industrial structural upgrading are aimed at responding to the new challenges presented in this section.

On the contrary, in Chapter 7, "Promoting local SMEs through GVCs: a framework and case study of Laotian SMEs," Vidavong and Otsubo introduce the difficulties that an Asian latecomer country, Laos, faces. They point out, by showing a so-called Smile Curve that portrays the value-added structure of typical GVCs, that latecomers like Laos are confined to the low-value-added product assembly-related segments of the value chains without much prospect for industry upgrading.

In Chapter 13, "Mechanisms and impacts of innovation on firm survival: evidence from Sub-Saharan Africa," Otchia explores the reasons for the observed differences in African firm survival in international markets. Using a unique dataset that matches firm-level panel data and intersectoral input-output linkages data, the research finds that product innovation and process innovation are strong determinants of firm survival in the international market, but the effect of process innovation is greater than that of product innovation. Chapter 13 establishes that the speed of propagation of technological innovation has a strong effect on firm survival, especially through backward linkages.

From the discussion presented in this section, it is obvious that the future direction of China's industrial development will certainly impact that of other developing economies. In Chapter 11, "'Made in China 2025' and the recent industrial policy in China," Akkemik and Yülek introduce China's Made in China 2025 master plan for industry upgrading and analyze its impact. After a long period of high economic growth and industrialization, the Chinese economy has recently entered a period of relatively low economic growth. Behind the past remarkable performance lies the government's ambitious and interventionist industrial policies. To ensure a swift transition and avoid falling into a middle-income trap, the Chinese government has recently devised a new industrial policy called "Made in China 2025." This strategy envisages that China will join the ranks of industrialized countries through a structural change toward high-tech industries and by nurturing domestic production and the adoption of "smart manufacturing" technologies. This new strategy favors domestic firms against foreign competitors and imposes strict domestic content requirements. In the past, these were essential characteristics of traditional industrial policies in East Asia (e.g., Japan, Korea, and Taiwan). But the scale of the Chinese economy ensures that such a policy will have a significant impact on the world economy. Chapter 11 overviews and evaluates contemporary industrial policies in China in conjunction with criticism from some advanced countries, which recently have led to trade frictions. Chapter 11 sets up a theoretical and analytical framework to analyze industrial policies in the context of the Chinese case.

1.6.3 Do we need modern/new industrial policies?

> How can we design a new partnership between business and development?
> How can we promote the role of public-private-partnership (PPP) for inclusive industrial development?

The recent literature on industrial policy tends to contrast modern versus old industrial policies. Modern industrial policy emphasizes the extent and nature of the collaboration between government and the private sector as fundamental to the effectiveness and success of industrial policy.[20] According to Devlin and Moguillansky (2013), modern industrial policy stresses that the most successful strategies and interventions emerge out of a social process of close alliance between the public and private sectors. The new thinking promotes public-private alliance as a way to design and implement industrial policy (Chang, 1994; Devlin & Moguillansky, 2013; Evans, 1995; Rodrik, 2004; Wade, 2004). This has changed the focus of the industrial policy debate from "what" to "how." As part of the coordination of management of industrial policies, the private sector contributes to the design, content, and implementation of industrial policies. The coordination of management of industrial policies enables us to solve two major weaknesses of the old industrial policy: coordination and monitoring within government (Devlin & Moguillansky, 2013), and market failure (Chang, 2015). Industrial policies should serve the purpose of a clear vision for development and structural change, based on consistent dialogue between the public and private sectors. To this end, modern industrial policy calls for a more proactive intervention, rather than the traditional top-down approach, where the government solely identified sectors to promote or protect. The concept of public-private partnership (PPP) is given many definitions, some of them dating from as early as the 1990s. More recently, Günther and Alcorta (2011) of UNIDO referred to industrial policy as the public and private sectors jointly identifying and lifting the constraints that impede the transformation of industry. To advance the discussion, it is important to create specific institutions that support PPP-related developments.

There have been some successful cases of public-private dialogue for industrial policy in Sub-Saharan Africa. For example, the government of Ethiopia and the private sector established the Ethiopia Public Private Consultative Forum (EPPCF) in 2010 to serve as a platform for public-private dialogue for industrial policy. The EPPCF also aimed to create an environment of mutual understanding, increase the level of trust between the government and the private sector, and enhance the key actors' capacities in light of evidence-based policy. It is decentralized at three levels (federal, state, and county). The dialogue is championed by the Ministry of Trade and Industry (on the government side) and the Ethiopian Chamber of Commerce and Sectoral Association (ECCSA). As of March 2015, the EPPCF had conducted two high-level national dialogues (chaired by the Prime Minister) and more than 15 dialogues of other types (Mihretu & Eyob, 2015). The EPPCF claims positive results in the areas of customs procedure, trade licensing, taxes, and trust among economic agents.

In Chapter 16, "A new partnership between business and development: a case study of Ethiopia's industrial development," Ohno and Uesu state that the interface between business and development cooperation activities is growing, and major donors have begun to introduce new instruments to promote PPPs for development. This is because, with accelerated globalization, private financial flows to developing countries have dramatically increased, superseding the volume of Official Development Assistance (ODA). Particularly after the 2008 financial crisis, multinational corporations (MNCs) actively expanded their business operations in emerging economies and developing countries. This chapter aims to review the recent trends of development partnerships with the private sector, analyze the practices of major donors (traditional donors such as Western donors and Japan, as well as non-traditional donors, such as China and Turkey) and MNCs, and draw implications for the industrialization of latecomer countries. In doing so, Chapter 16 consists of two main sections: (1) an overview of development partnerships with the private sector in recent years, and (2) a case study of Ethiopia, which is endeavoring to achieve inclusive and sustainable industrial development.

In Chapter 9, "Thailand's industrial policy: its history and recent development," Thaiprasert and Roidoung introduce the history and evolution of industrial development and *de facto* industrial policy for a country that has not officially recognized "industrial policy." The role of PPPs is explicitly discussed for this country where the relationships between business and government, and business and development have been closer, compared to those in the other ASEAN economies.

From the days of the East Asian miracle, industrial promotion in Thailand, like that in Indonesia, has been considered to be market-driven (private sector-driven) with minimal direct government intervention, as opposed to the widely known and well-studied models of Japan, South Korea, and Taiwan (World Bank, 1993). In reality, however, there exist conscious and unconscious efforts by the state to promote industrial growth and development. Chapter 9 introduces the history, issues, and initiatives of industrial promotion in the Kingdom of Thailand. It introduces: (1) the mix of direct and indirect interventions, modalities utilized, and the recent Thailand 4.0 initiative; (2) the roles of the US, Chinese immigrants, and Japan; and (3) the role of PPPs. Overall, Chapter 9 intends to provide the context for further discussion on whether industrial policies were/should be intentionally developed or occur spontaneously when opportunities arise in the constantly changing global economic environment.

1.6.4 Does today's developing world have industrial policy space under the WTO global rules?

Many economists argue that the current difficulties facing developing countries wishing to embark on the process of industrialization are related to the new rules of the game. There is still a debate on what should be the best "policy space" for developing countries to accelerate industrial development under the World Trade Organization (WTO) rules and the bilateral and regional trade and investment agreements.

Trade policies played a significant role in the East Asian miracle (Masuyama, Vandenbrink, & Yue, 1997). Governments of the countries involved used import protection to develop their infant industries, and then export promotion for their strategic industries to upgrade their productive structure and create new comparative and competitive advantages. Since the conclusion of the Uruguay Round trade negotiations in 1994 and the establishment of the WTO that followed in 1995, trade policy space for developing countries has been restricted, to the advantage of the neoliberal international economic order (Gallagher, 2005; Khan, 2007; Wade, 2003). Shadlen (2005) adds that the advanced countries have also used trade agreements to impose additional restrictions on developing countries. Under these circumstances, industrial policies in developing countries need to conform to commitments countries have made with their major trading partners and to the rules of the multilateral trade system. As a corollary, it has been argued that the WTO rules do not provide a greater policy space for industrial development, as they have reduced the ability of developing countries to achieve economic development.[21] The regulations that may reduce the range of policy options for developing countries include the General Agreement on Tariffs and Trade (GATT), the General Agreement on Trade and Services (GATS), the Agreement on Subsidies and Countervailing Measures (SCM), the Agreement on Trade Related Aspects of Intellectual Property Rights (TRIPS), and the Trade Related Investment Measures (TRIMS). For instance, policies such as import protection and export promotion, which were implemented by the East Asian economies to develop their infant industries and create comparative advantages, became illegal under the WTO rules (Chang, 2003; Di Maio, 2014). As far as import protection is concerned, the WTO regulations require that member countries limit their tariffs up to a ceiling. Despite the fact that developing countries were allowed to fix their ceiling at higher levels than their applied tariffs, authors such as Gibbs (2007) contend that it still reduces the ability of developing countries to adjust tariff protection with the improvement of technology, through a system of "cascading." Since the ceiling levels of tariffs are generally not allowed, developing countries have a limited amount of leeway to use tariff instruments when their economic structure changes or when they enter regional integration agreements.[22]

Similarly, WTO's SCM agreements are restricting the use of export subsidies and subsidies for domestic inputs (Di Maio, 2014; Rodrik, 2004; Shadlen, 2005), which had been the key interventions in the East Asian model of export-promotion-based growth. Rodrik (2004), in addressing the issue related to SCM agreements, contended that it renders export processing zones (EPZs) illegal. A clarification in this debate is provided by Shadlen (2005) and UNECA (2016), who state that developing countries can still use "actionable subsidies" as long as they do not create injury or cause adverse prejudice to the importing country's domestic industry or another country's export of the same product. UNECA (2016) adds that subsidies can still be used until they are challenged or countervailed, which can take 2 to 3 years.

Several other criticisms have been made of the introduction of TRIPS rules on copyrights, trademarks, industrial designs, trade secrecy, and patents. The criticisms stem from the fact that the TRIPS agreement has strengthened the patent rights and Intellectual Property Rights (IPRs) with regard to the developing countries whereas most of the developed economies—the USA, the European countries, Japan, Taiwan, and South Korea—had wide access to new technologies from other countries and could learn to imitate them to climb up the technological ladder and industrialize. Thus, TRIPS has been criticized for reducing the use of patents and is therefore responsible for a widening technology gap between developed and developing countries (Correa, 1999; UNDP, 2005). Other ambiguous effects of TRIM based on empirical studies include those found by Ahn, Hall, and Lee (2014) and Americo and Fredriksson (2007). For instance, Americo and Fredriksson (2007) find that the effects of TRIMs, using case studies in six countries, have been mixed or positive but small. We have to clarify what are the positive and negative effects. Static and dynamic impacts should also differ.

The WTO agreement of TRIMs which bans local content and performance requirements has mostly been criticized for restricting industrial policy toward foreign investment and reducing trade flows (Aggarwal & Evenett, 2014; Wade, 2003). The TRIMs agreement, however, does not limit the use of other regulatory investment measures, such as conditions for maintaining joint ventures with local firms, transfer of technology, and limitations on foreign equity ownership. These are important investment measures and can be used by developing countries to create a useful investment strategy.

In Table 1.4, we present a summary of indicative policy options for developing countries under the WTO global rules. We see that developing countries can still make use of industrial policies related to science and technology, regional development, the environment, infrastructure, human capital, and capacity building under the WTO regime. This corroborates the conclusion of UNECA (2016), which argues that the WTO rules restrict a few trade policy instruments and developing countries still have room for trade policy measures if they do not affect exports or imports. For instance, developing countries can fully apply the SCMs and TRIMS in services as the regulations cover only goods. The WTO rules and trade agreements give a restricted policy space for industrialization in manufacturing and agriculture. However, the service sector remains an interesting and promising frontier. Finally, the WTO rules might not be applied to certain industries in certain countries. For example, the TRIPs and GATS agreements have not been found to be of direct importance in the Malaysian and Thai automotive industries (Natsuda & Thoburn, 2014).

As WTO functions as the provider of negotiating tables and dispute settlement mechanisms, a proper understanding of the related rules and the cases of their applications including those handled under the Dispute Settlement mechanism

Table 1.4 Summary of policy options under the WTO

Import barriers	Tariffs and ODCs	Can be used for industrial policies, by virtue of "water." Countries can also renegotiate the bound tariffs for one or several products or apply the Government Assistance to Economic Development
	NTB (import quotas, import licensing, import prohibitions and local content requirements)	Local content requirements are not consistent with the Trade-Related Investment Measures (TRIMs) agreement (and so are likely to be challenged). Alternative strategies that can spur domestic production and are allowed under WTO rules must be sought (for example, offset clauses).
	Quantitative restrictions on imports	Accepted under the WTO Agreement of Agriculture (AOA) or for balance of payments reasons
	National treatment	Accepted only for government procurement
	GATS-inconsistent measures	Allowed to promote the establishment of a particular industry
	Anti-dumping measures	Can be applied
	Countervailing duties	Can be applied to offset the effect of a subsidy
Exchange rate policies	Exchange rate policies	Can be applied as no WTO agreement explicitly deals with exchange rates
Aid to enterprises	Subsidies for goods (SCM)/domestic content subsidies	Prohibited since 31 December 2002
	Subsidies for goods (SCM)/production subsidies	Accepted if it meets the specificity requirement
	Subsidies for R&D	Accepted under WTO rules (up to 75 percent of research costs and 50 percent of pre-competitive development), but fiscally expensive
	Upgrading of disadvantaged regions and to develop environmentally friendly technology	Allowed but WTO members are simply required to notify any new R&D measure granted in favor of the agricultural sector
	Human capital development	
Export promotion	Export subsidies	Accepted for developing countries with a per capita income of less than $1,000
	Export finance; export insurance; export guarantee	Allowed
	Export quality management	Allowed

Table 1.4 Cont.

	Export taxes and duties	Export taxes are not regulated by the WTO agreements. However, the imposition of a prohibitive tax may be tantamount to a quantitative restriction according to the terms of GATT Article XI
Investment measures and incentives	FDI and TRIMS	Export performance requirements, joint ventures measures, technology transfer and equity repatriation (foreign equity ownership) are allowed by WTO but limited by some trade agreements
	SEZ	Accepted under WTO rules
	Technology-related requirements on domestic firms	Accepted but contents and implementation of requirement remain vague
	FDI policy on performance requirements	Generally forbidden
	Facilitating reverse engineering and imitation	TRIPS requires domestic IPR institutions and protection

Source: Authors' compilation from various sources including Guadagno (2015) and Rodrik (2008b).

seems to be imperative for policymakers and scholars to support their policy-making. Human capital development in developing countries, including sharing talent in regional cooperation frameworks, should be promoted. In 419 WTO disputes up to 2018, no single case was brought against low-income countries, suggesting that industrial policies undertaken by those countries might not result in legal actions by other members. However, after 2018, the world has started to observe cases brought against developing countries, such as China and India. Other developing countries, middle-income countries in particular, should be ready to discuss and defend their initiatives for "inclusive" industrial promotion. Continuous efforts should be made for the low-income countries to be supported by preferential arrangements. Various case chapters in this book will deal with some of the related issues.

In Chapter 4, "A *de facto* industrial policy and its effects on the least developed countries," Matsunaga and Haraguchi address issues related to this "policy space." It has been argued that an increasing number of international arrangements have limited the "policy space" in industrial policies for developing countries. Such WTO rules as the TRIPS, TRIMS, and SCM made poor countries face more difficulties in devising and implementing industrial policies to develop their economies. However, scrutiny of international arrangements could make some developing countries enjoy a *de facto* industrial policy, thereby widening the policy space. The authors demonstrate that the Multi-Fiber Arrangement (MFA) and the Generalized System of Preferences (GSP) functioned as a *de facto* industrial policy to foster the export-oriented garment industry in one of the least developed countries, Bangladesh. The industry has had latent comparative advantage but was totally different from the known comparative advantage industry (jute products). This case defied the theory of comparative advantage yet eventually succeeded. Likewise, the policy space can be widened by studying the possible effects of international arrangements on developing economies and using them as a *de facto* industrial policy. Even Brexit and the recent US-China trade frictions may have similar effects. Researchers should play a role in devising these policies.

1.6.5 Should industry policies cater for "pro-poorness" and "inclusiveness" in addition to promoting economic growth?

As shown above, in Figure 1.1, the SDGs encompass goals of inclusive economic growth, industrial development, and reduced inequalities:

> Goal 1: End poverty in all its forms everywhere.
> Goal 8: Promote inclusive and sustainable economic growth, employment and decent work for all.
> Goal 9: Build resilient infrastructure, promote sustainable industrialization and foster innovation.
> Goal 10: Reduce inequality within and among countries.

This focuses thoughtful and concurrent attention on the provision of decent employment for all, the promotion of sustainable industrialization with innovation, and the reduction of inequalities as imperative or at least desired elements of today's industrial policymaking. Furthermore, industrial policies, narrowly defined industrial policies in particular, tend to create/increase inequalities and disparities across industrial sectors, labor segments, and geographical regions of a country. This, in turn, should force policymakers to pay more attention to the "inclusiveness" of their policy initiatives.

In Chapter 1 and Chapter 2, Otsubo and Otchia introduce general views on the impact of industrialization, centering on the expansion of manufacturing on economic growth (enlargement of total value-added) and employment. With a concise but integrated literature survey and presentation of historical facts related to value-added and employment generation, Chapters 1 and 2 point to the importance of manufacturing development and more integrated and linked promotion of higher-yielding agriculture/agro-product processing and manufacturing-related services supported by technological innovation, such as ICT and IoT. This, in turn, should widen the beneficiaries of modern industrialization to various segments of sectors and workers for a more inclusive economic growth.

In Chapter 3, "The importance of manufacturing development and structural change for pro-poor growth," Haraguchi and Amann highlight the relevance of manufacturing in promoting pro-poor growth pathways of industrial development. This is done by means of carefully disaggregating and analyzing structural change patterns, taking into account various sources of heterogeneities and variations. Their analysis highlights the continued importance of manufacturing and the key role of industrial policies in the process of industrialization. Chapter 3 furthermore explores the dynamics of structural change within manufacturing and delineates a path of inclusive manufacturing development for pro-poor growth. With regard to the role of manufacturing for pro-poor growth, they offer a review of the stylized views, present long-term (1965–2017) statistics to support a positive relationship between manufacturing development and increased per capital income relative to the other countries in the world, and accumulated employment creation by key sectors in manufacturing industry. The chapter goes on to analyze the patterns of industrial structural changes for pro-poor growth by identifying key manufacturing industries which are particularly associated with pro-poor growth (higher levels of employment generation for the similar path of value-added), based on pooled cross-country data for 153 countries between 1963 and 2015. In doing so, they consistently control for differences in income levels and brackets, and thus are able to identify impacts on the lower-income groups in comparison to those in higher-income segments.

In Chapter 5, "Toward pro-poor industrial policies in Indonesia: progress, challenges, and future directions," Gunawan, Pratikto, and Dartanto address the question, "What explains the successful and unsuccessful impacts of Indonesia's industrial policies on poverty reduction?" Indonesia had accomplished three decades of remarkable industrial development since the mid-1960s that took off as trade and investment liberalization boosted foreign and domestic investments in manufacturing sectors. Indonesia's living standards had significantly improved, the incidence of poverty had significantly decreased and inequality had been maintained at a low level. However, in the aftermath of the Asian Financial Crisis that hit Indonesia's economy in 1997/1998, Indonesia began to face deindustrialization even before industrialization had matured, i.e., the issue of "premature deindustrialization." Focusing on trade orientation and protection, upstream-downstream linkages, minimum wage regulation, and transportation infrastructure, Chapter 5 aims to investigate which of Indonesia's industrial policies, or absence of particular policies, tend to be "pro-poor" or "anti-poor," and which particular set of industrial policies should be adopted and implemented by Indonesia's policymakers.

Given the fact that most of the labor force in a developing country is employed in small and medium-sized enterprises (SMEs), discussing and analyzing industrial development and industrial policies in the context of SMEs leads to the discussion of "inclusive" industrial promotion. In Chapter 7, "Promoting local SMEs through GVCs: a framework and case study of Laotian SMEs," Vidavong and Otsubo analyze the impact of local SMEs' participation in global value chains (GVCs) as the government of Laos intends to promote industry upgrading by promoting participation of their local firms in global production networks. While an extension of the GVC network would be conducive to job creation and income growth in developing countries, participation in GVCs should also bring about upgrading of supply capacity on the part of local firms. For the local SMEs that have only limited exposure to global business practices, GVC participation could provide access to new technologies, innovations, and new markets. This, in turn, should lead to improvements in productivity and competitiveness. In reality, however, the benefits for local firms are not automatically created, and proper facilitation by the state and conscious efforts by local firms to upgrade their capacities are called for. Vidavong and Otsubo's statistical analyses based on their firm-level data collected in the field surveys do not identify increases in wages supported by productivity improvements brought about by GVC participation. The results confirm, instead, the sad reality in latecomer economies in Asia where GVCs look for lower-cost labor-intensive production with a large pool of the supporting unemployed or underemployed, unskilled labor force. A traditional industrial promotion strategy that depends on the existence of abundant cheap labor and foreign investment that capitalizes on it is not only losing the room to grow, but also not offering the desired benefits to the host economies.

For readers to further understand the background of these sad realities observed in Asia's latecomer economy of Laos, Chapter 6, "Industrial policy and development in Laos: trade, industrial estates, and enterprise development" by Vixathep and Phonvisay introduces the history of industrial promotion in Lao where industrial policy has been embedded in the National Socio-Economic Development Plans (NSEDPs), which can be viewed as *de facto* industrial policy. Their chapter evaluates the contribution of industrial policy to economic development in three areas: trade liberalization, special economic zone development, and SME promotion. It also agrees that more efforts are necessary to improve capacity building for government officials and thereby enhance effective policy implementation.

In Chapter 12, "Promoting exports by the ASEAN SMEs: impediments, drivers, and conducive policies," Jitsutthiphakorn and Otsubo look at impediments, drivers, and conducive policies in internationalizing SMEs in developing countries. Access to export markets often signifies higher productivity and competitiveness, leading to firms' ability to survive. Using the World Bank Enterprise Surveys of eight countries in ASEAN, the authors introduce export experiences of these eight ASEAN countries in comparison to those of the East Asian economies, focusing on SMEs' shares in total employment, exports, and GDP. The need for higher export performance by the ASEAN SMEs is discussed. This chapter analyzes the dynamic changes in the problems faced by ASEAN firms, separately by country, by firm size, and by sector. The issue is discussed in the context of internal factors (firm characteristics, access to finance, ICT) and external factors (trade facilitation, real effective exchange rate, policies conducive to SME promotion) that may influence the export activities of SMEs. The chapter then introduces key results obtained from econometric analyses on the drivers of SMEs' export activities.

For most developing countries where resources are limited to support more balanced industrial development in either the sectoral dimension or geographical dimension, industrial policies naturally create disparities and inequalities that, in turn, can undermine the attempts at "inclusive" industrial development.

In Chapter 18, "Promoting both industrial development and regional convergence: toward a regionally inclusive industrial policy," Mendez deals with this conflict between industrial promotion and regional disparities. Industrial policy boosts economic growth through targeted interventions that affect the allocation of skilled labor, output composition, and industrial productivity growth. A commonly omitted consequence of these changes is that, depending on the initial cross-regional distribution of income, policies aiming to foster industrial development may change regional inequality in unintended ways. In this context, this chapter aims to explore the interaction between industrial development and regional divergence/convergence. The ultimate goal of this exploration is to identify possible lessons that could guide the design and implementation of "regionally inclusive" industrial policies (RIIPs). The first part of Chapter 18 revisits some key facts about industrial development and regional divergence/convergence. Next, industrial and regional interactions are evaluated through the lens of an industry-based model of regional convergence. Chapter 18 concludes by outlining some lessons that may prove helpful to the design and implementation of "regionally inclusive" industrial policies.

1.6.6 What are the dimensions of integration in designing "integrated" industrial policies?

Regarding the dimensions and levels of "integration" that we have to take into consideration when designing "integrated," not piecewise, industrial promotion policies/initiatives for multiple goals of industrial promotion, discussions so far in Chapter 1 have already presented the most important factors. First of all, we discussed the multiple/combined goals of industrial promotion under the SDGs. Industrial policy should now target not only economic growth, but also employment generation (provision of decent work for all segments in society) and human capital development (making people more productive) in an inclusive and pro-poor manner. How can a "pro-poor" impact be secured/promoted in packaging policies? How should "sustainability" be treated in line with the SDG goal of promoting sustainable industrialization and fostering innovation (Goal 9)? Multiple goals, in principle, require a combination of multiple policies/initiatives.

Second, the types of industrial policies presented in Table 1.2 can/should be combined or integrated. When types/definitions of industrial policies are combined, we can categorize tools of policy interventions to be selected or combined as Weiss's classification (Table 1.3) nicely portrayed. The efficacy of the narrow and targeted industrial policies depends on the performance of broader and general policies such as preserving a stable and investment-conducive macroeconomic environment.

As the integration of old and new models of industrial policies, above we discussed the importance of the public-private partnership (PPP) in industrial promotion both in national policies and in international development cooperation. How should we view the "new PPP" as a coordination model of innovation, productivity, and international cooperation? How should "integrated" policies deal with coordination failure, market failure, and government (governance) failure?

Questions addressed in Section 1.6.1 and Section 1.6.2 point to the need to integrate certain segments of service (such as manufacturing-related services, transportation/logistics) and agriculture (such as agro-production and processing) into "industry" when we discuss industrial promotion. Advances in ICT and IoT that are highly desired for the future of manufacturing require strong support from the service sectors.

As we try to promote industries in developing countries in today's globalized world with the active extension of production and service networks of MNCs and GVCs, border policies (such as trade, investment, exchange rate policies) and domestic policies should be integrated. On the domestic front, goods/service market policies and policies that work on factor (capital and labor) markets should also be integrated.

Although the list of dimensions of integration seems endless, this book, in addition to the aforementioned elements of integration, also tries to shed some light on the following new dimensions.

1.6.6.1 Regional Comprehensive Economic Partnerships (RCEPs)

One new dimension of integration in designing industrial policy is related to the recent surge in super-national regional arrangements, such as the ASEAN Economic Community (AEC) in Asia and the reinforced Africa Union (AU) in Africa. Particularly when they take a form of Regional Comprehensive Economic Partnerships (RCEPs), industrial policies may well be coordinated together with coordination in trade and investment policies. In this sense, integrated designs of national and super-national regional industrial promotion policies are called for.

In Chapter 8, "The role of Thailand's industrial promotion in ASEAN," Amonvatana asserts that, as the ASEAN Economic Community (AEC) is now fully effective, the Thai government is obliged to help increase the region's competitiveness. Although the AEC Blueprint has attracted attention from researchers and policymakers, much attention has been placed on the impact on individual countries of this AEC Blueprint. For Thailand, economic growth is one clear positive result from the region's economic integration. Empirical studies also suggest a positive impact of poverty reduction in relation to this accelerated economic growth. However, what has been questionable is the relationship between economic growth and income disparity, especially between Bangkok and other regions. More importantly, what has been understudied is the impact of the industrial policy of particular countries on the growth and development of ASEAN as a whole. Taking into account the existing literature, this chapter looks at two levels of Thailand's industrial policies. First, it aims to analyze whether the policies that the Thai government adopted have helped to close the poverty gap or have instead created a wider gap and worsened Thailand's regional disparities. Second, it aims at examining whether the policies initiated by the Thai government have promoted regional growth and development for the AEC.

In Chapter 17, "Taking part in RCEP: CGE analysis focusing on industrial impact," Itakura conducts policy simulations in order to analyze the impacts of RCEPs and GVCs on the member economies' industrial development, using computable general equilibrium (CGE) models. CGE models are based on inter-industry input-output data, and therefore, are considered to be useful tools for industrial policy simulations. After all, most of the industrial policies aim to create industrial structural changes, often in favor of targeted sectors, by impacting the inter-industry (productive) resource flows. Multi-sector and multi-country models can also ensure macro-economic consistency, such as balancing investment and savings in a national and/or world/regional context. They are also suitable to evaluate the impacts of industrial promotion with international initiatives under the globalizing world economy. This chapter considers taking part in a mega-regional trade agreement (MRTA) as an industrial policy one country can adopt for industrial development. It takes the Regional Comprehensive Economic Partnership (RCEP) as a policy scenario for a CGE simulation. While some industries expand in the RCEP, other industries contract because of resource constraints. Three features in simulating RCEP are: (1) accommodation of GVCs; (2) liberalization of trade in goods and services; and (3) investment measures.

1.6.6.2 The service-tourism "industry"

Another dimension of integration is to include the designs of industrial promotion for the economies where manufacturing industries may not have many chances to grow into a key engine of development. In Chapter 10, "The process of change in the economic development model of the Pacific Island Countries under the influence of globalization," Umemura introduces a development model of the Service-Tourism "industry" for Small Island Developing States (SIDS) in the Pacific region. This is a good example of promoting non-manufacturing industry as industry to make it an engine of growth and inclusive development.

Although the Pacific SIDS achieved independence after WWII, economic development was initiated by the production of commodities under colonization and a subsistence economy. The main feature of the Pacific SIDS is the so-called "MIRAB" (Migration (MI), Remittance (R), Foreign Aid (A), and Public Bureaucracy (B)). These countries were affected by their small domestic markets and populations, and their remoteness from continents or developed countries. The MIRAB model has been developed into the "TOURAB" (Tourism (TOU), Remittance (R), Foreign Aid (A), and the Public Bureaucracy (B)) model and the "SITES" (Small Island Tourists Economies) model. In this chapter, economic development models of the Pacific SIDS are examined in three periods: (1) postwar independence; (2) the first wave of globalization in the 1990s when international trade had grown at a much faster pace than before; and (3) the second stage of globalization during the 2000s onward when international tourism had expanded. These changes in the international economic environment have affected the development policies and management of industrial promotion in the Pacific SIDS.

1.6.6.3 The presence of China

In the context of today's developing countries in Africa, and the same is true of Asia's latecomer economies, integrating the ever-increasing presence of China in their economies into their designs of industrial policies has become one crucial part of policymaking. In Chapter 15, "Is China's growing interest in Africa a blessing or curse for the continent's industrialization drive?," Osei-Assibey addresses this issue from the macro-economic viewpoint. He investigates the effect of increasing Chinese engagements in Africa on value-added manufacturing and industrial growth in Africa. More specifically, Chapter 15 investigates, first, the effects of China's investments, trade, loans, and financing of infrastructure in Africa on the manufacturing and on overall industrial sector growth in Africa. Second, it examines the potency or effectiveness of Chinese activities on industries within a differing enabling policy and institutional context (such as political stability, government effectiveness, control of corruption, or rule of law). Using data from 40 African countries that spans from 2003 to 2016 and applying an Autoregressive Distributed Lag model and a Pooled Mean Group estimator, the study reveals a range of interesting findings. The study finds generally that Chinese activities such as exports, FDI, and infrastructure contracts in Africa have had a positive impact on industry growth but only in the short run. In the long run, however, Chinese activities have a negative influence on manufacturing and industry GDP growth. Further, the negative impact becomes more pronounced in the context of weak institutions, such as government effectiveness and corruption. These findings suggest that without a stronger institutional and governance framework, Africa cannot benefit from China's growing influence on the continent.

In Chapter 14, "Local and Chinese-invested SMEs' contribution to industrial development through knowledge spillovers in Africa: the case of Tanzania," Maswana and Munisi address this issue from the micro-economic viewpoint. While spillover effects generated by the presence of large foreign firms have been well documented in the literature, little is known of the case of spillovers associated with small foreign-owned or returnee-migrant-owned enterprises in developing countries. Focusing on these two unaddressed aspects and based on a case-study approach, the authors outlined interviews of SMEs in Tanzania and examined their technology spillover mechanisms from the perspective of industrial development. Major findings indicate that, for the most part, entrepreneurs have little or no knowledge of how to upgrade the technical capabilities of their firms, and many of them end up with failed businesses that could have been profitable. Moreover, the lack of interactions with their counterparts owned by Tanzanian returnee migrants and Chinese-invested enterprises seems to have been hindering their opportunities for technology absorption and upgrading. For this reason, the presence of foreign- and returnee-owned firms might not be helping in the technology upgrading of SMEs. Therefore, policy priority should focus on overcoming some of the identified limitations of SMEs, such as through identification of their technological needs and strengthening their exchange of information through networking. There is a need for a platform of knowledge-sharing for entrepreneurs so that they can better manage the accumulation of technical knowledge. Therefore, similar to the macro-analyses in Chapter 15, firm-level micro-analyses in Chapter 14 also point to the need for capacity building on the part of the state to act as coordinators/facilitators of desired exchanges between local firms and foreign-invested (Chinese-invested) firms.

1.6.7 How can we properly assess the efficacy of industrial policies for evidence-based policymaking?

Evaluation of the causal effects of industrial policy on a selected outcome variable consists of assessing the difference between the value of the outcome variable after the policy has been implemented (or simulated) and the value of the outcome variable in the absence of the policy. Another possible method is to relate changes in the value of the industrial policy instrument with those of the outcome variables. However, the practice in the field has been to pick a successful case (or failure), demonstrate that a deliberate government policy existed, and make the case for (or against) the use of industrial policy (Haggard, 2015). Gathering sufficient empirical evidence on the causal effect of the industrial policy has been a key impediment in the debate on industrial policies. According to Rodrik (2008a), pro-industrial policies tend to select case studies where industrial policies worked to back up their argument whereas anti-industrial policies tend to make use of cross-industry econometrics. But at the end of the day, the empirical analyses leave us no better informed than when we started.

Leaving this discussion aside, the empirical assessment of industrial policy faces several unique challenges. The main challenge so far has been the difficulty in finding a credible counterfactual and the timing for the effect of the policy to materialize. Finding a credible counterfactual consists of finding a situation that we would observe, had the policy not been implemented. For instance, an ideal counterfactual to evaluate the impact of a government policy on infrastructure upgrading would be to compare what happened to firms who benefited from the infrastructure against what would have happened to them in the absence of the infrastructure. The results from such exercises will most likely depend on the nature of the data and the outcome variable(s), as well as the timing for the effect to materialize. For example, infrastructure development is likely to produce sizable effects many years after the completion of the project when income is used as the outcome variable. The effect can also vary when we compare the benefits for direct beneficiaries versus benefits for the region as a whole.

Even though the effects of industrial policy are likely to vary, three techniques have been widely used in the empirical evaluation or assessment of industrial policy, either ex-ante or ex-post. The most popular methods include control case studies, cross-firm regressions (cross-firm, cross-sector, cross-country, and their panel studies), and structural models (including input-output, econometric, and computable general equilibrium models). In this book, we offer piecewise and combined applications of those methods of assessment. The recent Nobel Economics Prize awarded to Professor Abijit Banerjee, Professor Esther Duflo, and Professor Michael Kremer jointly for their use of randomized controlled trials (RCTs) in the analyses of micro-policies/initiatives on micro-poverty outcomes heightened our expectation of a leapfrog advance in the assessment of industrial policies. However, even if we succeed in proving a causational relationship between a certain piece of industrial policy and a certain outcome variable such as increased profits or survivability of local firms, we still have to keep in mind that the multifaceted targets of industrial policies that we discussed here would still require tools to assess the superiority of designing and implementing more combined and integrated policies to work on multiple goals, such as growth and inclusiveness at the same time. How can/should we assess the efficacy of integrated (or coordinated) industrial policies in various dimensions against piecewise (uncoordinated) ones in order for us to avoid the "fallacy of composition" in designing integrated industrial policies for inclusive growth in today's globalized world?

Notes

1 Refer to the United Nations Resolution A/RES/70/1 of 25 September 2015, *Transforming Our World: The 2030 Agenda for Sustainable Development.* Official SDGs website available at: www.un.org/sustainabledevelopment/.

2 The MDGs period was from 2000 to 2015, but used 1990 as the reference year for goal settings. For the official account of the MDG results, visit the official MDGs website at: www.un.org/millenniumgoals/bkgd.shtml.

3 One can recall the Arab Spring of 2010–2012 that stormed North Africa and the Middle East regions. The lack of job creation that introduces young entrants to job markets was (and still is) considered to be a key trigger.

4 Asian Tigers, or the four Asian Tigers, refers to Hong Kong, Singapore, South Korea, and Taiwan.

5 OECD countries renewed industrial policies mainly as a direct response to 2008 economic and financial crisis (OECD, 2013). However, there is a growing discussion on industrial policy for industrialized countries, which can be understood as a strategy to promote "high-road competitiveness." In this context, industrial policy is expected to combine strategic policy in the field of advanced skills, innovations, supporting institutions, ecological ambition, and an active social policy to achieve "Beyond-GDP" Goals (Aiginger, 2015).

6 See, for example, Chang (1994), Peres and Primi (2009), and Di Maio (2014).

7 See, for example, Newman and Page (2017) for a recent discussion on industrial clusters in Africa.

8 Lall (2004) notes that the distinction between functional and selective industrial policy is not easy in practice.

9 Pareto efficiency refers to a state where resources cannot be further reallocated to improve one party's welfare without causing damage to the other party. It is a

notion of market efficiency. However, it does not guarantee equitable allocation of resources.

10 Studies on market imperfection include Acemoglu and Verdier (2000), Dustmann and Schönberg (2012), Krueger (1990), and Wasmer and Weil (2004).

11 For detailed theoretical arguments in favor of industrial policy, see Pack and Saggi (2006), Rodrik (2008a), and Lall (2004).

12 This group of 75 countries includes developed economies such as Australia and Iceland. In their study, 154 sample countries are divided into 34 high-core countries with exportation of "good products," another 28 high-core countries in the "middle products" trap, 17 low-core countries in the "middle products" trap, and the aforementioned 75 low-core countries in the "low products" trap.

13 Haraguchi and Amann (the UNIDO team) discuss the importance of manufacturing development and structural change for pro-poor growth in Chapter 3. For further reading on the role of manufacturing, see Amable (2000), Peneder (2003), Rodrik (2013), Szirmai (2012), and UNIDO and UNU-MERIT (2012).

14 Unfortunately, reliable cross-country data on manufacturing employment is not yet available. Observation years are chosen encompassing three recent decades and avoiding years affected by financial crises such as the Asian Financial Crisis and the Global Financial Crisis. Three-year averages are used.

15 Earlier, Ghani and O'Connell (2014) also found a similar changing pattern for three decades (the late 1980s, the late 1990s, and the late 2000s).

16 GDP value-added sectors have traditionally been trisected into Agriculture, Industry, and Service sectors. Industry is further split into Manufacturing and Non-Manufacturing industries. Non-Manufacturing industry normally includes Mining and Quarrying, and Public Utilities (electricity, gas, water supply). Although some earlier studies also included Construction in the Non-Manufacturing industry, it is included in the Service sector in this book. The coverage of economic activities of each subsector follows that of the United Nations International Standard Industrial Classification of All Economic Activities (ISIC), Rev. 4.

17 Conversely, the service sector has contributed to growth and employment in India, and has been playing an important role in Brazil and South Africa.

18 Analogous to the Asian Tigers, the term, "African Lions" has been used in the Africa Rising narrative, but unlike the Asian Tigers, African Lions do not refer to a specific group of countries.

19 The report by IDE-JETRO and World Trade Organization (2011) provides a clear picture of the trade patterns and GVCs in the East Asia region.

20 See Alvarez (2013), Herzberg and Sisombat (2016), and Devlin (2014) for a discussion of public-private collaboration. In Chapter 16, Ohno and Uesu discuss the new partnership between business and development in a PPP context, taking a case study from Ethiopia's industrial development.

21 For a recent detailed discussion, see UNECA (2016). Also, the issue of "policy space" for developing countries in their fight against poverty and inequality was actively discussed at the World Economic Forum 2016 in Davos, Switzerland.

22 Initially, this book planned to include a chapter by a WTO team in the subject area of policy space and the proper understanding of the global trading rules for developing countries. Heightened political tension due to the US-China trade disputes during 2018–2020, however, made it difficult for us to obtain a completed manuscript. WTO, however, offers online information sources and training courses for policymakers to aid proper understanding of their rules.

References

Acemoglu, D., & Verdier, T. (2000). The choice between market failures and corruption. *American Economic Review*, 90(1), 194–211.

ACET. (2014). *2004 African transformation report: Growth with depth.* Accra, Ghana: The African Center for Economic Transformation.

Aggarwal, V. K., & Evenett, S. J. (2014). Do WTO rules preclude industrial policy? Evidence from the global economic crisis. *Business and Politics*, 16(4), 481–509.

Agosin, M. R. (2007). Export diversification and growth in emerging economies. Working Paper No. 233. Department of Economics, University of Chile.

Ahn, S., Hall, B. H., & Lee, K. (2014). *Intellectual property for economic development.* Cheltenham: Edward Elgar Publishing.

Aiginger, K. (2015). Industrial policy for a sustainable growth path. In D. Bailey, K. Cowling, & P. Tomlinson (Eds.), *New perspectives on industrial policy for a modern Britain.* Oxford Scholarship, Online.

Altenburg, T. (2011). Industrial policy in developing countries: Overview and lessons from seven country cases. Discussion paper no. 4/2011. Bonn: German Development Institute.

Altenburg, T. (2013). Can industrial policy work under neopatrimonial rule? In A. Szirmai, W. Naudé, & L. Alcorta (Eds.), *Pathways to industrialization in the twenty-first century: New challenges and emerging paradigms.* Oxford: Oxford University Press.

Alvarez, C. V. (2013). Comments on "What's New in the New Industrial Policy in Latin America?" by Robert Devlin and Graciela Moguillansky. In J. E. Stiglitz & J. Y. Lin (Eds.), *The industrial policy revolution I: The role of government beyond ideology* (pp. 318–323). London: Palgrave Macmillan.

Amable, B. (2000). International specialisation and growth. *Structural Change and Economic Dynamics*, 11, 413–431.

Americo, B. Z., & Fredriksson, T. (2007). *Elimination of TRIMs: The experience of selected developing countries.* Geneva: United Nations.

Amin Guitierrez de Pineres, S., & Ferrantino, M. J. (2000). *Export dynamics and economic growth in Latin America.* Burlington, VT: Ashgate Publishing Ltd.

Anderson, K., & Strutt, A. (2014). Emerging economies, productivity growth and trade with resource-rich economies by 2030. *Australian Journal of Agricultural and Resource Economics*, 58(4), 590–606.

Chang, H.-J. (1994). *The political economy of industrial policy.* New York: St. Martin's Press.

Chang, H.-J. (2003). *Kicking away the ladder: Development strategy in historical perspective.* London: Anthem Press.

Chang, H.-J. (2010). Hamlet without the Prince of Denmark: How development has disappeared from today's 'development' discourse. In S. R. Khan & J. Christiansen (Eds.), *Towards new developmentalism: Markets as means rather than master.* Abingdon: Routledge.

Chang, H.-J., Andreoni, A., & Kuan, M. L. (2014). Productive capabilities transformation: Institutions, linkages and policies for manufacturing growth and employment. Background paper for World of Work Report, 2014— Developing with Jobs. Geneva: ILO.

Chang, J.-M. (2015). The Republic of Korea's financial support for small and medium-sized enterprises and venture businesses. In J. Felipe (Ed.), *Development and modern industrial policy in practice: Issues and country experiences* (pp. 247–278). Cheltenham: Edward Elgar Publishing.

Chenery, H., Robinson, S., & Syrquin, M. (1986). Structural transformation. In H. Chenery, S. Robinson, & M. Syrquin (Eds.), *Industrialization and growth: A comparative study*. New York: Oxford University Press.

Cimoli, M., Dosi, G., & Stiglitz, J. E. (2009). *Industrial policy and development: The political economy of capabilities accumulation*. Oxford: Oxford University Press.

Correa, C. M. (1999). Review of the Trips Agreement. *The Journal of World Intellectual Property*, 2(6), 939–960.

Crespi, G., Fernández-Arias, E., & Stein, E. (2014). *Rethinking productive development: Sound policies and institutions for economic transformation*. Washington, DC: Inter-American Development Bank.

Dadush, U. (2015). Is manufacturing still a key to growth? OCP Policy Paper No. 15/07. OCP Policy Center.

Devlin, R. (2014). Towards good governance of public-private alliance councils supporting industrial policies in Latin America. IDB Technical Note No. 615. Washington, DC.: Inter-American Development Bank.

Devlin, R., & Moguillansky, G. (2013). What's new in the new industrial policy in Latin America? In J. E. Stiglitz & J. Y. Lin (Eds.), *The industrial policy revolution I: The role of government beyond ideology* (pp. 276–317). London: Palgrave Macmillan.

Di Maio, M. (2014). Industrial policy. In B. Currie-Alder, R. Kanbur, D. M. Malone, & R. Medhora (Eds.), *International development: Ideas, experience, and prospects*. Oxford Scholarship Online.

Dustmann, C., & Schönberg, U. (2012). What makes firm-based vocational training schemes successful? The role of commitment. *American Economic Journal: Applied Economics*, 4(2), 36–61.

ESCAP. (2011). Sustaining recovery and dynamism for inclusive development: Connectivity in the region and productive capacity in least developed countries. Economic and Social Survey of Asia and the Pacific Bangkok: United Nations Economic and Social Commission for Asia and the Pacific.

Evans, P. (1995). *Embedded autonomy: States and industrial transformation*. Princeton, NJ: Princeton University Press.

Felipe, J., Kumar, U., & Abdon, A. (2010). How rich countries became rich and why poor countries remain poor: It's the economic structure ... Duh! Working Paper No. 644. The Levy Economics Institute.

Felipe, J., Kumar, U., Abdon, A., & Bacate, M. (2012). Product complexity and economic development. *Structural Change and Economic Dynamics*, 23(1), 36–68.

Felipe, J., Kumar, U., Usui, N., & Abdon, A. (2013). Why has China succeeded? And why it will continue to do so. *Cambridge Journal of Economics*, 37, 791–818.

Felipe, J., León-Ledesma, M., Lanzafame, M., & Estrada, G. (2009). Sectoral engines of growth in developing Asia: Stylized facts and implications. *Malaysian Journal of Economic Studies*, 46(2), 107–133.

Felipe, J., Mehta, A., & Rhee, C. (2014). Manufacturing matters ... but it's the jobs that count. ADB Economics Working Paper Series No. 420. Manila: Asian Development Bank.

Ferraz, J. C., Kupfer, D., & Marques, F. S. (2014). Industrial policy as an effective development tool: Lessons from Brazil. In J. M. Salazar-Xirinachs, I. Nübler, & R. Kozul-Wright (Eds.), *Transforming economies: Making industrial policy work for growth, jobs and development*. Geneva: International Labour Office.

Gabriele, A. (2010). The role of the state in China's industrial development: A reassessment. *Comparative Economic Studies*, 52(3), 325–350.

Gallagher, K. P. (2005). *Putting development first: The importance of policy space in the WTO and international financial institutions.* London: Zed Books.

Ghani, E., & O'Connell, S. D. (2014). Can service be a growth escalator in low income countries? Policy Research Working Paper, No. 6971. Washington, DC: The World Bank.

Gibbs, M. (2007). *Trade policy national development strategies: Policy notes.* New York: United Nations Department of Economic and Social Affairs

Greenwald, B. C., & Stiglitz, J. E. (1986). Externalities in economies with imperfect information and incomplete markets. *The Quarterly Journal of Economics*, 101(2), 229–264.

Greenwald, B. C., & Stiglitz, J. E. (2013). Learning and industrial policy: Implications for Africa. In J. Esteban, J. E. Stiglitz, & J. Y. Lin (Eds.), *The industrial policy revolution II: Africa in the 21st century* (pp. 25–49). Houndmills: Palgrave Macmillan.

Guadagno, F. (2015). Industrial policies in lower-middle-income countries. The E15 Expert Group on Reinvigorating Manufacturing. Geneva: International Centre for Trade and Sustainable Development (ICTSD).

Günther, T., & Alcorta, L. (2011). Industrial policy for prosperity: Reasoning and approach. Development Policy, Statistics and Research Branch Working Paper 02/2011. Vienna: UNIDO.

Haggard, S. (2015). The developmental state is dead: Long live the developmental state! In J. Mahoney & K. Thelen (Eds.), *Advances in comparative-historical Analysis.* Cambridge: Cambridge University Press.

Hallward-Driemeier, M., & Nayyar, G. (2018). *Trouble in the making? The future of manufacturing-led development.* Washington, DC: World Bank Group.

Hausmann, R., & Hidalgo, C. A. (2011). *The atlas of economic complexity: Mapping paths to prosperity.* Cambridge, MA: MIT Press.

Hausmann, R., Hwang, J., & Rodrik, D. (2007). What you export matters. *Journal of Economic Growth*, 12(1). 1–25.

Hausmann, R., & Klinger, B. (2006). Structural transformation and patterns of comparative advantage in the product space. Working Paper No. 128. Center for International Development, Harvard University.

Hausmann, R., & Rodrik, D. (2003). Economic development as self discovery. *Journal of Development Economics*, 72(2), 603–633.

Herzberg, B., & Sisombat, L. (2016). *State of play: Public-private dialogue.* Washington, DC: World Bank Group.

Herzer, D., & Nowak-Lehmann, F. D. (2006). What does export diversification do for growth? An econometric analysis. *Applied Economics*, 38, 1825–1838.

Hirschman, A. O. (1958). *The strategy of economic development.* New Haven, CT: Yale University Press.

IDE-JETRO, & World Trade Organization. (2011). *Trade patterns and global value chains in East Asia: From trade in goods to trade in tasks.* Geneva: World Trade Organization.

ILO. (2014). *Global employment trends 2014: Risk of a jobless recovery?* Geneva: ILO.

Kaldor, N. (1966). *Causes of the slow rate of growth of the United Kingdom: An inaugural lecture.* Cambridge: Cambridge University Press.

Khan, S. R. (2007). WTO, IMF and the closing of development policy space for low-income countries: A call for neo-developmentalism. *Third World Quarterly*, 28(6), 1073–1090.

Krueger, A. O. (1990). Government failures in development. *Journal of Economic Perspectives*, 4(3), 9–23.

Krueger, A. O. (1997). Trade policy and economic development: How we lean? *American Economic Review*, 87(1), 1–22.

Lall, S. (2004). Selective industrial and trade policies in developing countries: Theoretical and empirical issues. In C. Soludo, O. Ogbu, & H.-J. Chang (Eds.), *The politics of trade and industrial policy in Africa: Forced consensus?* New Jersey: Africa World Press & IDRC.

Lederman, D., & Maloney, W. F. (2007). *Natural resources: Neither curse nor destiny*. Washington, DC: The World Bank.

Lin, J. Y. (2012). *New structural economics: A framework for rethinking development and policy*. Washington, DC: The World Bank.

Lin, J., & Chang, H.-J. (2009). Should industrial policy in developing countries conform to comparative advantage or defy it? *Development Policy Review*, 27(5), 483–502.

Lin, J. Y., & Monga, C. (2010). Growth identification and facilitation: The role of the state in the dynamics of structural change. Policy Research Working Paper, No. 5313. Washington, DC: The World Bank.

Lin, J. Y., & Treichel, V. (2012). Learning from China's rise to escape the middle-income trap: A new structural economics approach to Latin America. Policy Research Working Paper No. 6165. Washington, DC: The World Bank.

Lo, D., & Wu, M. (2014). The state and industrial policy in Chinese economic development. In J. M. Salazar-Xirinachs, I. Nübler, & R. Kozul-Wright (Eds.), *Transforming economies: Making industrial policy work for growth, jobs and development*. Geneva: International Labour Office.

Manyika, J., Sinclair, J., Dobbs, R., Strube, G., Rassey, L., Mischke, J., ... Ramaswamy, S. (2012). *Manufacturing the future: The next era of global growth and innovation*. New York: The McKinsey Global Institute.

Masuyama, S., Vandenbrink, D., & Yue, C. S. (1997). *Industrial policies in East Asia*. Tokyo: Nomura Research Institute.

McMillan, M. S., & Harttgen, K. (2014). What is driving the 'African Growth Miracle'? Working Paper No. 20077. Cambridge, MA: National Bureau of Economic Research.

McMillan, M. S., & Rodrik, D. (2011). Globalization, structural change and productivity growth. Working Paper No. 17143. Cambridge, MA: National Bureau of Economic Research.

McMillan, M. S., Rodrik, D., & Verduzco-Gallo, Í. (2014). Globalization, structural change, and productivity growth, with an update on Africa. *World Development*, 63(0), 11–32.

Mihretu, M., & Eyob, T. T. (2015). ETHIOPIA: Ethiopian Public Private Consultative Forum (EPPCF). In Public-Private Dialogue 2015 Workshop, Copenhagen, Denmark.

Mishra, S., Lundstrom, S., & Anand, R. (2011). Service export sophistication and economic growth. Policy Research Working Paper No. 5606. Washington, DC: The World Bank.

Natsuda, K., & Thoburn, J. (2014). How much policy space still exists under the WTO? A comparative study of the automotive industry in Thailand and Malaysia. *Review of International Political Economy*, 21(6), 1346–1377.

Newman, C., & Page, J. (2017). Industrial clusters: The case for Special Economic Zones in Africa. WIDER Working Paper No. 2017/15. Helsinki: UNU-WIDER.

OECD. (2013). *Perspectives on global development 2013: Industrial policies in a changing world*. Paris: OECD Publishing.

Ohno, K. (2013). *Learning to industrialize: From given growth to policy-aided value creation*. London: Routledge-GRIPS Development Forum Studies.

Otsubo, S. (2009). *Globalization to Kaihatsu*. Tokyo: Keisoshobo.

Otsubo, S. (2016). *Globalization and development*, vol. I: *Leading issues in development with globalization*. London: Routledge.

Pack, H., & Saggi, K. (2006). Is there a case for industrial policy? A critical survey. *World Bank Research Observer*, 21(2), 267–297.

Page, J. (2012). Can Africa industrialise? *Journal of African Economies*, 21(suppl. 2), 86–124.

Peneder, M. (2003). Industrial structure and aggregate growth. *Structural Change and Economic Dynamics*, 14, 427–448.

Peres, W., & Primi, A. (2009). Theory and practice of industrial policy: Evidence from the Latin American experience. Productive Development Series 187 (LC/L.3013-P). Santiago, Chile: Economic Commission for Latin America and the Caribbean,.

Rodrik, D. (1995). Getting interventions right: How South Korea and Taiwan grew rich. *Economic Policy*, 10(20), 53–107.

Rodrik, D. (1996). Coordination failures and government policy: A model with applications to East Asia and Eastern Europe. *Journal of International Economics*, 40(1–2), 1–22.

Rodrik, D. (2004). Industrial policy for the twenty-first century. Paper prepared for UNIDO. Boston, MA: Harvard University.

Rodrik, D. (2008a). Normalizing industrial policy. Commission on Growth and Development. Working Paper No. 3. Washington, DC: World Bank.

Rodrik, D. (2008b). *One economics, many recipes: Globalization, institutions, and economic growth*. Princeton, NJ: Princeton University Press.

Rodrik, D. (2013). Unconditional convergence in manufacturing. *Quarterly Journal of Economics*, 128, 165–204).

Salazar-Xirinachs, J. M., Nübler, I., & Kozul-Wright, R. (2014). Transforming economies: Making industrial policy work for growth, jobs and development. Geneva: International Labour Office.

Shadlen, K. (2005). Policy space for development in the WTO and beyond: The case of intellectual property rights. Working Paper No. 05-06. Global Development and Environment Institute.

Stiglitz, J. E., & Monga, C. (2013). Introduction: The rejuvenation of industrial policy. In J. E. Stiglitz & J. Y. Lin (Eds.), *The industrial policy revolution. I. The role of government beyond ideology*. London: Palgrave Macmillan.

Szirmai, A. (2012). Industrialisation as an engine of growth in developing countries, 1950–2005. *Structural Change and Economic Dynamics*, 23(4), 406–420.

UNDP. (2005). *Human development report 2005*. New York: United Nations Development Programme.

UNECA (United Nations Economic Commission for Africa). (2014). Dynamic industrial policy in Africa: Innovative institutions effective processes and flexible mechanisms. ECA Policy Brief No. 011. Available at: http://repository.uneca.org/handle/10855/22765

UNECA. (2016). *Transformative industrial policy for Africa*. Addis Ababa, Ethiopia: Economic Commission for Africa.

UNECA, & AU. (2014). Dynamic industrial policy in Africa: Economic report on Africa. Addis Ababa, Ethiopia: UNECA. Available at: www.uneca.org/publications/economic-report-africa-2014

UNIDO. (2013). Sustaining employment growth: The role of manufacturing and structural change. Industrial Development Report 2013. Vienna: UNIDO.

UNIDO, & UNU-MERIT. (2012). *Structural change, poverty reduction and industrial policy in the BRICS.* Vienna: UNIDO.

Wade, R. H. (2003). What strategies are viable for developing countries today? The World Trade Organization and the shrinking of 'development space'. *Review of International Political Economy*, 10(4), 621–644.

Wade, R. H (2004). *Governing the market: Economic theory and the role of government in East Asian industrialization* (2nd ed.). Princeton, NJ: Princeton University Press.

Wasmer, E., & Weil, P. (2004). The macroeconomics of labor and credit market imperfections. *American Economic Review*, 94(4), 944–963.

Weiss, J. (2016). Industrial policy: Back on the agenda In J. Weiss & M. Tribe (Eds.), *Routledge handbook of industry and development* (pp. 135–150). New York: Routledge.

World Bank. (1993). *East Asian miracle.* Washington, DC: The World Bank.

2 The state of global manufacturing and risks of deindustrialization in the developing world

Christian Samen Otchia and Shigeru Thomas Otsubo

2.1 Introduction

Two of the most important developments in the global economy in recent decades have been the rapid integration of many poorer countries into global value chains (GVCs) and the rapid growth of automation. These unprecedented changes are forcefully pointed out by Baldwin (2019), who refers to the combined phenomena as "globotics." Alongside these developments are three striking and unprecedented global trends: (1) the emergence of new manufacturers in the highly concentrated group of manufacturing production; (2) significant deindustrialization, with developing countries losing industrialization opportunities at much lower levels of income, against large and persistent increases in high-value-added manufacturing production and export in developed countries; and (3) the growing importance of "industries without smokestacks."

For a variety of reasons, including the perception that industrial policy plays an important role in enhancing structural change and economic development, these global patterns have stirred up intense discussion among both policymakers and academics. This debate can broadly be summarized as a dispute between leapfrogging manufacturing and promoting industries without smokestacks as deindustrialization has occurred in many countries. In principle, and as discussed in Chapter 1, manufacturing has been the key to economic development. Nevertheless, the data seems to point to the changing role of manufacturing, especially in recent decades. As illustrated in panel (a) of Figure 2.1, global manufacturing employment generally followed an upward trend but remained below non-manufacturing employment until 2008 when non-manufacturing employment began to decelerate. Panel (b) furthermore shows that both global manufacturing value-added and non-manufacturing value-added have moved upward at a similar rate, but the growth rate of manufacturing value-added decelerated after 2008. The recent changes in the pace of manufacturing employment and value-added are even more dramatic when contrasted with the level of economic development. Using this metric, value-added and employment in manufacturing in many developing countries started to decrease prematurely at a lower level of GDP per capita before reaching the peak that is characteristic of early industrializers.[1] How has the trend of premature deindustrialization

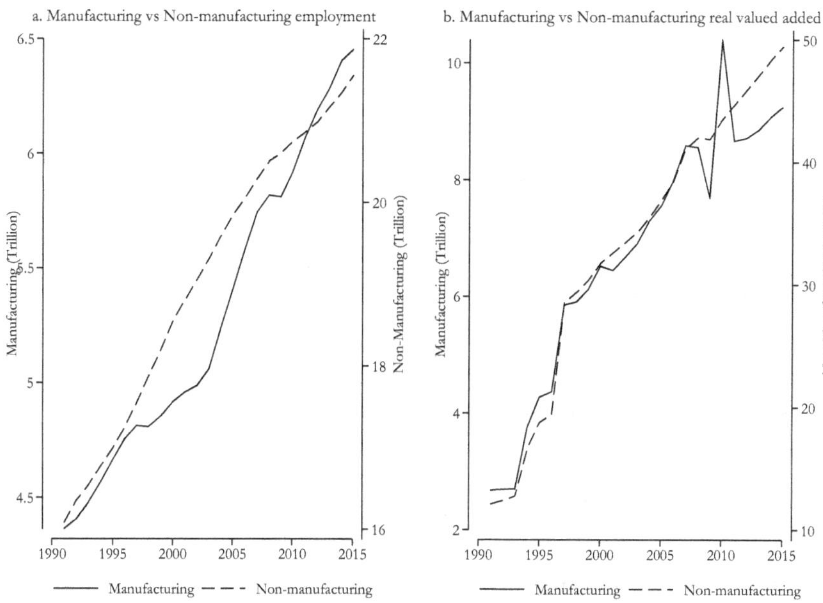

Figure 2.1 World manufacturing employment and real value-added

emerged in many parts of the developing world? How have the changing shares of manufacturing in total value-added, total employment, and international trade been associated with international income convergence/divergence? With the rapid technological upgrading and extension of GVCs for manufacturing, are there any spaces where developing countries can find a niche for manufacturing activities?

In this chapter, we provide an overview of the changing state of global manufacturing and manufacturing-related services as a first step toward answering these questions. We then present new empirical evidence on patterns in industrialization and structural change. In order to document these patterns, we exploit a variety of datasets on value-added and employment by income groups and geographical regions.[2] The choice of the database is dictated by the level of geographical coverage and the time dimension necessary for the analysis. Particularly useful data is provided by the World Development Indicators (WDI) from the World Bank, the UNSTAT National Accounts—Analysis of Main Aggregates (NAAMA),[3] the Groningen Growth and Development Center (GGDC) 10-Sector Database (Timmer, de Vries, & de Vries, 2015), the UNIDO Competitive Industrial Performance Database,[4] and the ILOSTAT Database.[5] For historical analyses, we use data from Mitchell (2007). This is a well-known international historical database that has been widely used for comparisons across both time and geography. We include data starting in 1780 extending through 2005.

The rest of this chapter is organized as follows. In Section 2.2, we present the changing state of global manufacturing, discuss the unconditional convergence in manufacturing and how focusing on medium and high-tech manufacturing can spur reindustrialization. In Section 2.3, we present evidence from a time series test of the patterns of industrialization, and document new findings on deindustrialization. Section 2.4 examines structural transformation and its potential effect on premature deindustrialization. Section 2.5 presents new evidence on servicification. Concluding remarks follow.

2.2 State of global manufacturing

The main aim of this section is to document changes in manufacturing by income groups and geographical regions. We mainly use per capita manufacturing value-added (MVA), that is, the total manufacturing value-added adjusted by the country's population, as our indicator for measuring progress in industrialization. The advantage of using this indicator is that it focuses on production, essentially the addition of value by manufacturing firms on their primary inputs.[6]

2.2.1 Heterogeneity in manufacturing growth

Traditionally, the manufacturing sector has been the engine of the economy in many countries. As discussed in Chapter 1, rapid and sustained economic growth has been strongly correlated with the expansion of manufacturing and the reallocation of resources to more productive activities. The key feature is that activities in this sector have a high capacity for productivity growth, externalities, and increasing returns to scale. Indeed, manufacturing has faster productivity growth than services and agriculture, pays the highest wages, and has strong spillovers (backward and forward linkages) to other sectors. This means that rapid growth in the manufacturing sector promotes productivity growth in other sectors of the economy and, as a result, leads to stronger economic growth. For resource-based economies whose exports depend on commodities, diversification of the export structure from primary commodities to manufacturing has been a key policy to strengthen resilience to external shocks and sustain growth. Table 2.1 illustrates this strong correlation between the expansion of world MVA and rapid economic growth, particularly evident before the 2010s. The per capita MVA growth in the last three decades is virtually identical to average per capita growth.

There is less consensus, however, on what the reasons for these correlations are. Many authors, including the editors of this book, put forward the argument that coordinated measures to promote and facilitate industrial upgrading and diversification have led countries to attain higher levels of development. Nonetheless, it is agreed that there are varying patterns of manufacturing growth across countries and across different periods. This is again illustrated in Table 2.1, but perhaps better visualized in Figure 2.2. Focusing on the geographical regions, East Asia and Pacific (EAP) and Europe and Central Asia (ECA) show remarkable improvements in per capita MVA while North America fell behind. In particular,

Table 2.1 Recent trends in global manufacturing output

	GDP per capita growth (annual %)			*Per capita manufacturing valued added growth*			*Manufacturing, value-added (% of GDP)*			*Industrialization intensity index*		
	1990s	*2000s*	*2010s*	*1990s*	*2000s*	*2010s*	*1990s*	*2000s*	*2010s*	*1990s*	*2000s*	*2010s*
Geographical region												
East Asia & the Pacific	2.2	3.0	2.6	3.7	4.0	2.9	14.2	12.9	12.3	0.37	0.41	0.41
Europe & Central Asia	1.2	3.3	2.2	0.0	2.8	2.7	17.7	13.7	12.6	0.38	0.38	0.40
Latin America & the Caribbean	1.7	1.7	1.3	0.8	1.3	–0.2	13.6	11.9	11.0	0.31	0.31	0.29
Middle East & North Africa	2.7	1.5	0.5	4.8	3.3	–2.5	16.9	18.4	14.5	0.28	0.30	0.30
North America	1.9	0.9	0.5	2.7	–1.9	–1.4	16.3	9.3	9.0	0.36	0.33	0.33
South Asia	3.2	4.2	3.5	3.3	3.7	3.4	12.5	12.4	11.4	0.26	0.28	0.26
Sub-Saharan Africa	1.0	2.4	1.5	0.2	1.9	2.2	11.1	10.4	10.1	0.22	0.21	0.21
Income group												
Low-income	–0.1	1.9	1.4	0.4	2.3	0.7	10.3	9.3	8.7	0.21	0.20	0.19
Lower middle-income	0.9	3.6	2.7	0.9	4.3	3.6	14.3	12.5	12.0	0.28	0.30	0.30
Upper middle -income	2.4	3.5	1.9	1.1	3.0	0.9	14.2	13.3	12.6	0.31	0.31	0.30
High-income	2.3	1.5	1.3	2.5	1.2	1.0	16.4	14.0	12.2	0.38	0.40	0.42
World	1.6	2.6	1.8	1.5	2.5	1.5	14.2	12.8	11.8	0.32	0.32	0.33

Notes: The industrialization intensity index was developed by UNIDO to capture the level of technological deepening and upgrading. It is computed as the average of the share of MVA in GDP and the share of medium and high-technology activities in MVA. The last year for the decade of the 2010s is 2017.

Source: Compiled by author using World Bank World Development Indicators and UNIDO Competitive Industrial Performance Database.

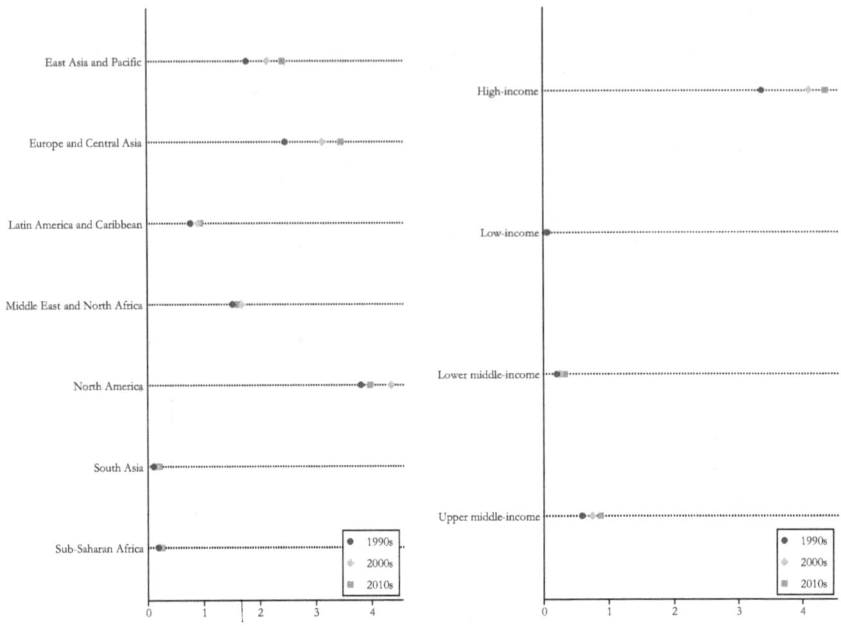

Figure 2.2 Log of per capita manufacturing value-added

EAP is the fastest industrializing region, with an average annual manufacturing growth of 3.7 percent in the 1990s, 4 percent in the 2000s, and 2.9 percent in the 2010s. Industrialization in East Asia was achieved by intensive use of industrial policy. This can be seen from the variations in the industrialization intensity index, which measures the technological complexity of production structures, technological capabilities, and knowledge intensity of production systems. In fact, the industrialization intensity rose from 0.37 in the 1990s to 0.41 in the 2000s. The experience of East Asia in designing and implementing industrial policies has been largely documented (Akkemik, 2009; Chang, 2006). In particular, Otchia (2015) pointed out that East Asian countries have diversified their exports into labor-intensive, export-oriented manufacturing due to the widespread availability of cheap labor, before starting to climb up the quality ladder. In recent years, these countries have been focusing on high-skill-dependent goods such as electronics, automotive products, heavy equipment, and consumer durable goods. China, as the leader of manufacturing exports, has been moving away from labor-intensive goods and specializing in automobiles, industrial equipment, and heavy machinery.

South Asia has followed a similar pattern of manufacturing growth to East Asia; per capita MVA grew almost constantly by a factor of about 3.3–3.7 percent. However, South Asia achieved this growth with lower industrialization intensity. The Middle East and North Africa (MENA) started with an average per capita manufacturing value added of 4.8 percent in the 1990s but eventually fell behind, with growth falling into negative territory. The industrialization intensity of the region, however, has increased from 0.28 to 0.30. Per capita manufacturing value-added in Sub-Saharan Africa (SSA) has experienced a significant increase since the 2000s. However, the industrialization intensity has been almost unchanged.

The manufacturing performance of African countries raises both enthusiasm and concern, depending on the circumstances of the specific country. African countries have low manufacturing value-added per capita and annual growth in manufacturing value-added has been stagnant or almost negative for many of them between 1990 and 2014. While China, Vietnam, and Cambodia have been very dynamic over the last two decades, some African countries have not given up the race to industrialization either. However, the process of structural transformation remains particularly difficult for African countries. Africa's efforts to industrialize and diversify are taking place in an interdependent global economy where industrialized countries have already accumulated both enabling and core productive capacities that give their firms considerable cost and productivity advantages and enable them to push the technological frontier through research and innovation.

We next turn our attention to the income groups. We use the World Bank classification of countries into high-income (HICs), upper middle-income (UMICs), lower middle-income (LMICs), and low-income countries (LICs). HICs stand out as the only income group where there is a clear decline in per capita manufacturing valued added growth (Figure 2.2). The bottom panel of Table 2.1 indicates that HICs experienced a significant per capita manufacturing value-added growth of about 2.5 percent in the 1990s but growth was reduced to 1.2 percent in the 2000s and 1 percent in the 2010s. The industrialization intensity index increased to 0.42 in the 2010s from 0.38 in the 1990s. One other feature is that LMICs started with low per capital manufacturing value-added growth (0.9 in the 1990s), but have been achieving high growth since the 2000s, at rates that are much higher than economic growth. Interestingly, Table 2.1 also illustrates that the 2000–2009 decade stands out as a notable industrialization period for UMICs and LICs, as the average per capita manufactured value-added rose to 3 percent and 2.3 percent, respectively, but the change was meaningful for UMICs, given the higher initial manufacturing valued added per capita (Figure 2.2).

To provide further insight on the heterogeneity in global manufacturing performance, it is useful to focus on exports. The main reason for this being that trade policy was a key driver of industrialization and economic development. Figure 2.3 plots the manufacturing exports index calculated from the UNIDO statistics as the ratio of the manufacturing exports to the manufacturing value-added and normalized to the year 1990. Starting with panel (a), which reports results by geographical regions, it is obvious that each geographical region has followed a different pattern, particularly after 2001. South Asia shows a very flat trend in the manufacturing exports index. There is little change over the period in the manufacturing exports index of SSA. What is striking is the significant change that occurred in Latin America and the Caribbean (LAC), which started expanding in 2002, but had been badly hit by the 2007–2008 global financial crisis, before experiencing a recovery in 2010. We expect exports to have played a role in EAP because of the reason mentioned earlier. The region experienced the second largest increase in the manufacturing exports index, following LAC. EAP experienced an increase in manufacturing exports of about 5 percent between 1990 and 2000, increasing its world share from 12.6 percent to 13.3 percent.

The bottom panel of Figure 2.3 shows some similarities in the evolution of the manufacturing exports index by income groups. In contrast to the geographical region, which depicted a flat trend between 1990 and 2000, the manufacturing exports index picked up quickly for all income groups, with the largest growth in UMICs and LMICs. Again, a sharp decline is observed in 2008 during the financial crisis and after 2014 due to the falling oil prices. The drop is much larger for HICs. Second, there is a perception that export-led growth strategies in developing countries face more constraints than in the past, in particular due to the slower growth of global demand, especially from industrialized countries (UNCTAD, 2016). Finally, Figure 2.3 shows that it has been difficult for LICs to maintain a positive trend by producing manufacturing products that are marketable in the global economy (as the declining indicator shows).

2.2.2 Global concentration of manufacturing production

Since the end of the global financial crisis in 2008, there has been strong growth in manufacturing value-added. According to the UNIDO (2017), global manufacturing value-added reached US$12.3 trillion (at constant 2010 prices) in 2016, thanks to strong growth in emerging and developing countries, whose MVA doubled between 2010 and 2016, rising from 21.7 percent to 44.6 percent. With this strong growth, the growth in MVA in emerging and developing countries continues to outpace that of developed countries. As a result, the share of developing countries in world MVA has been steadily increasing and is expected to reach 44.6 percent in 2016 compared to its share of only 26.5 percent in 2000. By far the most important changes are the increase in the share of the least developed countries in Asia and the Pacific and the sharp declines in Africa (6.5 percent to 4.4 percent) and Latin America (29.3 percent to 13 percent). China has been remarkably dynamic, increasing its manufacturing world share from 3 percent in 1990 to 25 percent in 2018 (UNIDO, 2019).

Figure 2.4 illustrates the way China is positioning itself as a global manufacturer due to a significant increase in its share of world MVA. For comparison purposes, we also include the G7, three other fast industrializers (India, Indonesia, and Korea), and the rest of the world. Between 2005 and 2017, China increased its share of value-added. In particular, its share moved from 20 percent in 2009 to reach 25 percent in 2015. Other emerging economies registered an increase in their shares in the world MVA but at a slower pace than China. This group,

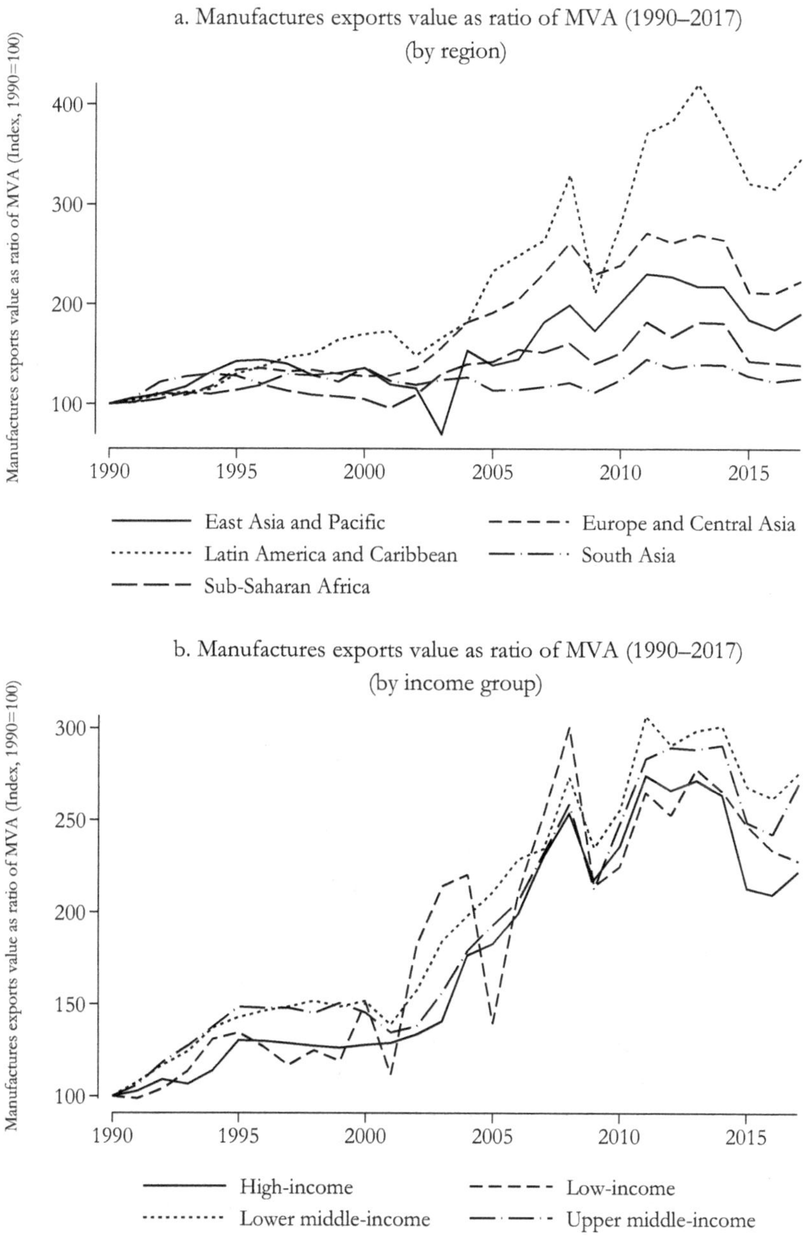

Figure 2.3 Manufactures exports

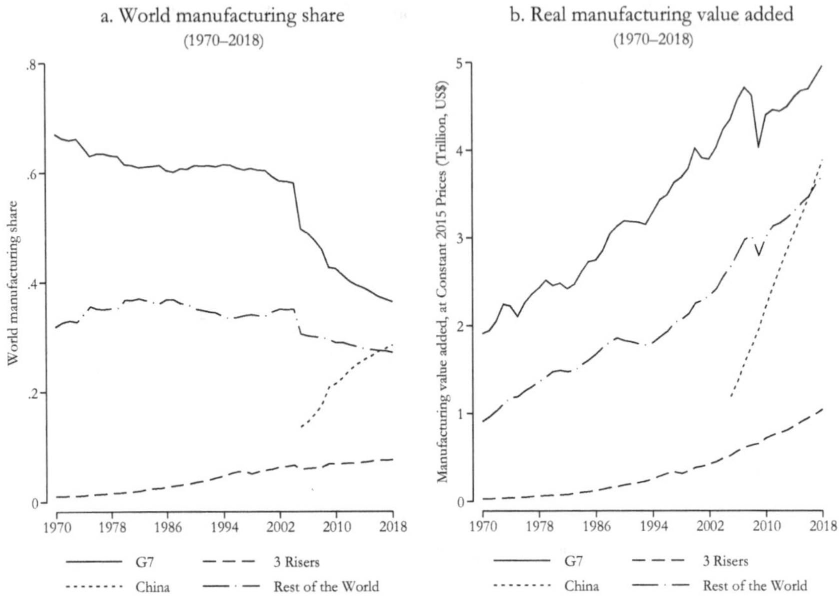

Figure 2.4 G7, China, and 3 Risers' share of world manufacturing and real value-added

which we label the "3 Risers," is India, Korea, and Indonesia. What is striking about Figure 2.4 is the dramatic decline in the G7's share of world MVA, especially since 2005. We thus see that manufacturing production became increasingly concentrated with the G7 losing their strong position.

In addition, we show a similar trend in Figure 2.4 panel (b), where we plot the per capita MVA using 2015 constant prices. It is important to note the G7 is losing its share but the per capita MVA has been rising. As will be discussed later, this is because the G7 is moving to higher value-added yielding manufacturing activities. What can be clearly seen in Figure 2.4 is that the convergence between G7 countries, China, and the 3 Risers is due to the fact that fast catching-up economies are industrializing faster than the former. For instance, there has been a sharp increase in the MVA of China from 2005 to 2017.

The case of China, India, Indonesia, and Korea demonstrates good catching-up validity. This raises interesting questions: Is the global industrial landscape changing? Can convergence occur between the most industrialized countries and the latecomers? Figure 2.5 presents an attempt to answer these questions, by plotting the MVA growth rate over 1990–2018 against the 1990 level of real per capita MVA and fitting a regression line within each income group. For presentation purposes, we group LMICs and UMICs together as middle-income countries. Consistent with Figure 2.3, late industrializers exhibit higher MVA growth compared to early industrializers. As one would expect, most

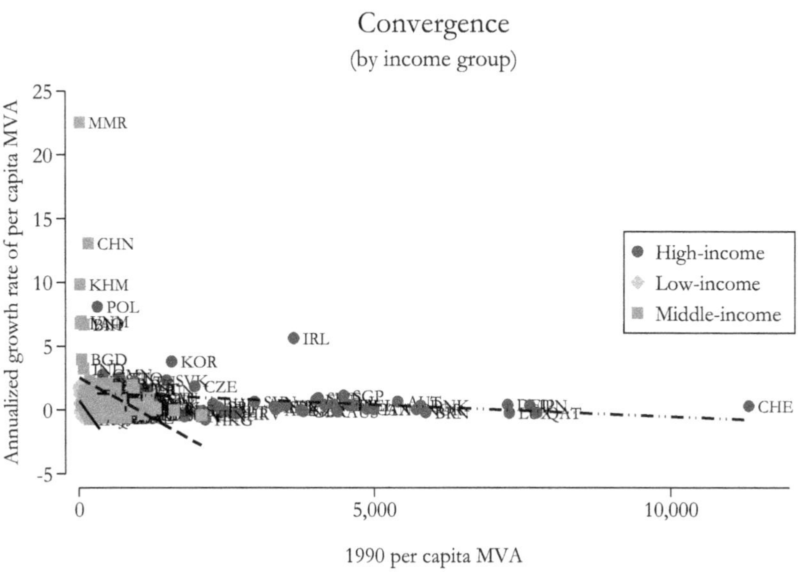

Figure 2.5 Convergence by income group

of them are Asian countries such as Vietnam and Cambodia. Poland has been listed by Baldwin, Ito, and Sato (2014) as part of the 6 Risers together with Korea, India, Indonesia, Thailand, and Turkey. The most interesting aspect of Figure 2.5 concerns, however, the catching-up behavior across income group. Despite variability in MVA growth rates, it is obvious that there is a negative relationship with MVA in the starting year and subsequent industrialization, implying that there is a catching-up behavior within income growth. A closer inspection evinces that there is strong catching-up behavior among LICs and MICs.

To better understand the patterns of catching-up, Figure 2.6 plots the relationship between growth rate of per capita MVA and per capita MVA for two time periods: 1990–2017 and 2000–2017. In both panels, the lines show a local polynomial regression without weights. Figure 2.6 is quite revealing in several ways. First, late industrializers were initially catching up because they were industrializing faster than industrialized countries. Second, convergence in the post-2000 period occurred because of rapid industrialization of late industrializers but also slow growth in industrialized countries. Third, the local polynomial fit shows that three groups of industrialization emerged in the post-2000 period. In addition to the group of industrialized countries such as Japan and the United States, where the local polynomial fit is decreasing, the second group, which is stagnant, includes India, Russia, and Brazil, while the fast-growing group includes Indonesia, Nigeria, and China.

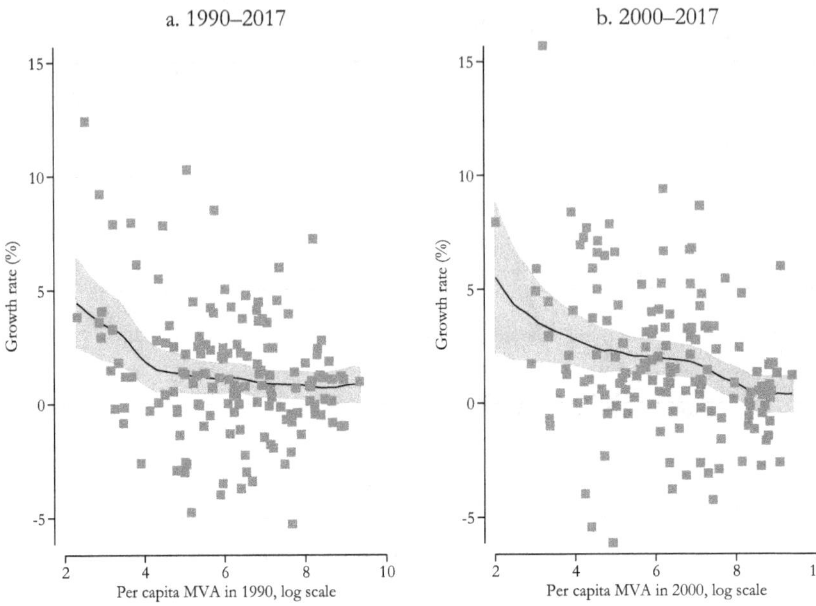

Figure 2.6 Convergence by time period

2.2.3 Relocation of manufacturing employment

The slowdown of MVA growth among early industrializers is particularly due to the fact that these countries are moving toward capital-intensive and technologically sophisticated industries. While manufacturing is generally a labor-intensive industry, the movement toward sophisticated industries will increase the demand for high-skilled workers and manufacturing-related services, thus decreasing manufacturing jobs. Figure 2.7 illustrates that as HICs are shifting to sophisticated industries, manufacturing jobs are being relocated to developing countries. In fact, as can be seen in panel (a) of Figure 2.7, HICs accounted for 21.4 percent of global manufacturing jobs in 1991, but this share decreased to 15.6 percent in 2005 and 13.4 percent in 2017. Panel (b) of Figure 2.7 shows that the reduction of manufacturing jobs was faster between 2000 and 2008 and then slowed down. The greatest beneficiary of the relocation of manufacturing jobs are UMICs such as China, where manufacturing employment's share of total employment increased slightly from 21.9 percent in 2007 to 22.7 percent in 2017. Furthermore, there seems to be a relocation to LMICs, especially since 2012. Panel (a) shows that LMICs are the only income group that exhibits a strong upward trend in manufacturing employment growth since 2010.

What remains to be understood is the extent to which the concentration in manufacturing production and relocation of manufacturing employment relate to labor productivity growth in the manufacturing sector. According to ILO (2019), the shift in employment toward sophisticated industries in HICs and

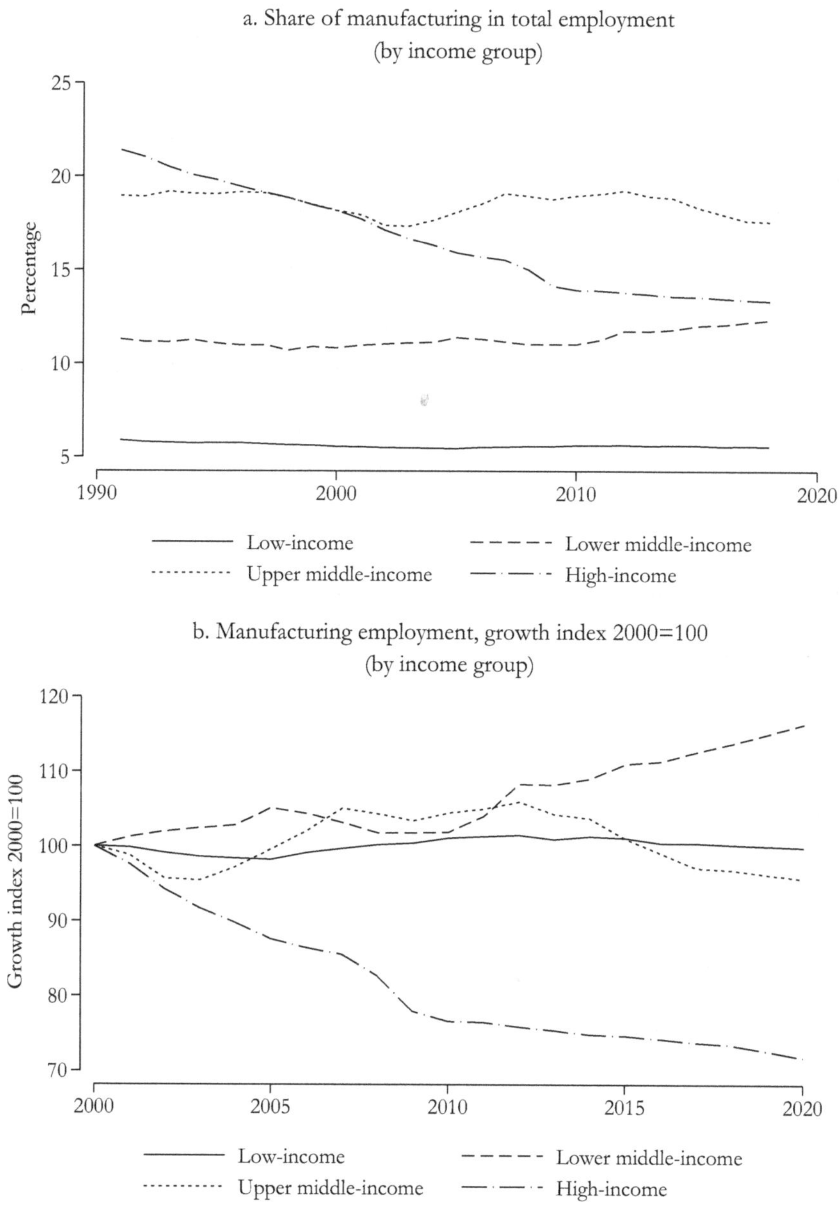

Figure 2.7 Manufacturing employment, growth index, and shares

the relocation of labor-intensive manufacturing to developing countries require an improvement in productivity. They further note that industrial policies that foster technology upgrading, skills development, and institutional capabilities are required to accelerate productivity growth. The evidence for the importance of industrial policy in accelerating industrialization for early industrializers and East Asia is well documented. An interesting recent study has taken advantage of the rapid growth in China to identify the impact of specific industrial policy that favored place-based policy. Lu, Wang, and Zhu (2019) looked at the incidence and effectiveness of Special Economic Zones (SEZs) in China. They found that establishing SEZs increased the number of firms in the designated areas and had an overall positive effect on capital investment, employment, output, and productivity. They found that these positive effects were driven by new firms.

One aspect that we wish to highlight is the unconditional convergence in manufacturing industries. There is substantial work in the growth literature on unconditional convergence in total output. Only recently has there been an interest in the convergence in manufacturing industries. Using a sample of 118 countries and 23 manufacturing (ISIC two-digit level) industries, Rodrik (2013), for instance, found that manufacturing exhibits strong unconditional labor productivity convergence, unlike the rest of the economy. The estimated beta-coefficient in these industries is close to 2–3 percent. However, Rodrik's findings are viewed as applying to formal parts of manufacturing because of data coverage. We contribute to this new strand of literature by documenting unconditional convergence using aggregated manufacturing data that goes back to 1960. In Figure 2.8, we plot the beta-coefficients from the unconditional convergence regression relating average growth of manufacturing labor productivity to its initial level. We see a clear pattern of unconditional convergence depicted by the statistically significant negative betas for both

Figure 2.8 Unconditional convergence in manufacturing labor productivity

the sample of all income groups and the sample that excludes HICs. The point estimates are qualitatively consistent among the two panels. While the period of analysis may be short, it is interesting the note that the unconditional convergence in labor productivity became weaker in the 1980s.

2.2.4 Manufacturing upgrading

Despite its role in accelerating structural transformation, manufacturing upgrading has also been praised for its role in sustaining growth. The empirical literature on industrialization and structural transformation has largely documented the structural transformation from agriculture to industry or from industry to service. An important but less highlighted regularity that recent research on patterns of economic growth has not shown is the process of diversification and expansion of the range of activities within manufacturing. The 2018 UNIDO report noted a significant change in the world's major manufacturing industries, the most important being food and beverages, chemicals and chemical products, base metals, computer, electronic and optical products, and motor vehicles, trailers and semi-trailers. The growing share of these manufacturing industries mainly reflects technological advances that are accelerating the specialization of industrialized and emerging countries in technology-intensive industries, leaving low-technology activities behind. This shift has also led to strong growth in manufacturing employment (UNIDO, 2018).

Figure 2.9 compares patterns of structural change within manufacturing. Panel (a) depicts the value-added share of medium and high-tech manufacturing against the per capita GDP in constant 2000 US$, while we plot the medium and high-tech manufactured exports share in panel (b). First note that panel (a) exhibits a positive and increasing relationship between medium and high-tech manufacturing value-added share and the log GDP per capita. These regularities underscore the importance of industrial development as an engine of economic growth. Panel (b) shows that the importance of manufacturing is even stronger when countries diversify into medium and high-tech manufactured exports. The unconditional *lowess* shows a strong correlation between high income and high MVA share. The relation is stronger for log per capita GDP of 6 and above because many developing countries have a low share of high MVA.

This finding supports existing research that points to the fact that economic diversification is needed to sustain growth and reduce poverty significantly. This argument is supported by the fact that export diversification toward manufacturing is linked to increased employment, exports, and GDP growth (Agosin, 2007; Herzer & Nowak-Lehmann, 2006; Lederman & Maloney, 2007). Moreover, recent theories on structural change suggest that producing high value-added products is a condition for sustained growth (Hausmann, Hwang, & Rodrik, 2006; Hausmann & Klinger, 2006; Hausmann & Rodrik, 2003). This is because development has been associated with the movement of resources from lower productivity sectors to higher productivity sectors (McMillan, Rodrik, & Verduzco-Gallo, 2014; McMillan & Rodrik, 2011).

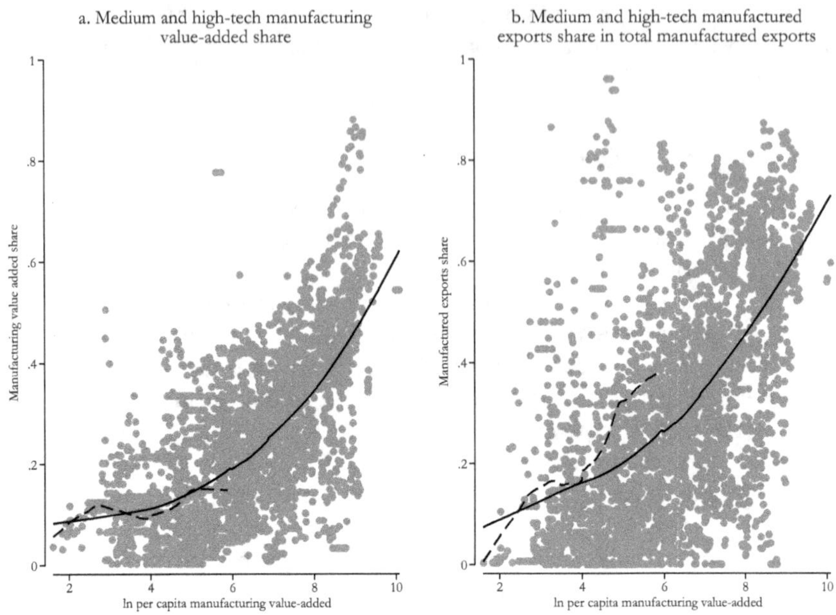

Figure 2.9 Medium and high-tech manufacturing value-added and exports

The good news for developing countries is that they can realize rapid economic development by increasing their share of high MVA in their exports. Figure 2.10 confirms that exports of medium and high technology goods as a share of total manufacturing exports tend to increase with the level of countries' industrialization. The gap between HICs and UMICs is large but has remained almost constant during the period of analysis. LMICs and LICs have increased their exports shares since 2011, closing the gap with UMICs. However, the single most striking observation to emerge from these charts is the spectacular catching-up of China, which has doubled its share within 10 years.

2.2.5 *Volatility*

Diversification toward higher value-added products is crucial for developing countries to reduce the volatility of their production and exports. While the experience of East Asia has validated the role of diversification into higher value-added products in sustaining economic growth, economic diversification has received plenty of attention in policy discussions and empirical research in recent decades, especially with regard to African economies. The argument in support of this is that the concentration of exports into few commodities exports has increased the volatility of export revenue, reducing the productivity and employment in these countries (Bleaney & Greenaway, 2001; Ghosh & Ostry, 1994).

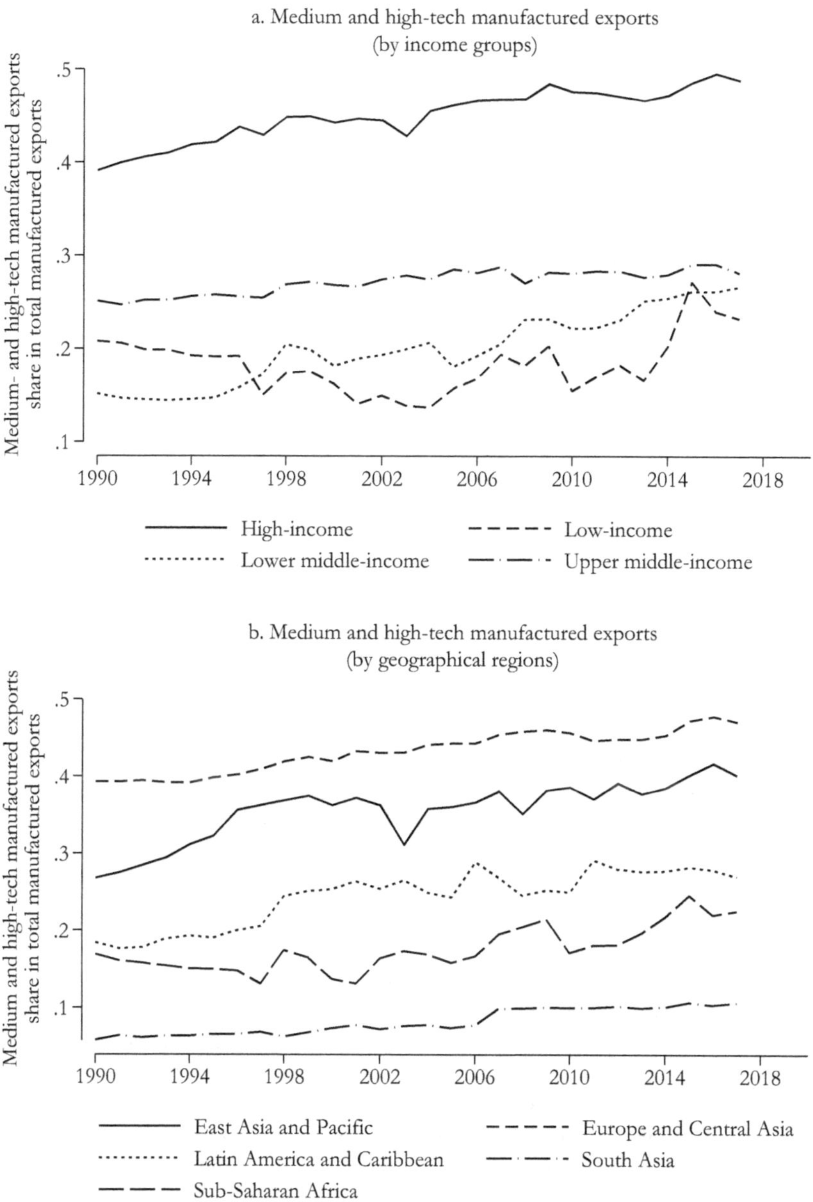

Figure 2.10 Medium and high-tech manufacturing value-added and exports by income groups and regions

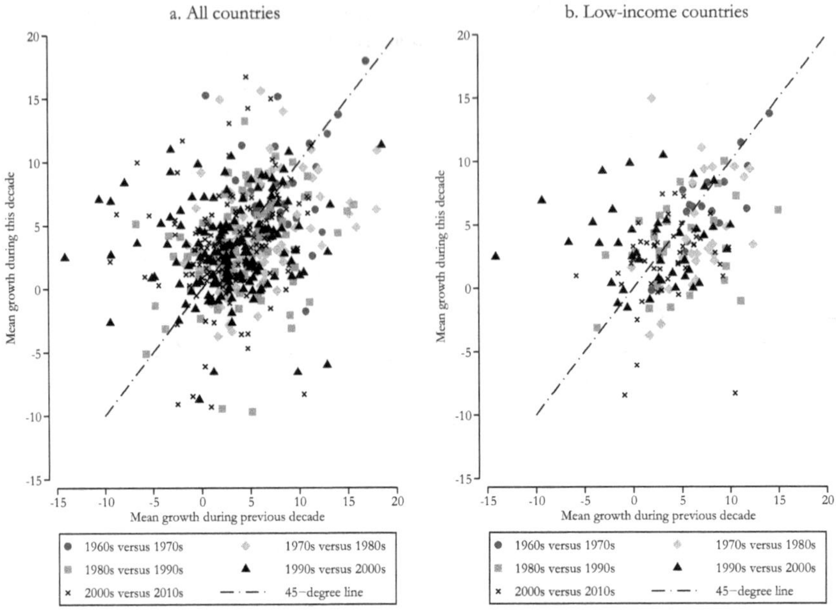

Figure 2.11 Correlation of per capita manufacturing value-added growth in consecutive decades

Recent evidence suggests that MVA is more volatile than GDP. UNIDO (2019), for instance, demonstrates that when the GDP growth rates were rising, MVA growth rates were rising even higher, and when GDP growth rates were declining, MVA growth rates were declining even lower. We analyze the volatility of manufacturing in detail through the lens of contrasting the growth rate for each decade with that from the previous decade from 1960. Figure 2.11 illustrates the volatility in the manufacturing growth rate for all countries (developed and developing) in the WDI and LICs. Comparison with the 45-degree line reveals the instability of manufacturing growth from one decade to another, especially since the 1990s. In order to assess the importance of volatility for developing countries, we also perform the same analysis for LICs. There is even more instability for LICs as Figure 2.11 shows the existence of a lesser density of points around the 45-degree line. The timing of instability seems also to start in the 1980s with many negative points. This is largely due to the advent of the debt crisis. Another shock for the decade of the 1990s was the 1989 fall of the Berlin Wall and the birth of transitional economies after the collapse of the former Soviet Union. The 1980s were also the decade of currency realignment (after the Plaza Accord of 1985) that triggered foreign direct investments (FDIs) to developing countries, starting with FDIs to Asian developing countries. The volatility of MVA growth results from the difficulties many countries face in sustaining long periods of industrial expansion. In Section 2.3, we will analyze the timing of deindustrialization in detail for selected countries.

2.3 Time series test of industrialization and deindustrialization

Given the facts so far presented in this chapter, the natural questions are why and when is deindustrialization happening? This section reports a time series test of the patterns of industrial growth. The time series test focuses on the differences in the rate of changes in the industrial structure between successive time periods. Put differently, this analysis compares time effects with a reference period to gauge the effects of common shocks felt by manufacturing in each of the time periods (Rodrik, 2016). Such calculations enable us to understand the speed of industrialization over time. A seminal work by Temin (1967) tested these patterns using 20-year intervals from 1870 to 1950 for nine countries. The findings indicate that the share of manufacturing has been rising over time, but no systematic evidence in the rate of change of the share of this sector between time periods was found. In the agriculture sector, on the other hand, the share of agriculture was falling over time, and importantly, it fell faster in the periods 1870–1890 and 1910–1930 than 1890–1910 and 1930–1950. In recent empirical studies, the main evidence typically cited for time series patterns of industrial growth is perhaps the premature deindustrialization documented by Dasgupta and Singh (2006). In their paper, Dasgupta and Singh document that the share of employment in manufacturing in developing countries is peaking at lower levels of GDP per capita than it does in present-day industrialized countries. In the same vein, Rodrik (2016) recently showed that the share of manufacturing has been decreasing faster in recent decades and at much lower levels of income for most countries in the analysis. This section revisits the classical analysis that was initiated by Dasgupta and Singh (2006). We provide new evidence using recent data with more coverage of countries.

2.3.1 *Which indicator to use?*

For a quantitative analysis of deindustrialization, it is useful to highlight some aspects of the measurement used, as a debate is taking place with respect to which indicator is the best proxy for industrialization. The three most common measures of economic activity at the sectoral level are labor force (Clark, 1940), consumption patterns, and value-added shares. Due to the availability of data for time series and cross-country analyses, labor force and value-added shares have been intensively used in the literature. While these two measures often coincide in their conclusion of industrialization patterns, there are cases in which they differ. For example, Felipe, Mehta, and Rhee (2019) draw on correlations between countries' average income per capita and their peak in manufacturing to conclude that manufacturing employment is a better predictor of eventual prosperity than is manufacturing output. While Felipe et al. (2019) use a large database of countries' manufacturing employment and output shares, their study does not consider the country fixed effect that affects the variability in manufacturing value-added shares. Other researchers such as Diao, McMillan, and Wangwe (2017) have preferred to use employment share as a measure of industrialization because of their interest in drawing lessons for employment creation, which is a policy priority in Africa.

Value-added share and employment share are both related to production. However, they can yield different results because they can contain different information. Surprisingly, there has been comparatively little research examining the issue of measurement in developing countries. It is clear that the roles of the informal sector and service-related manufacturing activities are underreported. Based on this discussion, several authors have been using both measures simultaneously or as a robustness analysis. For instance, Rodrik (2016) finds that advanced economies have lost considerable employment (especially of the low-skilled kind), but they have done surprisingly well in terms of keeping manufacturing output shares. Rodrik (2016) adds that the differential patterns may be due to globalization and labor-saving technological progress in manufacturing. These findings suggest that the decline in share of employment due to labor-saving technology implies that the manufacturing sector itself is not shrinking. Second, the loss of employment due to the shrinkage of manufacturing under globalization is a sign of deindustrialization. Third, the decreasing share of employment in the manufacturing sector is related to the worsening performance in aggregate productivity within the economy.

An important question for policy and practice is whether changes in value-added shares are correlated with changes in employment shares. Figure 2.12 plots the changes in manufacturing employment and value-added between 1990 and 2010. Four groups are clear. The first group of countries have experienced an increase in the share of manufacturing value-added and an increase in the share of manufacturing employment. This group of countries represents 15 percent of our sample

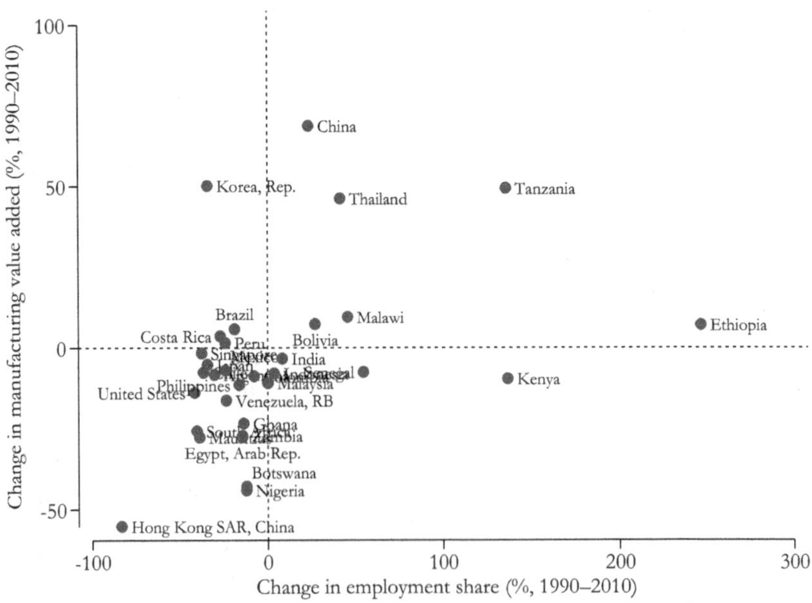

Figure 2.12 Correlation of employment share and manufacturing value-added share

and includes fast-growing economies, such as China, Thailand, Ethiopia, Kenya, Malawi, and Bolivia. A similar number of countries (13 percent) have experienced an increase in the share of manufacturing value-added alongside a decline in manufacturing employment. This pattern may signal a positive deindustrialization where improvements in labor efficiency are accompanied with increasing output of manufacturing. More importantly, 44 percent of countries have experienced a decline in both the share of manufacturing value-added and employment. Finally, the last group includes countries (28 percent) experiencing a decline in the share of manufacturing output but an increase in employment, a signal of a rise in inefficiency in the manufacturing sector. Taken together, these findings show that by utilizing both readily available measurements, value-added and employment, we not only can improve the robustness of the analyses but also can extract additional information on the patterns of structural changes surrounding manufacturing.

2.3.2 Time series test of patterns of industrialization

To put into context the discussion of deindustrialization, we take a small detour to revise early evidence (Temin, 1967) on the time of the pattern of industrial growth. We use data from Mitchell (2007), which provide historical statistics on 20-year intervals from 1870 to 2010 for nine countries (Australia, Canada, France, Germany, Italy, Sweden, the United Kingdom, Japan, and the United States). We extend the seminal work by Temin (1967) in two important ways. First, we extend the sample to include more recent years as Temin was only able to cover data until 1950. Second, we use a more robust econometric specification that includes a quadratic function of log GDP whereas Temin used a linear specification. His findings show that the industry sector was rising over time but there were no systematic differences in the rate of change of the share of industry between time periods.

We present our time trends in Figure 2.13, together with 95 percent confidence intervals around them. The increase in the industry value-added share is evident until the 1950s but we also find that the rate of change during this period is not statistically significant. As can be seen, this finding corroborates that of Temin (1967). Interestingly, however, we document a statistically significant negative time trend in the post-1950s period. Figure 2.13 shows a steady decline in the industry value-added share, but with large variations between countries. In Section 2.3.3, we extend this analysis for the period post-1960s and we cover developing countries.

2.3.3 Time series test of deindustrialization

Much research has documented time trend patterns of deindustrialization (Dasgupta & Singh, 2006; Rodrik, 2016) over recent decades. Using data up to the 2000s, Rodrik (2016) points to a steady decrease over time in manufacturing value-added and employment shares. Using a similar specification that controls for income trends and recent data, we show in Figure 2.14 that this general

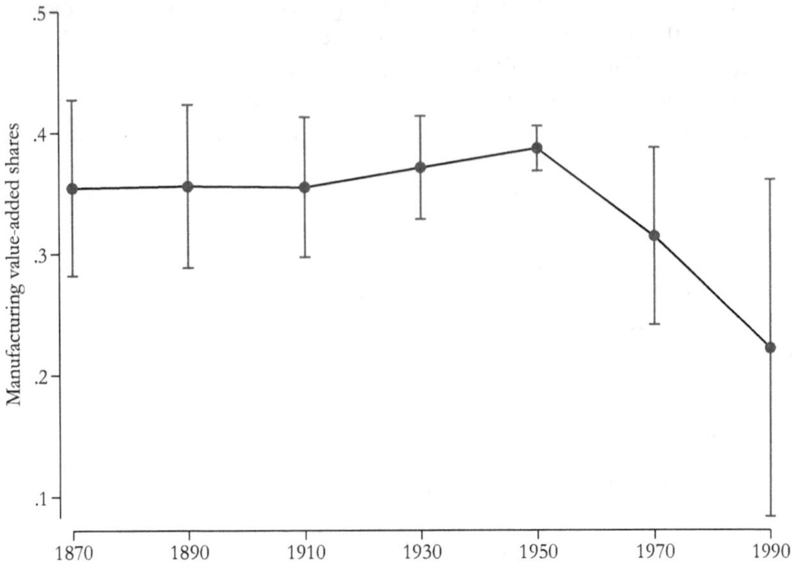

Figure 2.13 Industrialization: estimated period share in early industrialized countries

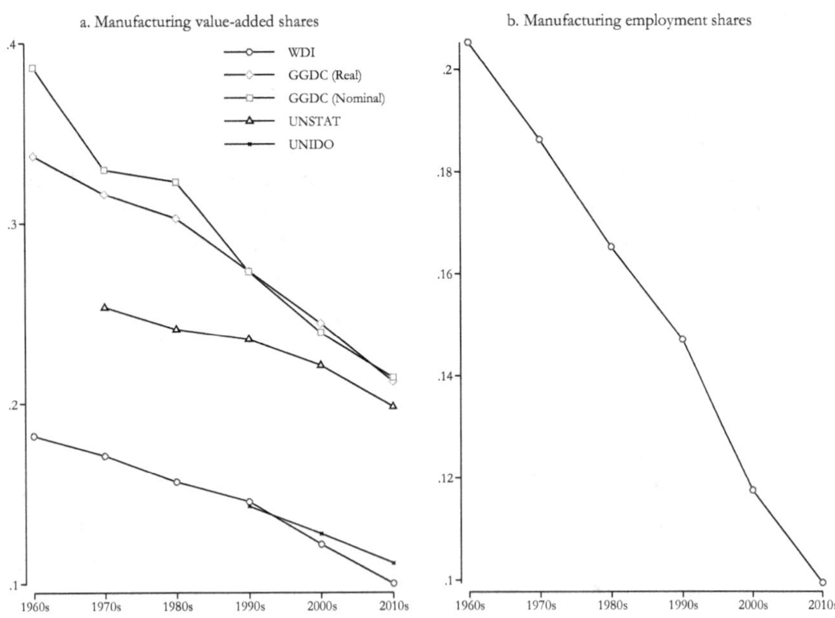

Figure 2.14 Deindustrialization: estimated period share, post-1960

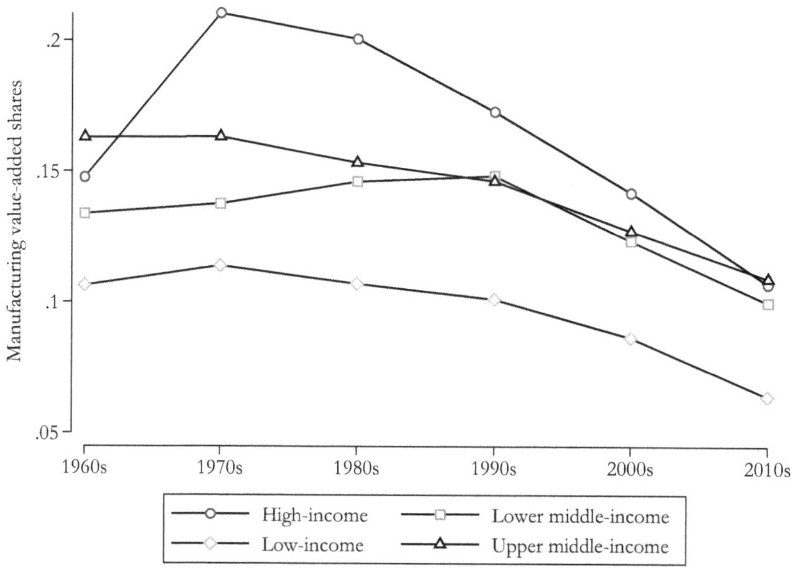

Figure 2.15 Deindustrialization: estimated period share by income group

decline in manufacturing value-added shares was more severe in the 2010s. While most of the data set shows that deindustrialization is particularly evident since the 1980s, the WDI has shown that the shares of MVA have exhibited a significant downward trend since 1960s, and this pattern does not appear to be random. One of the reasons for this difference may be the coverage in terms of countries. Similar to Rodrik (2016), Figure 2.14 panel (b) shows a systematic difference in the rate of manufacturing employment shares between periods, but the trend might have slowed since the 2010s.

Figure 2.15 presents the manufacturing value-added trends over time by income group. Here again, countries are divided into HICS, UMICS, LMICS, and LICS. The shares of manufacturing value-added increased in the 1970s for HICS, and then decreased. However, the decrease is not statistically significant. HIMCS and LMICS exhibit similar time trends, particularly since the 1990s. The striking observation is the manifest failure to industrialize among poor countries and the existence of deindustrialization at very low levels of manufacturing value-added share. After a stagnant period in the 1970s, LICs embarked on the processes of deindustrialization which accelerated after the 1980s.

In Figures 2.16 and 2.17 we present the deindustrialization patterns by geographical regions using value-added share.[7] The results point to different regional patterns. The first striking observation is that South Asia is the only region where the share of MVA has been increasing over time. The trend was to accelerate in the 1980s but decelerate in the 2000s. The share of MVA in ECA has been falling

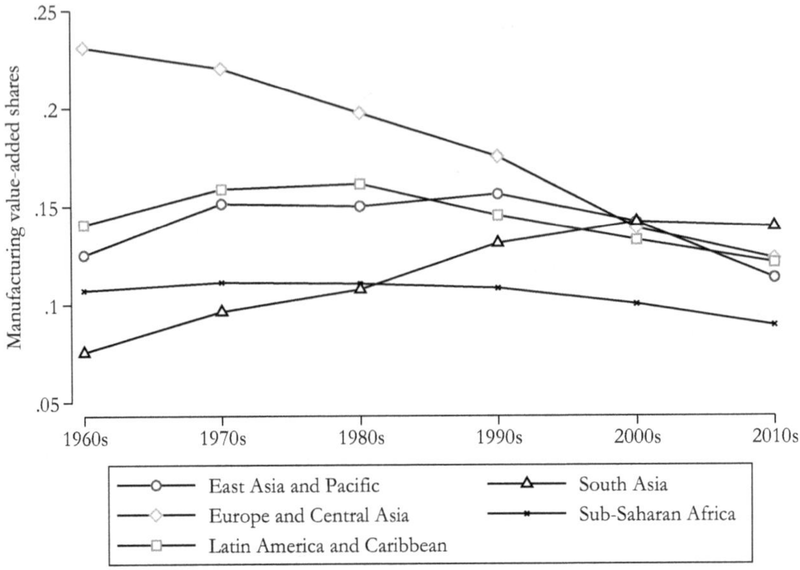

Figure 2.16 Deindustrialization: estimated period share by geographical region

over time and the trend is highly influenced by Northern Europe and Western Europe. In Central Asia, the share of MVA exhibited a rising trend from the 1960s to 1980s, then stagnated in the 1990s before steadily dropping. In LAC, even if the time trend increased slightly, it has declined steadily since 1980s. Within the region, it appears that the share of MVA in South America has been falling over time, particularly since the 1980s. The fall in the manufacturing sector in Central America started earlier in the 1970s but the speed of deindustrialization has been slower than in Central America. Finally, it is interesting to note that the Caribbean exhibits a time trend in deindustrialization.

We find no evidence of the existence of a time trend for deindustrialization in EAP, but the region exhibits a positive increase in the share of manufacturing value-added until the 1990s. In the sub-region, it is only Eastern Asia that exhibits a negative time trend in the manufacturing since the 1980s whereas there is no evidence for the time trend in Micronesia, Melanesia, and Polynesia. Interestingly, South-eastern Asia exhibits a significant positive time trend in all the period of analysis. The effect is higher for ASEAN but the speed does not significantly change. We also find no evidence of a time trend in SSA. On the contrary, Southern Africa exhibits a strong and positive time trend until the 2000s, but the effect is highly influenced by Botswana. Excluding Botswana shows that Southern Africa exhibits no time trend, expect in the 2000s when manufacturing falls.

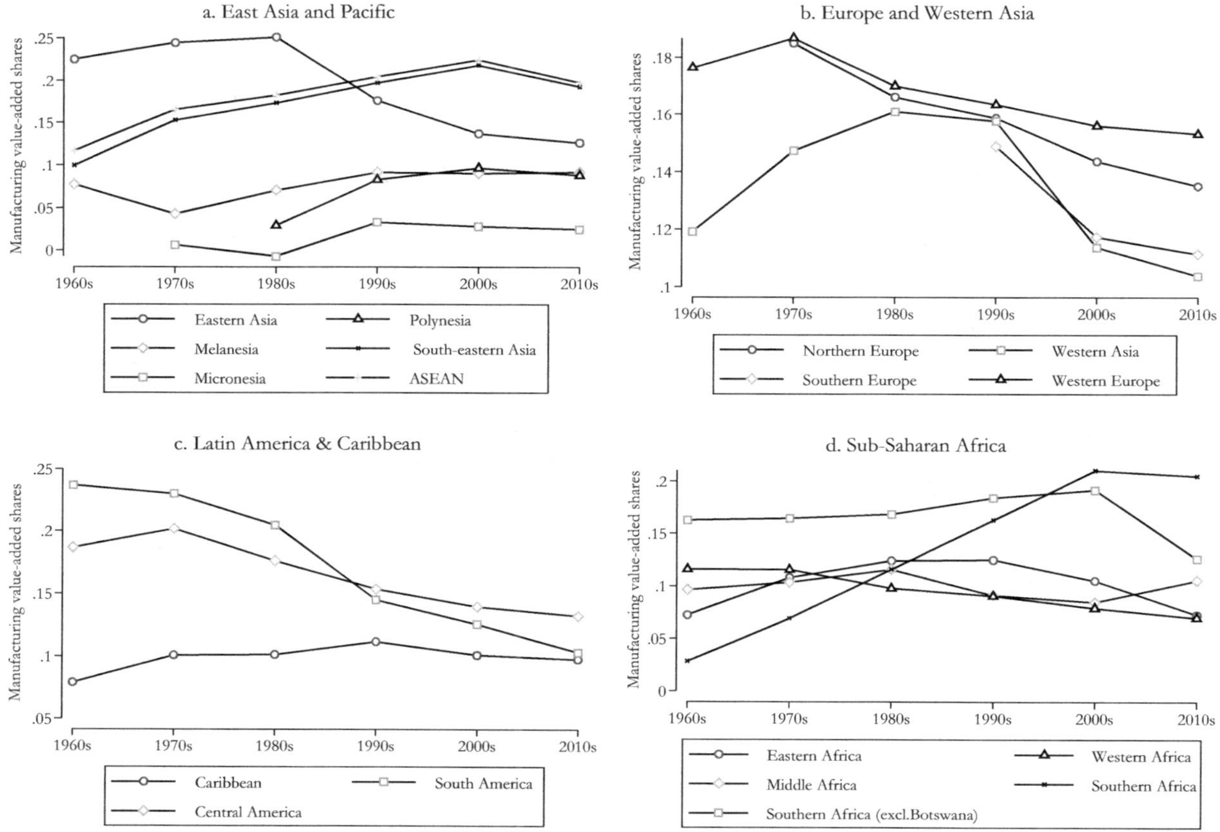

Figure 2.17 Deindustrialization: estimated period share by geographical sub-regions

2.4 Structural change and premature deindustrialization

The reallocation of resources and output away from agriculture toward industry and services is now a well-established fact in the growth literature (Chenery, 1960; Clark, 1957; Kuznets, 1966; Syrquin, 1988). Also documented as one of the most important facts about structural change; this theory generally states that the economic development of nations begins with a rise in industrial production and a relative decline of agriculture, followed by a decrease in the industrial sector and a sustained increase of services. The early research literature observed these patterns of structural change for the early industrializers and predicted that other regions would follow the same development pattern. Recent studies such as Herrendorf, Rogerson, and Valentinyi (2014) and Bah (2011) have also documented these development processes for the late industrializers. Together, these studies indicate substantial heterogeneities across countries. The previous section has clearly demonstrated that there has been a major change in the structure of manufacturing value-added for many developing countries, and that the speed of deindustrialization has been faster in recent decades. It is also clear that there has been an improvement in the quality and coverage of data so that it is worthwhile reexamining the stylized facts of structural transformation. This is what we do in this section.

2.4.1 Structural change and premature deindustrialization

As is standard in the growth literature, we start by presenting stylized facts about structural change for developed countries. Since we are interested in historical patterns, we use value-added shares as they are available in longer spans than employment shares. Specifically, we use a long time series of nine developed countries for the period 1870–2018 from Mitchell (2007) and the WDI to show a panel data with unequally-spaced intervals. Following Bah (2011), we regress the sectoral value-added shares of GDP against a quadratic log of GDP per capita and country fixed effects and we estimate corrected value-added shares by filtering out country fixed effects. In Figure 2.18, we plot the log of GDP per capita (solid line) together with the corrected share of each country during each time period and the confidence interval around the estimates (two dotted lines). We observe the well-known fact that as countries develop, agriculture value-added share monotonically declines, the share of services increases, and the share of industry follows a clear hump-shape pattern, that is to say, the share of industry increases for lower levels of GDP per capita, reaches a peak, and subsequently decreases.

Some other interesting aspects of Figure 2.18 are worth noting. First, a closer look shows that the corrected shares for all the countries lie within the two standard deviations' confidence interval, indicating that developed countries followed a similar process of structural transformation, as described by Kuznets (1973). Second, focusing on the hump shape, we see that the average peak share of manufacturing is 0.4 (40 percent) and occurs at log GDP per capita of 9 (about $8,100). Third, the speed of transformation differs across countries but

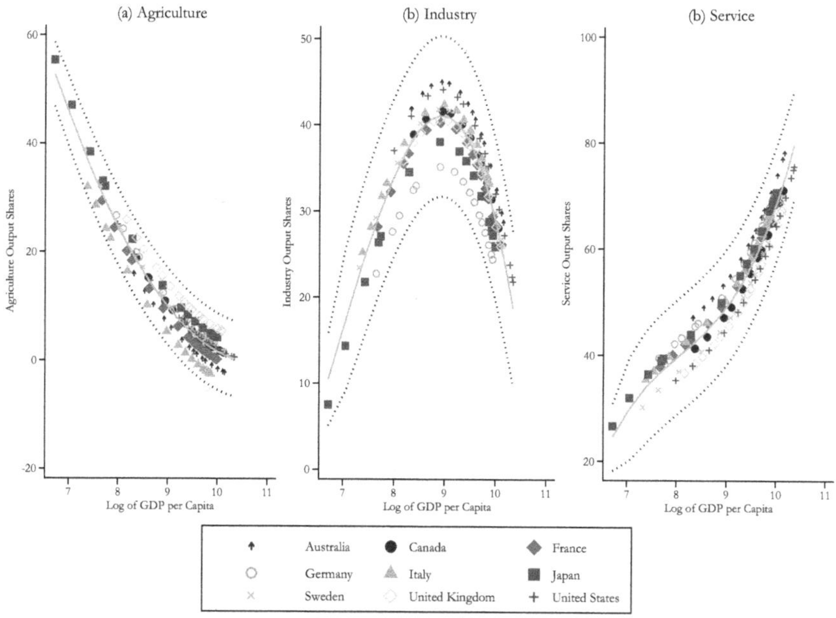

Figure 2.18 Structural change for developed countries

all countries exhibit a late acceleration after log GDP per capita of 9. For instance, Japan started low in the increasing part of the share of industry but converged faster to the levels of other developed countries. Using recent time series data, we are able to document that the speed of transformation for all developed countries is very fast at the decreasing part of the share of industry. This feature is consistent with our previous finding on the change in the speed of deindustrialization in recent years. Fourth, we document that the share of manufacturing expands more quickly than does the service sector at low levels of GDP per capita. Similar to Herrendorf et al. (2014), we document that the share for manufacturing peaks around the same log GDP per capita at which the share of the service sector accelerates, meaning that the acceleration of services goes hand in hand with the decline of manufacturing.

Moving on now to consider the case of developing countries, Figures 2.19, 2.20, and 2.21 compare the pattern of developed countries with developing countries of Asia, Latin America, and Africa, and for comparison, we plot the fitted curve of developed countries.[8] Figure 2.19 shows that Asia, with few exceptions, has been following similar patterns as the developed countries, but structural transformation has been happening at lower levels of log GDP per capita. For manufacturing, the pattern of Southeast Asia is very close to the one for developed countries, but deindustrialization seems to occur at a slower pace and acceleration occurs faster. South Asia followed a different pattern but started

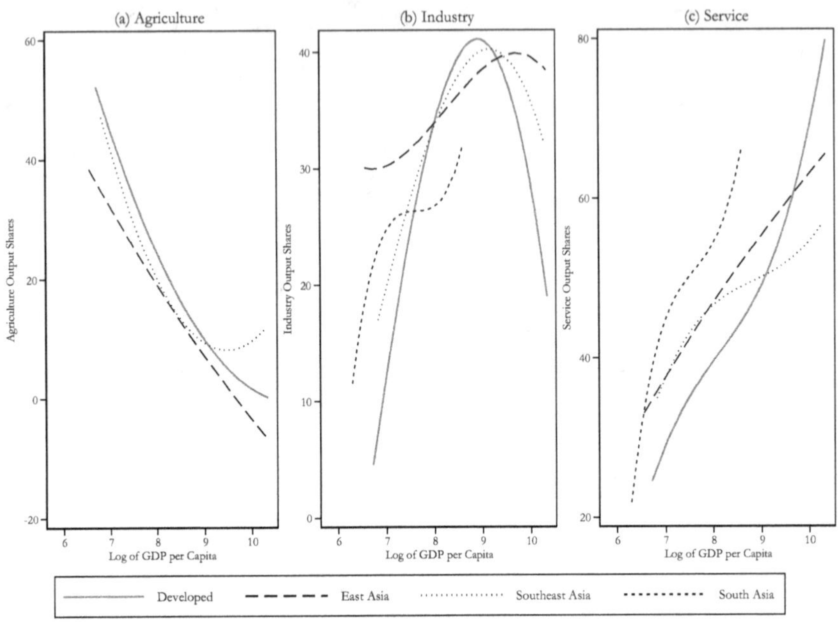

Figure 2.19 Structural change: within Asia comparisons

deindustrialization a little below 0.4 peak share. However, there are a lot of heterogeneities within East Asia, with Korea reaching the peak with a share of manufacturing larger than 0.4 and China still growing. Interestingly, South Asia is still in the first phase of industrialization driven by India and Sri Lanka.

Figure 2.20 presents the patterns for Latin America divided into Central America and South America. The region follows a similar path of developed countries in agriculture and industry. We observe a monotonic decline in agriculture while the share of manufacture shows a hump-shape. Both Central and South America started to deindustrialize at lower levels of GDP per capita and share of manufacturing. There is also large heterogeneity in Central America due to Mexico and Panama. Countries like Nicaragua and Honduras are at the first stage of industrialization. There is also large heterogeneity in South America, but they have done well in agriculture as their pattern converges with developed countries, especially after log per capita GDP of 9. Another important feature we observe is that deindustrialization is also taking place during periods of economic stagnation and even decline.

Finally, Figure 2.21 shows the results for Africa. We document a monotonic decline in the share of agriculture in Eastern Africa and Southern Africa, whereas Central Africa and West Africa are slow at starting agricultural transformation. We also observe a hump-shaped pattern of the share of industry in Southern Africa and less clearly in West Africa, but at very low levels of log GDP per capita.

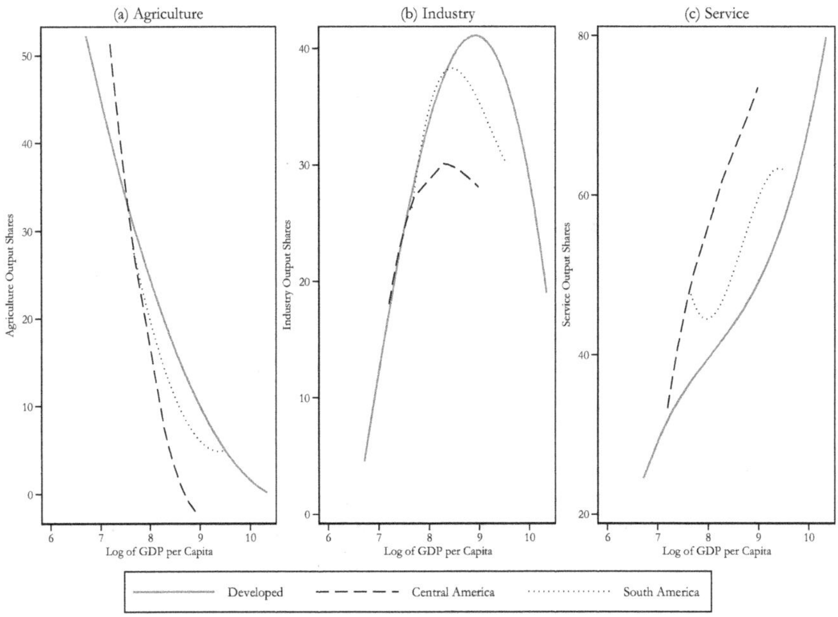

Figure 2.20 Structural change: within Latin America comparisons

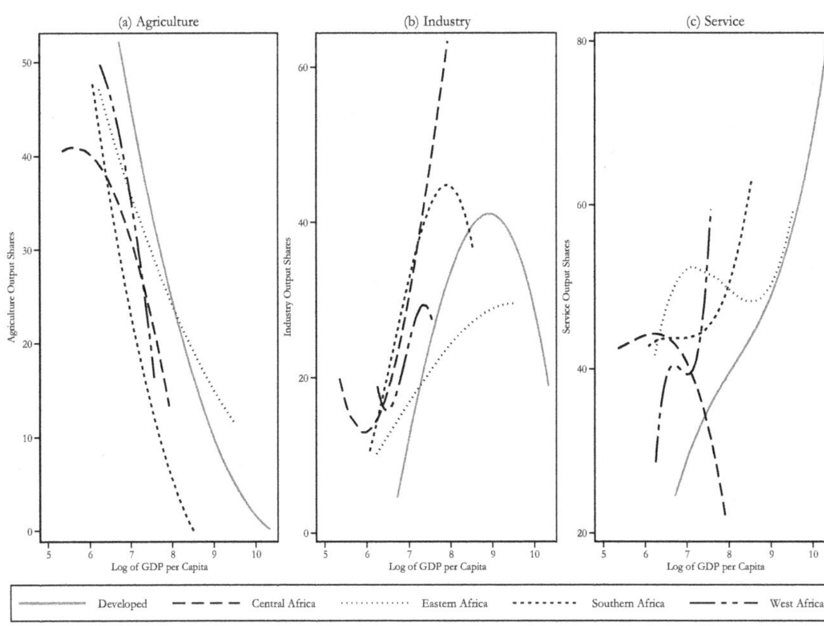

Figure 2.21 Structural change: within Sub-Saharan Africa comparisons

Compared to developed countries, Africa has started with a high share of service value-added at very low levels of GDP per capita. The qualitative pattern of the share of service is, however, very different across sub-regions. Here again, Southern Africa and Eastern Africa are following a close pattern but at the second phase of service growth. The plots also show that the qualitative patterns of structural change are very different to within Africa.

2.4.2 Flying geese and industrialization in Asia

There is a tradition among development economists that lessons from certain successful models should be applied to less successful countries. A popular academic finding suggests that Asian countries followed a different pattern for development that is closer to Japan, based on the "flying geese" patterns of development. According to this theory, the catching-up process of industrialization of latecomers can be explained by the subsequent relocation process of industries from advanced to developing countries during the latter's catching-up process. Arguably, this theory has been useful to explain growth and the pattern of FDI flows from Japan to East Asia and South Asia, but data limitations have constrained its validation. We test whether the East Asian model and the flying geese theory hold with the data for the Asia region, and whether convergence among the sub-regions (late industrializers) is possible. Our strategy is as follows. First, we refer to the Big Three (Japan, Korea, and Taiwan) as the East Asian model, following Chang (2006). Then, we simulate the industrialization path of the Big Three and test whether the latecomers are following a similar path by plotting the prediction bounds for the Big Three.

Figure 2.22 presents the patterns of structural change followed by the Big Three. The vertical axis is the share of value-added in agriculture, industry, and the services sectors. The horizontal axis is the log of GDP per capita in 1990 international dollars. The solid line represents the fitted curves while the dashed lines plot the upper and lower bounds at two standard deviations of the forecast values. These graphs in Figure 2.22 clearly show that the Big Three followed a more homogeneous pattern of structural transformation, whereby increases in GDP per capita were associated with a rapid decrease in the share of agriculture, a humped-shape pattern of the share of manufacturing, and an increase in the share of service. We also find that the decrease in the share of manufacturing is simultaneous with an acceleration in the increase in the share of service.

In Figure 2.23, we verify whether East Asia is following a similar pattern of structural transformation as that of the Big Three. Panels (a), (b), and (c) plot the corrected sectoral shares against the log of GDP per capita. Since our interest is to compare these patterns with the Big Three, we therefore also plot the fitted upper and lower bounds at two standard deviations of the forecasted values from the Big Three. Figure 2.23 shows that the basic qualitative patterns of structural transformation of the Big Three do not hold in East Asia. Specifically, the pattern of Hong Kong is outside of the prediction bounds for the Big Three. The first phase of the structural transformation of China shares the basic regularities of

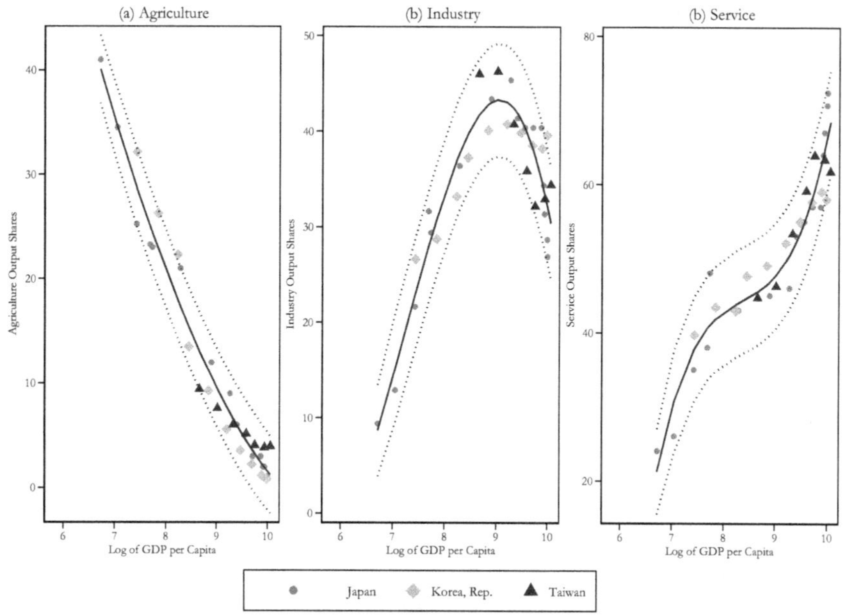

Figure 2.22 Structural change of the Big Three

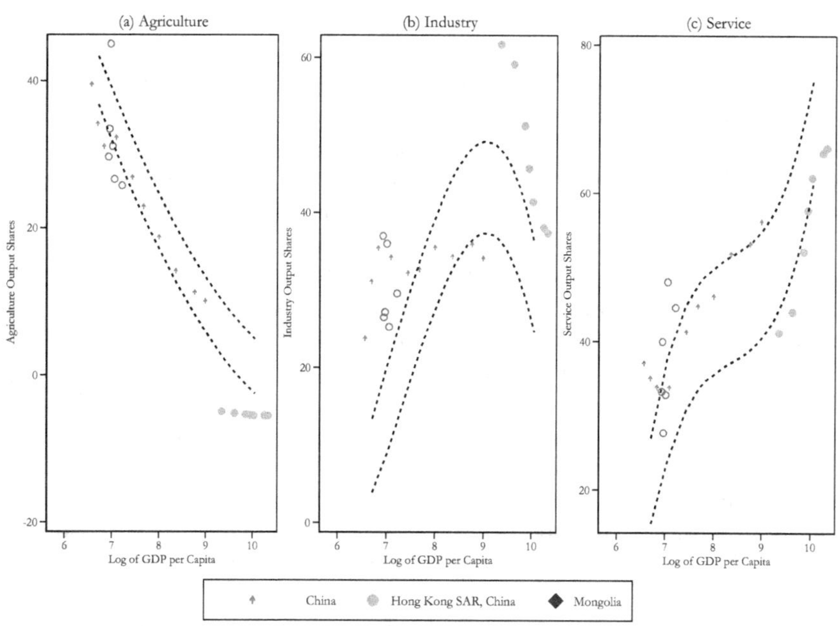

Figure 2.23 Structural change: comparing the Big Three and East Asia

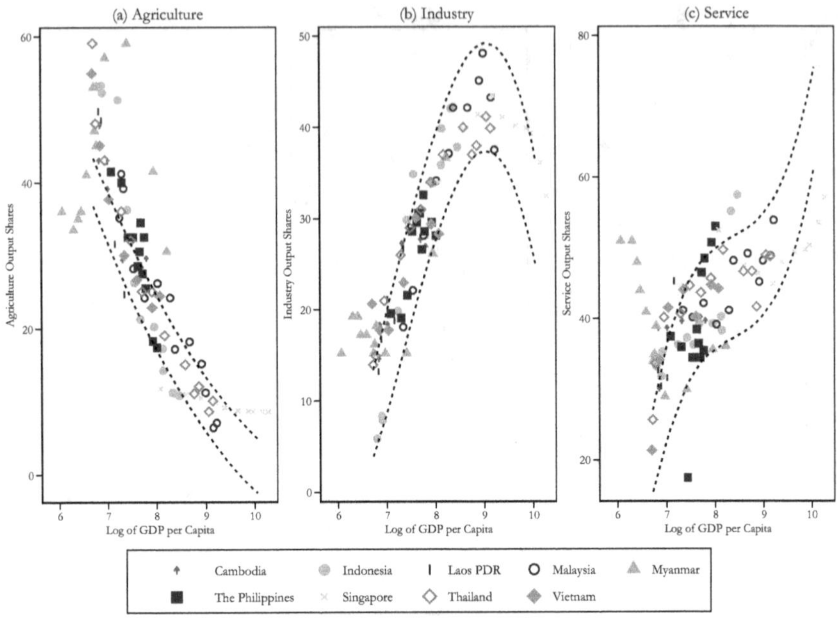

Figure 2.24 Structural change: comparing the Big Three and Southeast Asia

structural transformation as the share of agriculture converged to the bounds for the Big Three. We can also see a similar convergence in the service sector whereas these regularities do not hold in manufacture. China's value-added share of manufacture is flattening out but this started to happen at faster and at lower levels of manufacturing valued added and GDP than the Big Three. Interestingly, Mongolia seems to be following a similar pattern to China, with the difference being that Mongolia shows some signs of premature deindustrialization.

Figure 2.24 tests whether Southeast Asia is following a similar transformation as the Big Three. We can see that the plots reveal some qualitative regularities that we found for the Big Three. However, it is interesting to note that there are some outlier countries, such as Myanmar and Singapore. Agriculture and service value-added of Singapore have similar patterns to Hong Kong while its manufacturing is almost the same as the Big Three. However, Singapore has reached the roof of manufacturing value-added and has started to move to the second phase of structural transformation. Myanmar follows an irregular pattern that we have not observed before. In an analysis not reported here, we removed Myanmar and Singapore and found that most of the Southeast Asian countries are following the Big Three's patterns of structural change. Two patterns are observed: the agriculture value-added is decreasing (faster) with the level of development while the service value-added is increasing (slowly) with development. The manufacturing value-added is increasing but has not reached the maximum. Compared to Vietnam and the Philippines, Malaysia, Thailand, and Indonesia are closer

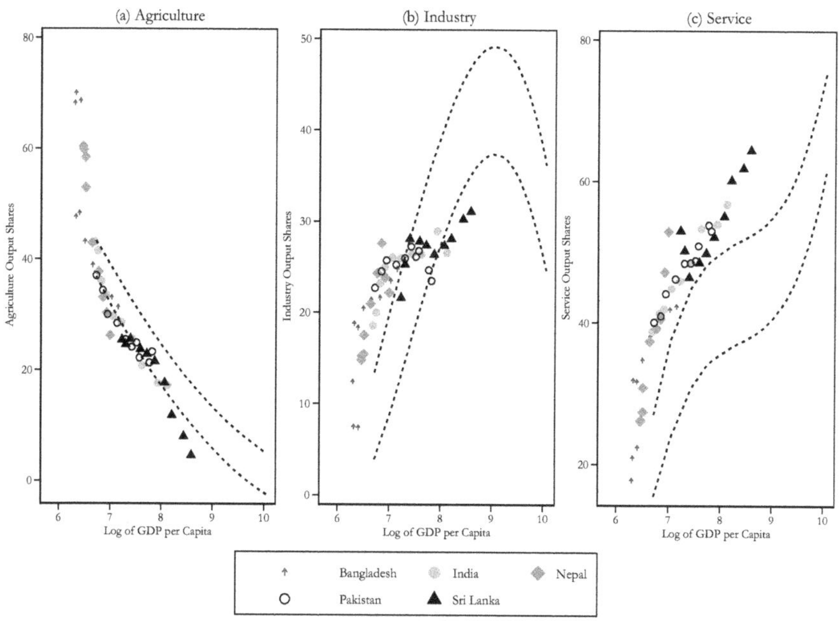

Figure 2.25 Structural change: comparing the Big Three and South Asia

to the maximum of manufacture value-added for the Big Three. However, the Philippines and Indonesia tend to show acceleration in service value-added, which can be a sign of exhausted manufacturing growth. As we need to further monitor structural changes in these countries, Chapter 5 analyses the Indonesian case in detail.

Figure 2.25 compares South Asia with the Big Three. The plots show that South Asia on average does not follow the same regularities as the Big Three. Nevertheless, some patterns of structural change are observed, specifically in the first phase. We see that agriculture value-added shares are decreasing with development while service value-added shares are increasing with development. It is important to highlight that Sri Lanka decreased the agriculture value-added shares very quickly because the initial values were also low. In this group, India, Sri Lanka, and Pakistan tend to follow the same patterns but Pakistan has started deindustrializing. We see that India seems to follow a similar pattern as China. We will come back to that later. Before that, we focus on Bangladesh and Nepal. Isolating Bangladesh and Nepal show some interesting features. While their level of development is still low, Bangladesh and Nepal are going through the first phase of structural change. The value-added shares of manufacturing are still increasing. Their patterns are parallel to the bounds for the Big Three. Our assumption is that they are more likely to follow the same pattern as India, Pakistan, and Sri Lanka. Sri Lanka might have experienced decreasing value-added shares in service when GDP was increasing. Figure 2.25 also shows high growth of the

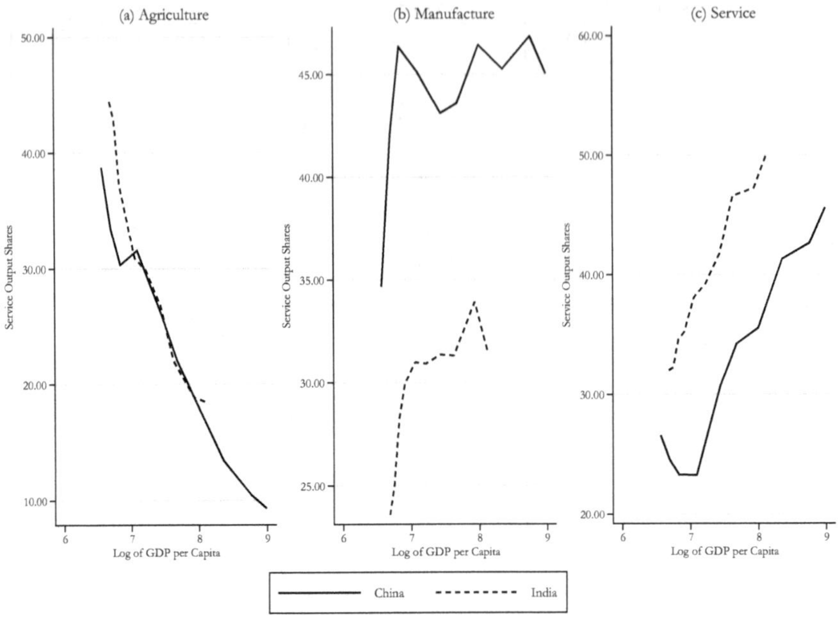

Figure 2.26 Structural change: comparing the Big Three and India and China

service sector due to a rapid decrease in the agriculture value-added shares. This pattern is also unusual.

2.4.3 *Structural change in China and India*

Finally, we compare whether China and India follow a unique pattern. In Figure 2.26, we simply plot the shares of value-added instead of corrected share. As discussed earlier, China and India seem not to follow closely the Big Three's patterns. However, they seem to move closer to the bounds for the Big Three when they reach higher levels of development. Their manufacture value-added shares point to the fact that China and India might have reached their maximum value-added share because it has flattened out. On a final note, India is following China's path but at lower levels of value-added shares, especially in manufacture. India, with its reputation as the "back office of the world" and traditionally high share of service value-added, may follow a new path to a high-yielding service (including medical services) and service-related manufacturing.

2.4.4 *Premature deindustrialization and manufacturing employment*

So far, we have used value-added shares in Sections 2.4.1–2.4.3 to present stylized facts on structural change and premature deindustrialization. In this approach, comparing the patterns of developed countries versus developing countries provides a direct test of premature deindustrialization. In contrast to early industrializers, latecomers have experienced falling manufacturing value-added shares at lower level of GDP per capita, without reaching the peak share of 0.4. As a result, the manufacturing sector in many developing countries has remained very small and not enough to generate productive jobs. Similarly, deindustrialization has reduced the potential of overall economic growth to generate employment and reduce poverty. According to UNCTAD (2013), countries with faster GDP growth achieved this with relatively less employment creation. In addition, employment elasticity declined to about half of the Least Developing Countries (LDCs) in the period 2000–2008, and that elasticity tended to fall more frequently in precisely those LDCs that were growing faster.

To determine the extent to which countries have been losing manufacturing employment after reaching the peak share of manufacturing value-added, we measure the timing of the deindustrialization in the year in which manufacturing employment begins to decline. Then, for each country, we calculate the growth rate of employment between the year of the peak in manufacturing shares and the last year of the data, which is 2018. Of the 182 countries with available data in the WDI, we found that 71 countries have already reached the employment peak and started to deindustrialize, while the share of manufacturing employment has been shrinking in 63 countries before 1960 and increasing in 48 countries. Figure 2.27 shows the average percentage reduction in the share of manufacturing employment between the peak year and the last year of data available. We can see that deindustrialization seems to be severe as many countries are losing more than 10 percent of manufacturing jobs.

2.5 Servicification

Changes in labor allocation across sectors are naturally dictated by the changes in demand for various goods and services that, in turn, are brought about by two factors: changes in income (income effect), and changes in relative prices of goods resulting from different speeds of productivity growth across sectors (Duarte & Restuccia, 2010; Ngai & Pissarides, 2007; Rogerson, 2008). Traditionally, a key feature of rapid economic growth is the movement of labor out of agriculture and into other sectors of the economy. Given the substantial impact of manufacturing job losses due to deindustrialization, a key question remains as to whether manufacturing can still be the engine of growth. While part of the answer to this question has already been given in Chapter 1 of this book, it merits its own consideration.

2.5.1 Servicification and manufacturing productivity differences

The premature decline of manufacturing and the subsequent growing importance of the service sector in both developed and developing countries provide ample evidence arguing that structural transformation has occurred in

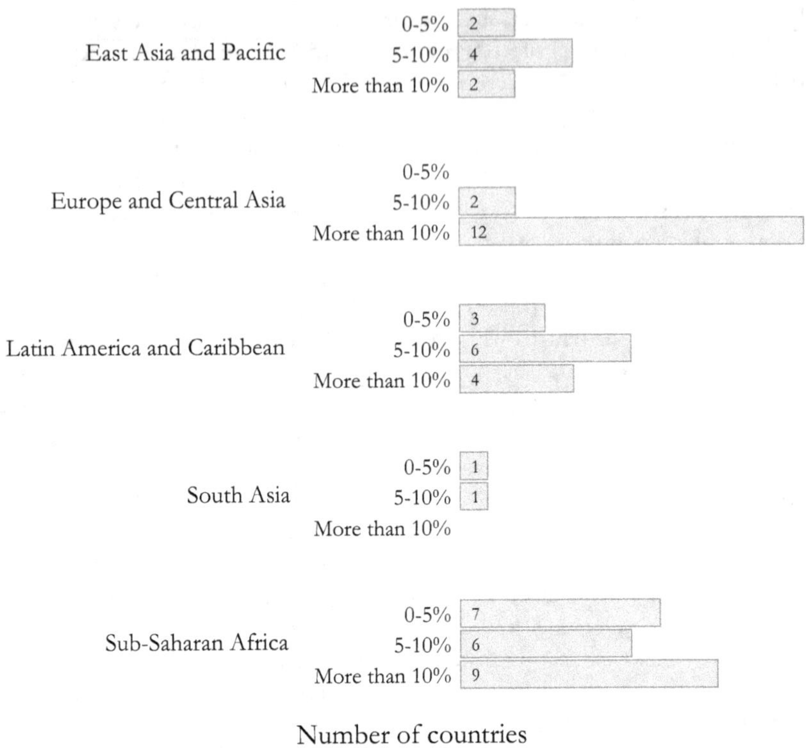

Figure 2.27 Reduction in the share of manufacturing employment since the peak year of manufacturing employment

the boundaries of manufacturing where the service sector has expanded due to technological innovation. The previous discussion has provided evidence of the increasingly important role played by the service sector in the international economy. It is also clear that this transition to the service economy has benefited less developed countries more. For instance, Newfarmer, Page, and Tarp (2018) argue that the future of Africa lies in the service sector because of the emergence of industries without smokestacks, such as agro-industrial and horticultural value chains; tourism; and business and trade services (including ICT- based services, and transport and logistics). Newfarmer et al. note that these sectors are growing in importance in the global economy and also in Africa. Figure 2.28 illustrates the growing importance of services, especially in the last decade. Historically, the service sector increased slowly in the early stages of development, and then accelerated when manufacturing sector reached the hump shape. Figure 2.28 shows that the share of service sector is moving to the left, meaning that the sector is becoming increasingly important for developing countries.

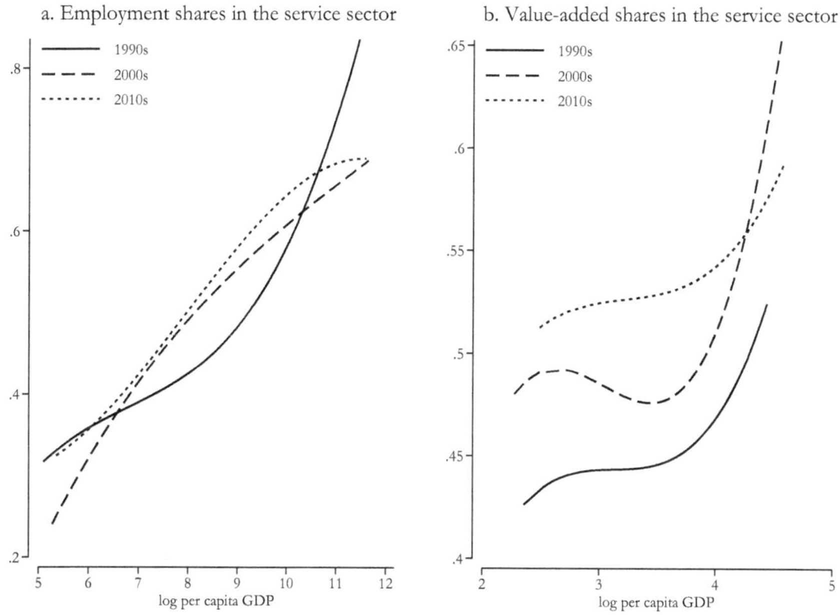

Figure 2.28 Changing landscape of the service sector

Perhaps the most dramatic structural change toward the service sector in developing countries is the growth-reducing structural change, as documented by McMillan et al. (2014). Using sector data on productivity and employment between 1990 and 2005, they identified the movement of labor from high-productive tradable sectors in agriculture and manufacturing to low (negative-productive non-tradable sectors in service. This movement was apparent in Africa and LAC while Asian countries exhibited a growth-enhancing structural change. The advances in technology and the current nature of global trade characterized by high productive service (manufacturing-related service) sectors create new conditions for developing countries to industrialize. While the shift began in tradable services, such as some industries without smokestacks, it appears that productivity in the service sector is still lagging.

Figure 2.29 provides a visual comparison of productivity growth across countries and sectors by plotting the annualized growth rate of labor productivity against the sectoral productivity growth rate. We see large differences in productivity growth between countries and over periods. Over the long run, agriculture and manufacturing productivity growth have been almost three times higher than productivity growth in the service sector. Our results are qualitatively similar to those found by Duarte and Restuccia (2010) using a sample of 29 countries for the period 1956–2004. Not surprisingly, China has made substantial progress in both manufacturing and non-manufacturing productivity growth and its performance has been sustained over time.

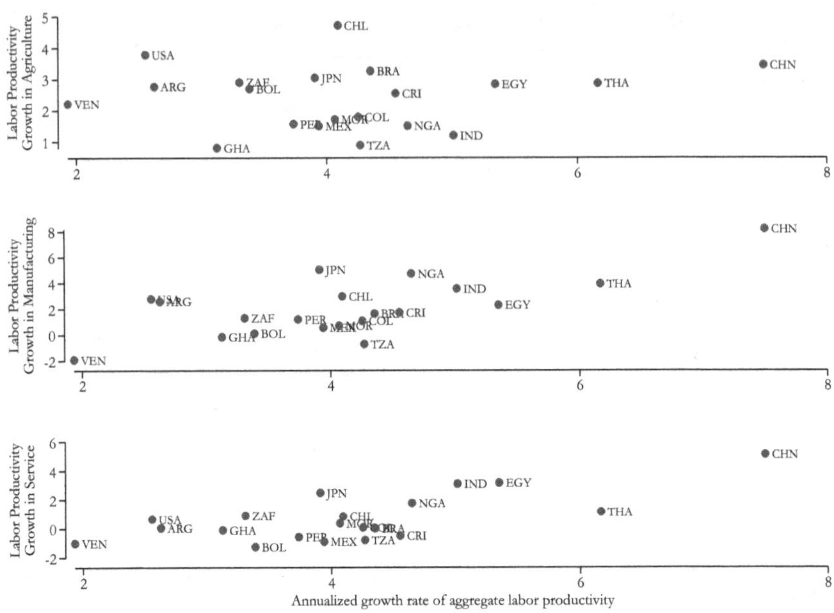

Figure 2.29 Sectoral growth rates of labor productivity

Stiglitz (2018) highlights that deindustrialization may occur when manufacturing is a victim of its own success, meaning when productivity exceeds the rate of increase in demand. Since labor flows from higher-productive sectors to lower-productive sectors, we can test whether differentials in productivity can explain the structural change observed. To do so, we explore the relationship between manufacturing labor productivity and employment in the service sector in Figure 2.30 and see clear correlations between labor productivity in manufacturing and share of employment in the service sector. This shows that the service sector can become an important tool for employment when a country industrializes. This confirms our previous findings on the structural change occurring between manufacturing and the service sector. Newfarmer et al. (2018) likewise use firm-level data for 580,000 firms in over 100 countries to show the considerable effects of services on manufacturing productivity. They find that, at an average level of services use, a 10 percent improvement in services productivity is associated with an increase in manufacturing productivity of between 0.3–0.6 percent, depending on country-specific fixed effect and institutional variables. However, it should be highlighted that manufacturing labor productivity exhibits strong unconditional convergence. According to Rodrik (2013), manufacturing labor productivity in poorer countries is on average catching up with manufacturing labor productivity in HICs, independent of the policies, qualities of institutions, education, or other growth determinants of low- and middle-income

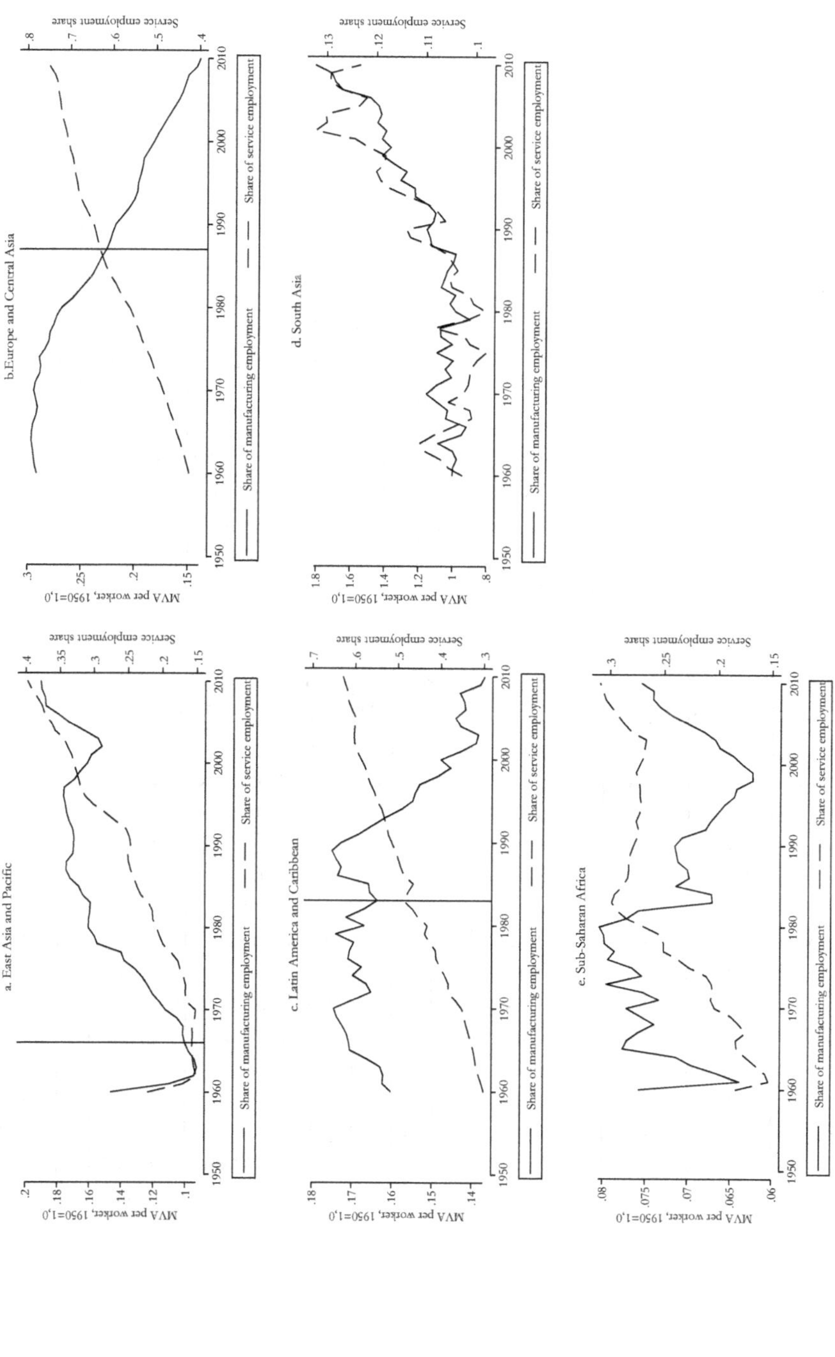

Figure 2.30 Manufacturing labor productivity versus manufacturing employment shares over time

countries. Describing these strongly correlated trends in manufacturing productivity and service employment in a different way, we reconfirm the ever declining share of labor in manufacturing value-added pointed out in Chapter 1.

2.5.2 *GVCs, deindustrialization, and reindustrialization*

The empirical economic literature has provided substantial evidence that the growing of servicification has been highly related to the development of value chains. According to Baldwin et al. (2014), the emergence of GVCs has contributed to the reduction in the role of manufacturing relative to the service sector through outsourcing certain tasks such as R&D, marketing, and design work. Similarly, joining value chains can help developing countries industrialize through offshoring of production. Baldwin et al., however, are concerned with the fact that innovations in ICT make it easy to distribute labor-intensive stages of the production process in low-wage countries and skill-intensive stages in skill-abundant countries. This issue is discussed and analyzed further in Chapter 7 of this book, taking GVCs in Laos as a case. This creates new patterns of production and specialization where countries can focus on stages or tasks that fit their comparative advantage, instead of focusing on the entire production process. Linking into these international production and distribution networks could, therefore, help developing countries initiate their industrialization with labor-intensive tasks and further upgrade to medium and high-tech manufacturing.

Guided by this assumption, a wide range of formal econometric tests using macro-, micro-, and firm-level data led to the conclusion that GVC participation has contributed to inclusive growth, reducing poverty, and increasing gender participation and equity in the workplace (UNIDO, 2018; World Bank, 2020). A key question for our purpose is whether there are any spaces where developing countries can find manufacturing activities with the rapid technological upgrading and extension of GVCs for manufacturing. To answer this question, we make use of the recent GVC linkages indicators proposed by the World Bank (2020). They proposed a measure of GVCs linkages based on the type of product the country exports and their participation in GVCs. These measures are classified into four types, namely, commodities, limited manufacturing, advanced manufacturing and services, and innovative activities.

Figure 2.31 presents four GVC linkages measures by income groups, in panel (a), and geographical regions, in panel (b). It is clear from panel (a) that the levels of GVC linkages are correlated with income groups. LICs are mainly engaged in commodities and to a lesser extent in limited manufacturing. Panel (b) clearly shows that this group is located in Africa, Central Asia, and Latin America. LMICs and UMICs are engaged in limited manufacturing and advanced manufacturing and services while HICs are also engaged in innovative activities. With regards to region, it appears that East Asia and Pacific, Europe, and North America are engaged in advanced manufacturing and services GVCs and innovative GVC activities.

Figure 2.32 panel (a) shows that countries that join limited manufacturing from commodities GVCs exhibit a positive and strong growth in the per capita

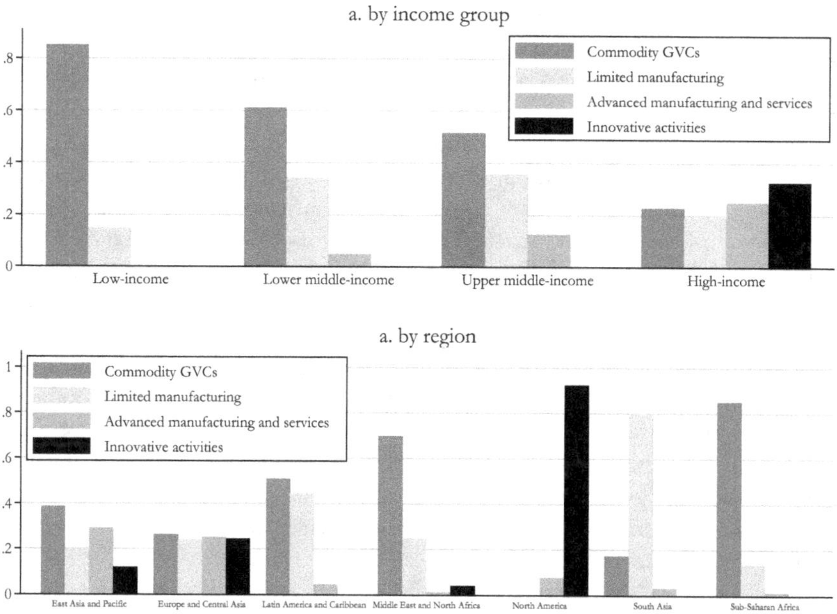

Figure 2.31 Global value chains linkages by income group and region

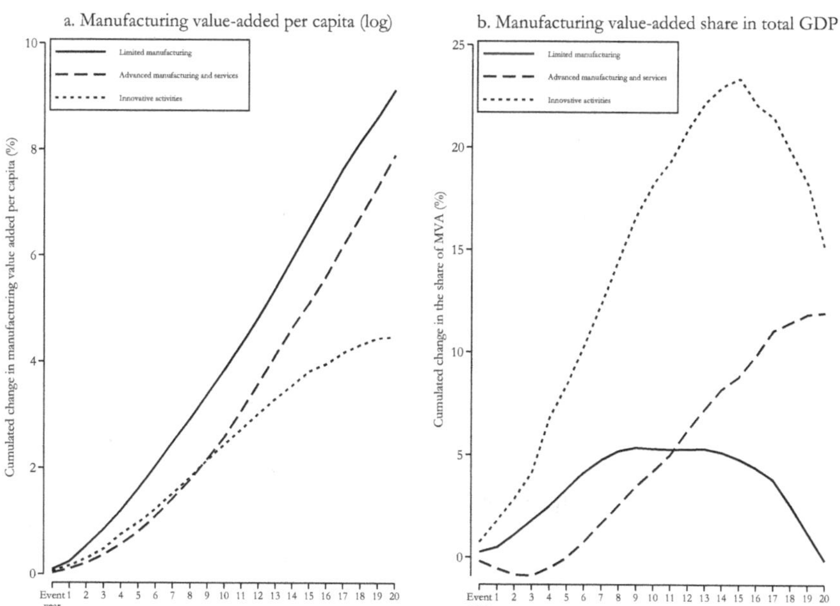

Figure 2.32 Impact of global value chains on manufacturing

MVA. Figure 2.32 suggests that such performance can be expected to continue over 20 years but at varying speeds. Panel (b) shows that the share of manufacturing increases after entering limited manufacturing GVCs but the effects tend to become smaller and even negative if countries do not upgrade. To achieve sustained industrialization, countries should upgrade from limited manufacturing to advanced manufacturing and services, and then into innovative tasks. This evidence suggests several promising ways to accelerate industrialization in developing countries, particularly in Sub-Saharan Africa. These regions have the lowest share of medium and high technology goods (as share of total manufacturing exports) but they have been closing the gap with other regions since 2011. This is a bit surprising given that the period coincides with a significant increase in commodity prices for oil, petroleum, and basic metals. Africa's industrial performance is weak but has strong growth potential. Agriculture, service sectors, and natural resources also remain at the heart of Africa's industrial development. Indeed, investment in the manufacturing and mining sectors has not crowded out investment in the agricultural sector, which means that Africa is attracting investment in the agricultural and non-agricultural sectors at the same time. Since these sectors differ in terms of resource endowment, Africa can develop by promoting labor-intensive industries and capital- or technology-intensive sectors simultaneously, as there is no competition and reallocation of resources between these industries. However, the economic difficulties and poor performance of industrial sectors and sub-sectors in developing countries are due to low productivity and lack of capacity at the firm level.

2.5.3 Are SEZs the solution?

In recent years, the rapid rise of SEZs has jump-started a multitude of countries as a strategy for industrialization: virtually every country or region wants to establish SEZs or other place-based policies such as industrial parks (IPs), export processing zones, eco-industrial parks (EIPs), technology parks (TPs), and innovation district (IDs), to achieve economies of agglomeration, attract (foreign) investment, alleviate unemployment, and implement special policy experiments. UNCTAD's inventory for its 2019 World Investment Report (UNCTAD, 2019) states that the rate of establishment of new SEZs is accelerating as governments increasingly compete for internationally mobile industrial activity. The report identified about 5,400 SEZs in 147 economies, and at least 500 more are in the pipeline. This number expanded from 500 in 73 countries in 1995 to 3,500 SEZs in 130 countries in 2006, before reaching 4,300 in about 140 countries in 2014. Impressively, the world has established more than 1,000 SEZs since 2014.

Has this dramatic expansion of SEZs helped build an industrial base? While research is at the embryonic stage in evaluating the impact of SEZs, we can obtain some insights about their potential using simple correlations. We do this in Figures 2.33 and 2.34 for MVA shares and employment, respectively. In each figure, we plot the growth rate over 1990–2018 against the accumulated number of SEZs up to 2018. The solid line is a linear regression fit line. Some

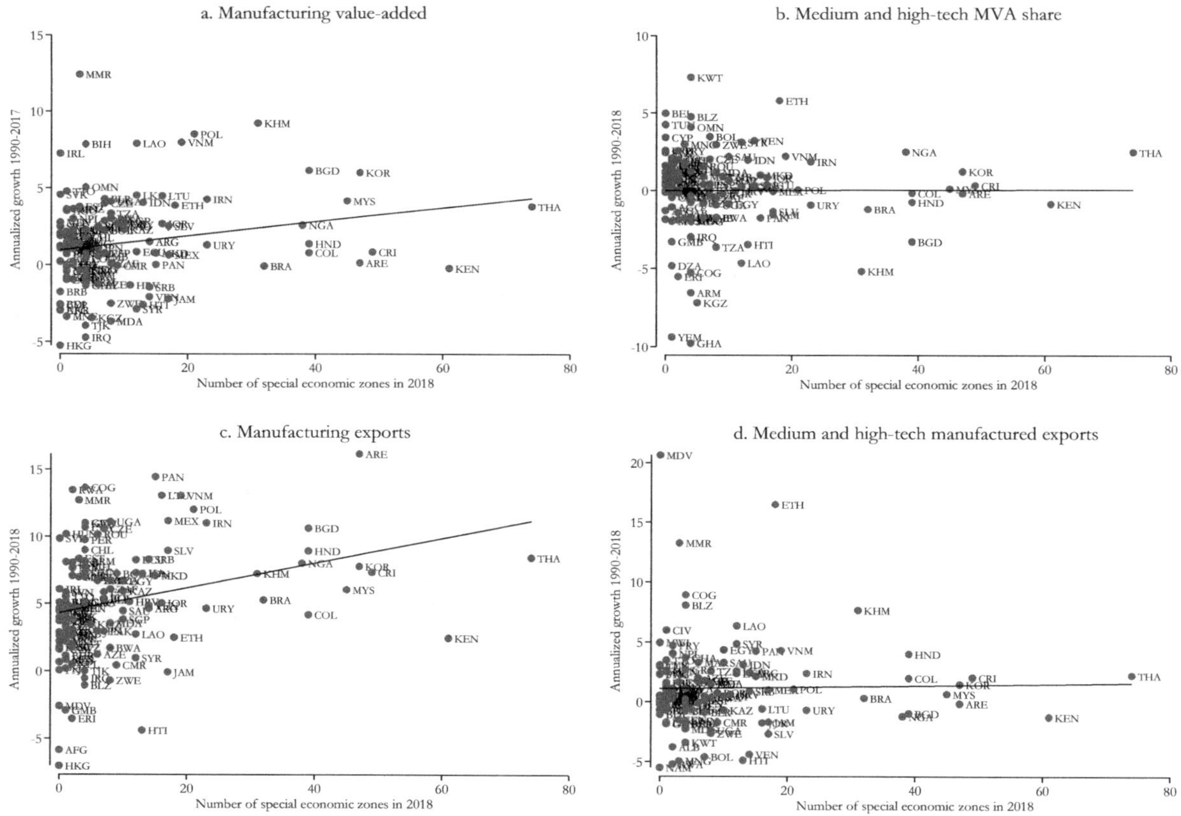

Figure 2.33 Special Economic Zones and manufacturing value-added

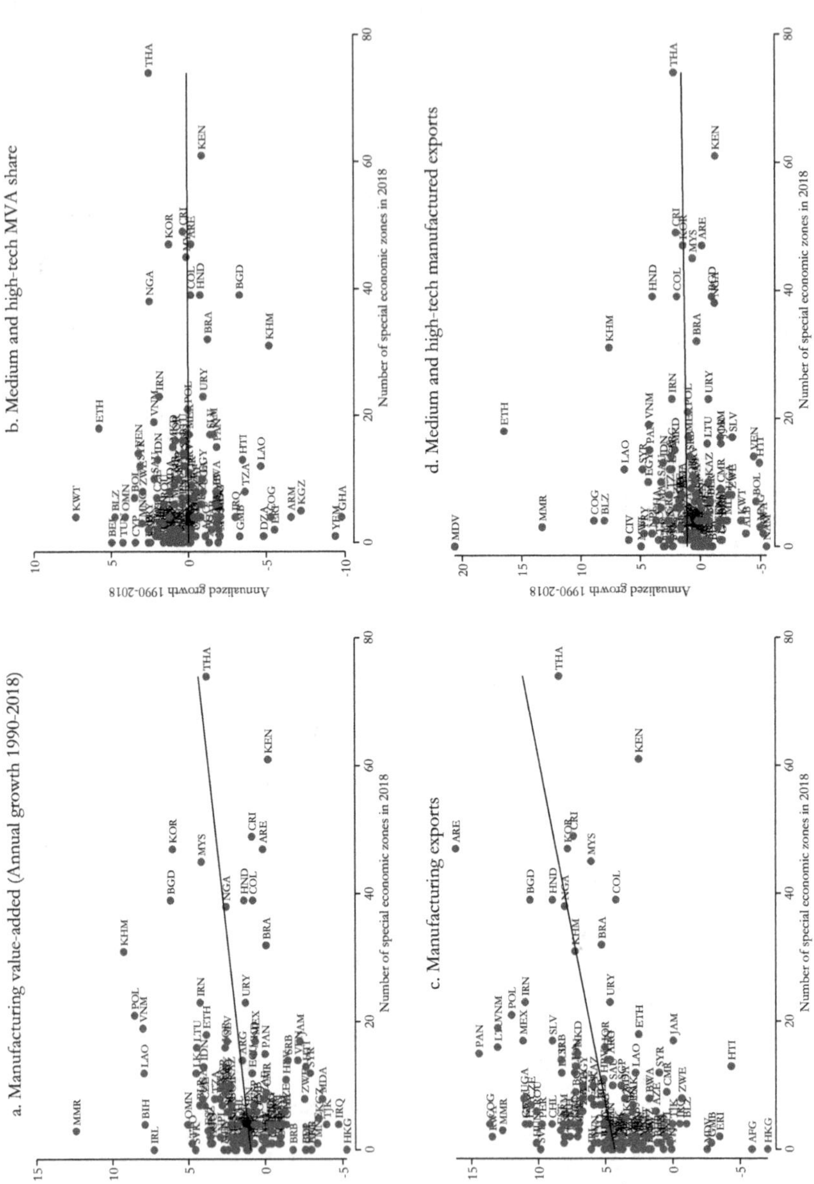

Figure 2.34 Special Economic Zones and manufacturing employment

interesting observations are immediately apparent. First, there is a positive correlation between the number of SEZs and MVA growth. This is rather expected because of the basic nature of SEZs. The results are highly driven by Asian countries like Thailand, Cambodia, Vietnam, and South Korea. Contrasting Thailand with Kenya, or Cambodia with Brazil, *ceteris paribus*, highlights the importance of other factors like the design and implementation of SEZs.

The results with respect to Asia and the contribution that manufacturing exports make to the process of industrialization suggest strongly that SEZs have been promoting industrialization through exports, and in particular, regardless of geographic location. Figure 2.33 panel (c) points to a stronger correlation between SEZs and manufacturing exports. The effect is more pronounced for certain countries such as Vietnam, Uganda, Mexico, Poland, and Panama, to name but a few. The case of Vietnam is worth noting, as it is based on a unique dual non-overlapping system governed by the central government and the provincial government. The central government establishes industrial zones providing generous corporate tax incentives while local governments promote industrial clusters with land rent incentives. The industrial clusters are designed to promote local business activities but they play a key role in supporting the export-oriented industrial zones through linkages and spillovers. This can be seen in Figure 2.33 as SEZs tends to be highly correlated with both MVA and manufacturing exports in Vietnam.

Like Vietnam, there is evidence that the development of SEZs in Ethiopia has generated industrial-based and manufacturing exports. Figure 2.34 shows that Ethiopia is one of the few African countries to have achieved high growth of MVA between 1990 and 2018, and the MVA is highly correlated with manufacturing exports. Similar to Vietnam, SEZs in Ethiopia have been piloted by the prime minister.

Even if Figure 2.34 shows little evidence of the relationship with medium and high-tech MVA to draw general conclusions, some notable patterns are revealing. SEZs can be a tool for resource-rich countries to industrialize. Figure 2.34 shows that Iran, Indonesia, Nigeria, Saudi Arabia, Venezuela, and Kuwait have both high growth in medium and high-tech MVA and the number of SEZs. Among them, Nigeria stands out. Second, some countries, like Ethiopia, have been leapfrogging from agriculture to medium and high-tech MVA using labor-intensive SEZs. Figure 2.33 panel (b) confirms the findings from the MVA that the industrialization of Ethiopia in both MVA and medium and high-tech MVA is happening through SEZ-led exports. Laos, Myanmar, and Cambodia also stand out.

Figure 2.34 presents the correlations between employment in manufacturing and the accumulated number of SEZs in a short-run spell (2000–2010) and long-run spell (1990–2010) using GGDC data. Figure 2.34 confirms that SEZs are correlated with manufacturing employment growth, and, in particular, that these correlations are even larger in the long run. In addition, all African economies plotted in Figure 2.34 lie above the linear regression fit line, suggesting larger SEZ-led employment for Africa. These calculations are only suggestive as we do not claim any causality with this simple analysis for Africa. But the implication is clear for policymakers who are striving to promote employment and welfare. Furthermore, this finding is consistent with existing evidence that finds strong and positive effects of SEZs on employment and industrialization.

2.5 Conclusion

Following the presentation of the leading issues in industrial promotion in today's globalized world in Chapter 1, this chapter introduced a variety of facts and trends pertaining to industrial structural changes. As our UNIDO team looks into the manufacturing industries in detail in Chapter 3, we tried to present a more holistic picture of structural change surrounding manufacturing.

In Section 2.2, we portrayed the state of global manufacturing with the use of substantial and diverse empirical evidence. There is a great degree of heterogeneity in manufacturing growth across time and across regions. In its diversity in the patterns of structural changes, we found ongoing concentration and convergence in manufacturing activities and the roles of manufacturing. The early industrializers are losing their share in global manufacturing with China and a small number of emerging economies taking over. Late industrializers are growing at a faster pace relative to that of early industrializers. However, most of them focus on labor-intensive manufacturing. Production of medium and high-tech manufacture products is concentrated in HICs. As we have shown here, the core of global manufacturing value-added has shifted away from traditional labor-intensive manufacturing into products that embody higher technology. Industrial promotion today, thus, calls for facilitations for industrial (manufacturing) upgrading, rather than a mere expansion of low-tech labor-intensive manufacturing activities.

In Section 2.3, we used historical data combined with recent panel datasets to examine how the trend of premature deindustrialization emerged in many parts of the developing regions. We took advantage of our data coverage in examining heterogeneity in the timing of deindustrialization among regions. Furthermore, we provided new evidence on the timing of (de)industrialization by examining historical data of early industrializers. The patterns that we found are rather robust to a variety of measures (i.e., value-added, employment, exports) and across the different datasets we used. The peaks of industrialization, measured in manufacturing value-added (MVA) shares in total value-added, are much lower for the income groups of developing countries as compared to the peaks experienced by the early industrializers (over 40 percent in today's HICs). And these peaks tend to come at earlier stages of development (at lower levels of per capita income).

We extended this method of analyzing structural changes to characterize the patterns of (de)industrialization in Asian countries that followed the so-called "flying geese" pattern where Asia's later industrializers follow the Big Three (Japan, Korea, and Taiwan) in their industrial structural transformation as the leading industries of the Big Three move out to East and South-East Asian economies in sequences as newer and higher technology manufacturing (new leading industries) develops in the economies of the Big Three. The structural changes in China and India were also analyzed in the same manner, as both of these economies have been following a similar pattern with an element of uniqueness identified for India. India, with its reputation as the "back office of the world" and with its traditionally high share of service value-added, may follow a new path to a high-yielding service (including medical services) and manufacturing-related service (including call centers for manufacturing/service enterprises). This is related to the servicification and the growing share of service trade in global transactions. Africa and other regions are similarly analyzed for their patterns of (de)industrialization.

In Section 2.4, we looked at the process of servicification, both within manufacturing and outside manufacturing, with a consideration of how GVCs and SEZs could provide spaces where developing countries can find manufacturing activities. Here we portrayed a seemingly strong correlation between trends in manufacturing productivity and service employment. This reconfirms the ever-declining share of labor in manufacturing value-added pointed out in Chapter 1.

Regarding the roles of GVCs that could provide spaces for manufacturing in developing countries can grow into, we analyzed the time frameworks of increases and decreases of value-added shares of manufacturing activities after GVC participation, categorized by technology intensity (low-tech to innovative manufacturing activities) of participating manufacturing activities. The results suggest that premature deindustrialization tends to emerge when countries are confined to low-tech manufacturing even when they can participate in GVCs.

For the use of SEZs in promoting manufacturing value-added, employment, and exports, our analyses indicate a great potential, particularly if the promotion of SEZs is coupled with facilitation of technology/product/activity upgrading on the part of the participating local firms.

We hope that readers keep these identified facts and trends in mind as the context for the following chapters of this book.

Notes

1 This is illustrated in Figures 1.4 and 1.5 of Chapter 1.
2 Available at https://unstats.un.org/unsd/snaama/Index.
3 Available at https://stat.unido.org/database/CIP%202019.
4 Available at https://ilostat.ilo.org/data/.
5 Andreoni, Chang, Konzelmann, and Shipman (2018) provide a useful discussion on why economists should re-focus on production.
6 Figure 2.17 in particular follows the UN Department of Economic and Social Affairs' classification of sub-regions, see (https://esa.un.org/MigFlows/Definition%20of%20regions.pdf).
7 We followed the World Bank's classification of income groups and geographical regions. For income groups, the 2020 fiscal year uses the 2018 Gross National Income per capita, calculated based on the Atlas method, to define countries as low-income economies (US$1,025 or less), lower middle-income economies (between US$1,026 and US$3,995), upper middle-income economies (between US$3,996 and US$12,375),

and high-income economies (US$12,376 or more). The regions are divided into East Asia and the Pacific, Europe and Central Asia, Latin America and the Caribbean, Middle East and North Africa, South Asia, and Sub-Saharan Africa.

8 Results on the heterogeneity within each group are available up on request.

References

Agosin, M. R. (2007). Export diversification and growth in emerging economies. Working Paper No. 233. University of Chile, Department of Economics.

Akkemik, K. A. (2009). *Industrial development in East Asia: A comparative look at Japan, Korea, Taiwan, and Singapore.* Singapore: World Scientific Publishing.

Andreoni, A., Chang, H.-J., Konzelmann, S., & Shipman, A. (2018). Introduction to the Special Issue: Towards a production-centred agenda. *Cambridge Journal of Economics, 42*(6), 1495–1504.

Bah, E.-h. M. (2011). Structural transformation paths across countries. *Emerging Markets Finance and Trade, 47*(suppl. 2), 5–19.

Baldwin, R. (2019). *The globotics upheaval: Globalisation, robotics, and the future of work.* London: Weidenfeld & Nicolson.

Baldwin, R., Ito, T., & Sato, H. (2014). *Portrait of a factory: Production network in Asia and its implication for growth—the "smile curve."* Joint Research Program Series No. 159. Chiba: Institute of Developing Economies, Japan External Trade Organization (IDE-JETRO).

Bleaney, M., & Greenaway, D. (2001). The impact of terms of trade and real exchange rate volatility on investment and growth in Sub-Saharan Africa. *Journal of Development Economics, 65*(2), 491–500.

Chang, H.-J. (2006). *The East Asian development experience: The miracle, the crisis and the future.* London: Zed Books.

Chenery, H. B. (1960). Patterns of industrial growth. *The American Economic Review, 50*(4), 624–654.

Clark, C. (1940). *The conditions of economic progress.* London: Macmillan.

Clark, C. (1957). *The conditions of economic progress* (3rd ed.). London: Macmillan.

Dasgupta, S., & Singh, A. (2006). Manufacturing, services and premature deindustrialization in developing countries: A Kaldorian analysis. United Nations University Research Paper, No. 2006/49. UNU-WIDER.

Diao, X., McMillan, M., & Wangwe, S. (2017). Agricultural labour productivity and industrialisation: Lessons for Africa. *Journal of African Economies, 27*(1), 28–65.

Duarte, M., & Restuccia, D. (2010). The role of the structural transformation in aggregate productivity. *The Quarterly Journal of Economics, 125*(1), 129–173.

Felipe, J., Mehta, A., & Rhee, C. (2019). Manufacturing matters… but it's the jobs that count. *Cambridge Journal of Economics, 43*(1), 139–168.

Ghosh, A. R., & Ostry, J. (1994). Export instability and the external balance in developing countries. *IMF Staff Papers, 41*, 214–235.

Hausmann, R., Hwang, J., & Rodrik, D. (2006). What you export matters. NBER Working Paper.

Hausmann, R., & Klinger, B. (2006). Structural transformation and patterns of comparative advantage in the product space. Working Paper No. 128. Center for International Development, Harvard University.

Hausmann, R., & Rodrik, D. (2003). Economic development as self-discovery. *Journal of Development Economics, 72*(2), 603–633.

Herrendorf, B., Rogerson, R., & Valentinyi, Á. (2014). Growth and structural transformation. In P. Aghion & S. N. Durlauf (Eds.), *Handbook of economic growth* (2, pp. 855–941). Oxford: Elsevier,

Herzer, D., & Nowak-Lehmann, F. D. (2006). What does export diversification do for growth? An econometric analysis. *Applied Economics*, 38, 1825–1838.

ILO. (2019). *World employment and social outlook: Trends 2019.* Geneva: ILO.

Kuznets, S. (1966). *Modern economic growth.* New Haven, CT: Yale University Press.

Kuznets, S. (1973). Modern economic growth: Findings and reflections. *The American Economic Review*, *63*(3), 247–258.

Lederman, D., & Maloney, W. F. (2007), *Natural resources: Neither curse nor destiny.* Washington, DC: The World Bank.

Lu, Y., Wang, J., & Zhu, L. (2019). Place-based policies, creation, and agglomeration economies: Evidence from China's economic zone program. *American Economic Journal: Economic Policy*, *11*(3), 325–360.

McMillan, M., & Rodrik, D. (2011). Globalization, structural change and productivity growth. NBER Working Paper No. 17143.

McMillan, M., Rodrik, D., & Verduzco-Gallo, Í. (2014). Globalization, structural change, and productivity growth, with an update on Africa. *World Development*, *63*, 11–32.

Mitchell, B. (2007). *International historical statistics 1750–2005: Europe.* Basingstoke: Palgrave Macmillan.

Newfarmer, R. S., Page, J., & Tarp, F. (2018). Industries without smokestacks: Industrialization in Africa reconsidered. In *UNU-WIDER studies in development economics.* Oxford: Oxford University Press.

Ngai, R., & Pissarides, C. (2007). Structural change in a multi-sector model of growth. *American Economic Review*, *97.*

Otchia, C. S. (2015). Mining-based growth and productive transformation in the Democratic Republic of Congo: What can an African Lion learn from an Asian Tiger? *Resources Policy*, *45*, 227–238.

Rodrik, D. (2013). Unconditional convergence in manufacturing. *Quarterly Journal of Economics*, *128*, 165–204.

Rodrik, D. (2016). Premature deindustrialization. *.Journal of Economic Growth*, *21*(1), 1–33.

Rogerson, R. (2008). Structural transformation and the deterioration of European labor market outcomes. *Journal of Political Economy*, *116*(2), 235–259.

Stiglitz, J. E. (2018). From manufacturing-led export growth to a twenty-first-century inclusive growth strategy: Explaining the demise of a successful growth model and what to do about it. WIDER Working Paper 2018/176.

Syrquin, M. (1988). Patterns of structural change. In H. Chenery & T. N. Srinavasan (Eds.), *Handbook of economic development.* Amsterdam: Elsevier Science Publishers.

Temin, P. (1967). A time-series test of patterns of industrial growth. *Economic Development and Cultural Change*, *15*(2), 174–182.

Timmer, M. P., de Vries, G. J., & de Vries, K. (2015). Patterns of structural change in developing countries. In J. Weiss & M. Tribe (Eds.), *Routledge handbook of industry and development* (pp. 65–83). London: Routledge.

UNCTAD. (2013). *Least developed countries report 2013: Growth with employment for inclusive and sustainable development.* New York: United Nations Publications.

UNCTAD. (2016). *Trade and development report.* Geneva: UNCTAD.

UNCTAD. (2019). *World investment report 2019: Special economic zones.* New York: United Nations Publications.

UNIDO. (2017). *Industrial development report 2018: Demand for manufacturing: driving inclusive and sustainable industrial development.* Vienna: UNIDO.

UNIDO. (2018). *Global value chains and industrial development.* Vienna: UNIDO.

UNIDO. (2019). *Industrial development report 2020: Industrializing in the digital age.* Vienna: UNIDO.

World Bank. (2020). *The world development report 2020: Trade for development in the age of global value chains.* Washington, DC: World Bank.

3 The importance of manufacturing development and structural change for pro-poor growth

Nobuya Haraguchi and Juergen Amann

3.1 Introduction

The analysis presented in this chapter highlights the dynamic and heterogeneous nature of structural change within manufacturing and delineates a path of inclusive manufacturing development for pro-poor growth. In doing so it illustrates the continuous importance of manufacturing development and the key role of industrial policy design.

In the first part of the chapter we revisit the current debate on whether the importance of manufacturing for economic development has changed or not, and discuss both past contributions as well as more recent advances in the related literature to emphasize the continued importance of manufacturing and the key role of industrial policies.

The second part of this chapter elaborates on the importance of industrial structural change by highlighting the relevance of manufacturing development and emphasize pro-poor growth pathways of industrial development. Our analysis is informed by a careful dis-aggregation of structural change patterns, and provides a detailed account of generally industry-level heterogeneities, their inter-temporal dynamics, as well as employment linkages to other industries and sectors of the economy before touching on the question of manufacturing sustainability. The fourth and final section offers a conclusion.

3.2 The importance of manufacturing development

3.2.1 Manufacturing as the engine of growth: An empirical regularity

It is universally acknowledged in both the theoretical and empirical economic literature that manufacturing is widely regarded as a shaping and growth-promoting factor at early stages of a country's economic development and that it undergoes notable structural change as economies grow richer, see, among others, Kuznets (1953), Lewis (1954), Kaldor (1967), and Matsuyama (1992) as well as Bluestone and Harrison (1982), and Brady and Denniston (2006). This observation of

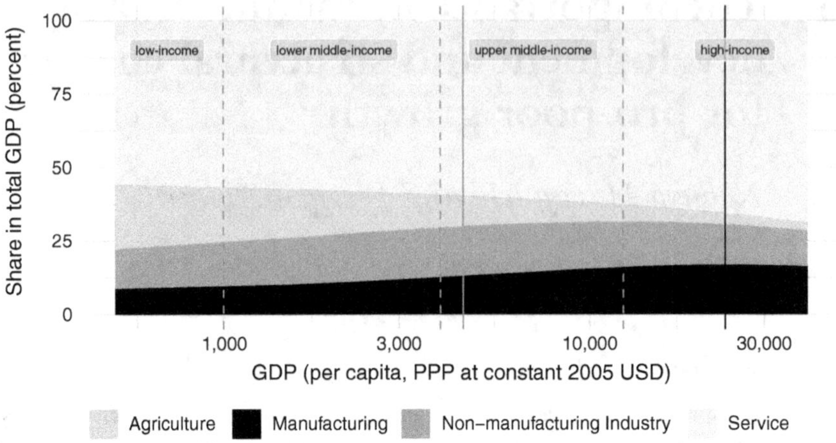

Figure 3.1 GDP composition by income and sector

Note: Constructed using pooled data for 153 countries, 1950–2017. Vertical lines in grey (black) identify the highest contributing share of non-manufacturing industries (manufacturing) and the equivalent GDP per capita level of USD 4,500 (USD 23,000), respectively. X-axis in logs. Income group cut-offs identified by the dashed vertical lines at USD 995, USD 3,896 and USD 12,375 as defined by World Bank Country and Lending Groups (World Bank 2019a).

Source: Calculations based on World Development Indicators (World Bank 2019b) and Penn World Tables 9.1 (Feenstra, Inklaar, and Timmer, 2015) following IDR (2013).

the "classical" (de-)industrialization pattern is illustrated in Figure 3.1. There, a first noteworthy increase in both the share of manufacturing as well as non-manufacturing-related industries at lower-income levels, followed by a steady decline of both sector shares at higher-income levels is shown. The turning point at which the sectoral contribution of both industry-related aggregates reduces can be identified by the two vertical lines at a GDP per capita of around US$4,500 for the non-manufacturing industries and at roughly US$23,000 for manufacturing respectively. This means that, by and large, developing countries have typically experienced a steady increase in the share of manufacturing at around 20 percent, after which deindustrialization patterns can historically be observed for higher-income economies.

Similar to the works on the sectoral composition of the economy, the history of research on sectoral structural change in manufacturing is long and influential.[1] One of the first attempts to identify regularities of growth differentials across industries within the manufacturing sector was undertaken by Chenery (1960). In this seminal contribution and through further works with Taylor and Syrquin,[2] the authors attempted to identify the underlying forces in the transformation processes of developing countries and to quantify how structural change manifests itself through compositional changes of the manufacturing sector. For example, Chenery and Syrquin (1975) investigate development patterns in a cross-country setting and identify country size in particular as having a significant impact on the development pattern of countries: Large countries are found to transform their economic structure at earlier points of their development process than small countries, which implies that small countries "catch up" to bigger economies at higher-income levels.[3] Unfortunately, attempts to understand the development patterns of manufacturing at the level of its industries have received somewhat less attention after the works of Chenery and Syrquin. In the years after their study, most structural change analyses were based on broad economic sectors with little systematic investigation of the development patterns of manufacturing industries. Most recently, Haraguchi and Amann (2020b) reconnect to this earlier strand of the literature through a synthesis of revisiting some key findings of the founding works of this field and by expanding on the empirical analysis with more comprehensive data.

3.2.2 *Manufacturing as the engine of growth: Running out of steam?*

As already noted in Syrquin and Chenery (1989a), advances in the field of industrial development have shown that the dynamics of the industry sector in general, and of manufacturing in particular, are not only subject to changes in the income level but seem to have an intertemporal dimension as well. In more recent history, these trends have been found to be more pronounced. For example, Haraguchi (2015) observes that the contribution of manufacturing to GDP along the income trajectory was more dynamic between the 1960s and the 1980s than during more recent periods. Similar observations were made by Rodrik (2016) and Palma (2014). Both authors note that the hump-shaped relationship between manufacturing-related employment and the value-added shares has moved to a lower tipping point at lower-income levels for more recent periods. This corresponds to a projected decline of employment and value-added shares at earlier stages of economic development than experienced by earlier industrializers. Palma (2014) also notes that the hump-shaped relationship for employment seems to collapse in more recent periods.

In this vein, visual evidence presented in Figure 3.2 lends support to this notion: While the pre-2000s follow a similar industrialization with deindustrialization tendencies at higher-income levels, the post-2000s see a notable reduction in the structural change dynamics (through a flattening of the regression line in Figure 3.2) for both middle-income country aggregates as well as the group of high-income countries. What is more, the positive relationship between manufacturing and income seems to break down completely for low-income economies in the post-2000s. Against this backdrop, doubts have been cast on the continuing importance of manufacturing as a shaping factor of economic prosperity for future development: It is the identification of these time-related patterns of premature deindustrialization that has led researchers to argue that manufacturing-led growth has become a more difficult path for currently developing countries to follow as they "are running out of industrialization opportunities sooner and at much lower levels of income compared to the experiences of earlier industrializers" (Rodrik, 2016, p. 1).

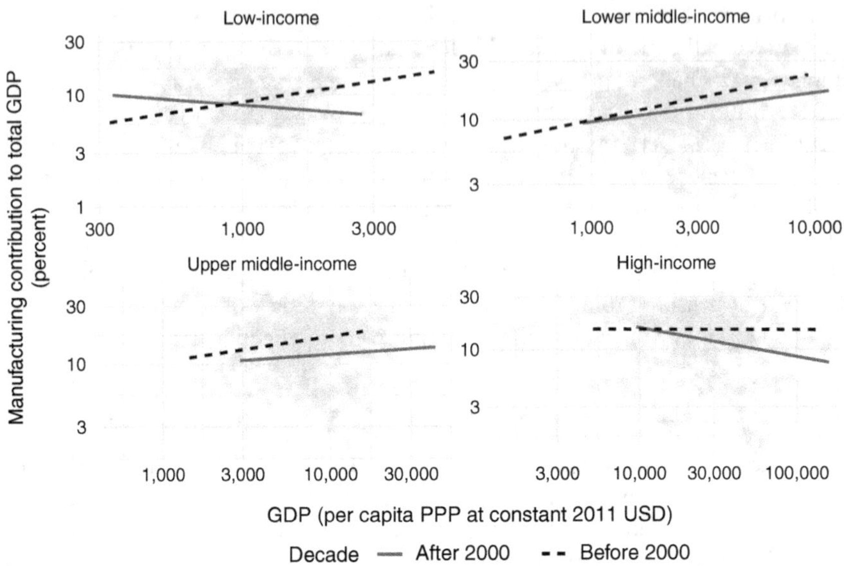

Figure 3.2 Manufacturing value-added contribution to GDP, 1950–2017
Note: Constructed using pooled data for 153 countries. Country classification following World Bank (2019a). X- and y-axis in log scale.

Source: Calculations based on World Development Indicators (World Bank 2019b) and Penn World Tables 9.1 (Feenstra, Inklaar, and Timmer 2015).

3.2.3 Manufacturing as the engine of growth: A more complex future ahead

While aggregated inter-temporal dynamics may paint a rather bleak picture for manufacturing's capacities for promoting growth for the road ahead, recent research also shows that these stylized findings are far from universal and to a notable degree the result of heterogeneities and fragmentation both across countries and industries alike.

3.2.3.1 Fragmentation across countries

Findings in Rodrik (2016) seem to suggest that there is indeed (regional) heterogeneity among developing countries.[4] Rodrik explains the variation in manufacturing-related growth outcomes as being the consequence of comparative advantages. He finds that countries with a strong comparative advantage, i.e., extensive manufacturer exporters, have experienced much less pronounced reduction in manufacturing value-added shares and employment figures than their less competitive, i.e., non-exporting counterparts. In the same vein, Dasgupta and Singh (2006) describe the three pillars of premature industrialization as: (1) lower-income level turning points as well as (2) "jobless growth" in manufacturing combined with comparatively faster-growing services for low(er)-income countries. Noting significant regional discrepancies in their analysis, the authors argue that this development may be due to "nonconforming structures unable to satisfy changes in consumer demand" (Dasgupta & Singh, 2006, p. 1) and that departures from historic trajectories could suggest that the service industry in some countries might be gaining more importance in earlier stages of economic development.

Discussing evidence of hampered industrial development in the more recent past, Ghani and O'Connell (2014) reason that the low pick-up rate of industrial development in less developed countries may be due to productivity gains by means of better technology and demand side effects. The same argument is also made in Rodrik (2016), who identifies both changes in preferences as well as technology, as the driving forces behind deindustrialization. Ghani and O'Connell (2014) also stress that the "third industrial revolution" has been much more about a well-thought integration of industry, services, and trade and that the globalization of services may provide a different experience for currently developing countries compared to other past experiences. This is an important observation. It goes without saying that the last decades have brought about many changes in the political and economic environment, which have been fuelled by technological progress and globalization. Through the emergence of the fourth industrial revolution with smart technology and fully integrated and automated production processes, i.e., the *smart factory* in the domain of *industry 4.0*, these tendencies will only accelerate and bring new challenges for developing economies (UNIDO, 2020). Yet, given the observation that "the dividing line between manufacturing and services is becoming increasingly blurred" (Ghani & O'Connell, 2014, p. 4), doubts may be raised about the definite statement that premature deindustrialization, as observed in the aggregate, leads to both a decline in manufacturing's importance as an engine of growth or the argued redundancy of political ramifications of policy-led industrial development.

Emphasizing the challenges of the changing global environment, researchers have indicated the more complex, multi-dimensional nature of industrial development of the more recent past. For example, Szirmai and Verspagen (2015) stress the importance of industrial development and manufacturing with regards to productivity, capital accumulation, and economies of scale as well as linkages, spillovers, and demand-side effects, and state that manufacturing is an important contributor to inclusive labor-force mobilization. The latter argument is very important as strong linkages between manufacturing and services are found for advanced economies and, in some cases, dependence structures have been identified where manufacturing provides a necessary foundation for service activities (Guerrieri & Meliciani, 2005). What is more, the composition of linkages is also strongly connected to the degree of development of an economy. Consequently, not accounting for intersectoral linkages in employment, output will not fully represent the employment impact of the manufacturing industry in its full context (UNIDO, 2013).

Lin and Monga (2010) discuss industrial development in the context of government-led industrial policy interventions and argue that exploiting comparative advantages should be an important objective in well-targeted industrial development. The authors show that attempts at copying too advanced economies (measured by the percentage difference of GDP) may do the economy of the industrializing country more harm than good. Consequently, they stress the importance of a policy-led framework for growth identification and facilitation of potential industries based on comparative advantage. In other words, the authors make a strong case that successful industrialization is the result of careful and far-sighted policy interventions to "identify industries that are appropriate for a given country's endowment structure and level of development" (Lin & Monga, 2010, p. 4).

3.2.3.2 Heterogeneity within manufacturing

Finally, in order to fully understand the nature of patterns of industrialization as well as (premature) de-industrialization alike, it is imperative to unravel the dynamics in manufacturing itself. This is because an aggregated analysis alone is not sufficient to assess whether deindustrialization tendencies can be attributable to country-specific policy-related factors, or if they are the consequence of a long-term shift in the global economic structure. Haraguchi, Cheng, and Smeets (2017) argue that opportunities for manufacturing development have not changed as the global contributions of employment as well as value-added have not decreased for developing countries over the last four decades. They explain that industrial development remains strong for developing countries with certain characteristics. Rather than losing its development potential, the authors identify a shift of manufacturing activities to a relatively small number of populous countries, which leads to a concentration of manufacturing-related industries for a distinct group of developing countries. In other words, when not aggregating manufacturing and employment figures on a country level, but globally, they find no evidence of a reduction of either employment or value-added to the global aggregate over the last four decades. Since those populous successful countries, China, in particular, are now mostly at the upper middle-income levels and likely to follow a normal pattern of deindustrialization in the future, hitherto less successful developing countries could experience faster manufacturing development if they implemented the right policies.

Haraguchi and Amann (2020b) discuss sectoral differences in patterns of innovation. The authors connect Pavitt-type classifications with structural change, thus linking technology classes with manufacturing industries. Their analysis reveals a substantial degree of heterogeneity in manufacturing as far as development patterns are concerned. The authors make the important argument that the aggregate figures on deindustrialization in advanced economies can be misleading. Some high-technology sectors continue to grow at high levels of income, while others do not. They also document that the effect of premature deindustrialization and productivity growth varies significantly across manufacturing industries and that notable heterogeneities can also be associated with exogenous factors such as resource endowment and country size.

To summarize, the importance of manufacturing as an engine of growth is of a quite dynamic nature. Not only is it subject to changes with regards to the income level of an economy, it is also found to vary considerably over time. There is little doubt that the growth dynamics of manufacturing as a contributory factor to economic development have become more stagnant on an aggregated level. The reasons for this can be found in the "classical argument"—at higher-income levels, industrially developed countries become more and more service-oriented—with its unarguable effect on aggregated statistics. Additionally, further empirical evidence seems suggestive of the fact that deindustrialization also appears to occur at lower-income levels and is accompanied by decreasing employment opportunities; however, it is subject to striking regional differences. All of this seems to suggest that more recent industrial development is more complex than how it was experienced by the early industrializing nations in the past, and the reasons for this may be the same ones that are argued to be among the driving patterns behind industrial change itself: technological progress, global trade, and specialization as well as demand-side effects. What remains unchanged is that finding the right policy mix and targeting the right industry present industrializing countries with a complex challenge which some will cope with more successfully than others.

3.2.3.3 The role of manufacturing for pro-poor growth: A stylized view

While the previous discussion has added a bit of nuance to the debate on manufacturing development by stressing the complex nature of manufacturing development, little has been said about the connection between a strong manufacturing base and pro-poor growth in particular. In order to get a more contextualized understanding of the two, Figure 3.3 compares the evolution of per capita GDP levels of two selected groups of countries against the quintile distribution of global per capita GDP from 1965 to 2017. Consequently, the lowest dashed line indicates the GDP per capita level of the poorest country at any given time, the next dashed line indicates the same GDP per capita measure where 20 percent fall below (and 80 percent remain above). Given this representation, we can easily assess the growth performances of the group of selected countries vis-à-vis the overall performance of all world economies as a whole, thereby indicating which countries have "climbed the income ladder" relative to others.[5]

As the upper panel in Figure 3.3 reveals, the two country aggregates start off at a very similar and relatively low-income level, putting both countries into the lowest per capita income quintile in 1966. However, while the set of (climbing) countries move to around the 40th percentile in per capita GDP by the mid-2010s, the other (non-climbing) group remains within the lowest quintile. See Figure 3.4 for the individual country series. The lower panel of Figure 3.3 contrasts this with the average sectoral shares for both sets of aggregates over the same time period. Most interestingly, both aggregates are found to start with a rather similar share of services and agriculture with a much lower contribution for manufacturing and (non-manufacturing) industry. However, while both see a robust share of roughly 20 percent for the climbing aggregate, these sectors remain largely undeveloped for the group of non-climbing economies. What is more, the non-climbing aggregate shows a moderate shift from agriculture into services for the post-2000s with both the (non-manufacturing) industry and manufacturing sector remaining stagnant over the same time window. This is

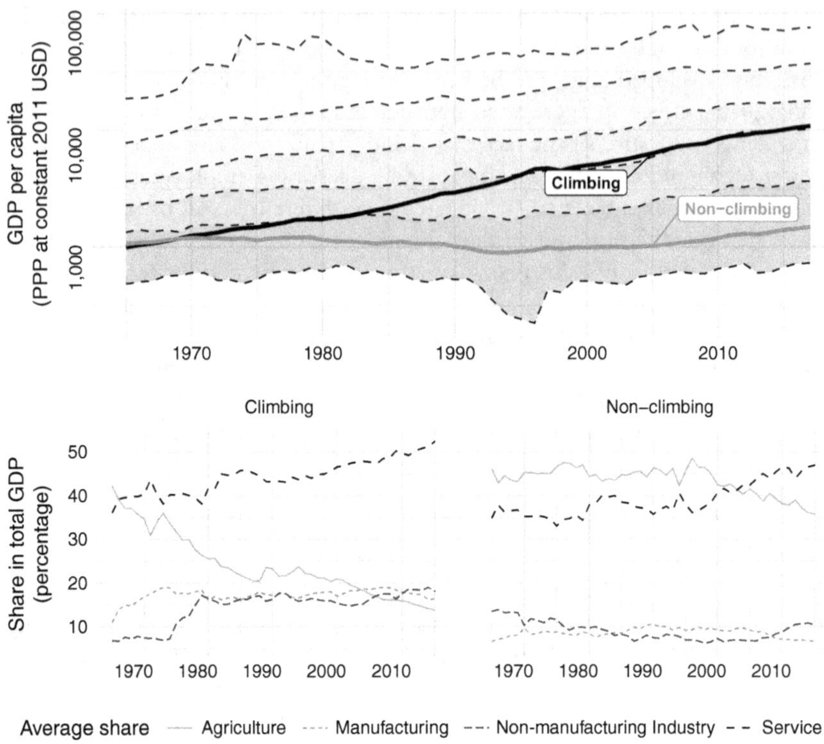

Figure 3.3 Pro-poor growth over time

Upper panel: Quintile Distribution of per Capita GDP, 1965–2017. Lower panel: Sectoral GDP Composition by Sectors over Time for Selected Countries, 1965–2015.

Note: Upper panel based on pooled data for 182 countries for quintile distribution. Selected countries by group are highlighted by solid lines. Y-axis in log scale. Lower panel shows sectoral composition of selected countries by group. Selected countries included: Botswana, Bosnia and Herzegovina, China, Egypt, Thailand Republic of Korea, Indonesia, Bhutan, Cabo Verde, Lao People's DR, Viet Nam, Myanmar, India, Cambodia Lesotho (*climbing*) and Nepal, Uganda, Rwanda, Burkina Faso, Mali, Togo, Ethiopia, Guinea-Bissau, Madagascar, Malawi, Niger, Liberia, Burundi, Central African Republic (*non-climbing*). See Figure 3.4 for individual country series.

Source: Own calculations based on World Development Indicators (World Bank 2019b) and Penn World Tables 9.1 (Feenstra, Inklaar, and Timmer 2015).

in line with the point made by Dasgupta and Singh (2006) regarding the service industry potentially gaining more importance in earlier stages of economic development than in the past. Yet with the shift from agriculture into services, it does not appear as if these dynamics translate well into increases in income as the overwhelming majority of surveyed non-climbing economies seem to have lost in relative income compared to the global trend, as can be seen in Figure 3.4. The bigger relative reduction in agriculture reflects the argument made by Szirmai and Verspagen (2015) that manufacturing is an important contributor to inclusive

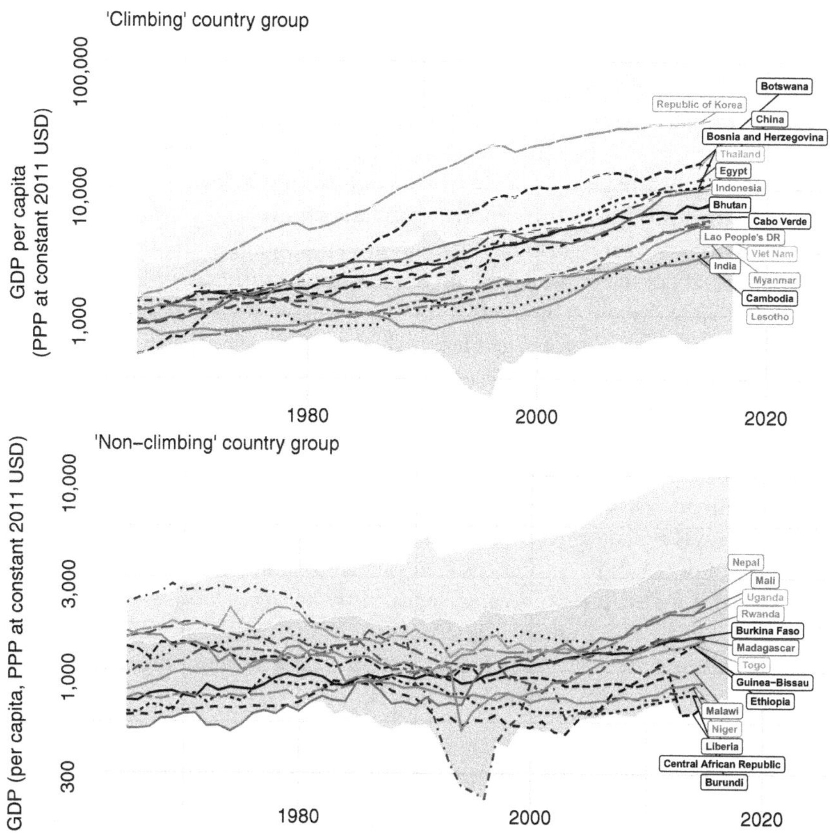

Figure 3.4 Quintile distribution of per capita GDP, 1965–2017; individual country series by group

Note: Quintile distribution based on pooled data for 182 countries for quintile distribution. Y-axis in log scale.

Source: Own calculations based on World Development Indicators (World Bank 2019b) and Penn World Tables 9.1 (Feenstra, Inklaar, and Timmer 2015).

labor-force mobilization with strong backward linkages to the primary sector for developing countries which we illustrate in Section 3.4. Before this, however, Section 3.3 will expand on designated structural change patterns for pro-poor growth in manufacturing.

3.3 Designated patterns of structural change for pro-poor growth

Ideally, rapid economic growth will lead to a broad and stable generation of employment as well as value-added in all industries, thereby creating quantitatively high and qualitatively diverse jobs across all industries. This goes hand-in-hand with an increase in the demand for jobs that require different skill sets and will both reduce unemployment rates as well as enable people to transition from subsistence into the labor force. As the previous discussion has shown, structural change dynamics depend on multiple different and often counteracting sources, making it a highly complex topic. What is more, while robust growth patterns have been found not to be the general rule of growth patterns (Pritchett, 2000), it is worthwhile investigating ways in which manufacturing development could be made more inclusive by putting special emphasis on exploring pro-poor growth patterns. Since structural change dynamics are strikingly different for low- and middle-income countries versus high(er-)income countries, we illustrate the structural change dynamics by concentrating on the low end of the income range. For a more general discussion, see Haraguchi and Amann (2020b).

To this end, in this section we identify key manufacturing industries which are particularly associated with pro-poor growth. The analysis benefits from an up-to-date data set on global manufacturing at the industry level which is used to provide a detailed account of structural change dynamics in manufacturing. The novelty of our analysis comes from the uniquely compiled manufacturing industry data set which is based on INDSTAT (2017) and improves upon other data sets by its level of detail and comprehensiveness (Haraguchi & Amann, 2020a). The nine industries we analyze in greater depth in this chapter have been chosen to be reflective of the representative performance of the numerous components of the manufacturing sector.[6] A detailed discussion on the methodology used in this part of the chapter is provided in Appendix B.

3.3.1 A pro-poor path of manufacturing development: An overview

Figure 3.5 visualizes the relationship between the value-added and employment share contribution of selected manufacturing industries in total manufacturing at different income levels and illustrates the compositional changes of the manufacturing sector as countries grow richer. The projections start at a per capita income level of US$500 and, in increments of US$1,000, move up to US$15,000. The final projection point of US$15,000 is identified by the connecting label. Using Figure 3.5, one can also infer the speed of structural change: For each sector aggregate, the connecting lines indicate the projected trajectory of employment or value-added as the income level of the economy rises by US$1,000. Consequently, the greater the distance between two connecting points, the bigger the structural change of the sector with respect to either value-added (by a strict horizontal movement), employment (by a strict vertical movement) or both (a combination of both).

For low-income countries, low-technology industries are of particularly high importance relative to medium and high-technology industries in terms of their value-added and employment generation, as they offer a noteworthy accelerator in both domains. Arguably, this is because of low unit labor costs and comparative advantages. While *food and beverages* are found to be remarkably robust with regards to changes in income per capita, both *wearing apparel* and *textiles* are highly affected by structural change along both dimensions. However, at least for durable consumer products, this advantage is short-lived. While, at low-income levels, *wearing apparel* is found to increase its relative employment share in manufacturing, this sector experiences a decline in both value-added and employment generation at moderate incomes. The industry-level pattern of deindustrialization is even more pronounced for *textiles*. While this is the second most important sector for low-income countries right after *food and beverages*, a steady decrease in its relative importance can be observed for increasing income levels. This transformation is also quite fast, as can be seen in Figure 3.5. The rationale behind this is simple from an economic point of view: If comparative advantages are the driving mechanism for these sorts of goods, durability implies that countries compete more internationally and small differences in a country's cost structure can have a considerable impact on its sectoral performance. Non-durable and domestic-oriented industries like food and beverages, on the other hand, are less substitutable and hence more demand-inelastic. Particularly for *food and beverages*, consumption may be innately informed by consumer taste which can be more heterogeneous and country-specific and, consequently, might

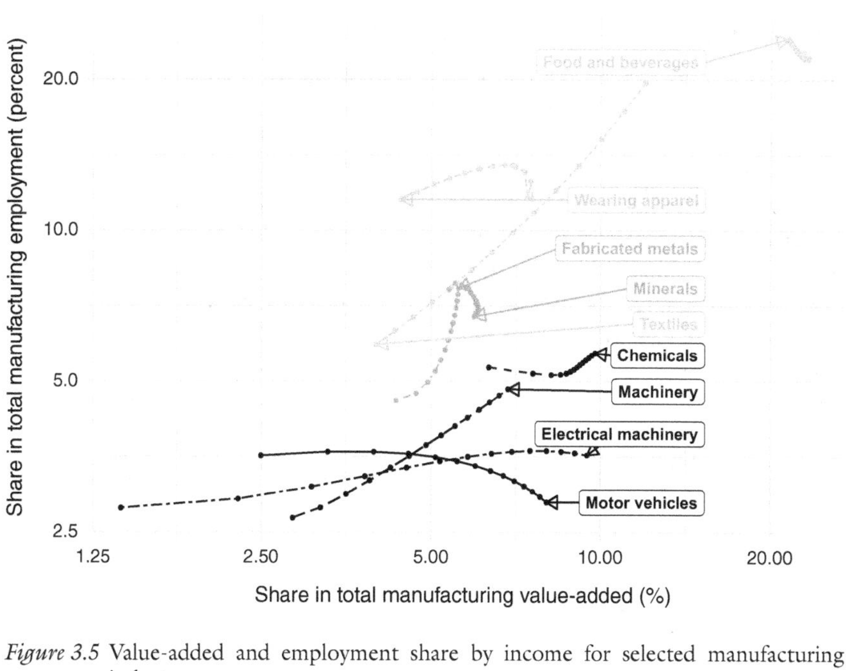

Figure 3.5 Value-added and employment share by income for selected manufacturing industry

Note: Based on pooled cross-country data for up to 153 countries between 1963 and 2015. Projections from per capita GDP USD 500 up to USD 15,000 in increments of USD 1,000. Final projection point at USD 15,000 is highlighted by the connecting label.

Source: Calculations based on INDSTAT (2017) and Penn World Tables 9.1 (Feenstra, Inklaar, and Timmer 2015) following Haraguchi and Amann (2020a).

be less affected by changes in income structure. In general terms, however, while being of the utmost importance at low-income levels, the importance of low-technology industries producing durable products decreases dramatically in terms of its contribution to value-added and employment of the manufacturing sector. In Figure 3.5, this is illustrated by a downward-sloping trajectory from the upper-right to the lower-left corner.

At the same time, while being the most underdeveloped industries at low-income levels, high-technology industries see a continuous growth in value-added contribution as well as in employment (for *chemicals*, *machinery*, and *electrical machinery*). At the upper middle-income levels, these industries have surpassed their low-technology counterparts in terms of value-added contribution while they remain below in terms of employment, thereby displaying their immense scalability potential. As far as medium-technology industries are concerned, these are typically identified as the least dynamic technology aggregate. However, it has to be noted that particularly these industries are subject to significant country-specific variation due to the difference in resource endowment (Chenery & Syrquin, 1975) which naturally is not fully exploited by an aggregate analysis similar to the one presented here.

3.3.2 Development patterns in manufacturing

Based on the discussion so far, two observations seem worthy of being pointed out. On the one hand, evidence based on a disaggregated analysis of the nine individual manufacturing industries shows a notable difference in development patterns across industries: Some aggregates seem to be subject to deindustrialization tendencies at much lower income levels than others. On the other hand, evidence presented so far does not make any inference regarding the contribution of any manufacturing industry in absolute terms, as a rising share of one industry could simply be the result of a lower negative growth rate of this particular industry relative to the manufacturing sector as a whole. To address this issue, the analysis in this section differs from the one in Section 3.3.1 as it looks at the actual contribution of each industry to value-added per capita, as well as the employment-to-population ratio. This approach is preferred for an in-depth analysis as it is not influenced by any volatility of other industries and hence is better suited to shed light on actual industry characteristics.

3.3.2.1 The baseline case

Figure 3.6 and Figure 3.7 highlight the trajectory of selected manufacturing industries as countries' per capita income levels increase. At very early stages of development, the low technology industries are of central importance in order to promote both employment and value-added growth. Particularly from the lowest levels of income, *food and beverages* as well as *textiles* and *wearing apparel* are found to have by far the highest contribution to value-added and employment generation. Among other industries that develop substantial employment

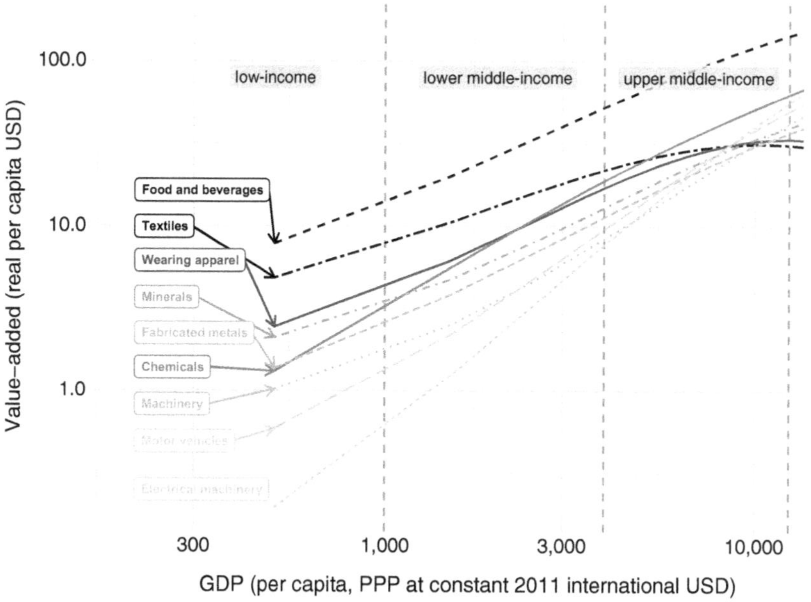

Figure 3.6 Value-added by income for selected manufacturing industry
Note: Based on pooled cross-country data for up to 153 countries between 1963 and 2015. Income group cut-offs identified by the dashed vertical lines at USD 995, USD 3,896 and USD 12,375 as defined by World Bank Country and Lending Groups (World Bank 2019a).

Source: Calculations based on INDSTAT (2017) and Penn World Tables 9.1 (Feenstra, Inklaar, and Timmer 2015) following Haraguchi and Amann (2020a).

dynamics at the lowest income margins are chemicals—which is identified as the most dynamic industry at low income levels in value-added generation—as well as *(non-metallic) minerals*. This is because they produce important input factors such as fertilizers, dyes, or soap as well as building materials such as glass, cement, and bricks—all of which, together with *food and beverages* as well as *textiles* and *wearing apparel*, are of the utmost importance at low development levels as they all accommodate the basic needs of the country's citizens. These goods can be seen as necessary requisites for stable, long-run development and poverty reduction: Only if these input factors are both abundant and cheap, can more advanced industries develop free of constraints or limitations. What is more, particularly *food and beverages* as well as chemicals have been identified as retaining their growth potential even at high-income levels and over time, thereby indicating their critical role as cornerstones of well-balanced and successful industrial development. The low technology group is also the most labor-intensive in its production processes. This fact is illustrated in Figure 3.7 which shows the striking impact of the low technology group in the creation

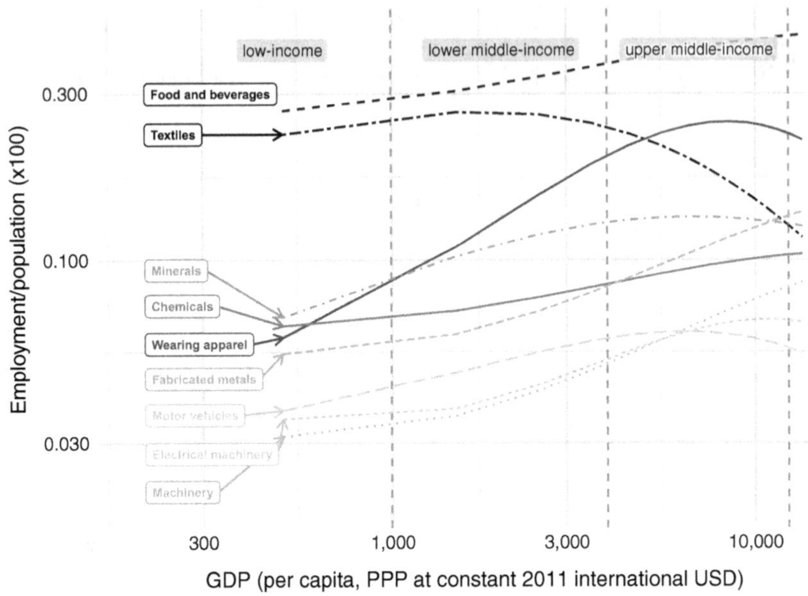

Figure 3.7 Employment-to-population by income for selected manufacturing industry
Note: Based on pooled cross-country data for up to 153 countries between 1963 and 2015. Income group cut-offs identified by the dashed vertical lines at USD 995, USD 3,896 and USD 12,375 as defined by World Bank Country and Lending Groups (World Bank 2019a).

Source: Calculations based on INDSTAT (2017) and Penn World Tables 9.1 (Feenstra, Inklaar, and Timmer 2015) following Haraguchi and Amann (2020a).

of formal manufacturing employment for often agrarian economies. Among these labor-intensive, low-technology industries, it is particularly the *food and beverages* industries that can sustain long-run growth in employment whereas both *textiles* and *wearing apparel* experience significant employment reductions at lower-middle as well as upper middle-income levels, respectively. In other words, labor-intensive industries seem to be crucial for the development of employment opportunities at low incomes and early stages of industrial development. As the population moves from agriculture into formal, paid employment, labor-intensive industries offer a pivotal option to facilitate big movements in the labor force and accommodate the productive absorption of job-seekers. Particularly at the early development stage of an economy, there is also ample opportunity for capital accumulation which, however, as economies transition to and beyond the group of upper middle-income countries, becomes restricted to *food and beverages*. In Haraguchi (2012), the previously mentioned industries were classified as "original," as they both exist in almost all countries and meet citizens' basic needs even before industrialization. Consequently, the production processes of these industries are very likely to be notably different in low-income versus high-income countries. It is thus necessary for developing countries to carefully modernize these "original" industries while continuously developing and promoting new industries in order to sustain the growth trajectories in value-added as well as employment generation. In this context, Figure 3.6 and Figure 3.7 also illustrate an interesting point regarding the dynamics within the low technology aggregate. Already at low-income levels, *textiles* experience a reduction in employability which, together with the observation that their value-added growth potential remains strong in the lower-income ranges, become more capital-intensive at very early stages of economic development. What is more, *wearing apparel* is the first industry that develops its employment base relative to other industries: This industry displays a moderate employment potential at lowest incomes but experiences significant employment growth with increases in a country's income level. It can be argued that modernization and success in this industry may represent a first experience of how industrialization can make a difference to a country's development.

High technology industries, on the other hand, consistently develop at medium to late stages of development while they are typically the most fast-growing industries in terms of their value-added generation across all manufacturing industries, even at low-income levels. Medium technology industries share common elements of both the low-technology as well as the high-technology group. They are particularly robust for countries within the range of upper middle-income countries while we also acknowledge their pivotal position as an integral building block of an evolving economy: Producing bricks, cement, and glass, the *minerals* industries are largely driven by domestic demand. Similar to low-technology industries, they are further typical early developers in both employment and value-added. Different from the set of low-technology industries, however, and apart from *food and beverages*, *minerals* retain their value-added growth at much higher income levels while also experiencing only a slight reduction in employment. In general, medium-technology industries offer investment potential for middle-income as well as upper middle-income countries and may potentially remain significant at high-income levels. Even though they do not develop employment opportunities as early along the income trajectory as low-technology industries, they do offer more robust and stable development opportunities at higher-income levels. On top of that, they are typically high-productivity industries and provide ample investment opportunities (UNIDO, 2013).

3.3.2.2 Development classification

Based on the previous discussion, this section summarizes the industry dynamics based on the relative importance in generating both employment and value-added at early stages of development.[7] Rearranged in this way we can see that the major contributors to both value-added (Figure 3.8) and employment (Figure 3.9) are the two low-technology industries *textiles* as well as *wearing apparel*. They remain the strongest players in the generation of value-added up to a per capita income of US$4,000 and about US$10,000 for employment. At their peaks, *textiles* and

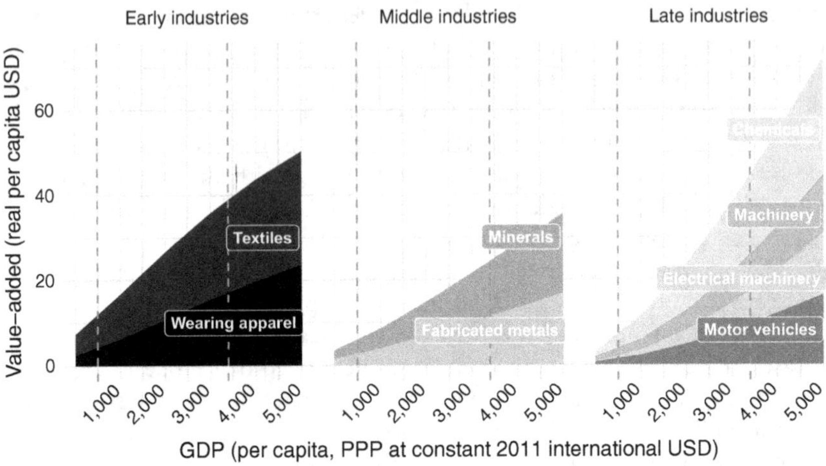

Figure 3.8 Accumulated value-added by income for selected manufacturing industry
Note: Based on pooled cross-country data for up to 153 countries between 1963 and 2015. Income group cut-offs identified by the dashed vertical lines at USD 995 and USD 3,896 as defined by World Bank Country and Lending Groups (World Bank 2019a).

Source: Calculations based on INDSTAT (2017) and Penn World Tables 9.1 (Feenstra, Inklaar, and Timmer 2015) following Haraguchi and Amann (2020a).

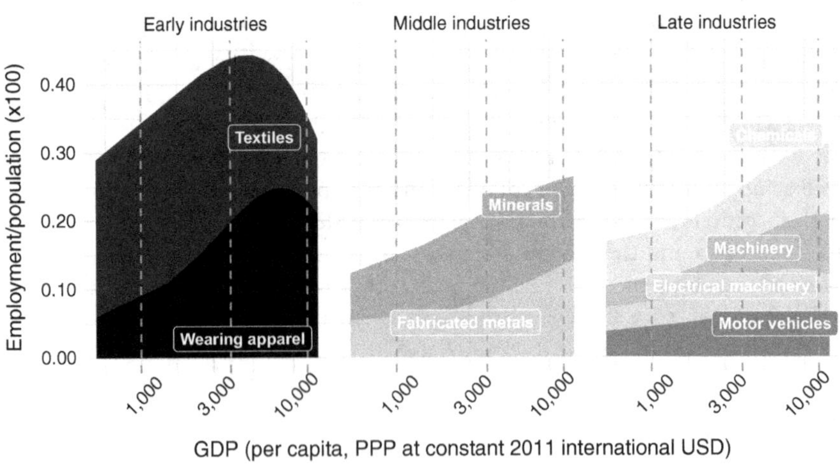

Figure 3.9 Accumulated employment by income for selected manufacturing industry
Note: Based on pooled cross-country data for up to 153 countries between 1963 and 2015. Income group cut-offs identified by the dashed vertical lines at USD 995, USD 3,896 and USD 12,375 as defined by World Bank Country and Lending Groups (World Bank 2019a).

Source: Calculations based on INDSTAT (2017) and Penn World Tables 9.1 (Feenstra, Inklaar, and Timmer 2015) following Haraguchi and Amann (2020a).

wearing apparel alone employ more people than all other manufacturing industries (except for *food and beverages*) combined. In light of this, it is argued that for low-income countries, successful development of the *wearing apparel* industry could provide an incredibly important boost to both value-added generation and labor force mobilization with the positive side effects of promoting personal income growth, firm growth, and increases in firm profits, as well as government revenue for investment in better education and infrastructure, which as a whole could make an important contribution to poverty reduction. In other words, successfully developing the *wearing apparel* industry will also have a significantly positive effect in the context of institutional development as well as policy and managerial learning as these early experiences of industrial development will thereafter provide a fruitful foundation for continuous and future industrial development efforts.

Since there are no middle or late industries that are comparable to the early, low-technology group in terms of their labor force absorption capacity, Figure 3.9 emphasizes that a country needs to develop middle and late industries more broadly in order to compensate for the decline of the major employment sources provided by the low-technology group at earlier income stages. Particularly the extent and direction of substitutability of capital and labor in the context of comparative advantages should serve as a warning sign for developing countries not to wait too long before diversifying their industrial portfolio when approaching the US$10,000 mark. Consequently, middle and late industries need to play an increasingly important role in the context of industrial development to ensure that the country remains on a prosperous growth trajectory by creating new employment opportunities and increasing growth potential and also to counterbalance reductions in employment experienced by the low technology/early industries. In other words, with increasing income levels, manufacturing development paths become more complex and diverse: In order to retain the initial boost in employment and value-added generation, developing economies have to develop several middle and late industries simultaneously.

3.3.2.3 Substitutability of input factors

It is one of the characteristics of the manufacturing sector that production processes become more capital-intensive as income rises and production becomes more elaborate. This substitutability between the input factors of labor and capital is one of the driving factors that explains the extensive scalability of manufacturing production. Given the very strong heterogeneity of manufacturing industries, it should not be surprising that notable differences can also be observed in that respect.

Figure 3.10 illustrates the income elasticities of value-added and the employment-to-population ratio of *electrical machinery* and *wearing apparel.* These elasticities reflect the change in each of these variables expressed in changes of per capita GDP. One of the unique characteristics of the *wearing apparel* industry is its limited potential to substitute production factors. This means, even

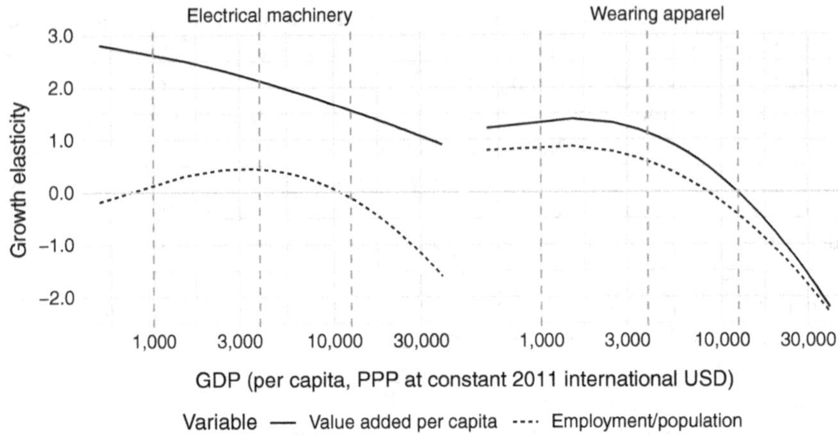

Figure 3.10 Growth elasticities of value-added and employment/population by income for selected manufacturing industry

Note: Based on pooled cross-country data for up to 153 countries between 1963 and 2015. Income group cut-offs identified by the dashed vertical lines at USD 995, USD 3,896 and USD 12,375 as defined by World Bank Country and Lending Groups (World Bank 2019a).

Source: Calculations based on INDSTAT (2017) and Penn World Tables 9.1 (Feenstra, Inklaar, and Timmer 2015) following Haraguchi and Amann (2020a).

at high(er) income levels, *wearing apparel* will always remain relatively labor-intensive compared to other industries with fewer opportunities to substitute labor for capital. Put differently, as this industry loses its comparative advantages due to increasing labor costs, value-added-led growth patterns brought about by a more rigorous utilization of capital—which can be witnessed in more capital-intensive industries such as late and high technology industries—are not feasible for this industry. Therefore, once a country reaches an upper middle-income level, it tends to lose competitiveness in the industry and reduces both value-added and employment relatively quickly. With low-wage labor being the key input factor, *wearing apparel* has little scope for productivity increase. The almost parallel decline of value-added and employment-to-population changes indicates only limited room for this industry to substitute capital for labor. This stands in sharp contrast to the *electrical machinery* industry where the estimated patterns show significant potential for such a substitution. Even though labor input declines, the increase in labor productivity helps to sustain the value-added growth of the industry.

3.3.3 Premature deindustrialization across manufacturing industries

The previous sections established the heterogeneous development of manufacturing industries and highlighted the importance of a set of key industries in the early stages of economic development. We now shift to the question of whether these general dynamics have remained unchanged over time or if the most recent decades have seen a transformation in the development patterns of manufacturing industries. We do this by revisiting the topic of premature deindustrialization and identify emerging characteristics within manufacturing by estimating Equation (3.1) in Appendix A separately for the 1970s, the 1980s and the 1990s as well as the period from 2000 onwards; see Appendix B. We will also refer to these four distinct periods as decades for the remainder of this section. As before, we limit the discussion to the same sub-sample of representative industries and the low-income to upper middle-income range.

In Figure 3.11 we can identify some time-dependent dynamics for value-added in the low-technology group and in particular for *textiles*. As a matter of fact, this industry seems to be most affected by a decrease in average value-added contribution in the last 20-odd years. However, Figure 3.11 also indicates that this trend seems far from general. Particularly for high technology industries, development potentials appear very robust in the post-2000s compared to earlier

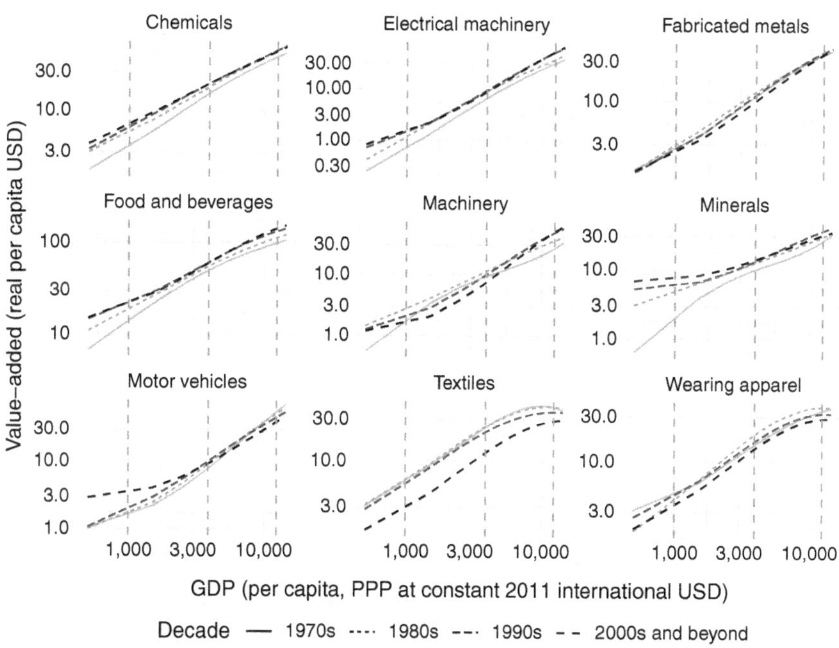

Figure 3.11 Changes in value-added over time by income for selected manufacturing industry

Note: Based on pooled cross-country data for up to 153 countries between 1970 and 2015. Income group cut-offs identified by the dashed vertical lines at USD 995, USD 3,896 and USD 12,375 as defined by World Bank Country and Lending Groups (World Bank 2019a).

Source: Calculations based on INDSTAT (2017) and Penn World Tables 9.1 (Feenstra, Inklaar, and Timmer 2015) following Haraguchi and Amann (2020a).

decades. When looking at employment patterns in Figure 3.12, we see a less uniform picture. Among low-technology industries, employment in *textiles* as well as *wearing apparel* has been markedly lower in more recent decades. For both industries, we can see a reduction in the hump-shaped relationship as well as a shift of the tipping point of maximum employment generation to earlier industries. Particularly for the *textile* industry, the employment trajectory has become much more stagnant compared to earlier periods. Another observation is that across most industries, the employment potential appears less dynamic at lower-income levels. In other words, at lower-income levels, employment generation across most industries in the post-2000s is not at the level of earlier periods. The effect is particularly strong for low-skilled manual labor industries. While these findings are in line with the results of Haraguchi, Cheng, and Smeets (2017) and could hint at the centralization of certain industries in a handful of large, populous countries, an alternative explanation could be that improvements in production technologies simply have resulted in a much more capital-intensive initial industrialization kick-off than observed in earlier decades.

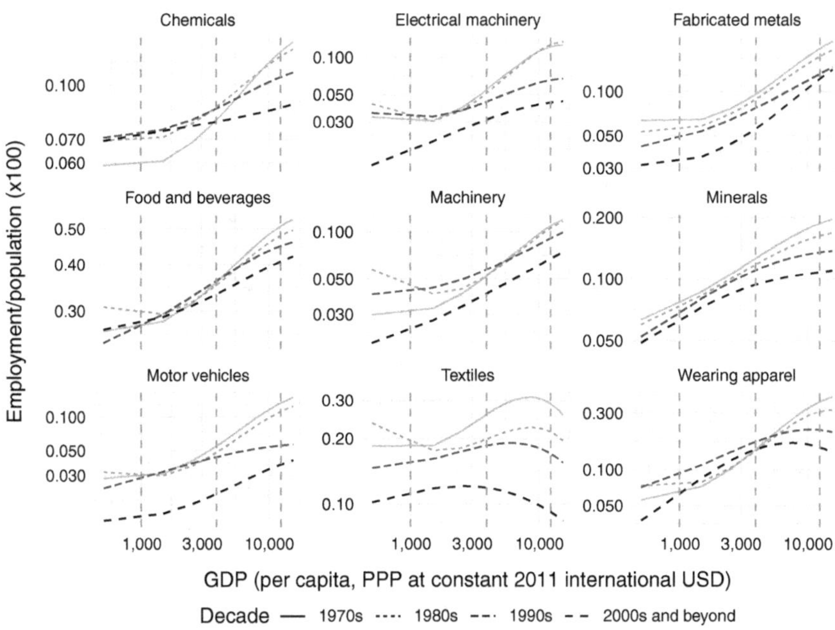

Figure 3.12 Changes in employment over time by income for selected manufacturing industry

Note: Based on pooled cross-country data for up to 153 countries between 1970 and 2015. Income group cut-offs identified by the dashed vertical lines at USD 995, USD 3,896 and USD 12,375 as defined by World Bank Country and Lending Groups (World Bank 2019a).

Source: Calculations based on INDSTAT (2017) and Penn World Tables 9.1 (Feenstra, Inklaar, and Timmer 2015) following Haraguchi and Amann (2020a).

Based on these observations, a natural question is whether the overall contribution of manufacturing in the value-added and employment generation has increased as an aggregate from the 1970s to the 2000s and onwards. We present the aggregated figures in Figure 3.13 and Figure 3.14, respectively. Overall, a notable change in the composition of the industries can be seen by a bump-up and increase in particularly high-technology/late industries in the later decades. What is more, *textiles* seems to have lost in relative importance based on its contribution to value-added and also very notably in employment generation; see Figure 3.14. As a whole, manufacturing structural change over time has strongly been subject to increase in capital intensity. What is interesting is the observation that this trend seems to mainly have happened between the 1970s to 1990s, as the last 25 years have seen very little change in the levels of the employment-to-population ratio across industries with overall peak employment being roughly the same from the early 1990s onwards. What is more, we see the industry-level

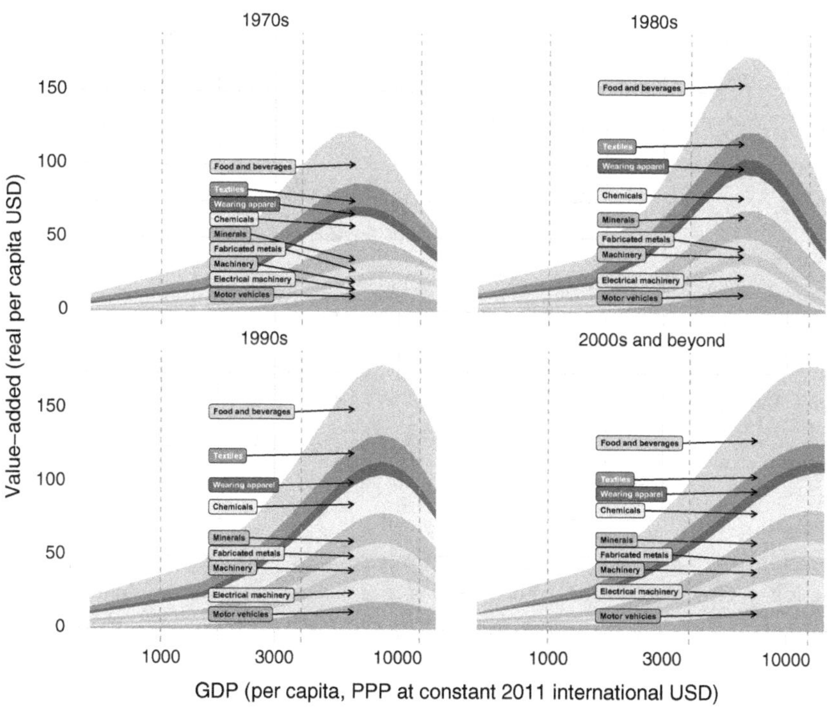

Figure 3.13 Changes in accumulated value-added by income for selected manufacturing industry

Note: Based on pooled cross-country data for up to 153 countries between 1970 and 2015. Income group cut-offs identified by the dashed vertical lines at USD 995, USD 3,896 and USD 12,375 as defined by World Bank Country and Lending Groups (World Bank 2019a).

Source: Calculations based on INDSTAT (2017) and Penn World Tables 9.1 (Feenstra, Inklaar, and Timmer 2015) following Haraguchi and Amann (2020a).

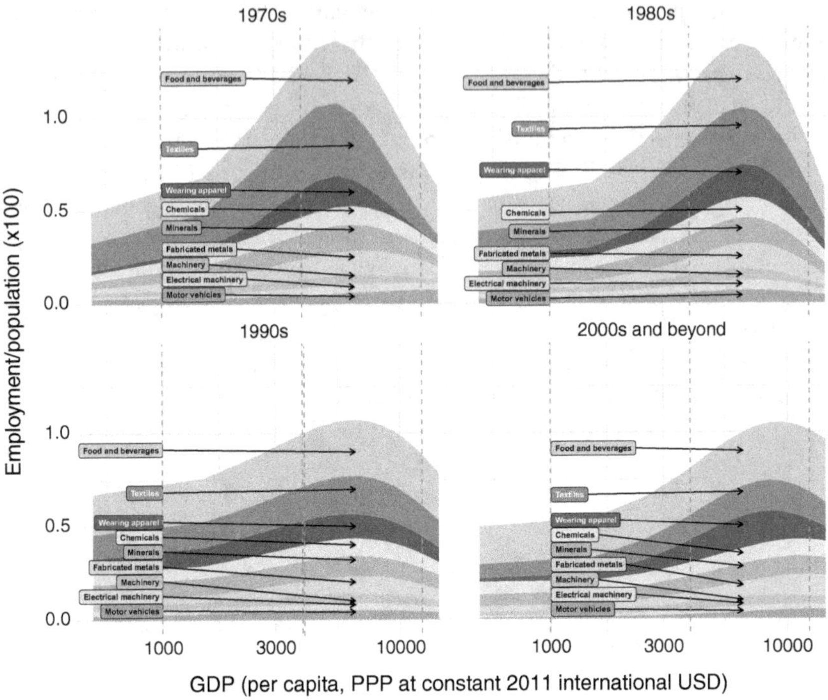

Figure 3.14 Changes in accumulated employment by income for selected manufacturing industry

Note: Based on pooled cross-country data for up to 153 countries between 1970 and 2015. Income group cut-offs identified by the dashed vertical lines at USD 995, USD 3,896 and USD 12,375 as defined by World Bank Country and Lending Groups (World Bank 2019a).

Source: Calculations based on INDSTAT (2017) and Penn World Tables 9.1 (Feenstra, Inklaar, and Timmer 2015) following Haraguchi and Amann (2020a).

contribution has changed significantly over time as well and most notably for the low-technology group. Whereas *food and beverages* have remained a strong and stable developer over time, particularly the *textile* industry appears to be hit the hardest by inter-temporal structural change. Even though it still remains a significant industry, particularly in the early stages of development, its relative share in total employment generation has experienced a steady decline. Another very interesting observation can be made with regards to *wearing apparel* which, because of its unique characteristics, has shown little signs of capital intensification. This emphasizes the important position this industry has in the context of sector-level, manufacturing development of low-income countries.

The above analysis suggests a significant shift and reduction in the importance of the *textile* industry mainly brought about by technological advances and higher capital intensity over the last decades. Among the other low-technology industries, *food and beverages* as well as *wearing apparel* increase their fundamental importance for successful industrial development in relative terms. Whereas the former serves as one of the biggest promoters of employment and value-added for all income levels, the latter retains its predominant position as the first industry that should specifically be targeted by policymakers to improve industrial growth dynamics from early levels of economic development onwards, due to its impact on both growth and poverty reduction. In addition to these two main pillars, chemicals play an additional integral role in the development of an economy and have to be highlighted for their unprecedented growth potential for value-added across all income ranges of development.

3.3.4 Employment mobilization beyond manufacturing

It goes without saying that the development impact of manufacturing is not restricted to value-added and employment in manufacturing alone but is well integrated in the grand scheme of the economy (Szirmai & Verspagen, 2015). With this in mind, it may be reasonable that a particular manufacturing industry may see a reduction in industry-level (direct) employment while total industry-induced employment is actually on the rise, due to particularly strong employment links to other parts of the economy. In this section we examine the extent and nature of such manufacturing industry-related employment links on the sector level in Figure 3.15. For more information on data and methodology, see Appendix C.

Manufacturing industries are very different in terms of their employment links (Figure 3.15). Particularly, low technology industries like food, beverages, and tobacco or *textiles*, *wearing apparel*, and *leather* have very strong links to the primary sector. Not surprisingly, food, beverages, and tobacco are found to have the strongest employment-inducing effect toward the primary sector underscoring their importance in contributing to inclusive labor-force mobilization. The medium-technology industries (such as *minerals* or *fabricated metals*) only show very moderate links to other sectors of the economy. This is an important result as these industries, despite their robust growth and important position in the creation of raw material necessary to further economic development (such as glass or concrete), are less connected to other parts of the economy through the employment process but remain so through their production output. While low technology industries have particularly pronounced links to the primary sector, high technology industries are much more connected to services. These results appear particularly noteworthy in the context of the more difficult separation of manufacturing- and service-related production (Ghani & O'Connell, 2014).[8]

Another important insight is that the linkage structure of manufacturing industries dramatically changes depending on the development stage of the economy. This is stressed in Figure 3.17 which contrasts the share of employment backward-linkages across sectors for advanced and emerging economies. A particular feature of manufacturing industries is that their employment linkages typically move from more primary-related to more service-related business at higher-income levels: Irrespective of the industry, manufacturing induces notable employment in the primary sector for emerging industries while notable business

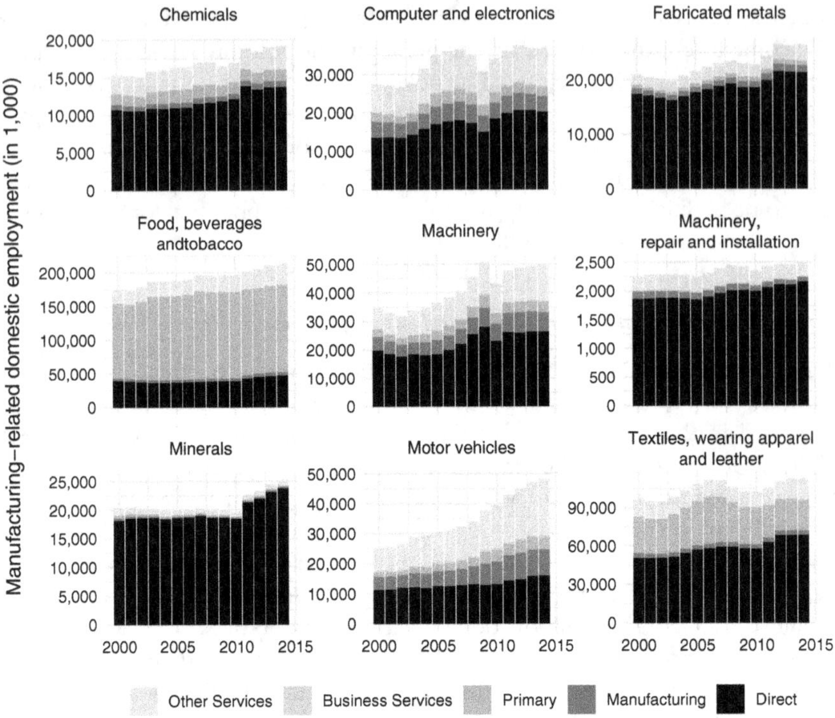

Figure 3.15 Domestic employment linkages over time by selected manufacturing industry
Note: World Input-Output Table based on 28 EU countries and 15 other major countries in the world for the period from 2000 to 2014. Domestic employment linkages within the same industry is referred to as direct employment. The remaining four categories in this figure sum up domestic linkages of the corresponding sectors, respectively. See Appendix C for more information on data and methodology.

Source: Calculations based on World Input-Output Database (WIOD) Release 2016 (Timmer et al., 2015).

upgrading and a stronger connection with the service sectors can be observed across the vast majority of industries at higher incomes.

This insight is particularly useful and important when analyzing the growth trajectory for industrializing countries, as this aggregated analysis shows that thoughtful industrialization plays an integral role in the development of manufacturing-related employment opportunities for developing and developed countries alike. In other words, industrial development not only helps an economy to fully integrate its employment potential at lower incomes but it also generates more employment opportunities within as well as outside of manufacturing. This positive acceleration effect of manufacturing, where medium- and high-technology industries, particularly those sustaining high value-added growth at high(er) incomes, do not only make up for the overall decline of manufacturing jobs as illustrated above, but also compensate by generating modern jobs in services and

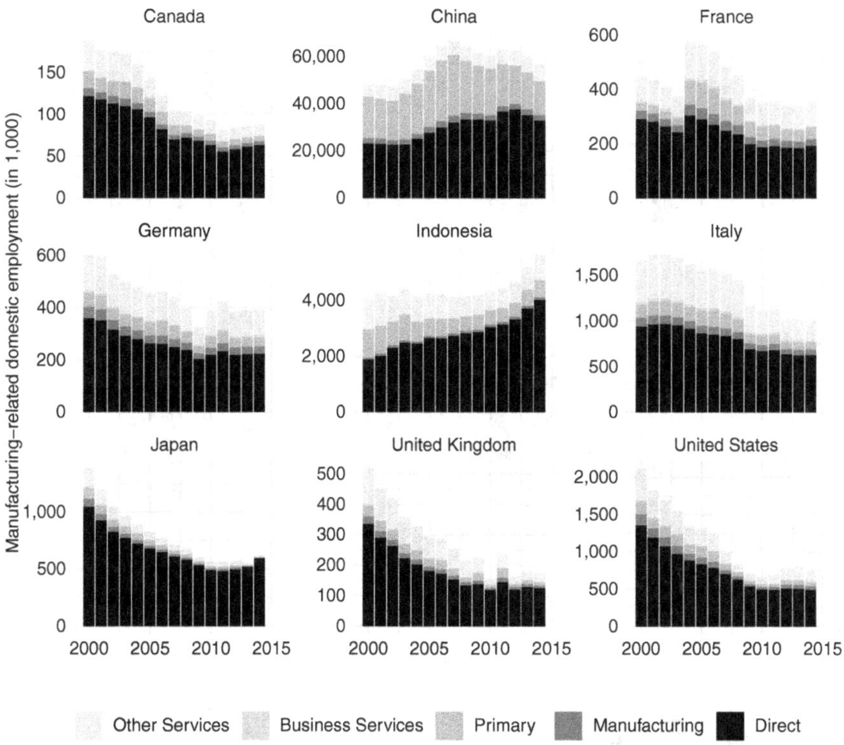

Figure 3.16 Domestic employment linkages: textiles, wearing apparel and leather industry over time for selected countries

Note: World Input-Output Table based on 28 EU countries and 15 other major countries in the world for the period from 2000 to 2014. Domestic employment linkages within the same industry is refereed to as direct employment. The remaining four categories in this figure sum up domestic linkages of the corresponding sectors, respectively. See Appendix C for more information on data and methodology.

Source: Calculations based on World Input-Output Database (WIOD) Release 2016 (Timmer et al., 2015).

other manufacturing-related industries. Therefore, careful and targeted manufacturing development is not only necessary in order to unleash manufacturing's full employment potential across all its industries, but it also plays a crucial role in using and promoting innovative service activities which, in turn, are by themselves of increasing importance as an economy moves along its income trajectory.

3.3.5 Sustainability and manufacturing development: An inevitable trade-off?

Discussing industrial growth policies in the twenty-first century is incomplete without discussing its implications with regards to sustainability in general and climate change in particular. For developing economies, there are meaningful

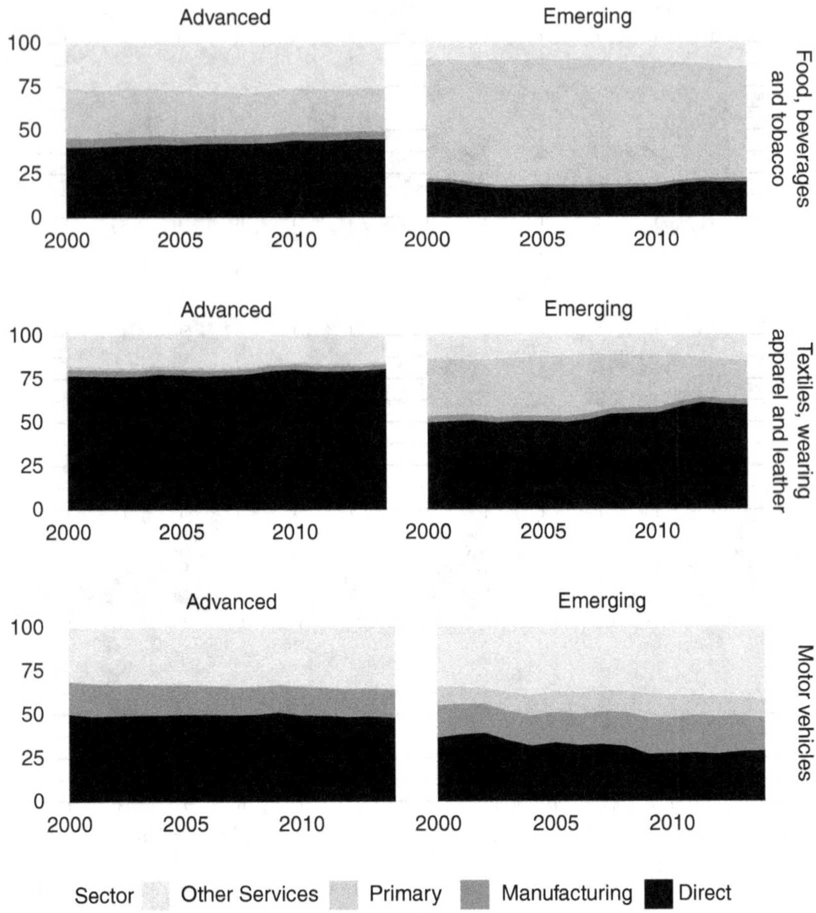

Figure 3.17 Domestic employment linkages: shares over time by economic development and selected manufacturing industry

Note: World Input-Output Table based on 28 EU countries and 15 other major countries in the world for the period from 2000 to 2014. Domestic employment linkages within the same industry is refereed to as direct employment. The remaining four categories in this figure sum up domestic linkages of the corresponding sectors, respectively. See Appendix C for more information on data and methodology. Country classification following World Bank (2019a).

Source: Calculations based on World Input-Output Database (WIOD) Release 2016 (Timmer et al., 2015).

trade-offs to consider. On the one hand, environmental stress tends to have disproportionately negative impacts on less developed economies as a strong association between (climate change) adaptation and economic development has been reported in the literature; see among others, Klien, Schipper, and Dessai (2005); Schipper and Pelling (2006). Jerneck and Olsson (2008); Pouliotte, Smit, and Westerhoff (2009). On the other hand, climate change mitigation in emerging and developing countries might pose a challenge from a development perspective if it requires more costly, low-carbon energy sources (Jakob & Steckel, 2014).

We expand the conceptual approach proposed in UNIDO (2016) as we express the environmental sustainability of manufacturing industries by measuring their industry-level value-added per unit of carbon dioxide emission. Even though this measure does not fully capture all the necessary characteristics of environmentally friendly development, it is argued that it may serve as an important proxy as it has taken the centerstage in much of the policy debate in the most recent past, such as at the 2019 Sustainable Development Impact Summit in New York or the Climate Summit in Madrid in the same year. General trends on an aggregated level of manufacturing as in Figure 3.18 seem to suggest a non-linear relationship between environmental sustainability and economic growth, following the concept of the environmental Kuznets (1955) curve where environmental indicators are typically found to deteriorate first with economic development before improving again at higher incomes (Grossman & Krueger 1995).

Rather than on the aggregate, the interest of this section is to illustrate the industry-level dynamics of CO_2 emissions. This is done in Figure 3.19. In Figure 3.19, an industry is considered environmentally sustainable the lower the emission per unit of real value-added is and steep, downward-sloping lines indicate improvements in emission patterns as economies move up the income trajectory.

It should not go unnoticed that many manufacturing industries generally improve their emission performance as countries move up to higher incomes.

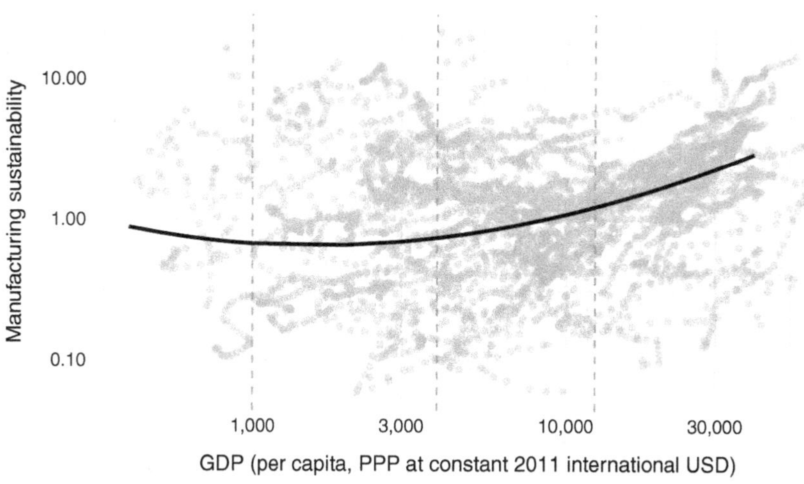

Figure 3.18 Manufacturing environmental sustainability

Note: Based on 5-year averages for 98 countries between 1970 and 2014. Manufacturing sustainability is calculated as the log of constant manufacturing value-added per tonne of emitted carbon dioxide.

Source: Calculations based on INDSTAT (2017) and Penn World Tables 9.1 (Feenstra, Inklaar, and Timmer 2015) and CAIT Climate Data (WRI 2015) following IDR (2016).

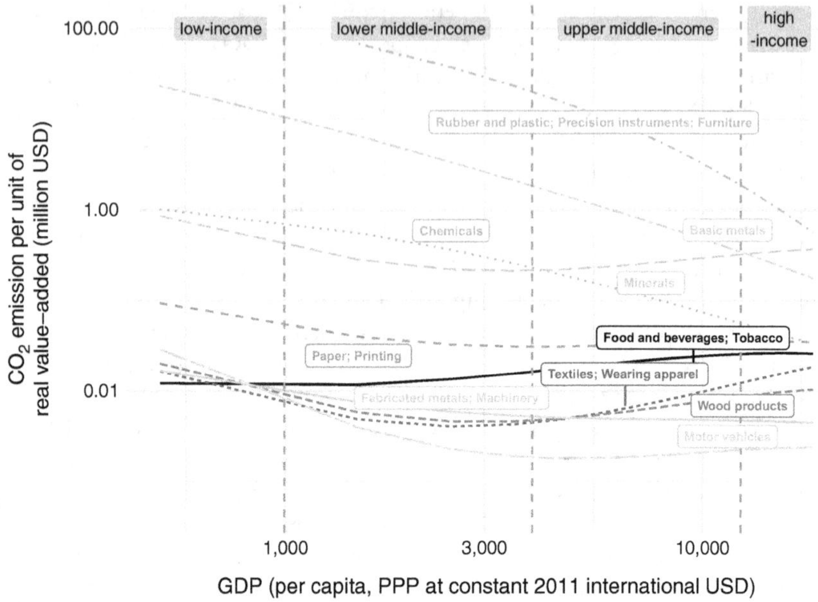

Figure 3.19 Manufacturing industry-level CO_2 emission per unit of real value-added
Note: Real value-added series calculated following Haraguchi and Amann (2020a).

Source: Calculations based on INDSTAT (2017) and Penn World Tables 9.1 (Feenstra, Inklaar, and Timmer 2015) and IEA (2015).

The decrease in emissions is particularly strong for the heavier emitters at early development stages such as the aggregate rubber and plastic; precision instruments; furniture as well as basic metals and *chemicals*. Second, there is also a notable dispersion in the degree of CO_2 emissions across industries. In particular, the earlier industries stand out. While they have by and large moderate emission rates at lower-income levels, their carbon intensity increases at upper middle-income levels again, which can be attributed both to the higher energy demand and, more extensively for *food and beverages and tobacco*, changes in the direction of a more meat-heavy diet (Carlsson-Kanyama & González, 2009). At the same time initial industrialization for low-income countries can be achieved through environmentally sustainable, industrial growth. This holds particularly true when recognizing the heavy emitters at low incomes such as *chemicals* that also play a crucial role in the development of an economy and therefore should be given special attention. Our analysis indicates that initial industrialization for low-income countries can be achieved through environmentally sustainable industrial development without compromising growth objectives under the right policy environment. It goes without saying that even if low-technology, labor-intensive industries may not be among the heavy emitters, this does not imply that emissions for the economy as a whole may not be subject to an increase as it transitions from an agriculturally-dominated state to a more industrially developed stage.

3.4 Conclusion

In this chapter we set out to elaborate on the importance of manufacturing development by discussing the dynamics of structural change within manufacturing itself. In doing so, we have first tried to shed light on the aggregated dynamics of structural change by paying close attention to the recent literature on premature deindustrialization and linking them to more as well as less successful stories of economic development in the recent past.

Section 3.2 carefully breaks down structural change patterns to the industry level in manufacturing. We do so by describing paths of sustainable manufacturing development for pro-poor countries by carefully addressing industrial development dynamics at the low(er)-income spectrum. We illustrate that manufacturing is a highly complex and dynamic sector with an important mandate to promote and retain economic success at different stages of economic development. It is stressed in this chapter that not accounting for these growth potentials by not capturing the underlying dynamics in manufacturing adequately may result in a suboptimal allocation of resources which, in turn, may adversely affect development opportunities for countries. This is particularly true in the context of manufacturing-induced employment *outside* of manufacturing. Having said this, it is of even more importance to understand the dynamics and inter-connectivity of industrial development within manufacturing. Whereas it might appear as if, in aggregated terms, manufacturing might have lost parts of its reputation as the engine of growth over the past decades, a more in-depth analysis proposed in this chapter has attempted to shed light on the complex growth dynamics in manufacturing and across different aggregates and periods. In doing so, it has tried to touch on some of the fundamental principles of industrial development by reflecting on the ideas of structural change and (premature) deindustrialization in the most important dimensions identified in the literature. This has resulted in an outline of a possible road map for inclusive and sustainable industrial growth for the twenty-first century and a clear mandate for the importance of manufacturing as an important contributor to sustainable and long-term economic growth for decades to come.

Notes

1 To this end we refer to the economic aggregates that correspond to sub-sectors of manufacturing as "industries." For more information on the classification of these respective industries, see Appendix A.

2 See, among others, Chenery and Taylor (1968); Chenery and Syrquin (1975); Chenery (1982); Syrquin and Chenery (1989a); and Syrquin and Chenery (1989b).

3 Additionally, Chenery and Syrquin (1975) observe that development processes in smaller countries are typically (more) affected by trade factors, such as capital inflows and external markets. More importantly, small countries with a primary export orientation stemming from their rich endowment in resources experience a notable delay in their average transformation of their export structure and fail to close this gap for manufacturing exports compared to more industry-oriented, non-oil-exporting small economies.

4 As the author reports, even though developed countries have kept a relatively constant share in real manufacturing value-added, its nominal counterpart as well as

manufacturing employment have experienced big losses in the past. There are sharp contrasts between Asia and Latin America as well as Sub-Saharan Africa (excluding Mauritius). Whereas the former group has managed to perform well in manufacturing production and employment, both Latin American and Sub-Saharan African countries have seen prolonged and significantly negative trends in the evolution of employment and manufacturing value-added generation.

5 We do not include countries which have experienced strong income growth brought about by the extraction of fossil fuel or gas in this analysis.

6 These are *food and beverages* (ISIC Rev. 3 code 15); *textiles* (17); *wearing apparel* (18+19); *chemicals* (24), *(non-metallic) minerals* (26); *machinery and equipment* (29+30); *electrical machinery and apparatus* (31+32); and *motor vehicles* (34+35). More information on the industry aggregates is provided in Appendix A.

7 To this end, we define them as early, middle, and late industries based on their highest, moderate, and low contribution to employment and value-added generation at early income stages. Coincidentally, but not very surprisingly, this classification almost perfectly overlaps with the technology classification introduced in the earlier sections of this chapter. In some arguable cases, e.g., chemicals, we retain the technology classification approach for the sake of keeping the analysis concise and the fact that the industries in question retain their relative importance even at later stages of development. Furthermore, recognizing the unprecedented role of the food and beverage industry as one of the most important industry throughout all the development stages of an economy, we exclude this particular industry from the subsequent analysis as this allows us to better look at the dynamics within and across the aggregates. It goes without saying that we will, of course, include the food and beverages industry when talking about policy implications and recommendations.

8 It is important to note that Figure 3.15 shows aggregate figures of total employment across the set of available countries through the WIOTS database. This makes the patterns only partly comparable with the regression analysis of the previous section, which are based on average patterns. The differences in findings (for example, by the robust performance of the *textiles* and *wearing apparel* industry since the 1990s) can, to a noteworthy extent, be attributed to a concentration of some industries in a handful of large, populous economies (Haraguchi, Cheng, & Smeets, 2017) such as China or Indonesia, which are also included in this analysis; see Figure 3.16.

References

Bluestone, B., & Harrison, B. (1982). *The deindustrialization of America: Plant closings, community abandonment, and the dismantling of basic industry.* New York: Basic Books.

Brady, D., & Denniston, R. (2006). Economic globalization, industrialization and deindustrialization in affluent democracie. *Social Forces.* https://doi.org/10.2307/ 3844417.

Carlsson-Kanyama, A., & González, A. J. (2009). Potential contributions of food consumption patterns to climate change. *The American Journal of Clinical Nutrition*, 89(5), 1704S–1709S.

Chenery, H. (1960). Patterns of industrial growth. *The American Economic Review*, 50(4), 624–654.

Chenery, H. (1982). Industrialization and growth: The experience of large countries. World Bank Staff Working Paper No. 539.

Chenery, H., & Syrquin, M. (1975). Accumulation and allocation processes. In H. Chenery & M. Syrquin (Eds.), *Patterns of development, 1950–1970.* New York: Oxford University Press.

Chenery, H., & Taylor, L. (1968). Development patterns: Among countries and over time. *The Review of Economics and Statistics*, 50(4), 391–416.

Dasgupta, S., & Singh, A. (2006). Manufacturing, services and premature deindustrialization in developing countries. *UNU-Wider*. 7.

Feenstra, R., Inklaar, R., & Timmer, M. (2015). The next generation of the Penn World Table. *American Economic Review*, 105(10), 3150–3182. https://doi.org/10.1257/aer.20130954.

Ghani, E., & O'Connell, S. D. (2014). Can service be a growth escalator in low-income countries? http://papers.ssrn.com/sol3/papers.cfm?abstract/_id=2470231.

Grossman, G. M., & Krueger, A. B. (1995). Economic growth and the environment. *The Quarterly Journal of Economics*, 110(2), 353–377.

Guerrieri, P., & Meliciani, V. (2005). Technology and international competitiveness: The interdependence between manufacturing and producer services. *Structural Change and Economic Dynamics*, 16(4), 489–502.

Haraguchi, N. (2012). Pro-employment manufacturing development in large countries. UNIDO Working Paper, Development Policy, Statistics and Research Branch.

Haraguchi, N. (2015). Patterns of structural change and manufacturing development. In J. Weiss & M. Tribe (Eds.), *Routledge handbook of industry and development* (pp. 36–64). London: Routledge,

Haraguchi, N., & Amann, J. (2020a). Measuring structural change for developing countries: A new approach to analysing manufacturing value added with application. UNIDO Working Paper, forthcoming.

Haraguchi, N., & Amann, J. (2020b). Sectoral dynamics. In *New perspectives on structural change*. Forthcoming.

Haraguchi, N., Cheng, C. F. C., & Smeets, E. (2017). The importance of manufacturing in economic development: Has this changed? *World Development*, 93, 293–315. https://doi.org/10.1016/j.worlddev.2016.12.013.

IEA (International Energy Agency). (2015). Energy flow charts. Available at: www.iea.org/ data-and-statistics.

INDSTAT. (2017). INDSTAT 2 based on International Standard Industrial Classification (ISIC), Revision 3. *UNIDO Statistics*. Available at: https://unstats.un.org/unsd/cr/registry/regcst.asp?Cl=2.

Jakob, M., & Steckel, J. C. (2014). How climate change mitigation could harm development in poor countries. *WIREs Climate Change*, 5(2), 161–168. https:// doi.org/10.1002/wcc.260.

Jerneck, A., & Olsson, L. (2008). Adaptation and the poor: Development, resilience and transition. *Climate Policy*, 8(2), 170–182.

Kaldor, N. (1967). *Strategic factors in economic development*. Ithaca, NY: Cornell University Press.

Klien, R. J. T., Schipper, E., & Dessai, S. (2005). Integration mitigation and adaptation into climate and development policy: Three research questions. *Environmental Science and Policy*, 8, 579–588.

Kuznets, S. (1953). International differences in income levels: Reflections on their causes. *Economic Development and Cultural Change*, 2(1), 3–26.

Kuznets, S. (1955). Economic growth and income inequality. *The American Economic Review*, 45(1), 1–28.

Lewis, W. A. (1954). Economic development with unlimited supplies of labour. *The Manchester School*, 22(2), 139–91. https://doi.org/10.1111/j.1467-9957.1954.tb00021.x.

Lin, J. Y., & Monga, C. (2010). Growth identification and facilitation: The role of the state in the dynamics of structural change. *World*, May.

Matsuyama, K. (1992). Agricultural productivity, comparative advantage, and economic growth. *Journal of Economic Theory*. https://doi.org/10.1016/0022-0531(92)90057-O.

OECD. (2011). ISIC Rev. 3 Technology Intensity Definition. OECD Directorate for Science, Technology and Industry; Economic Analysis and Statistics Division. Available at: www.oecd.org/ sti/ind/48350231.pdf.

Palma, J. G. (2014). De-industrialisation, 'premature' de-industrialisation and the Dutch disease. Available at: http://stat.ijie.incubadora.ufsc.br/index.php/necat/article/view/3118.

Pouliotte, J., Smit, B., & Westerhoff, L. (2009). Adaptation and development: Livelihoods and climate change in Subarnabad, Bangladesh. *Climate and Development*, 1(1), 31–46.

Pritchett, L. (2000). Understanding patterns of economic growth: Searching for hills among plateaus, mountains, and plains. *The World Bank Economic Review*, 14(2), 221–250.

Rodrik, D. (2016). Premature deindustrialization. *Journal of Economic Growth*, 21(1), 1–33. https://doi.org/10.1007/s10887-015-9122-3.

Schipper, L., & Pelling, M. (2006). Disaster risk, climate change and international development: Scope for, and challenges to, integration. *Disasters*, 30(1), 19–38.

Syrquin, M., & Chenery, H. (1989a). *Patterns of development, 1950 to 1983.* Washington, DC: World Bank.

Syrquin, M., & Chenery, H. (1989b). Three decades of industrialization. *The World Bank Economic Review*, 3(2), 145–181. https://doi.org/10.1093/wber/3.2.145.

Szirmai, A., & Verspagen, B. (2015). Manufacturing and economic growth in developing countries, 1950–2005. *Structural Change and Economic Dynamics*, 34, 46–59. https:// doi.org/10.1016/j.strueco.2015.06.002.

Timmer, M., Dietzenbacher, E., Los, B., Stehrer, R., & Gaaitzen, J. (2015). An illustrated user guide to the world input-output database: The case of global automotive production. *Review of International Economics*, 23(3), 575–605. https:// doi.org/10.1111/roie.12178.

UN. (2014). National account statistics: Analysis of main aggregates. Available at: http://unstats.un .org/unsd/snaama/Introduction.asp.

UNIDO. (2013). Sustaining employment growth: The role of manufacturing and structural change. Industrial Development Report (IDR), United Nations Industrial Development Organization (UNIDO).

UNIDO. (2016). The role of technology and innovation in inclusive and sustainable industrial development. Industrial Development Report (IDR), United Nations Industrial Development Organization (UNIDO).

UNIDO. (2020). Industrializing in the digital age. Industrial Development Report (IDR), United Nations Industrial Development Organization (UNIDO).

World Bank. (2019a). World Bank country and lending groups. Available at: https://datahelpdesk.worldbank.org/knowledgebase/articles/906519-world-bank-country-and-lending-groups.

World Bank. (2019b). *World development indicators 2019.* Washington, DC: World Bank. https://datacatalog.worldbank.org/dataset/world-development-indicators.

WRI. (2015). World Resource Institute. Climate analysis indicators tool: WRI's climate data explorer. Available at: http://cait2.wri.org.

Appendix A: Manufacturing industry classification

The data used for the industry analysis within manufacturing builds on the International Standard Industrial Classification (ISIC), Revision 3 data base by the United Nations Statistics Division (INDSTAT, 2017). Out of the 18 manufacturing industries that are representative of manufacturing, nine industries are analyzed in greater detail, and have been chosen to be reflective of the representative performance of the numerous components of the manufacturing sector. These are *food and beverages* (ISIC Rev. 3 code 15); *textiles* (17); *wearing apparel* (18+19); *chemicals* (24), *computer and electronics, (non-metallic) minerals* (26); *machinery and equipment* (29+30); *electrical machinery and apparatus* (31+32);

Table 3.1 Manufacturing industry classification based on ISIC Revision 3

ISIC Rev.3 Code	*ISIC Rev.3 Industry Description*	*Abbreviation*	*Technology group*
15	*Manufacture of food products and beverages*	*Food and beverages*	*Low*
16	Manufacture of tobacco products		Low
17	*Manufacture of textiles*	*Textiles*	*Low*
18+19	*Manufacture of wearing apparel and leather*	*Wearing apparel*	*Low*
20	Manufacture of wood and of products of wood and cork		Low
21	Manufacture of paper and paper products		Low
22	Publishing, printing and reproduction of recorded media		Low
23	Manufacture of coke, refined petroleum products and nuclear fuel		Medium
24	*Manufacture of chemicals and chemical products*	*Chemicals*	*High*
25	Manufacture of rubber and plastics products		Medium
26	*Manufacture of other non-metallic mineral products*	*Minerals*	*Medium*
27	Manufacture of basic metals		Medium
28	*Manufacture of fabricated metal products*	*Fabricated metals*	*Medium*
29+30	*Manufacture of machinery and equipment (incl. office, accounting and computing machinery)*	*Machinery*	*High*
31+32	*Manufacture of electrical machinery and apparatus and radio television and communication equipment*	*Electrical*	*High*
33	Manufacture of medical, precision and optical instruments		High
34+35	*Manufacture of motor vehicles, trailers, semi-trailers and of other transport equipment*	*Motor vehicles*	*High*
36	Manufacture of furniture; manufacturing n.e.c.		Low

and *motor vehicles* (34+35) and account for around 75 percent of manufacturing value-added and employment within manufacturing.

With regards to the technology classification of the industries, all manufacturing industries are further classified by their technology intensity following the technology classification of the Organisation for Economic Co-operation and Development (OECD), which is based on research and development (R&D) intensity relative to value-added and gross production statistics (OECD, 2011). The OECD classifies manufacturing industries into four categories of high-technology, medium high-technology, medium low-technology, and low-technology industries. For the purpose of this analysis, high-technology and medium high-technology industries are combined and referred to as "high-technology" sub-sectors, while low-technology and medium-low technology sub-sectors are categorized as "medium-technology" sub-sectors respectively; see Table 3.1 for a detailed description.

Appendix B: Data and methodology regression analysis

Data

For the industry-level analysis, we combine manufacturing-level data from INDSTAT (2017) with Penn World data 9.1 (Feenstra, Inklaar, & Timmer, 2015). The construction of the real value-added series follows Haraguchi and Amann (2020a). Country-level classification is based on the World Development Indicators (World Bank, 2019a).

The sustainability analysis in Section 3.4 is based on National Account statistics (UN, 2014) as well as CAIT climate data (WRI, 2015) and from the International Energy Agency (IEA 2015), respectively. The industry definitions in Figure 3.4 are based on IEA (2015) data and follow a slightly different industry-level aggregation.

Regression model

The basic empirical set-up for the industry-level analysis of this chapter expands on Haraguchi's (2015) study. More specifically, we estimate a panel fixed effects model in order to analyze the development patterns for 18 industries of manufacturing of which the group of nine industries (see Table 3.1) is discussed in greater depth. For each industry i we estimate

$$y_{cit} = \alpha_{ci} + \beta_i \mathbf{X}_{cit} + \tau_{it} + \varepsilon_{cit} \tag{3.1}$$

where y_{cit}, is either the log of real value-added per capita or the log of the employment-to-population ratio of country c's industry i in period t. Note that this model is estimated separately for all i individual industries and we retain subscript i to highlight this feature of our model. Furthermore, the employment-to-population ratio is defined as the ratio of country c's employment head count in

Table 3.2 Input-output table structure of n-sector economy

	$Sector_1$	…	$Sector_i$	…	$Sector_n$	$Foreign_1$	…	$Foreign_i$	…	$Foreign_n$	*Final demand*	*Output*
$Sector_1$	z_{11}	…	z_{1i}	…	z_{1n}	x_{11}	…	x_{1i}	…	x_{1n}	f_{d1}	y_1
…	…	…		…			…		…	…	…	…
$Sector_i$	z_{i1}	…	z_{ii}	…	z_{in}	x_{i1}	…	x_{ii}	…	x_{in}	f_{di}	y_i
…	…	…		…			…		…	…	…	…
$Sector_n$	z_{n1}	…	z_{ni}	…	z_{nn}	x_{n1}	…	x_{ni}	…	x_{nn}	f_{dn}	y_n
$Foreign_1$	imp_{11}	…	imp_{1i}	…	imp_{1n}	…	…	…	…	…	…	…
…	…	…	…	…	…	…	…	…	…	…	…	…
$Foreign_i$	imp_{i1}	…	imp_{ii}	…	imp_{in}	…	…	…	…	…	…	out_i
…	…	…	…	…	…	…	…	…	…	…	…	…
$Foreign_n$	imp_{n1}	…	imp_{ni}	…	imp_{nn}	…	…	…	…	…	…	out_n
Value-added	v_{a1}	…	v_{ai}	…	v_{an}							
Output	y_1	…	y_i	…	y_n							

industry *i* at time *t* relative to its population, that is $(\text{employment}_{\text{cit}} \,/\, \text{population}_{\text{ct}})$. The explanatory variables in **X** contain the logs of real GDP per capita (in constant PPP 2011 international US dollars) and are added in their linear, quadratic, and cubic representation. Furthermore, α_{ci} and τ_{it} denote country and time effects. We retain this rather simple specification in our attempts to identify different forms of heterogeneities by means of sub-sample analyses throughout this chapter. Finally, we use the predictions obtained through the above model to analyze the compositional changes in terms of their absolute contribution to per capita GDP and employment over a grid of a GDP per capita level of US$500 to US$15,000.

In order to investigate the time dynamics of the manufacturing sector in Section 3.3, we interact the right-hand side of Equation (3.1) with a dummy identifier for each decade $TD_d, d = \{1970s, 1980s, 1990s, 2000 \, \textit{and beyond}\}$ where we eliminate the 1960s for the sake of robustness from the data.

Sustainability analysis

In order to analyze the impact of industrial production and CO_2 emissions, we modify the basic regression set-up in Equation (3.1) by defining manufacturing sustainability in y_{cit} as the log of manufacturing value added per tonnes of emitted carbon dioxide (CO_2). For Figure 3.19, industry-level CO_2 emission per unit of real value-added is utilized as the dependent variable.

Appendix C: Data and methodology input-output analysis

Data

The input-output analysis is based on World Input-Output Tables (WIOT, Release 2016) by Timmer et al. (2015). There, we represent the evolution of reported, domestic employment for each industry over time as direct employment. The remaining four categories in this figure sum up domestic linkages of the corresponding sectors respectively, e.g., manufacturing is comprised of domestic linkages to other domestic manufacturing industries across all countries considered for this analysis.

Methodology

Table 3.2 shows the structure of the input-output table of an n-sector economy. For convenience, Table 3.2 can be written as

$$Z + FD = X$$

Table 3.3 Employment contribution table structure of n-sector economy

	$Sector_{j,1}$	…	$Sector_{j,I}$	…	$Sector_{j,n}$	$Sector_{k,1}$	…	$Sector_{k,i}$	…	$Sector_{k,n}$
$\text{Sector}_{\text{j,1}}$	$n_{j,1}$	…	$n_{j,1} \times a_{j,1i}$	…	$n_{j,1} \times a_{j,1n}$	$n_{j,1} \times b_{j,11}$	…	$n_{j,1} \times b_{j,1i}$	…	$n_{j,1} \times b_{j,1n}$
…	…	…	…	…	…	…	…	…	…	…
$\text{Sector}_{\text{j,i}}$	$n_{j,i} \times a_{j,i1}$	…	$n_{j,i}$	…	$n_{j,i} \times a_{j,in}$	$n_{j,i} \times b_{j,i1}$	…	$n_{j,i} \times b_{j,ii}$	…	$n_{j,i} \times b_{j,in}$
…	…	…	…	…	…	…	…	…	…	…
$\text{Sector}_{\text{j,n}}$	$n_{j,n} \times a_{j,n1}$	…	$n_{j,n} \times a_{j,ni}$	…	$n_{j,n}$	$n_{j,n} \times b_{j,n1}$	…	$n_{j,n} \times b_{j,ni}$	…	$n_{j,n} \times b_{j,nn}$
$\text{Sector}_{\text{k,1}}$	$n_{k,1} \times b_{k,11}$	…	$n_{k,1} \times b_{k,1i}$	…	$n_{k,1} \times b_{k,1n}$	$n_{k,1}$	…	$n_{k,1} \times a_{k,1i}$	…	$n_{k,1} \times a_{k,1n}$
…	…	…	…	…	…	…	…	…	…	…
$\text{Sector}_{\text{k,i}}$	$n_{k,i} \times b_{k,i1}$	…	$n_{k,i} \times b_{k,ii}$	…	$n_{k,i} \times b_{k,in}$	$n_{k,i} \times a_{k,i1}$	…	$n_{k,i}$	…	$n_{k,iv} a_{k,in}$
…	…	…	…	…	…	…	…	…	…	…
$\text{Sector}_{\text{k,n}}$	$n_{k,n} \times b_{k,n1}$	…	$n_{k,n} \times {}_{k,ni}$	…	$n_{k,n} \times b_{k,nn}$	$n_{k,n} \times a_{k,n1}$	…	$n_{k,n} \times a_{k,ni}$	…	$n_{k,i}$

where Z denotes the (international) transaction matrix and FD and X denotes the final demand and output, respectively. The above expression can also be rewritten as

$$AX + FD = X$$

with $A_{ij} = \dfrac{Z_{ij}}{Xj}$ to arrive at

$$X = (I - A)^{-1} FD \tag{3.2}$$

Using Equation (3.2) and the employment multiplication EM = *Employment/ Output*, manufacturing-related employment can be recovered as

$$\begin{aligned} Employment &= EM \times X \\ &= EM \times (I - A)^{-1} F \ (3) \end{aligned} \tag{3.3}$$

where the row sums of each line correspond to total employment of the respective sector and the column sums correspond to the backward linkages in terms of employment.

In order to differentiate between domestic and foreign effects, the latter are obtained by summing up all backward linkages from abroad. For domestic effects, direct linkages are replaced with reported employment. The resulting structure is presented in Table 3.3 for an n-sector economy and two countries $\{j, k\}$.

Part III

Designing integrated industrial policies in Africa

13 Mechanisms and impacts of innovation on firm survival

Evidence from Sub-Saharan Africa

Christian Samen Otchia

13.1 Introduction

Understanding the mechanisms underlying firms' survival is one of the major challenges in developed and developing countries in relation to the promotion of industrial development. This is certainly the case in Africa, where governments have increasingly developed and implemented strategies to promote high-growth entrepreneurship. The region accounted for about 30 percent of the global regulatory business reform between 2014 and 2015, with a large percentage aimed at reducing the complexity and the cost of regulatory processes as well as strengthening legal institutions for local entrepreneurs (World Bank Group, 2016). To date, these policies have been quite successful in promoting self-employment rather than promoting an entrepreneurial culture, business and job creation, and earnings increases (Cho & Honorati, 2014; Grimm & Paffhausen, 2015; McKenzie & Woodruff, 2014). For instance, a study by McKenzie and Paffhausen (2017), which uses a sample of 14,000 firms, observed in 16 panel surveys from 12 different countries, finds that half of all firms are likely to fail and close after six years. Additional evidence (Brenton, Cadot, & Pierola, 2012) shows that African firms suffer from low survival in export markets, as exports originating from Sub-Saharan Africa survive just over two years.

While the issue of firm survival has generated a vast body of literature, we know far too little about the phenomenon outside of the developed countries in order to inform policy in Africa. In addition, much of the research in Africa has tended to focus on the characteristics of surviving firms, whether in international markets (Brenton et al., 2012; Cadot, Iacovone, Pierola, & Rauch, 2013) or otherwise (McKenzie & Paffhausen, 2017). A variety of studies, such as McKenzie and Paffhausen (2017) and McGowan et al. (2017), among others, have established that factors such as profitability and productivity growth are important drivers of any attempt to overcome firm failure. However, causal factors leading to firm survival remain speculative, and far too little attention has been paid to the most salient feature of globalization and international trade, that is, innovation. In this chapter, we show that this feature is key to understanding the low survival rate of African firms in international markets as well as the variation in the innovation propagation effects across countries.

To fulfill this aim, we construct a unique dataset by merging firm-level panel data of African firms across eight sectors from the World Bank Enterprise Surveys (WBES) and sector-level information on input-output linkages from the Global Trade Analysis Project (GTAP) dataset. We also exploit the predetermined nature of innovation variables for identification. Our empirical analysis proceeds in three steps. First, we use the export history of firms to construct measurements of firm survival, as in Lederman et al. (2016). Ideally, one would estimate firms' time survival using longitudinal data on their participation in the export market. However, such data does not exist for African countries. Therefore, we proxy for firm survival using export spells, i.e., the extent to which firms remain exporters in the interim between different survey rounds. We establish that firm survival rate is very low but also varies between countries. For example, the survival rate is smaller in poor countries than rich countries (Figure 13.1). This feature is consistent with the pattern observed in other firm surveys (Brenton et al., 2012). A lesser-known stylized fact supported by our data is that the survival rate of African firms in international markets has been increasing in previous years. Figure 13.2 plots the survival rate of firms by year, and Figure 13.3 focuses on sectors to better visualize the trend by industry. Both figures show a rising trend.

In a second step, we test whether countries with faster technological innovation experience faster increases in their firm survival rate. Since the association between innovation and firm survival could be partly biased because of reverse causality, measurement error, and selection bias, we apply a structural equation

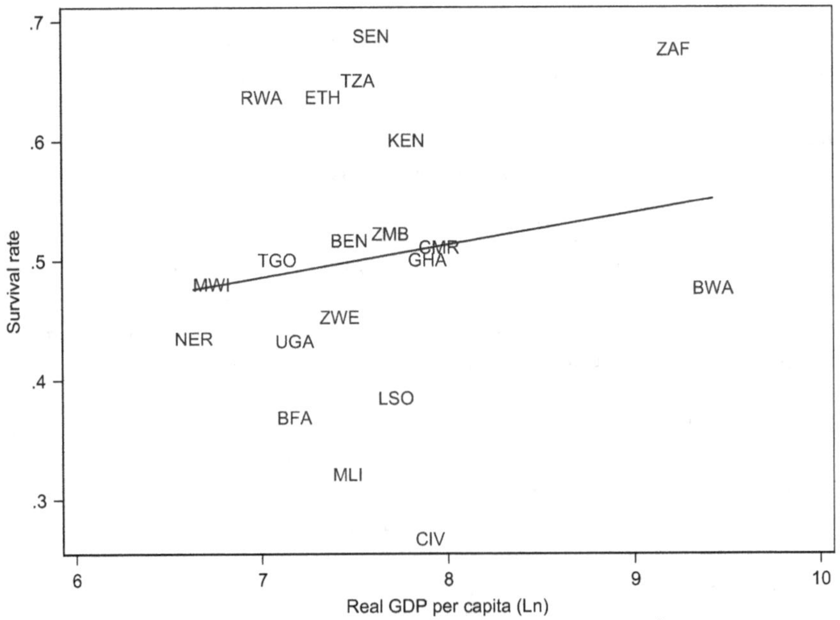

Figure 13.1 Firm survival by real GDP per capita (ln)

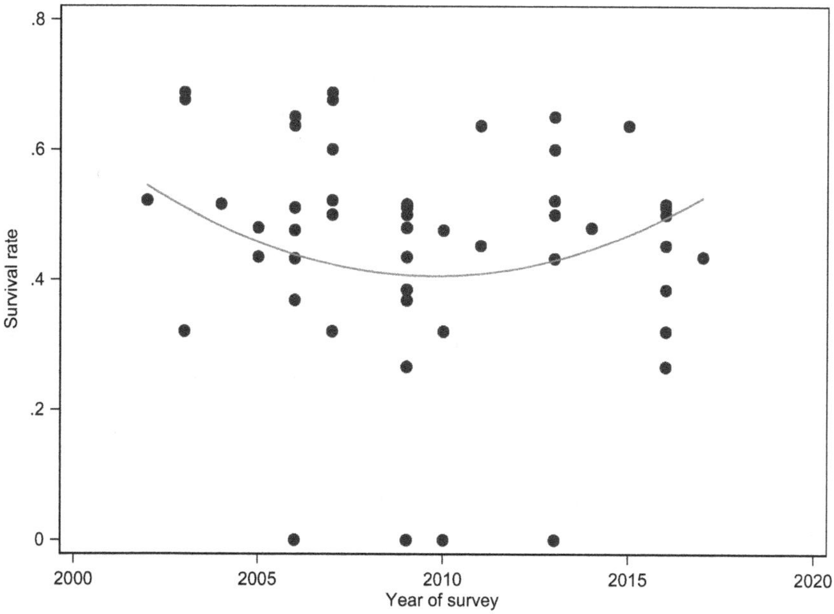

Figure 13.2 Firm survival by year

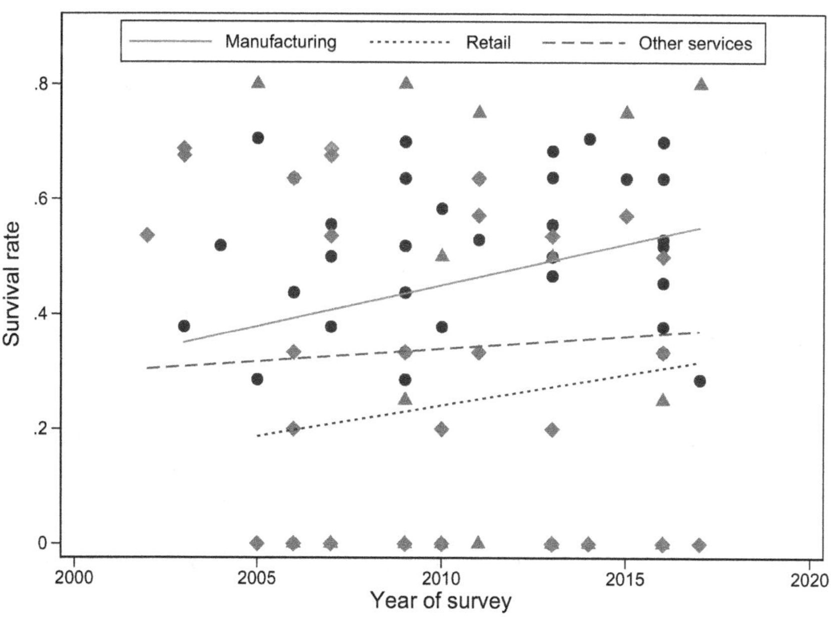

Figure 13.3 Firm survival by sector and by year

model that builds on the framework put forward by Crepon et al. (1998), but with two points of departure. First, our model jointly links knowledge inputs (such as ICT adoption) to innovation outputs (product and process innovation) and innovation outputs to firm survival. Second, we explicitly distinguish two innovation output functions and allow each function to depend on varying determinants. We find that product and process innovations increase firm survival, but the magnitude of process innovation is significantly greater than product innovation. We then analyze whether product and process innovation can be complementary and find that their interaction term is positive but not large in magnitude. Our findings suggest that the impacts of innovation are heterogeneous by country.

Finally, we discuss a potential mechanism that may underlie the relation between innovation and firm survival using the sectoral linkages derived from the input-output tables. In our model, innovation is propagated through backward and forward linkages, as well as the self-induced input and output effect. Our argument builds on the fact that African firms have a broad perception of innovation that may even include simple imitation. In this context, economic linkages can propagate the speed of innovation across countries. Indeed, we find that countries with higher propagation of innovation experienced higher firm survival. The effects of backward linkages are greater than forward linkages, while self-induced output seems to have a greater effect than self-induced inputs. Our estimates imply that structural transformation toward strengthening domestic value chains may amplify the effects of innovation on firm survival.

This chapter is organized as follows. Section 13.2 presents the related literature and Section 13.3 presents the data. Section 13.4 discusses the empirical strategy. Section 13.5 presents and interprets the estimation results, and Section 13.6 presents the mechanisms. The chapter concludes in Section 13.7.

13.2 Related literature

Our work is connected with the literature on firm heterogeneity and international trade, which emphasizes that heterogeneity in productivity, size, and other characteristics is systematically related to trade participation, with exporters larger and more productive than non-exporters, even prior to entering export markets (Bernard, Jensen, Redding, & Schott, 2012; Melitz & Redding, 2014). This literature has a long tradition of linking the value of innovation to firm growth and survival (Becker and Egger, 2013; Hopenhayn, 1994; Jovanovic & MacDonald, 1994; Klepper, 1996).[1] Evidence from the vast majority of studies, which were primarily conducted in the U.S. and Europe, suggests three main mechanisms through which innovation can affect firm survival (Hayashi, Li, & Wang, 2015):

1 *The production costs channel*: technological innovation tends to bring down production costs, which generates margins for firms to be competitive and reduce prices. Lower competitive prices increase profit, which helps firms to grow and survive.

2 *The technology gap channel*: technological innovation tends to increase the technology gap between firms. Two scenarios are worth noting. If the inter-firm technology gap becomes very large, then technological innovation will result in a shakeout, whereas a small number of firms survive and enjoy market expansion. If the diffusion of technology innovation is faster and the number of producers engaged in innovation is higher in the economy, other firms will be more likely to absorb innovation and can survive longer.
3 *The speed of the diffusion of innovation.* If a country has put in place tariffs and other commercial incentives, firms can innovate faster than they would in the absence of these conditions. The import structure may also affect innovation and firm survival through the intermediate inputs effect.

We contribute to this literature by providing evidence for all of these mechanisms in the developing country context. Finally, our empirical analysis also examines the role played by technological change and the propagation of technological innovation.

The idea that the propagation of innovation is vital for technology diffusion began to attract more empirical attention as a consequence of the linking of input-output tables with firm-level data. A series of studies by Javorcik (2004) and Barrios, Görg, and Strobl (2011), among others, argued that economic linkages can accelerate the spread of innovation by connecting foreign firms to domestic firms. Other researchers, such as Dietzenbacher (2000), linked innovation diffusion to sector growth to show that inter-industrial linkage channels can be operated in an economy in which technology is generated by a particular firm. This hypothesis also receives support from theoretical research presented by Caves (1974), who showed that innovation diffusion is linked to productivity growth. Other recent studies have also shown that economic linkages can amplify the effect of policy on domestic firms as well as output (Bartelme & Gorodnichenko, 2015; Pierce & Schott, 2016). Thus, our work builds on this literature to assess the mechanism and the effect of innovation on firm survival, focusing on economic linkages. In this setting, we predict that, when the economic linkages are higher, an increase in the number of innovations leads to an increase in firm entry and survival in the export market.

In terms of empirical strategy, our chapter adopts the framework put forward by Crepon et al. (1998), which has been extensively applied in research that links innovation to productivity. However, a growing number of studies have extended the Crepon, Duguet, and Mairesse (CDM) model to include different firm performance variables, such as productivity, sales, profit margins, market values, and export performance (Halpern & Muraközy, 2012). Our work extends this model in several ways: we link innovation outputs to firm survival rather than productivity; we explicitly distinguish two different types of innovations, namely, product and process innovation; we allow for each innovation function to depend on varying firm characteristics and determinants, which might not be very similar; and we apply a new estimation procedure—the Stata Extended Regression Models—to simultaneously address the econometric issues of sample selection and error in variables. To our knowledge, this is the first time that the survival approach and the innovation approach have been integrated in a single estimation procedure.

Finally, our work is related to recent empirical papers studying the determinants of ICT adoption, the role of ICT adoption in promoting technological innovation, and links between product and process innovation (Becker & Egger, 2013; Van Beveren & Vandenbussche, 2010).

13.3 Data and variable construction

We draw information from two datasets: the WBES on firm exports, and the GTAP data for the social accounting matrices. This section provides summary information on data construction and measurement. It then provides descriptive statistics.

13.3.1 Firm data

The first dataset is the WBES data by firm, in a two-digit harmonized system category, and in panel form. The WBES provides a rich environment for the analysis of firm exports and survival, as well as how it is related to policy variables such as innovation, agglomeration, institution, etc. The WBES data captures detailed information on firms, including firm and manager characteristics, innovation activities and labor, and it is administered in manufacturing and services. The sample for each country is stratified by industry, firm size, and location within the country. Weights are provided in the survey to ensure that the sample is representative of the non-agricultural private sector of the economy. While the surveys are conducted in different years according to the countries, we favor the panel structure as we are interested in export behavior between two or more rounds. We draw our sample from a panel of 23 countries and 7,108 firms. The sample periods vary by country but run roughly from 2006 to 2017. Table 13.1 lists the countries and years in our sample. The dataset that we use is a balanced panel of plants that were in operation in two or more rounds of the sample years and that have necessary data on innovation. This includes data based on firms' experiences and perceptions of the environment in which they operate. In principle, the data is collected at the plant level. However, the distinction between plants and firms is not important in this analysis, as we use it as a variable in some models. Of the sample plants, 19 percent are owned by firms that had only a single plant. In the rest of the study, we will use the word "firm" to refer to the individual observation in our sample.

The predictions in this study are primarily concerned with two variables: survival and innovation.

13.3.1.1 Survival

The procedure we use to construct measures of firm survival in the export market is as follows. All firms were asked questions regarding export status in each survey

Table 13.1 Sample description

Country	*2002*	*2003*	*2004*	*2005*	*2006*	*2007*	*2009*	*2010*	*2011*	*2013*	*2014*	*2015*	*2016*	*2017*
Angola					183			183						
Benin			69				97						62	
Botswana					119			119						
Burkina					88		88							
Cameroon					95		209						160	
Cape Verde					53		53							
Côte d'Ivoire							145						145	
DRC					105			197		92				
Ethiopia									372			372		
Ghana						31				31				
Kenya						151				151				
Lesotho							61						61	
Malawi				77			164				87			
Mali		69				197		193					97	
Niger				80			103							57
Rwanda					70				70					
Senegal		74				74								
South Africa		191				191								
Tanzania					115					115				
Togo							60						60	
Uganda					209					209				
Zambia	73					225				152				
Zimbabwe									302				302	

Source: Calculations based on WBES, World Bank.

Table 13.2 Transition matrix

Period t	*Period t+1*		
	Exporter	*Non-exporter*	*Total*
Exporter	39.48	60.52	100
Non-exporter	50.87	49.13	100
Total	49.27	50.73	100

Source: Calculations based on WBES, World Bank.

round. Since these questions assess if a firm exports directly or indirectly, we combined them into whether a firm exports or not. Next, we use the first wave as base year *t* and compare transitions using the export status in the second wave, which we call $t + 1$. Table 13.2 displays the transition rate from each status for the entire sample. Two patterns are clear. First, a firm that does not export has a probability of 0.508 that it will become an exporter, whereas the probability of remaining a non-exporter is 0.491. There is a significant number of firms that stay in the status of non-exporting over time, implying that half of the non-exporting firms in year *t* are likely to start exporting. If a firm is an exporter in year *t*, it has a probability of 0.394 that it will remain an exporter in year *t+1* percent, where the probability of exiting the export market is large and is estimated at 0.605. The transition patterns reported in Table 13.2 illustrate the need to define a comparator against which the effect of survival can be estimated. We separate the exporting pattern into two decisions. One is that we compare the likelihood of entering the export market against the likelihood of not entering, and on the other hand, the decision to survive is compared against the non-survivors. This is because the determinants of survival among exporters are different than those of the novice exporter. This study departs from the previous literature, for example, Lederman et al. (2016), in comparing survivor with non-survivor.

Table 13.3 presents the export patterns for the entire sample and by country. Five specific elements are worth noting. First, export participation rates are very low, except for South Africa. The top three countries with the lowest export participation rates include Angola (7.65 percent), Cape Verde (9.41 percent), and Democratic Republic of the Congo (DRC) (12.69 percent). Second, the turnover rate (entry and exit) tends to be higher in countries with high export participation rates: four countries with high turnover rates appear to belong in the top five countries with high export participation rates. These countries are Ghana (35.48 percent), South Africa (34.03 percent), Togo (33.33 percent), and Kenya (25.83 percent). Third, the average survival rate—that is, the share of firms exporting in period *t* and *t+1*—is 9.48 percent in our sample. Among the surviving firms, there is a high variation within countries. The rate of surviving firms is the highest in South Africa (38.22 percent), Senegal (29.73 percent), and Kenya (19.87 percent). They are followed by Togo and Ghana, where the surviving rates respectively reach 18.33 percent and 16.13 percent. Firms in the

Table 13.3 Export patterns

Country	*Not exporting*	*Exit*	*Entry*	*Survive*	*Total*
Angola	92.35	4.37	3.28	0.00	100
Benin	65.65	11.45	10.69	12.21	100
Botswana	77.31	9.24	5.04	8.40	100
Burkina	72.73	13.64	5.68	7.95	100
Cameroon	68.24	9.02	13.33	9.41	100
Cape Verde	90.57	5.66	3.77	0.00	100
Côte d'Ivoire	82.07	7.59	7.59	2.76	100
DRC	87.31	6.09	6.60	0.00	100
Ethiopia	81.18	3.23	9.95	5.65	100
Ghana	48.39	16.13	19.35	16.13	100
Kenya	54.30	13.25	12.58	19.87	100
Lesotho	68.85	13.11	9.84	8.20	100
Malawi	76.83	7.93	7.93	7.32	100
Mali	74.53	11.32	8.81	5.35	100
Niger	72.99	9.49	10.22	7.30	100
Rwanda	77.14	5.71	7.14	10.00	100
Senegal	48.65	13.51	8.11	29.73	100
South Africa	27.75	18.32	15.71	38.22	100
Tanzania	69.57	6.09	13.04	11.30	100
Togo	48.33	18.33	15.00	18.33	100
Uganda	72.25	10.05	10.05	7.66	100
Zambia	70.22	9.78	9.33	10.67	100
Zimbabwe	71.85	7.62	14.24	6.29	100

Source: Calculations based on WBES, World Bank.

rest of the sampled countries survive below 15 percent. Among them, Tanzania, Rwanda, and Senegal have an interesting feature, with low exit rates, but relatively high survival. Finally, countries with low entry also realize low survival rates.

13.3.1.2 Innovation

This study uses two measures of innovation, both based on the direct self-reports from a set of questions in the innovation module. One is product innovation, that is, the transformation of ideas into new products and services. Product innovation is ascertained from the two questions on whether the establishment introduced new or significantly improved products or services and whether the establishment introduced any new or significantly improved methods for the production or the supply of products or services. We define a firm as a product innovator if it improved the products or the methods of production or supply in the last three years preceding the survey. The other is a measure of process innovation introduced by firms also in the last three years. In fact, the WBES asked firms to report on the process innovation related indicators, such as: (1) whether this establishment introduced any new or significantly improved logistics, delivery, or distribution methods for inputs, products, or services; (2) whether this

Table 13.4 Distribution of innovation by country

Country	*Product innovation*	*Process innovation*
Angola	13.66	0.00
Benin	27.19	16.67
Botswana	17.65	0.00
Burkina	5.11	0.00
Cameroon	29.74	12.28
Cape Verde	0.00	0.00
Côte d'Ivoire	21.03	6.21
DRC	25.38	10.91
Ethiopia	61.96	56.72
Ghana	38.71	41.94
Kenya	62.25	40.73
Lesotho	4.10	4.10
Malawi	20.12	20.73
Mali	10.97	10.79
Niger	17.08	12.08
Rwanda	54.29	42.86
Senegal	0.00	0.00
South Africa	0.00	0.00
Tanzania	68.26	30.43
Togo	40.00	9.17
Uganda	50.00	38.04
Zambia	23.33	22.44
Zimbabwe	50.99	47.52

Source: Calculations based on WBES, World Bank.

establishment introduced any new or significantly improved supporting activities for processes, such as maintenance systems or operations for purchasing, accounting, or computing; (3) whether this establishment introduced new or significantly improved marketing methods; and (4) whether this establishment had introduced new or significant organizational structure in last three years. Those who report that they conducted any of these four activities are coded as process innovators. Finally, innovator firms are generated using the two indicators of product and process innovations. We define innovator as a firm who introduced either a product innovation or a process innovation in the last three years.

Results of the construction are presented in Table 13.4, where we compare the rate of innovation by country. An inspection of Table 13.4 indicates significant variations in innovation activities across countries and firms. Firms report the highest innovation activities in Tanzania, Kenya, Rwanda, Uganda, Zimbabwe, and Ghana. The middle group of innovators include countries where at least one-fifth of the firms innovate. Countries that belong to this group include Malawi and Zambia. At the lowest extreme, firms in countries like DRC, Angola, and Cape Verde have introduced product innovation but none them have introduced process innovation. Table 13.5 provides summary statistics of all the variables used in this study.

Table 13.5 Descriptive statistics

	Sample		*Non-resource*		*Fragile*	
	Mean	*SD*	*Mean*	*SD*	*Mean*	*SD*
Survival rate	0.51	0.50	0.49	0.50	0.37	0.48
Investment	0.45	0.50	0.43	0.49	0.42	0.49
Employment growth	0.04	0.12	0.04	0.12	0.02	0.14
Sales growth	0.08	0.20	0.07	0.18	0.09	0.19
Product innovation	0.31	0.46	0.37	0.48	0.28	0.45
Process innovation	0.22	0.42	0.28	0.45	0.21	0.41
Firm size	3.18	1.39	3.13	1.39	3.00	1.30
Exporter	0.29	0.45	0.28	0.45	0.24	0.43
Foreign ownership	0.14	0.35	0.12	0.32	0.13	0.34
Competition	0.09	0.29	0.11	0.32	0.11	0.32
Large city	0.50	0.50	0.44	0.50	0.47	0.50
Firm age	4.40	1.77	4.50	1.75	4.56	1.82
Manager's experience	3.16	0.39	3.19	0.40	3.19	0.40
Credit constrained	0.01	0.11	0.02	0.13	0.02	0.14
Part of larger firm	0.20	0.40	0.20	0.40	0.27	0.45
ICT adoption	0.63	0.48	0.64	0.48	0.60	0.49
Inadequately educated workforce	1.28	1.29	1.18	1.27	1.28	1.30

Source: Calculations based on WBES, World Bank.

13.3.2 Social accounting matrices (SAM)

We assemble a new dataset originated from the input-output tables and social accounting matrices to measure changes in innovation spillover, trade spillover, and import spillover across sectors in the sampled countries. Our main source of data is the GTAP data. We use several versions of the data, including the GTAP 9.1 database, which corresponds to the global economy of 2011 with 140 countries and 57 industries. For countries without the individual social accounting matrix (SAM), we use the region they belong to in the GTAP. These data were complemented by national SAM where they were absent from the GTAP.[2] To ensure comparability between the two datasets, we aggregated the input-output tables into eight broad sectors. The SAMs include information on the inter-industry linkages as well as final demand. Here, we define the key variables used in our analysis.

Our measure for backward spillover follows the traditional literature estimating spillovers from the foreign direct investment (FDI) (Caves, 1974; Javorcik, 2004). This literature uses the input-output structure of the economy to measure productivity spillovers to host countries from foreign firms. Following Javorcik (2004), we compute the proxy horizontal spillover to measure the exposure to innovative firms that produce product and process innovations in the same sector. This variable is computed as the share of outputs from innovator firms to the total sector output. Specifically, it is written as follows:

$$Horizontal\, INNOV_{jt} = \frac{\Upsilon_{jt}^{f}}{\Upsilon_{jt}}, \tag{13.1}$$

Since we consider the spillover effect of innovation across sectors, it is important to measure the propagation effect of innovation to the other sectors of production. An example of potential propagation of innovation effects is found in an interesting study by Dietzenbacher (2000), where social accounting matrices are used to compute different measurements of economic influence of innovation in one sector. We follow a similar approach and use the social accounting matrices to compute four measures of economic influence, namely, backward and forward linkages, as well as the self-induced effects in inputs and outputs. Then, we build the following proxies for potential propagation of innovation effects as:

$$Backward\, INNOV_{jt} = \sum_{k} \alpha_{kj}^{IO}\, Horizontal\, INNOV_{jt}, \tag{13.2}$$

$$Horizontal\, INNOV_{jt} = \sum_{k} \beta_{kj}^{IO}\, Horizontal\, INNOV_{jt}, \tag{13.3}$$

$$Self-input\, INNOV_{jt} = \sum_{k} \gamma_{kj}^{IO}\, Horizontal\, INNOV_{jt}, \tag{13.4}$$

$$Self-output\, INNOV_{jt} = \sum_{k} \varphi_{kj}^{IO}\, Horizontal\, INNOV_{jt}, \tag{13.5}$$

where α_{kj}^{IO} and β_{kj}^{IO} represent backward and forward linkages, respectively. Likewise, γ_{kj}^{IO} and φ_{kj}^{IO} are self-induced input and self-induced output changes generated from a unitary injection in sector *k*. Here, *k* denotes the manufacturing sectors, and sector *j* is a firm's main sector of activity. Summary statistics suggest a large variation across sectors with innovation having high spillover effects in food and chemicals. Finally, we provide a correlation matrix of our measures of innovation spillover in Table 13.6. We find positive and statistically significant correlations in all of the cases. One key point to highlight is a lower correlation between self-input innovation and the other measures.

13.4 Empirical strategy

We aim to prove the hypothesis that the surge in firm survival in the African export market in recent years was not simply the result of external factors caused by improvement in the business climate and macro-prudential policies in the 2000s. Rather, it can also be attributed to the marked and rapid adoption of innovation technologies, which is favored by high propagation, as evidenced

Table 13.6 Correlation matrix

	Self-induced percentage change	*Self-induced percentage change*	*Weighted backward linkage*	*Weighted forward linkage*
Self-induced percentage change	1			
Self-induced percentage change	0.71***	1		
Weighted backward linkage	0.81***	0.42***	1	
Weighted forward linkage	0.75***	0.48***	0.98***	1

Source: Calculations based on GTAP database, Purdue University.

by the sharp increase in the inter-industry linkages within countries. The basic approach is thus to regress the firm survival on a set of indicators for each type of innovation, as expressed in Equation 13.6.

$$Survival_{jt} = \mathbf{X}_{jt}\beta + \varepsilon_{jt}, \tag{13.6}$$

where *Survival* represents the survival of firms relative to exit, and $\mathbf{X}_{jt}$ is a vector of innovation types. The prediction is that the β in Equation 13.6 is positive, so technological innovation leads to firm survival. However, we cannot identify the impact of innovation by simply comparing innovation activities with survival and not survival status straightforwardly. The first issue is related to nonrandom selection into export as survival, and exit in the export market is observed only for firms who choose to export. Second is the issue of endogeneity and reverse causality due to the fact that innovation output might be a result of internal choices made by firms, or it might be that innovation embeds the use of certain types of new technologies that firms choose to introduce when they judge that it will spur innovation more than other technologies. Last is the issue of data quality. The WBES includes many subjective variables which are measured with error or without precision. This introduces an error-in-variables problem, which will likely cause endogeneity of innovation outputs in the production function (Mairesse & Mohnen, 2010). The ideal dataset for studying the issues discussed in our identification strategy is a longitudinal dataset covering a long period of time, while at the same time containing information on innovation inputs and outputs, market structure and competition, and information to correct for firm-specific effects. Unfortunately, such data is scarce or is not readily available for much of Africa. In lieu of longitudinal data, we built a panel dataset with few successive waves that partially satisfy these requirements using the WEBS. One advantage of the WEBS is that it contains qualitative information well suited to study the dynamics of innovation.

Our estimation approach builds on the work of Crepon et al. (1998), with two important points of departure. The Crepon, Duguet, and Mairesse (CDM) framework is a structural model that jointly analyzes the relationship between investment in knowledge and productivity by linking knowledge inputs (such as R&D and ICT adoption) to innovation outputs and innovation outputs to productivity. The idea behind the model is that innovation input affects firm performance through the generation of knowledge, also called innovation output. The basic version of the CDM structural model has three components: (1) the knowledge equation (or innovation input equation), which aims at estimating the determinants of R&D; (2) the innovation outcome equation; and (3) the productivity equation, which also depends on innovation outcomes. The structural specification of the CDM makes it possible to correct for selectivity and endogeneity as well as make good use of both quantitative and qualitative variables provided in the innovation surveys (Hall & Mairesse, 2006). As such, the CDM model is well fitted to the type of data we have, i.e., panel data with a very small number of successive waves, firms without R&D that innovate, and several qualitative variables.

Our structural model sits on four components, as shown in Equations 13.7a–13.7e. The primary identification challenge is that firms do not decide to innovate randomly. Firms' decision to innovate depends on both its internal practices and the external environment, but the literature has generally highlighted the importance of R&D efforts, firm size and competition pressure, and foreign ownership, among others (Baldwin & Hanel, 2003; van Beers, Kleinknecht, Ortt, & Verburg, 2008). We start by looking at the determinants of technology adoption, which govern the self-decision of firms to select (or not) a certain type of technology. We write the technology adoption equation of firm in Equation 13.7a, where *ict* is a dummy variable for reported technology adopted by firm i in industry j and during time period t. x'_{1ijt} is a vector of the predetermined firm-level characteristics and the environment in which the firm operates. Firm characteristics include variables such as firm size and ownership, competition pressure, exporter status, and location. We then analyze the determinants of innovation in Equations 13.7b and 13.7c, through which the ICT adoption variable and other factors feed into the different types of innovation outcomes to address endogeneity concerns regarding those correlation patterns. We estimate two equations: one with the product innovation as the dependent variable, and one with process innovation as the dependent variable. The estimated equation includes technology adoption as inputs in addition to other control variables, such as firm size, market structure, foreign ownership, and the quality of the workforce. The last component connects innovation outcomes to firm survival. Once we have obtained the estimation of the innovation outcomes as a function of innovation inputs in Equations 13.7b and 13.7c, we need to determine how innovation affects firm survival. Firm i chooses the type of innovation that improves productivity and survival. Firms can adopt product innovation or process innovation. Similarly, firms can adopt two types of innovation when they believe that the two types of innovations are complementary. We estimate two versions of the survival equation: one that control for sales growth, and one that controls for employment growth.

$$ict_{ijt} = x'_{1ijt}\beta_1 + \mu_{1ijt}, \tag{13.7a}$$

$$produc\_in_{ijt} = ict_{ijt} + x'_{2ijt}\beta_2 + \mu_{2ijt}, \tag{13.7b}$$

$$process\_in_{ijt} = ict_{ijt} + x'_{3ijt}\beta_2 + \mu_{2ijt}, \tag{13.7c}$$

$$survival_{ijt} = produc\_in_{ijt} + process\_in_{ijt} + x'_{4ijt}\beta_1 + \mu_{ijt}, \tag{13.7d}$$

$$exporter_{ijt} = \left(x'_{5ijt}\beta_1 + \mu_{ijt} > 0\right), \tag{13.7e}$$

The general procedure to estimate the CDM model had been to use asymptotic least squares, 3SLS, sequential 2SLS, or maximum likelihood (Lööf, Mairesse, & Mohnen, 2017). However, we follow a different approach. Instead of estimating the equations separately, we make use of the Stata's Extended Regression Model commands (StataCorp, 2017), which provide new features for fitting models with endogenous covariates, sample selection, and nonrandom treatment assignment. The model uses an equation sample selection (Heckman) model or the exporter and non-exporter. In the empirical analysis, we estimate several models based on the specification of the survival equation. Model 1 corresponds to the baseline regression, which only includes our innovation variables to capture the effect of innovation on firm survival without any covariates. Models 2 and 3 report the corresponding estimates for the three specifications, with controls for firm performance variables, such as sales growth and employment growth. Model 4 reports the model with interaction between product and process innovation to test for the complementarity effect. Models 5 and 6 present the results by two country sub-groups: non-resource-rich countries and fragile and conflict-affected countries. Since standards errors are likely correlated at the firm level, we cluster standard errors accordingly.

13.5 Innovation and firm survival

This section contains the empirical analysis of the determinants of technological innovation and its impact on firm survival in Africa. We exploit self-selection through the decision to adopt technologies and imitation that lead to technological innovation. We first consider the determinants of ICT adoption.

13.5.1 Determinants of ICT adoption

Table 13.7 reports the results from the estimations of Equation 13.7a, with ICT adoption, as opposed to non-adoption, as the dependent variable. Column 1 presents the basic results from ERM regression of the CDM model. We find that all firm-level characteristics and the environment in which the firm operates are

Table 13.7 Determinant of ICT adoption

	Model 1	*Model 2*	*Model 3*	*Model 4*	*Model 5*	*Model 6*
Panel A: Dependent variable is ICT adoption						
Firm size	0.1983***	0.1983***	0.1985***	0.1985***	0.1901***	0.2193***
Exporter status	–0.6591***	–0.659***	–0.659***	–0.659***	–0.6524***	–0.6842***
Foreign ownership	0.1716***	0.1721***	0.1712***	0.1711***	0.1703***	0.2068***
Competition	0.0275**	0.02755**	0.02707**	0.02705**	0.008454***	0.07699***
Larger city	–0.0236***	–0.0236***	–0.02393***	–0.02393***	–0.01169***	–0.03271***
Constant	0.0720	0.0719	0.0716	0.0716	0.05264***	–0.1063**
Panel B: Dependent variable is exporter status						
Firm size	.3518***	.3516***	.3521***	.3521***	.3449***	.3817***
Firm age	.02299**	.02316**	.02266**	.02265**	.0251*	–0.0106
Manager's experience	–.1511***	–.1515***	–.1521***	–.1521***	–0.1129	–0.0925
Credit constrained	–.2698***	–.2692***	–.2715***	–.2716***	–.2567***	–.2221***
Foreign ownership	.3543***	.3554***	.3525***	.3522***	.4002***	.4817***
Part of larger firm	–.1321***	–.1329***	–.1326***	–.1326***	–.1328**	–.2205**
Constant	–1.628***	–1.627***	–1.624***	–1.624***	–1.715***	–1.763***
Small control	No	Yes	Yes	Yes	Yes	Yes
Large control	No	No	Yes	Yes	Yes	Yes
N	2833	2833	2833	2833	1880	903
AIC	10382	10383	10375	10381	7235	3478
BIC	10405	10413	10392	10416	7251	3487

Notes: The marginal effects are estimated in Extended Regression Models with standard errors clustered at firm level. *** $p<0.01$, ** $p<0.05$, * $p<0.1$.

important for adoption of ICT. The log of the number of employees, used as a measure of firm size, is significant and has a positive impact on a firm's decision to adopt ICT adoption. Empirical evidence generally supports a strong relationship between firm size and ICT adoption (Fabiani, Schivardi, & Trento, 2005; Hollenstein, 2004; Morgan, Colebourne, & Thomas, 2006). Consistent with the FDI and domestic spillover theories, foreign-owned firms are far more likely to adopt ICT practices than domestic firms. With regard to competition pressure, our results indicate that the presence of competitive pressure increases the probability of small and medium-sized enterprises (SMEs) adopting ICT. Our findings corroborate those of Bayo-Moriones and Lera-López (2007) and Dasgupta et al. (1999), among others, who find a positive and significant relation between competition pressure and ICT adoption. Surprisingly, export-oriented firms and firms located in business cities and capital cities are less likely to make use of ICT practices. One would expect the coefficient of business city and large city to be positive. However, the negative sign may imply that these cities are not technological frontiers as the literature highlights that location near the technological frontier is an important determinant of firm survival (Fontana & Nesta, 2009).

The results from both non-resource rich countries (column 5) and from fragile, conflict-affected countries (column 7) suggest that the effect of business cities and large cities on ICT adoption varies significantly by country groups. Though firms located in business cities and large cities are less likely to adopt ICT practices in fragile and conflict-affected countries, we see that the adoption of ICT practices is higher in businesses and large cities across non-resource-rich countries. These findings may be due to the high cost of purchasing and installing these technologies.

The ICT adoption portion of our model uses a sample selection equation model for the exporting decision. The results of estimating this model using the maximum likelihood with robust standard errors clustered on the firm are shown in panel B of Table 13.7. Overall, the estimation shows that the structural characteristics of firms are significant determinants of exporter status. Larger and older firms are more likely to be exporters. The magnitude of firm size seems to be larger in fragile and conflict-affected countries than in non-resource-rich countries. On the other hand, the link between firm age and exporting status does not appear to be statistically significant for firms in fragile and conflict-affected countries. Regarding the experience of the top manager, our results show that the manager's experience in the sector is statistically significant but negatively associated with exporting. There are many reasons for this. First, the age of the firm and the years of experience of the top manager might be both proxy for measuring the accumulation of experience in general in the sector but not the manager's export experience. For instance, Sala and Yalcin (2015) find that managers' international experience is equally important regarding the likelihood that the firm starts exporting as productivity and fixed costs are associated with exporting. Another reason might be that older and incumbent firms have learning advantages, due to their experience with previous generations of technology, and are more likely to focus on the domestic market, where gains are higher.

When running foreign-owned dummy variables against firm export behavior, we find that the effect is positive and statistically significant. This indicates that firms owned by foreigners are more likely to be exporters. Furthermore, the magnitude of the foreign-owned firms is larger in fragile and conflict-affected countries than in non-resource-rich countries, at magnitudes of 0.4817 and 0.4002, respectively. While the status of the proprietorship of a firm is a good measure of proprietorship in general, such a variable ignores the possibility that only plants might have export capability by exporting directly or indirectly through the headquarters. We therefore use a dummy of whether the firm is part of a larger company as an alternative measure of proprietorship. We find that firms that are part of a large company are less likely to be exporters. The variable of interest thus proves to be robust to changes in definition. Another interesting result from the export status regression is that access to finance appears to play an important role on explaining the export status. Our estimations indicate that credit-constrained firms are less likely to be exporters. This is in line with Muûls (2015), who finds that firms are more likely to be exporting if they enjoy lower credit constraints and stresses the importance of financial development for international trade. It is worth noting that the empirical literature at best provides mixed evidence of the association between credit constraints and firm export behavior, depending on countries and measurement (Stiebale, 2011; Todo, 2011). Our results also indicate great heterogeneity between countries, as we find larger magnitudes in non-resource-rich countries compared to fragile and conflict-affected countries.

13.5.2 Determinants of innovation

Table 13.8 panel A reports the results from the estimations of Equation 13.7b, with product innovation as the dependent variable. We find that the use of ICT practices is positive but not statistically significant. On the other hand, we find that product innovation is also positively associated with being located in a larger city. We also find a strong association between competition and product innovation. The link between firm size and product innovation is positive but not statistically significant. Similarly, foreign-owned firms are insignificantly more likely to introduce product innovation. An inadequately educated workforce appears to be the only variable negatively related to product innovation. That is, firms perceiving an inadequately educated workforce as a major constraint have a lower likelihood of introducing new product innovation.

Now we turn our attention to the determinant of process innovation. Table 13.8 panel B shows our estimation results, with process innovation as the dependent variable. We find that the effect of ICT adoption on process innovation is statistically significant and positive in all specifications. This indicates that firms that adopt ICT practices are significantly more likely to introduce new processes of production or significantly improve the existing ones. Comparison of the results in panels A and B suggests that ICT adoption yields a higher effect of the likelihood to introduce process innovation than product innovation. The estimated effect of product innovation is between 0.2894 and 0.2950 percentage

Table 13.8 Determinant of technological innovation

	Model 1	*Model 2*	*Model 3*	*Model 4*	*Model 5*	*Model 6*
Panel A: Dependent variable is product innovation						
ICT adoption	0.2892	0.2894	0.2946	0.2950	0.3398	0.4380
Inadequately educated workforce	–.01847**	–.01845**	–.01849**	–.01853**	.05166***	0.0210
Firm size	0.0655	0.0654	0.0649	0.0648	0.0755	0.0976
Competition	.1814***	.1814***	.1798***	.1798***	.2241***	.1261**
Foreign ownership	0.0624	0.0627	0.0611	0.0606	0.0896	0.1921
Larger city	.06596***	.06599***	.0653***	.06554***	.244*	.238*
Panel B: Dependent variable is process innovation						
ICT adoption	.8204***	.8204***	.8307***	.8293***	.9435***	1.372***
Inadequately educated workforce	–.01379**	–.01385**	–.01422***	–.01414***	.05656*	0.0006
Firm size	0.0406	0.0402	0.0388	0.0392	.05948***	–0.0810
Competition	0.0650	0.0655	0.0634	0.0630	.1361*	–0.0345
Foreign ownership	–.2113*	–.2114*	–.2132*	–.2132*	–0.1750	–.3563*
Larger city	.129*	.1295*	.1284*	.1282*	.269***	.2448***
Small control	No	Yes	Yes	Yes	Yes	Yes
Large control	No	No	Yes	Yes	Yes	Yes
N	2833	2833	2833	2833	1880	903
AIC	10382	10383	10375	10381	7235	3478
BIC	10405	10413	10392	10416	7251	3487

Notes: The marginal effects are estimated in Extended Regression Models with standard errors clustered at firm level. *** $p<0.01$, ** $p<0.05$, * $p<0.1$.

points, meaning that the upper bound for product innovation is lower than the lower bound for process innovation. This implies that ICT adoption is the strongest predictor of process innovation. Consistent with the product innovation model, we find that firms located in larger cities are more likely to introduce process innovation, whereas the effect of an inadequately educated workforce reduced the likelihood of introducing process innovation. Competition and firm size also have a positive but not statistically significant effect. Finally, our results indicate that foreign-owned firms are more likely to introduce new process innovation, especially in fragile and conflict-afflicted countries.

13.5.3 The impact of innovation on firm survival

Now we extend the analysis to explore whether product or process innovation plays a role in determining firm survival. Table 13.9 reports the results from the probit estimations. Overall, we find that innovative firms are more likely to survive than non-innovative firms are. The results indicate that product innovation is positively associated with firm survival. It is worth noting, however, that the coefficient of product innovation remains unchanged with respect to the findings in column 1. We also find that process innovation is positive and statistically associated with firm survival. Our findings appear to be consistently robust across different specifications. The magnitude of this coefficient would seem to suggest that process innovation is more important for firm survival than product innovation.

Table 13.9 Determinant of firm survival

	Model 1	*Model 2*	*Model 3*	*Model 4*	*Model 5*	*Model 6*
Product innovation	.05992***	.0599***	.04914***	.05609**	0.0159	–0.1698
Process innovation	.2575***	.2641***	.2606***	.2369**	.1425***	0.3724
Product innovation # Process innovation				0.0197		
Constant	19.8900	21.1700	18.17*	17.74*	9.8400	23.8900
Small control	No	Yes	Yes	Yes	Yes	Yes
Large control	No	No	Yes	Yes	Yes	Yes
N	2833	2833	2833	2833	1880	903
AIC	10382	10383	10375	10381	7235	3478
BIC	10405	10413	10392	10416	7251	3487

Notes: The marginal effects are estimated in Extended Regression Models with standard errors clustered at firm level. *** $p<0.01$, ** $p<0.05$, * $p<0.1$.

One natural question in this context is whether there is a complementarity in introducing both types of innovation. To explore this possibility, our estimation strategy is to introduce an interaction between product and process innovation. The results of the model with interaction (column 4) yield interesting results. We find that the interaction term is positive, albeit small in magnitude and statistically not significant. This implies that there is a certain complementarity effect between the two types of innovations. While the point estimate of product innovation is smaller than in the previous specifications, the joint effect with the interaction term indicates that product innovation yields a higher probability for surviving in the presence of process innovation than otherwise. This suggests that the joint effect of product and process innovations contributes positively to firm survival. The finding regarding the interaction effect between competition and product innovation is particularly interesting in light of the revived discussion of industrial policy and regional integration efforts in Africa.

13.6 Mechanisms

In the preceding section, we explored the significant increase in the survival of African firms in the export market, and this change was likely caused by the introduction of product and process innovation. As predicated by our structural model, this finding is linked to the decision to adopt innovation inputs such as ICT technologies. However, the decision to innovate is not the only explanation for increased firm survival. Imagine that the government implements policies that increase the vertical integration of firms within the value chain so that it enables smooth upstream and downstream flow of know-how from innovative firms to non-innovative firms and increases the overall firm survival. Some pieces of evidence also point to this explanation. First, we have documented that controlling for country-level firm characteristics should reduce the magnitude of product and process innovations. Second, we also find that both product and process innovation interaction positively (but not significantly) affect firm survival. Third, allowing innovation to depend on technology adoption, we find that ICT adoption does not increase product innovation but only process innovation. Instead, we find that firm location and credit constraints have larger effects on product innovation. In this section, we present some additional analyses designed to provide insight into what may lead to these differences.

To understand the ways in which innovation improves firm participation and survival in exports, we explore the potential propagation effect. Previous work has shown that economic structure and linkages are strongly associated with the propagation effects of innovation. In this section, we estimate the effect of four propagation proxies on the innovation indicators by linking the WBES data and social accounting matrices data. We extend the model presented in Equations 13.7a–13.7e to include the variables reflecting the propagation effect of innovation through backward and forward linkages as well as self-induced effects in inputs and outputs. Results from the regression analysis with the full set of controls show that the backward propagation effects of innovation are positive and significant for both firm entry and survival, meaning that higher backward spillovers of innovation increase the probability of exporting and survival in the export market. The estimated coefficient is higher for entry than for survival, as 0.896 is compared to 0.142. With respect to forward propagation, we find that the coefficient for entry is highly positive and significant. The estimates for forward propagation are also positive and significant in the model of firm survival, but the magnitude of the coefficient is smaller. Our results demonstrate that the greater impact of forward propagation for entry is consistent with earlier findings that the effects of innovation were the greatest among the upstream sectors. This is particularly important, given that the concept of innovation as perceived by developing countries includes both radical innovators and simple imitators.

We next examine the propagation effects of innovation as measured by the self-induced changes. Column 5 in Table 13.10 contains the estimations of firm entry and shows that the marginal effect of self-induced output propagation is 1.821. Column 6 shows the estimates for export survival. This coefficient is smaller than for firm entry, as 1.821 is compared to 0.212. Finally, columns 7 and 8 contain the estimates for the self-induced input propagation. The pattern of the coefficient remains the same, but the coefficient in the model of export survival is not statistically significant. Nevertheless, these results consistently demonstrate that the propagation effects of innovation are important mechanisms through which innovation is likely to affect firm entry and survival in exports.

13.7 Conclusion

This study exploits export spells in different rounds of firm-level WBES panel data to explore the role of innovation in improving the export survival of African firms. The estimation of the CDM-type structural model that links innovation input and output and innovation output to firm survival addresses most concerns about the potential identification problems in estimating innovation as subjectively perceived by the firm. The remaining concerns about sample selection and reverse causality are addressed through the Stata Extended Regression Models. We establish empirically that product and process innovation lead to firm survival of African firms, highlighting the role of ICT technology adoption in generating process innovation. The evidence strongly suggests that the effect of process innovation is greater than product innovation, especially in fragile and conflict-affected countries. We then examine the complementarity in introducing both product and process innovation and find that the interaction term is positive but not significant. However, the combination of product innovation and the interaction term is greater in magnitude and jointly significant, meaning that product innovation may yield higher impact on firm survival when combined with process innovation. Our findings are qualitatively robust across country groups.

We then examine the mechanism through which innovation is likely to improve firm survival by combining firm-level data with sectoral information from the input-output tables. The data shows that inter-industrial linkages have

Table 13.10 Mechanism

	Entry *(1)*	*Survive* *(2)*	*Entry* *(3)*	*Survive* *(4)*	*Entry* *(5)*	*Survive* *(6)*	*Entry* *(7)*	*Survive* *(8)*
Backward propagation	0.896***	0.142**						
	(0.056)	(0.069)						
Forward propagation			1.156***	0.142*				
			(0.046)	(0.082)				
Self-induced output					1.821***	0.212***		
					(0.254)	(0.254)		
Self-induced input							1.174***	0.130
							(0.254)	(0.119)

Notes: The marginal effects are estimated in Extended Regression Models with standard errors clustered at firm level. *** $p<0.01$, ** $p<0.05$, * $p<0.1$.

drastically changed, which might have significantly improved the propagation of innovation across sectors. We find that the difference in economic linkages affects the propagation of innovation, whereas firm survival is higher in the presence of vertically integrated sectors within countries. The finding that the self-induced input and output appear to translate into a mechanism for innovation impacts on firm survival is also noteworthy, suggesting that policy for structural change matters in maximizing the effect of innovation.

Taken together, our results have significant implications for understanding the determinants of firm survival and the role of policy in fostering firm survival. The findings that product and process innovations have differential effects on firm survival suggest that some types of innovation are important during the stage of economic development, and their contribution to firm survival might change based on the direction and speed of structural transformation. Moreover, adoption of ICT might promote process innovation but not product innovation. A key policy priority should therefore be to design innovation policies that match the need of the industry and create competitive advantage. Finally, the mechanism of the propagation effect of innovation through economic linkages highlights the government's need to coordinate industrial policy to support firms that are successful and will survive.

Notes

1 See Sutton (1997) and Caves (1998) for a comprehensive theoretical and empirical discussion on the determinants of firm survival.

2 For countries which are not available in the GTAP, such as DRC, we use the data from 2013. Data from Rwanda is from 2014.

References

Baldwin, J. R., & Hanel, P. (2003). *Innovation and knowledge creation in an open economy: Canadian industry and international implications.* Cambridge: Cambridge University Press. https://doi.org/10.1017/CBO9780511510847.

Barrios, S., Görg, H., & Strobl, E. (2011). Spillovers through backward linkages from multinationals: Measurement matters! *European Economic Review*, *55*(6), 862–875. https://doi.org/10.1016/j.euroecorev.2010.10.002.

Bartelme, D., & Gorodnichenko, Y. (2015). Linkages and economic development. National Bureau of Economic Research Working Paper Series, No. 21251. https://doi.org/10.3386/w21251.

Bayo-Moriones, A., & Lera-López, F. (2007). A firm-level analysis of determinants of ICT adoption in Spain. *Technovation*, *27*(6), 352–366. https://doi.org/10.1016/j.technovation.2007.01.003.

Becker, S. O., & Egger, P. H. (2013). Endogenous product versus process innovation and a firm's propensity to export. *Empirical Economics*, *44*(1), 329–354. https://doi.org/10.1007/s00181-009-0322-6.

Bernard, A. B., Jensen, J. B., Redding, S. J., & Schott, P. K. (2012). The empirics of firm heterogeneity and international trade. *Annual Review of Economics*, *4*(1), 283–313. https://doi.org/10.1146/annurev-economics-080511-110928.

Brenton, P., Cadot, O., & Pierola, M. D. (2012). *Pathways to African export sustainability*. Washington, DC: World Bank.

Cadot, O., Iacovone, L., Pierola, M. D., & Rauch, F. (2013). Success and failure of African exporters. *Journal of Development Economics*, *101*, 284–296. https://doi.org/10.1016/j.jdeveco.2012.12.004.

Caves, R. E. (1974). Multinational firms, competition, and productivity in host-country markets. *Economica*, *41*(162), 176–193. https://doi.org/10.2307/2553765.

Caves, R. E. (1998). Industrial organization and new findings on the turnover and mobility of firms. *Journal of Economic Literature*, *36*(4), 1947–1982.

Cho, Y., & Honorati, M. (2014). Entrepreneurship programs in developing countries: A meta regression analysis. *Labour Economics*, *28*, 110–130. https://doi.org/10.1016/j.labeco.2014.03.011.

Crepon, B., Duguet, E., & Mairesse, J. (1998). Research, innovation and productivity: An econometric analysis at firm level. *Economics of Innovation and New Technology*, *7*(2), 115–158. https://doi.org/10.1080/10438599800000031.

Dasgupta, S., Agarwal, D., Ioannidis, A., & Gopalakrishnan, S. (1999). Determinants of information technology adoption: An extension of existing models to firms in a developing country. *Journal of Global Information Management*, *7*(3), 30–40. https://doi.org/10.4018/jgim.1999070103.

Dietzenbacher, E. (2000). Spillovers of innovation effects. *Journal of Policy Modeling*, *22*(1), 27–42. https://doi.org/10.1016/S0161-8938(97)00107-5.

Fabiani, S., Schivardi, F., & Trento, S. (2005). ICT adoption in Italian manufacturing: Firm-level evidence. *Industrial and Corporate Change*, *14*(2), 225–249. https://doi.org/10.1093/icc/dth050.

Fontana, R., & Nesta, L. (2009). Product innovation and survival in a high-tech industry. *Review of Industrial Organization*, *34*(4), 287–306. https://doi.org/10.1007/s11151-009-9210-7.

Grimm, M., & Paffhausen, A. L. (2015). Do interventions targeted at micro-entrepreneurs and small and medium-sized firms create jobs? A systematic review of the evidence for low and middle income countries. *Labour Economics*, *32*, 67–85. https://doi.org/10.1016/j.labeco.2015.01.003.

Hall, B. H., & Mairesse, J. (2006). Empirical studies of innovation in the knowledge-driven economy. *Economics of Innovation and New Technology*, *15*(4–5), 289–299. https://doi.org/10.1080/10438590500512760.

Halpern, L., & Muraközy, B. (2012). Innovation, productivity and exports: The case of Hungary. *Economics of Innovation and New Technology*, *21*(2), 151–173. https://doi.org/10.1080/10438599.2011.561995.

Hayashi, F., Li, B. G., & Wang, Z. (2015). Innovation, deregulation, and the life cycle of a financial service industry. IMF Working Paper No. 15-08.

Hollenstein, H. (2004). Determinants of the adoption of Information and Communication Technologies (ICT): An empirical analysis based on firm-level data for the Swiss business sector. *Structural Change and Economic Dynamics*, *15*(3), 315–342. https://doi.org/10.1016/j.strueco.2004.01.003.

Hopenhayn, H. (1994). The shakeout. University of Rochester Working Paper.

Javorcik, B. S. (2004). Does foreign direct investment increase the productivity of domestic firms? In search of spillovers through backward linkages. *American Economic Review*, *94*(3), 605–627. https://doi.org/10.1257/0002828041464605.

Jovanovic, B., & MacDonald, G. M. (1994). The life cycle of a competitive industry. *Journal of Political Economy*, *102*(2), 322–347. https://doi.org/10.1086/261934.

Klepper, S. (1996). Entry, exit, growth, and innovation over the product life cycle. *The American Economic Review, 86*(3), 562–583.

Lederman, D., Olarreaga, M., & Zavala, L. (2016). Export promotion and firm entry into and survival in export markets. *Canadian Journal of Development Studies/Revue canadienne d'études du développement, 37*(2), 142–158. https://doi.org/10.1080/02255189.2016.1131671.

Lööf, H., Mairesse, J., & Mohnen, P. (2017). CDM 20 years after. *Economics of Innovation and New Technology, 26*(1–2), 1–5. https://doi.org/10.1080/10438599.2016.1202522.

Mairesse, J., & Mohnen, P. (2010). Using innovation surveys for econometric analysis. In B. H. Hall & N. Rosenberg (Eds.), *Handbook of the economics of innovation* (vol. 2, pp. 1129–1155). Amsterdam: North-Holland. https://doi.org/10.1080/10438599800000031.

McGowan, A. M., Andrews, D., & Millot, V. (2017). The walking dead? Zombie firms and productivity performance in OECD countries. OECD, Economics Department Working Paper No. 1372.

McKenzie, D., & Paffhausen, A. L. (2017). Small firm death in developing countries. World Bank, Policy Research Working Paper No. 8236.

McKenzie, D., & Woodruff, C. (2014). What are we learning from business training and entrepreneurship evaluations around the developing world? *The World Bank Research Observer, 29*(1), 48–82. https://doi.org/10.1093/wbro/lkt007.

Melitz, M. J., & Redding, S. J. (2014). Heterogeneous firms and trade. In G. Gopinath, E. Helpman, & K. Rogoff (Eds.), *Handbook of international economics* (vol. 4, pp. 1–54). Oxford: Elsevier. https://doi.org/10.1016/B978-0-444-54314-1.00001-X.

Morgan, A., Colebourne, D., & Thomas, B. (2006). The development of ICT advisors for SME businesses: An innovative approach. *Technovation, 26*(8), 980–987. https://doi.org/10.1016/j.technovation.2005.09.001.

Muûls, M. (2015). Exporters, importers and credit constraints. *Journal of International Economics, 95*(2), 333–343. https://doi.org/10.1016/j.jinteco.2014.12.003.

Pierce, J. R., & Schott, P. K. (2016). The surprisingly swift decline of US manufacturing employment. *American Economic Review, 106*(7), 1632–1662. https://doi.org/10.1257/aer.20131578.

Sala, D., & Yalcin, E. (2015). Export experience of managers and the internationalisation of firms. *The World Economy, 38*(7), 1064–1089. https://doi.org/10.1111/twec.12222.

StataCorp. (2017). *Stata Extended Regression Models reference manual: Release 15*. College Station, TX: Stata Press.

Stiebale, J. (2011). Do financial constraints matter for foreign market entry? A firm-level examination. *The World Economy, 34*(1), 123–153. https://doi.org/10.1111/j.1467-9701.2010.01306.x.

Sutton, J. (1997). Gibrat's legacy. *Journal of Economic Literature, 35*(1), 40–59.

Todo, Y. (2011). Quantitative evaluation of the determinants of export and FDI: Firm-level evidence from Japan. *The World Economy, 34*(3), 355–381. https://doi.org/10.1111/j.1467-9701.2011.01331.x.

van Beers, C., Kleinknecht, A., Ortt, R., & Verburg, R. (Eds.) (2008). *Determinants of innovative behaviour: A firm's internal practices and its external environment*. New York: Palgrave Macmillan.

Van Beveren, I., & Vandenbussche, H. (2010). Product and process innovation and firms' decision to export. *Journal of Economic Policy Reform, 13*(1), 3–24. https://doi.org/10.1080/17487870903546267.

World Bank Group. (2016). *Doing business 2016: Measuring regulatory quality and efficiency*. Washington, DC: World Bank.

14 Local and foreign-owned SMEs' contribution to industrial development through knowledge spillovers in Africa

The case of Tanzania

Jean-Claude Maswana and Hawa Munisi

14.1 Introduction

In many developing countries, in recent years, there has been a great increase in initiatives to promote the diffusion of technology for the sake of promoting industrial development. The literature on industrialization in low-income countries often addresses only large firms and capital flows while ignoring the movement of labor, such as that of foreign workers and host countries' returnee migrants. For instance, Akamatsu's theory of follower-country (Akamatsu, 1962) implicitly assumes that foreign investment (mostly by large firms) will flow to a low-cost country and thus use the local cheaper labor. While spillover effects generated by the presence of large foreign firms have been well documented in the literature, little is known of the case of spillovers associated with small foreign-owned or returnee-migrant-owned enterprises in developing countries. Importantly, unaddressed issues in this regard include two major observations.

First, as the result of increasing global labor mobility associated with globalization, there has been a growing presence of cheap Chinese labor inflows into, for instance, African countries. Most of these Chinese labor migrations into Africa have been linked to the creation of small enterprises in host countries. Although data to illustrate the magnitude of this global mobility is not available, it can be argued that this unprecedented trend may represent not only opportunities for industrialization but also challenges for the competitiveness of local African SMEs. In regions such as Africa, where SMEs are the largest contributors to GDP, there has been renewed interest in opportunities and risks brought about by the new global patterns of foreign investment.

Another unaddressed issue is the crucial role of returnee migrants in spreading technical knowledge. It has been shown, for instance, that returnee migrants represent an important source of capital, advanced technology, and new ideas, and that this has profound implications for China in regard to building national technological capability (Lin, 2010).

These unaddressed concerns are critical for the formulation of industrial policies at the firm level. It is obvious that the inability to acknowledge this concern has resulted in local industries being unable to enhance productivity despite repeated industrial policy efforts, "mainly because there was no emphasis on technological change at the firm level" (UNCTAD, 2015). Industrial policies, whether in traditional or new sectors, cannot be put in place without promoting technological upgrading and capacity at the firm level.

As the need for research in this area emerges, it has become crucial to study the potential for industrial development brought about by the aforementioned trends in the context of a typical African country, namely, Tanzania, in order to identify factors that promote technology adoption as well as those that hinder it.

Based on a descriptive and interview approach, implemented at the firm level in Tanzania, the present chapter attempts to infer technology spillovers happening as the result of international and returnees' interactions with the typical local SMEs, from the perspective of the traditional channels of technology transfer and industrial spillovers addressed in the literature. Specifically, it addresses how local enterprises interact with their counterparts owned by Tanzanian returnee migrants and those that are owned by Chinese-invested enterprises, and the potential of such interactions for the country's industrial policies. In a qualitative case-study approach via in-depth interviews, it attempts to acquire a basic understanding of how the global influence of foreign-owned and returnee-owned firms is helping or hindering one of the key components of industrial policies (e.g., technological upgrading of SMEs) in Tanzania.

The chapter is organized as follows: Following the Introduction, Section 14.2 presents the institutional environment, especially knowledge-enabling agencies and policies as well as a brief review of relevant literature. Section 14.3 looks at methodological considerations, and Section 14.4 describes the business environment in which SMEs operate, in terms of enabling and constraining factors. Section 14.5 presents case studies of firms based on the main conceptual channels of technology transfer. Section 14.6 discusses and interprets the findings, while Section 14.7 presents general conclusions.

14.2 Technology-enabling context and institutions for SMEs

In the context of Tanzania, small-scale enterprises are defined as those that have 5–49 employees, and medium-sized enterprises are defined as those with 50–99 employees. Generally, therefore, we use a working definition of an SME as a company with 6–99 employees (URT, 2002). One of the specific features of SMEs is the monopoly of managerial decisions made by the manager-owner regarding financial and economic power. Given that entrepreneurial activity involves both arbitrage of opportunities and exploitation of new opportunities created by the manager (Kirzner, 1973), the very purpose of any industrial policy is to act through the manager and employees so that the technical capabilities of the firm can be enhanced. This in turn contributes to productivity growth, job creation, and economic growth.

Regardless of a firm's technical capabilities and its job creation potential, its actual performance depends on whether it operates in an environment that enables technology upgrading or in one that hinders it. To better understand technology-enabling environments for SMEs, we start by giving an overview of Tanzania's performance based on the World Economic Forum's (WEF) Global Competitiveness Index (GCI). The GCI is an annual assessment of the factors that drive countries' productivity and prosperity. It details the performance of countries over a wide range of competitiveness factors, ranging from institutions and infrastructure to business sophistication and innovation. Although Tanzania remains among the lowest in terms of economic development, the country was ranked 116th in the GCI in 2016–2017, which, surprisingly, is above the average for Sub-Saharan African countries.

It is also interesting to note that Tanzania has a relatively good ranking when it comes to the innovation pillar of the GCI (75th) compared to its general ranking. The breakdown of the innovation pillar reveals a relatively poor human resources condition (availability of scientists and engineers), which is required for successful technology adoption triggered by foreign firms. It can be argued that this performance results from the policy objectives Tanzania has designed for the promotion of technology for SMEs. In this regard, it should be pointed out that the objective of Tanzania's 2003 SME development policy was "directed toward technology and promises to facilitate acquisition and adaptation of technologies as well as enhance networking between R&D institutions and SMEs in a bid to upgrade technologies to raise the productivity and competitiveness of the sector" (UNIDO, 2012).

Past experience in technology upgrading in developing countries has been associated with four types of institutions or agencies: (1) SME development agencies that aim for expansion of such enterprises in general, in which case, technical upgrading is seen as one step toward the goal and the agency plays the supportive role of information dissemination and technical training; (2) agencies that play a more active role in adjusting or localizing technologies sourced externally, to make them easy to adopt by local SMEs; (3) research institutions whose aim is to create new technologies and spread them to local SMEs; and (4) training agencies whose role consists of providing both technical and managerial knowledge to managers of SMEs, in addition to serving as "knowledge enablers."

The knowledge transfer activity for an SME may take place through a knowledge enabler which makes it easier for the SME to adopt a specific technology. A knowledge enabler can be a different firm in the network or an institution expressly designed for that role. In the context of Tanzania, institutions that constitute the main support framework for SMEs include the National Income Generation Program (NIGP); Pride Tanzania; Mennonite Economic Development Associates (MEDA), and the Industries Development Organization (SIDO). SIDO also aims to develop the small-industry sector in Tanzania, which is expected to fulfill a very wide range of functions, from policy formulation to direct support to industries, and to hands-on involvement in the establishment of SMEs in both rural and urban areas.

Among SIDO's activities are the establishment of technology development centers, training, rent/purchase schemes for equipment, technology development, technology transfer through twinning arrangements, and exchanges with industries in Europe and Asia. More importantly, SIDO has a Business and Technology Incubator Program, which is a service center that aims to support entrepreneurs who have innovative and creative business or industrial ideas by nurturing them to develop their ideas to the level of commercial business undertakings. The incubator provides entrepreneurs with work premises, technical advice, access to information through an information and communications technology (ICT) facility, and financial support through loans, along with other business development services on demand, in order to enable a smooth start, growth, competitiveness, and sustainability of enterprises (UNIDO, 1999).

Private-sector institutions have also been promoting membership with the aim of strengthening capacity. One such organization that supports small industries is TAFSIO, the Tanzanian Federation of Small Industries Organizations (UNIDO, 1999). Other key organizations for the promotion of industrial development are the Tanzania Engineering and Manufacturing Organization (TEMDO), the Center for Agricultural Mechanization and Rural Technology (CAMARTEC), and the Technology Development and Transfer Centre of the University of Dar es Salaam, as well as the Tanzania Industrial Research Development Organization (TIRDO). The latter organization has three main objectives: (1) provision of training, extension, and advisory services to the industry; (2) carrying out applied research and prototype development; and (3) technology transfer to the industry for commercial purposes. Finally, there is the Confederation of Tanzanian Industries (CTI), whose mission is "to advocate for a conducive business environment and provide excellent value adding services to enhance competitiveness and profitability of the manufacturing and service industries through dedicated efforts and innovative solutions" (UNIDO, 1999).

In order to coordinate the R&D strategy and policy, Tanzania set up the Commission for Science and Technology (COSTECH) in 1986, which operates under the ministry which is responsible for science and technology and has the general objective of coordinating science and technology activities in the country. Specifically, COSTECH has been tasked to promote, coordinate, monitor, and evaluate scientific research and technology development and technology transfer activities. Also, COSTECH is responsible for acquiring, storing, and disseminating scientific and technological information and popularizing science and technology.

The aforementioned institutional setting in Tanzania accommodates various theories of technological development, especially those on the central role attributed to entrepreneurship in the process of economic growth. In the Solow model (1956), growth comes from new and larger plants (economies of scale), while in the Romer model (1990), it comes from new and growing firms (knowledge spillovers). Acs Braunerhjelm, Audretsch, and Carlsson (2009) illustrate the many ways in which knowledge spillovers drawn from investment in research generate opportunities for entrepreneurs. The presence of new firms serves as an indicator of entrepreneurship that leads to higher economic growth and productivity, higher employment, and more technological innovations (Klapper, Amit, Guillén, & Quesada, 2007).

Nevertheless, it should be admitted that in relation to technology, traditional SMEs (as opposed to technology-based SMEs) tend to treat technology as a contingency, something that appears suddenly and needs to be dealt with if it cannot be avoided. A major concern is the reluctance of SME managers to face technology-related problems in a proactive way. This is perhaps one of the reasons for the lack of demand for technology brokerages. This fact must be taken into account by public agencies when promoting technology transfer to SMEs (Albors, Sweeney, & Hidalgo, 2005). It is also a key success factor for agencies that aim to support technical upgrading in SMEs. There are three major factors that influence an SME's aspiration to adopt technical upgrading: (1) the owner's previous work experience and related professional capacities developed over a period of years (Romijn & Albaladejo, 2002); (2) the attributes of the owner, particularly his/her attitude toward risk and capacity for taking risks (Hadjimanolis, 2000); and (3) the extent of the SME's network. Networks enable SMEs to access resources and to share their risks and costs (Gronum, Verreynne, & Kastelle, 2012).

Before proceeding further, some definitional matters should be clarified. First, industrial policy can be seen as a policy selection mechanism that targets particular industries, or even firms, over others in terms of market signals, usually to enhance efficiency and promote productivity growth of the targeted industries while managing those that are declining (Chang, 2011). Resources (e.g., human and capital) of declining industries or firms can be put to use in new types of activities if the required technology is available.

Second, technology is defined by Stewart (1977) as "skills, knowledge and procedures required for making, using and doing useful things. Technology, therefore, includes the software of production—managerial and marketing skills—and extends to services: administration, health, education and finance." Obviously, defining technology is a complex endeavor, which in turn is reflected in the way SMEs acquire technology. Moreover, it has also been recognized that the ability of SMEs to understand and acquire new technology matters a great deal (e.g., Komoda, 1986). Technology acquisition requires pre-existing technical capabilities on the part of the recipient firm or nation, in the same way that seeds require fertile soil to flourish. In sum, for SMEs to acquire or be effective in their pursuit of technology acquisition, there must also be capabilities such as a learning environment. The learning process is a very important element in the technology acquisition process.

This understanding of "technological capabilities" has implications for the way that knowledge and technology can be acquired. In contrast to a physical product, technology cannot easily be transferred to a firm or a developing country without the active learning of related management and production processes. Thus, the mere provision of equipment, operating instructions, designs, or patents will not guarantee the effective use of the technology without the presence of adequate capabilities within the recipient organization (Szogs, 2010).

Ideally, technology acquisition should involve adaptation by the recipient firm, especially in the way the firm participates in or co-develops the technology. In the traditional and limited view, technology transfer is a one-way process—from donor to recipient—in which a benefiting firm obtains new technology from the donor through contracts, patents, license agreements, etc., and the technology is seen as hardware or a physical product. Relatedly, at the firm level, technology upgrading depends a great deal on the creativity and intuition of entrepreneurs, as well as on their ability to combine existing technical knowledge in order to develop new products or, perhaps more often, to adapt existing products to the specific needs of particular market niches (Buratti & Penco, 2001).

In the context of African countries, the extent to which a local SME can capitalize on technology upgrading via a network in its neighborhood depends on its initial conditions or absorptive capacities (Cantner & Pyka, 1998). The initial conditions of a domestic firm (i.e., the strength of its absorptive capacity and its ability to affect performance) play a crucial role in reaping the benefits of available technologies in the immediate environment of that firm.

The empirical literature has identified three dimensions of absorptive capacity (technology, networks, and human factors) which have been found to have a moderate effect on firm performance. Consequently, with high absorptive capacity being a precondition for effectively reaping external spillovers, this finding could be interpreted to mean that the extent to which a firm can exploit SEZ-induced spillovers is likely to be limited. Perhaps more importantly, the observed synergistic effect further highlights the risk associated with limited absorption of SEZ-induced spillovers (Maswana & Davies, 2014).

14.3 Methodological considerations

This research used a case-study approach aimed at assessing technology spillovers between SMEs. In particular, the study attempted to detect enablers and barriers to technology transfer between typical locally owned SMEs and foreign-owned/returnee-owned SMEs in Dar es Salaam in Tanzania. The main tool used in data/information collection is in-depth interviews in addition to the World Bank's Enterprise Survey.

We conducted six case studies and some additional company interviews for this study. Additional information was gathered from background interviews with industry actors (e.g., COSTECH and SIDO) and policymakers in Dar es Salaam. These discussions provided insightful background information on the studied phenomenon, helped to focus the study, and aided in drawing policy conclusions. The participants were selected from three categories of SME owners: returnee migrant owners, local owners, and Chinese owners.

The design of the interview questions follows the technology-transfer literature, which basically posits that the presence of SMEs owned by foreigners or returnee migrants may affect local firms through several mechanisms: imitation effects, technical information sharing, increased competition, and labor turnover. Specifically, channels such as supply, procurement, industry association membership, products, and management practices help local firms learn about new technology, new products, or new marketing techniques (Wang & Blomstrom, 1992). Local SMEs may hire workers who were previously employed and trained by foreign firms or returnee-migrant firms and thus have better knowledge of and experience with technology and business practices (Fosfuri, Motta, & Ronde, 2001). Furthermore, increased competition from foreign-owned and returnee-migrant-owned SMEs may induce local firms to reduce their inefficiencies and allocate more resources to learning from foreign-owned and returnee-migrant-owned SMEs and adopting new technology (Wang & Blomstrom, 1992).

Following these theoretical arguments, the questions outlined below were chosen as the core of the interview (not including non-exhaustive prompts and follow-up questions).

Questions asked of local firms:

- Does your firm interact with foreign SMEs or returnee-migrant SMEs? If yes, is this as a supplier or as a customer?
- Has your firm been receiving training from foreign partners? If so, have your employees put their learning into effect when back on the job?
- Were there noticeable and measurable changes in the activities and performance of the trainees when back in their roles?
- Did employees use the relevant skills and knowledge?
- Did employees demonstrate greater technical skills after interaction with foreign-owned/returnee-owned firms?
- Did the overall efficiency of the plant increase after interacting with foreign-owned/returnee-owned SMEs?
- Did the quality of manufactured products improve after the interaction/competition with foreign-owned/returnee-owned SMEs?
- Was the new software implemented after the foreign collaboration more effective than that which was previously used?
- Did the adaptability of the organization (i.e., its capacity to adjust to or update technical knowledge or products) increase as a result of interacting with foreign-owned/returnee-owned SMEs?
- Did the firm step up efforts to develop its own technology?

Questions asked of Chinese-owned or returnee-owned firms:

- Is the firm interacting with local SMEs? If yes, as a supplier or as a customer?
- Is there any exchange of technical knowledge (e.g., procedures, steps, quality, strategies)?
- Has the interaction with local firms met your expectations?
- Has your firm been able to apply knowledge learned from other SMEs?
- Was your firm able to transfer its learning to a local SME?
- Did your firm recommend some changes in the products, services, or raw materials provided by your supplier?

- Have you provided any technical training/explanation to any of your local partner SMEs?
- Did you see any improvement in your local partner SMEs after sharing technical knowledge with them? If not, what are possible reasons for that?

Some interviews were recorded, but the majority were not. Where recording was not possible because of technical issues or was not welcomed by interviewees, detailed notes were taken and interview notes were written up after the interview was complete. All interviewees agreed to speak to us on the basis of confidentiality and anonymity.

14.4 Business environment: Enabling and constraining factors

The assessment of the broad business environment's enabling and constraining factors was based on data from the Enterprise Surveys conducted by the World Bank (2018), which serve as indicators of various dimensions of technology use and innovation, including characteristics of the workforce employed in the non-agricultural private economy. The first set of indicators measures the extent to which firms invest in obtaining recognized certificates of production and accounting practices. Obtaining international quality certifications can open doors to technology and innovation and provide a sign of high quality that may open markets. The second set of technology-related indicators demonstrates the use of information and communications technologies (ICT) in business transactions. These technologies are important tools for all firms because they provide enterprises with the ability to reach international markets at low cost.

Another key indicator is employment growth. In general, the private sector in Tanzania, and its SMEs in particular, has experienced high employment growth. Between 2010 and 2012, the growth rate of employment in the private sector in Tanzania was 10 percent per annum. This is comparable to the annual growth rate between 2004 and 2006 (9 percent) and higher than the average for low-income countries and for all countries with ES data (6 percent). Small firms (with 5–19 employees) and medium-sized firms (with 20–99 employees) grew the fastest, adding jobs at annual rates of 11 percent and 10 percent, respectively. Large firms (with more than 100 employees) were also characterized by a positive dynamic, with an annual employment growth rate of 5.8 percent (Figure 14.1). Furthermore, real annual growth in sales by SMEs has been higher in Tanzania (23 percent) than in Africa overall (with an average of 19 percent).

A higher proportion of firms in Tanzania were exporting (directly or indirectly) in 2012 than in 2006 (14 percent vs 5 percent, respectively). During that period, the ratio of exports to total sales grew as well, from 2 percent in 2006 to 7 percent in 2012, which is close to the average for low-income economies and all countries with ES data. At the same time, growth in labor productivity has been around 25 percent, with small and medium-sized firms growing at a slightly higher pace than large firms. Moreover, foreign ownership (defined as at least

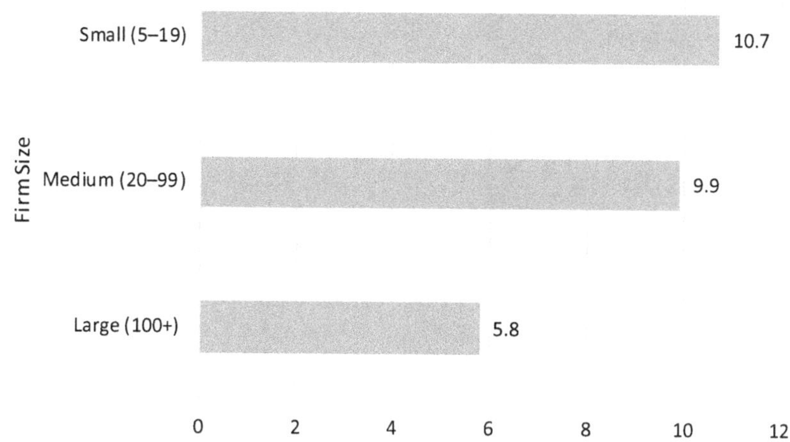

Figure 14.1 Annual employment growth (%)

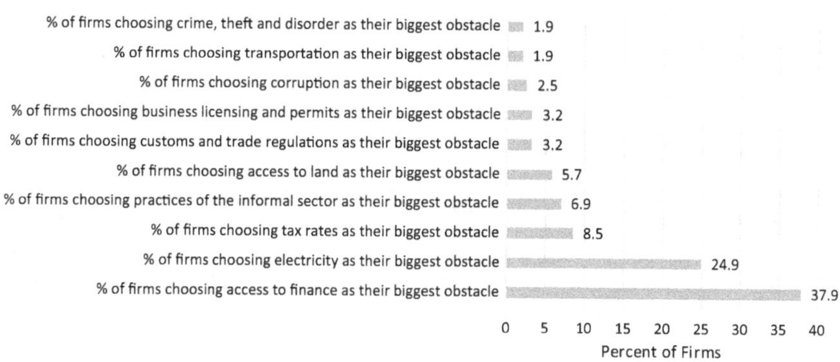

Figure 14.2 Ranking of the top business obstacles for firms

10 percent of foreign ownership) remains lower among SMEs (around 4 percent) than in large firms (around 16 percent).

The biggest obstacles faced by firms in their day-to-day operations are shown in Figure 14.2, the top three being access to finance, electricity shortages, and taxes.

Surprisingly, foreign content in production processes of SMEs in Tanzania is relatively higher than the overall average for Africa (52 percent). Roughly 60 percent of SMEs use material inputs and/or supplies of foreign origin (Figure 14.3). Also, a higher share of firms in Tanzania are using inputs of foreign origin than previously (48 percent in 2006 vs. 63 percent in 2012).

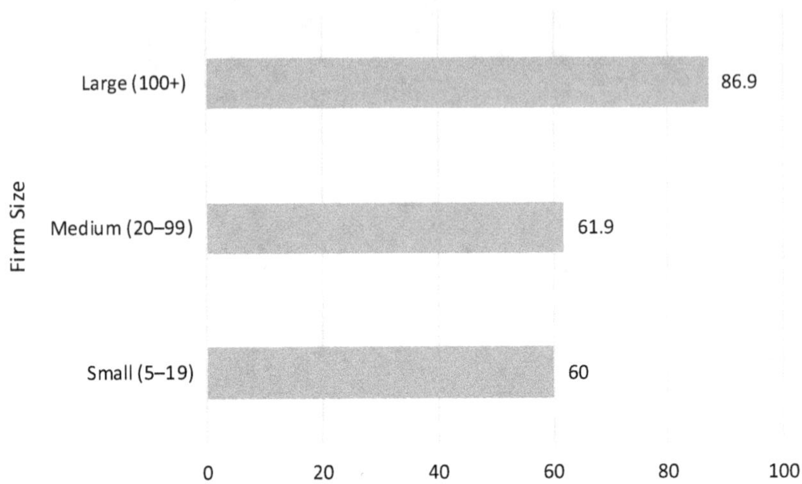

Figure 14.3 Proportion of inputs of foreign origin

Power supply in Tanzania improved between 2006 and 2012. The average number of hours without power in a month declined from 71 in 2006 to 58 in 2012. However, Tanzania still lags behind other countries. Globally, power outages occur for a total of 29 hours per month on average. The same pattern emerges regarding losses in sales due to electrical outages. On average, firms in Tanzania lost 5.5 percent of annual sales in 2012 on account of electrical outages, which is down from 7 percent in 2006 but still above the global average (2.6 percent). Furthermore, in Tanzania there is wide variation—from one region to another— in losses due to power outages, with the higher percentages of losses in Mwanza and Dar es Salaam.

The use of bank financing by firms in Tanzania is still limited by international standards. The proportion of firms that use banks to finance investment in Tanzania (21 percent) is higher than in other low-income countries but lower than the global average (25 percent). Furthermore, in 2012, around 17 percent of firms had a loan or a line of credit from a bank, compared to the averages of 20 percent for low-income economies and 34 percent for all countries with ES data. On the deposit side, fewer firms in Tanzania had a checking or savings account in 2012 (74 percent) than in 2006 (86 percent). Undercapitalization not only makes SMEs reluctant to invest in R&D but, more often, slows the pace of technological development through acquisition of external technologies.

Quite surprisingly, the proportion of firms identifying an inadequately educated workforce as a major constraint is quite a bit higher than the low-income country average of 30 percent. As seen in Figure 14.4, 38 percent of small enterprises and 47 percent of medium-sized firms indicate this workforce issue as a major constraint. Relatedly, as a remedy to this constraint, 27 percent of small enterprises

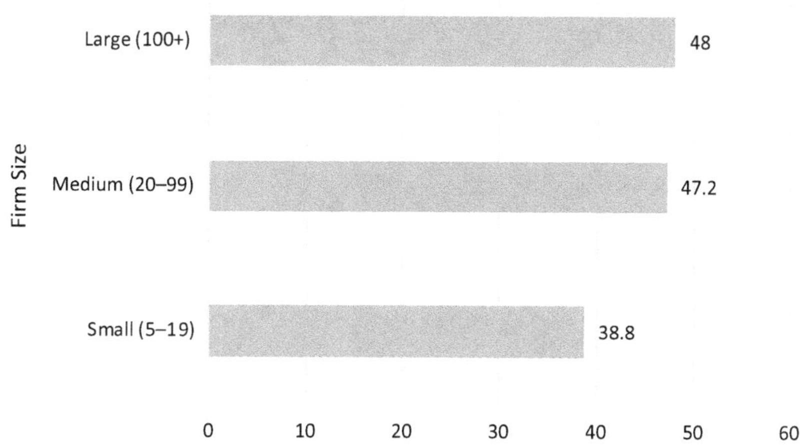

Figure 14.4 Inadequately educated workforce as a major constraint

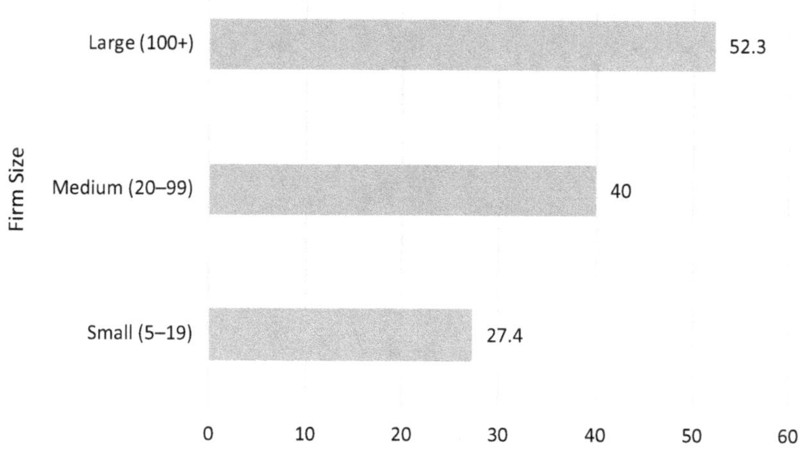

Figure 14.5 Formal training

offered formal training, compared to 40 percent in the case of medium-sized enterprises (Figure 14.5).

Also, the proportion of firms using technology licensed from foreign companies was around 5 percent for small enterprises and 16.5 percent for medium-sized firms. As expected, the proportion of firms that spend on R&D was around 10 percent among small enterprises and 16 percent for medium-sized enterprises, compared to 49 percent for large firms (Figure 14.6).

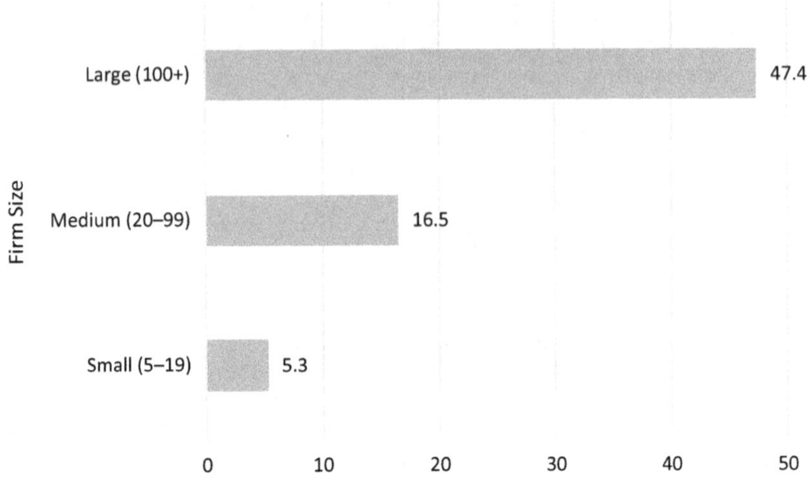

Figure 14.6 Use of foreign technology

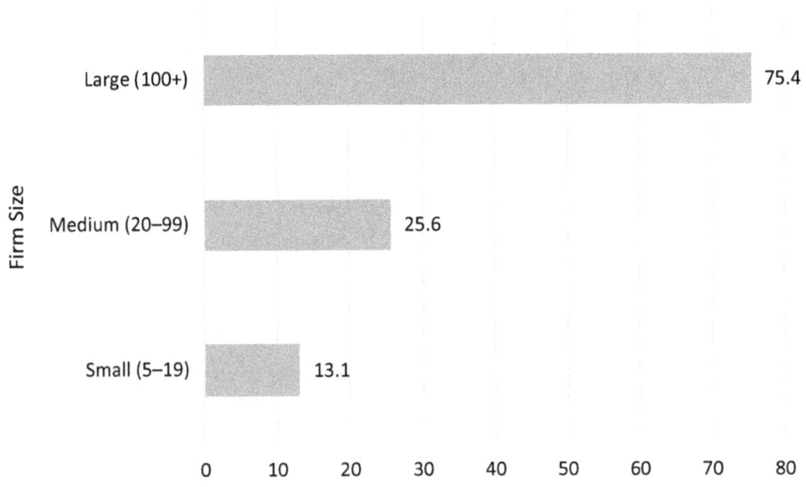

Figure 14.7 Internationally recognized quality certification

The share of firms with an internationally recognized quality certification is low: 13 percent for small firms and 25 percent for medium-sized firms, compared to 75 percent for large firms (Figure 14.7). This low level may undermine the reputation of SMEs or their brand and thus may discourage buyers, particularly in the export market.

In sum, the barriers and challenges encountered by SMEs in Tanzania are enormous. These challenges stem mostly from unpredictable electricity supply, stringent entry regulations, lack of knowledge and specialization, corruption, heavy taxation, limited access to investments and financing, persistent lack of efficient infrastructure, and outdated technology. In such a weak business environment, not only can SMEs not thrive and prosper, but they may not be able to capitalize on incentives offered as part of the country's industrial policies.

14.5 Case studies

To assess technology spillovers among SMEs from the perspective of industrial policies, in-depth interviews were conducted with six SMEs in Dar es Salaam in 2017–2018. Information obtained in those interviews is summarized below.

14.5.1 Happiness Furniture

Happiness Furniture is a family business, was established in 1997, and currently has 30 employees (7 Kenyans and 23 Tanzanians), of which 5 are in management positions. Happiness Furniture purchases machines from Kenya. The owner is a returnee from Kenya, where she lived for 25 years and was trained in the furniture business. Once she had enough capital, she returned home and brought the seven Kenyan experts with her.

New local employees get some informal training from the Kenyan experts employed by the company. The company does not interact with other local companies in the same business, so the transfer of knowledge, skills, and techniques from Happiness Furniture to other furniture businesses takes place through employees who leave the company to either establish their own firms or find employment with other companies.

The owner does not go back to Kenya or any other country for training. Only the Kenyan experts return to their homeland, which they do when their work visa expires and they must have it renewed. During their visit to Kenya, they often get in touch with other people in the profession. In this way, it is possible that these workers learn though their professional networks and upgrade their technology-related knowledge (often much more so than through any formal training). The interview with the owner also revealed that a culture of learning and co-operation is present among employees of this SME.

It was reported that managers are not aware of their company's technological needs. Even if they were, this SME has limited resources for upgrading of technology. This is largely due to the lack of information on alternative and the latest available technologies. Furthermore, the company does not co-operate with any specific providers of advice (business support agencies, consulting companies, universities, etc.) in this area. Another source of learning pointed out by the interviewee is through the customers (because of technological requirements of the customers that the company needs to meet). Lastly, the use of email and social media, libraries in which to carry out searches on technical details, and so on remains limited.

Finally, the interviewee was asked to identify the most pressing skills/competence deficits in her business. Accounting and quality control were mentioned as the biggest constraints, in addition to electricity shortages and employee turnover. Consequently, the frequent replacement of personnel has often led to considerable productive time wasted, since the owner has to train new employees instead of devoting time to other pressing tasks.

14.5.2 Speshoz

Established in 2012, Speshoz is a tailoring and dry-cleaning company with a workforce of 102 Tanzanian workers. The management team consists of only two people, a husband and wife.

By and large, the company does not interact with other local companies, so limited exchange of knowledge takes place via this channel. There has been a case of one employee quitting his job to start his own tailoring business, and this could be the only way knowledge has been transferred to other local companies. Also, the company hires both skilled and experienced workers but also candidates who are new to the art of clothing design and construction.

The company purchases machines and materials from China, which the owners frequently visit in order to select and purchase various materials but also to learn better and more modern ways of making clothes and to improve their designs. Nevertheless, cross-cultural relationships with the Chinese counterparts have been rather limited, and hence one of the inhibitors of managerial knowledge spillovers. Obviously, frequent and fluid communication, as well as cross-cultural understanding, are important elements that lead to knowledge spillovers. The company has a wide customer base in Tanzania, including celebrities, brides and grooms, as well as other members of wedding parties, and schools and companies that need uniforms.

Except for the use of email, the interview revealed little evidence of the use of websites, social media, or any other sources by employees to become informed of design details that are available. Some of the reasons for this are inadequate business processes, lack of knowledge of Internet usage, limited Internet connections, lack of trust and security in Internet usage, and computer maintenance costs.

The interview also revealed that certain social skills are also missing, especially the ability to transfer knowledge throughout the organization and a culture of learning and co-operation. Lastly, even though numerous business support organizations exist in Dar es Salaam, they are not perceived by Speshoz as being important players in the learning ecosystem.

14.5.3 National Estates & Designing Consultancy (NEDCO)

Established in 1968, NEDCO is a consulting company that provides services in the areas of design and supervision. It employs 27 full-time workers, plus 4 managers who are responsible for architecture, operations, and engineering, respectively. The company is located in Ada Estate, Kinondoni, in Dar es Salaam. In the past, two of the directors have sometimes worked in Kenya and Uganda. Currently, NEDCO is involved in joint ventures with both local and international firms (from Sweden, Italy, etc.).

The company has received training from foreign partners, mostly in software and expertise through a joint venture scheme. Fortunately, the company was able to detect noticeable and measurable changes in the activities and performance of the trainees when back in their roles in the company. Relatedly, employees demonstrate greater technical skills after interaction with foreign firms in that joint ventures help improve the possibility of being awarded contracts for future jobs.

Remarkably, thanks to the exposure to foreign designs and interaction with foreign/returnee-owned SMEs, the quality of manufactured products has improved. Overall, the adaptability of the organization (i.e., its capacity to regularly adjust or update technical knowledge or products) has increased to a certain extent.

Also, the firm stepped up efforts to learn and develop its own technology. Lastly, in terms of skills shortages, the interview revealed that employees lack management skills, especially in areas such as marketing and sales. Certain social skills are also missing, including the ability to transfer knowledge throughout the organization and a culture of learning and co-operation. However, employees have been active in online activities such as sharing business information, maintaining business relationships, and conducting business transactions.

14.5.4 Basix East Asia Ltd.

Basix East Africa, which focuses on security systems and drilling, was established in 2008, employs 25 workers, and is managed by 5 directors: one each for finance and human resources, sales, technology, and legal. Notably, the firm has been interacting with local SMEs, both as a supplier of CCTV cameras and as a user of multiple services provided by local SMEs. There is some degree of interaction and exchange of technical knowledge (e.g., procedures, steps, quality, strategies). The firm was initially owned by a US citizen; when it closed down in 2016, the new owner purchased the machinery and software from the original owner and had its employees stay on.

The firm provides technical knowledge to other SMEs, such as a local cigarette company that needed their expertise in setting up a lottery to promote their products. Importantly, experiences brought by the returnee manager have sometimes enabled him to provide technical advice to various local SMEs. Also, Basix East Africa Ltd. has been actively attracting managerial personnel with overseas training. For instance, one of the directors is a Harvard graduate, and another one, who is currently studying in Sweden, has brought knowledge that did not previously exist in the company. Through these experts, the company has expanded its market from previously offering security services only to individual customers to providing solutions to security services to other companies.

Basix East Africa was able to transfer its learning to a local SME in the form of an employee transfer. In addition to this, there have been cases of technical workers moving to establish their own businesses. Hence, this can be considered as a form of technical knowledge transfer. Recently, however, the company has not recommended any change in their products or services, or in the raw materials provided by suppliers. For large projects, such as providing traffic lights for the Zanzibar Ministry of Finance, they had to order from abroad. For small projects, they purchase locally. There has been no need for improvement, as machines that have been ordered from the company meet customers' requirements.

No specific activities have been provided to local SME customers, as training is provided only to fresh graduates employed by the company. Nevertheless, noticeable improvement in the sharing of technical knowledge with one local partner SME occurred after eight employees left Basix East Africa and joined another company, which enabled that company to get better jobs as a result of the knowledge received from those employees.

14.5.5 TTR Auto

Established in 2014, TTR Auto focuses on car updates, employs 15 full-time employees, and has two managers (a husband and wife). They train all their employees, and they focus on offering jobs to recovering addicts, former thieves, unemployed youth, etc.

The firm imports supplies, such as car lights and spanners, from other countries. Also, the managers have received, and continue to receive, special training in countries, such as Malaysia and Dubai. While visiting these countries, they would take an expert to lunch or dinner and use that occasion to update their knowledge. They look for special exhibitions in Dubai or Malaysia to target the kind of knowledge they seek to acquire. The ultimate outcome has been a noticeable and measurable change in the activities and performance of the managers, and the managers' improving technical skills have in turn attracted many young apprentices and interns interested in boosting their skills.

The firm has not yet done anything in the way of spreading their newly acquired technical knowledge around, although there have been numerous attempts by people from local SMEs, who have tried to approach them and make inquiries. Because of the bond built between the managers and their employees, very little in the way of technical details has been shared by the company's employees to others.

As to whether the company has been the recipient of recommendations for changes in the company's products or services, or in the raw materials provided from suppliers, the interviewee indicated that this was often the case with their Chinese suppliers of spare parts. Although the Chinese companies are potential sources of knowledge spillover via spare parts, spillovers of this type of knowledge are very limited on account of the specific nature of these supplies. For instance, most of the time spare parts are ordered according to specification, with no need to modify or improve them. This has rendered workers of the company passive intermediates rather than active co-developers of technologies embedded in those spare parts.

Some personnel from other local companies have tried to copy the work of TTR Auto, but its personnel are not willing to share their knowledge and techniques with other companies.

There was a lot of discussion in the key-informant interviews about the skills of which TTR Auto workers are lacking. The most cited were management skills, economic knowledge, and specific skills such as marketing and sales, in addition to a culture of learning and co-operation.

It should also be noted that while workers use email for interacting with partners, modern communications technologies do not influence the company's technical designs. The Internet has not been used as a source of technical ideas or details; it still operates in the traditional fashion, which consists of relying on the existing skills of workers rather than on their creativity or on improvements in its methods of repairing cars.

14.5.6 Spring City Enterprise

Spring City Enterprises is a car repair company that was established in 2002 and employs 45 workers, all Tanzanians. There are nearly 20 Tanzanian workers with certificates from VETA (a government vocational training institute), but they rarely stay. Sometimes they get offers from other companies, mostly Indian-owned ones. The machines it uses are mostly ordered from China. Initially, spare parts were imported, but in the past two years spare parts have been bought from local suppliers. Spring City Enterprises interacts with local SMEs mainly as a service provider. Sometimes other garages, such as those that use glass fibers, do not have certain skills and rely on local providers and a Kenyan competitor.

Rather than exchanging technical knowledge (e.g., procedures, steps, quality, and strategies), the garage outsources to other companies. The only actual exchange of technical knowledge takes place during the purchase of spare parts. Although there is no explicit exchange of knowledge with local SMEs, labor mobility is the largest form of sharing of technology-related knowledge. Other SMEs have improved as a result of the skilled workers from Spring City who have left to accept employment with other firms. Since its establishment, almost 300 youths have passed through the garage and acquired better skills than those that are available elsewhere in the Tanzanian market.

Information and communications technologies have no significant impact on the acquisition of knowledge by employees. In terms of changes in the company's products or services, or in raw materials provided by suppliers, there have been some cases of outsourcing in order to ensure that end products meet the expectations of customers.

Lastly, based on our interview, local organizations that support technical upgrading of SMEs are not seen as effective. The firm has been experiencing difficulties in finding a public agency that best suits its needs, and it has often been hampered by time-consuming administrative procedures.

14.6 Summary of findings

In general, our case studies indicate that the majority of the interviewed SMEs are young, have little experience, and often work far from the technological frontier. Nevertheless, most of them have been very successful in their respective business sectors. As expected, most of them have been experiencing high worker turnover, which means that labor mobility is the most effective mechanism of knowledge spillovers. The side effect of the high turnover is the disincentive for firms to provide training to their workers. Not surprisingly, interviews reveal that most SMEs neither design training plans nor document the training needs of their workers. There is no evidence of vocational training being organized either by management or by the workers, despite the reasonably high level of need for technical training. This is worsened by the lack of information on training possibilities reported by most interviewees. Linked to this was an issue that came up across all the case studies: workers' motivation and dedication to technical learning. More worrisome, the interviews also revealed that some workers are still desperately looking for employment elsewhere and consider their current employment as their last choice. Such an attitude inhibits employee effort as well as the SME's competitive stance.

The case studies also show that there is limited competition with Chinese-owned enterprises. The latter are rather used as enablers of technical progress, especially in their role as suppliers, that is, in their roles as explainers of technical specifications to local entrepreneurs. Furthermore, there was a lot of discussion in the key-informant interviews on the role played by Chinese SMEs. These interviews suggest that although Chinese-owned SMEs are potential sources of new technical knowledge, the spillover may be very limited because the local SMEs are primarily passive users of inputs provided by Chinese enterprises. Limited interactions with Chinese-owned enterprises may be a consequence of technological gaps combined with skills deficits in local SMEs. The institutional environment may not be conducive to synergistic links between local firms and Chinese-owned enterprises, in the sense that none of the existing industrial development agencies aims to help in establishing links between the two types of enterprises.

In addition to making use of advice provided by industrial development agencies, to some extent, the owners and entrepreneurs can upgrade their technology-related knowledge through their professional networks (which often include professionals from competing companies or from firms in other countries). Most interviewees considered these professional networks across borders to be a much better method of technical knowledge upgrading than any formal training. Customers are another important source of interaction with external bodies, because of the technological requirements of customers that a company has to meet.

Interactions for the purpose of technology upgrading have been rendered more challenging by the enormous skills deficits in SMEs. In this regard, participants were asked to identify the most pressing skills/competence deficits prevalent in

SMEs, including management skills, marketing and sales, creativity, accounting, and even concentration and patience. Therefore, to improve workers' technical skills, SMEs also need management skills, economic knowledge, specific skills such as marketing and sales, and certain social skills such as the ability to transfer knowledge throughout the organization, and a culture of learning and co-operation. The existing lack of these skills may be hindering the process of industrial development, which requires workers' willingness to take risks and the company's ability to manage complex processes.

The interviews also highlighted the international aspect of technical information sharing. In this regard, it was found that SMEs owned by returnee migrants are the ones that are more likely to upgrade their technical expertise. Importantly, there was a noticeable difference between typical locally owned SMEs and those owned by migrant returnees in terms of acceleration of technology diffusion and strengthening of links between foreign technical know-how and that of local SMEs. SMEs run by returnees as well as those that interact with Chinese/foreign counterparts are more likely to be aware of their technological needs than the typical local SMEs are. This advantage of SMEs managed by returnees is well exemplified in the case of Basix East Africa, where managers with a high level of education are more likely to transfer knowledge to their networks than firms whose managers have a relatively low level of education.

The aforementioned points hint at the reasons for the inability of most SMEs to take advantage of technical details that are available in the public domain, such as on the Internet. First, owing to their lack of scientific and technological knowledge, they have difficulty in engaging in science and technology networks of foreign-owned enterprises, such as those that are Chinese owned. Second, information and communications technologies are seldom used by workers for technical learning. These two observations are even more troublesome in a knowledge-based economy, as the Internet plays a strategic role in skills leveraging, the self-learning function, and the innovative capabilities of workers. Moreover, the Internet provides an efficient platform for e-learning that could be provided by industrial promotion agencies. This relates to the discussion about how interviewees see industrial development agencies.

Some SMEs have limited interaction with any specific industry-promoting agency. Often, SMEs have had to contend with a series of hurdles when it comes to finding the public agency that best suits their needs, and they often get lost in time-consuming administrative procedures. Hence these agencies are not perceived as important players in industrial development and technical knowledge transfer by some of the interviewed SMEs.

Consideration of the aforementioned factors begs the questions of how difficulties in the technological development of SMEs could be overcome and how sustained industrial development could be achieved. One solution could be assisted technology transfer (ATT). Prior to the implementation of ATT, SMEs should be made aware of their technology needs as well as the related skills deficits. It thus follows that to be successful and effective, industrial policies should lead to firms' awareness of their technological needs and of the existence and potential benefits of new technologies. Second, specific measures should be taken in the form of consultancy services, recruitment of university graduates and qualified personnel, awareness of new ideas and new technologies, incentive mechanisms and institutional frameworks for improving business-to-business collaboration through networks, and the creation of technology-based pilot projects.

Third, industrial agencies should provide general-purpose technology, such as the Internet, while also ensuring that more specialized agencies offer sectoral technical support in the form of either alleviating constraints facing SMEs (e.g., lack of financing and electricity shortages) or providing assistance in achieving specific goals (e.g., know-how to increase the export performance of products in which a prior technical improvement has occurred).

Fourth, there is a need for SMEs (those that are locally owned and their foreign partners) to co-develop technology themselves, rather than simply using it, and thus to further enable their creativity. This could take the form of SMEs promoting creativity in their workers by providing incentives such as bonuses and awards.

Ultimately, while industrial development strategies aim to develop high-technology sectors, stimulate job growth, and eradicate poverty, the characteristics of individual SMEs determine how their performance can be improved by technological development. Therefore, it should be clearly understood that a synergistic environment for industrial development led by technology upgrading rests with the SMEs.

14.7 Conclusion

In a case-study approach, this chapter outlined interviews of SMEs in Dar es Salaam and examined their technology spillover mechanisms from the perspective of industrial development. Major findings indicate that a supportive business environment for SMEs is still weak. On the whole, local SMEs have limited technical knowledge-related interactions with their counterparts owned by Tanzanian returnee migrants and with Chinese-invested enterprises. For this reason, the presence of foreign-owned and returnee-owned firms might not be helping in the technology upgrading of SMEs.

For the most part, entrepreneurs have little or no knowledge of how to upgrade technical capabilities of their firms, and many of them end up with failed businesses that could have been profitable but lack technology. In particular, SMEs could play a key role in Tanzania's industrial development if they were to overcome some of the constraints and limitations identified in this study, such as skills shortages, technical knowledge limitations, weaker absorptive capacity, financial constraints, and inability to capitalize on the knowledge base that exists in their network.

Under these circumstances, renewed attention should be directed toward overcoming some of the identified limitations of SMEs, such as through identification of their technology needs and strengthening of their exchange of information through networking. There is a need for a platform of knowledge-sharing for entrepreneurs so that they can better manage the accumulation of technical knowledge.

Another policy priority should be focusing on improving the financing of SMEs by developing venture capital and facilitating the accumulation of bank credit by SMEs for the specific purpose of enhancing their technical capabilities. Eventually, new financial instruments and leasing options should be made available to SMEs that have insufficient financial resources but are eager to finance a technology upgrading plan. Meanwhile, other initiatives to be considered include tax incentives for new activities; risk capital funds through either venture capital or a development bank for new high-risk activities; and a process of sector reviews to identify bottlenecks in individual sectors.

Of utmost importance should be the creation of technology-diffusion parks. These parks should offer a support program organized around three functions: (1) an information function that would present recent technologies in different target sectors to allow ownership by business owners; (2) the introduction of methods for tests and trials to be carried out in regard to adaptation of technologies by individual enterprises; and (3) support for companies that have successfully taken these steps and are in the process of increasing their markets and passing on their successes to their network partners.

It is important to realize that there is a need for SMEs themselves (those that are locally owned and those that are owned by foreign partners) to become involved in the country's design of industrial policy, which until now has essentially been designed by government officials alone, most of whom may lack an in-depth understanding of the constraints facing individual enterprises. SMEs are the most important stakeholders in technology upgrading and development of a successful industrial ecosystem in low-income countries such as Tanzania.

Going forward, technology development for SMEs needs to be modified to reflect the specific situation of Tanzania. This means that SMEs should be supported by policies oriented toward improving their business environment and developing their technical capabilities through local and global networks. As globalization is rapidly opening national markets to foreign medium- and small-sized enterprises, the success of industrial policies that aim to improve the competitiveness of locally owned firms depends, at least in part, on the effectiveness of initiatives to promote the diffusion of technology among SMEs.

References

Acs, Z. J., Braunerhjelm, P., Audretsch, D. B., & Carlsson, B. (2009). The knowledge spillover theory of entrepreneurship. *Small Business Economics*, *32*, 15–30.

Akamatsu, K. (1962). Historical pattern of economic growth in developing countries. *The Developing Economies*, *1*, 3–25.

Albors, J., Sweeney, E., & Hidalgo, A. (2005). Transnational technology transfer networks for SMEs. A review of the state-of-the art and an analysis of the European IRC network. *Production Planning & Control*, *16*(4), 413–423.

Buratti, N., & Penco, L. (2001). Assisted technology transfer to SMEs: Lessons from an exemplary case. *Technovation*, *21*, 35–43.

Cantner, P., & Pyka, A. (1998). Absorbing technological spillovers: Simulations in an evolutionary framework. *Industrial and Corporate Change, 7*, 369–397.

Chang, H-J. (2011). Industrial policy: Can we go beyond an unproductive confrontation? In J. Lin & B. Pleskovic (Eds.), *Annual World Bank Conference on Development Economics 2010, Global: Lessons from East Asia and the Global Financial Crisis.* Washington, DC: World Bank.

Fosfuri, A., Motta, M., & Ronde, T. (2001). Foreign direct investment and spillovers through workers' mobility. *Journal of International Economics, 53*(1), 205–222.

Gronum, S., Verreynne, M. L., & Kastelle, T. (2012). The role of networks in small and medium-sized enterprise innovation and firm performance. *Journal of Small Business Management, 50*(2), 257–282.

Hadjimanolis, A. (2000). A resource based view of innovativeness in small firms. *Technology Analysis and Strategic Management, 12*(2), 263–281.

Kirzner, I. M. (1973). *Entrepreneurship and competition.* Chicago: University of Chicago Press.

Klapper, L., Amit, R., Guillén, M. F., & Quesada, J. M. (2007). Entrepreneurship and firm formation across countries. World Bank, Policy Research Working Paper No. 4313.

Komoda, F. (1986). Japanese studies on technology transfer to developing countries: A survey. *The Developing Economies, XXIV*, December.

Lin, X. 2010. The diaspora solution to innovation capacity development: Immigrant entrepreneurs in the contemporary world. *Thunderbird International Business Review, 52*, 124–136.

Maswana, J. C., & Davies, M. (2015). Predicting the determination and performance impact of absorptive capacity in China's SEZ prospects in Zambia and Mauritius. *International Journal of Economics and Business Research, 9*(1), 80–99.

Romer, P. M. (1990). Endogenous technological change. Journal of Political Economy, *98*(5), S71–S102.

Romijn, H., & Albaladejo, M. (2002), Determinants of innovation capability in small electronics and software firms in Southeast England. *Research Policy, 31*, 1053–1067.

Solow, R. M. (1956). A contribution to the theory of economic growth. The Quarterly Journal of Economics, *70*(1), 65–94.

Szogs, A. (2010). *Technology transfer and technological capability building in informal firms in Tanzania.* Lund, Sweden: CIRCLE, Lund University.

UNCTAD. (2015). Technology and Innovation report 2015: Fostering innovation policies for industrial development. New York: United Nations. Available at: https://unctad.org/en/PublicationsLibrary/tir2015overview_en.pdf

UNIDO. (1999). *Tanzania small and medium-scale enterprise policy proposals.* Washington, DC: UNIDO.

UNIDO. (2012). *Tanzania SME Development Policy 2003 "ten years after", implementation review.* Dar es Salaam, Tanzania: UNIDO.

URT. (2002). *Small and medium enterprise development policy 2002.* Dar es Salaam: Ministry of Industry and Trade.

Wang, J. Y., & Blomstrom, M. (1992) Foreign investment and technology transfer a simple model. *European Economic Review, 36*, 137–155.

World Bank. 2018. Enterprise surveys. Available at: www.enterprisesurveys.org.

15 Is China's growing interest in Africa a blessing or a curse for the continent's industrialization drive?

Eric Osei-Assibey

15.1 Introduction

Over the last two decades or so, China's interest in Africa has been growing by leaps and bounds. This sustained but obviously unequal relationship between Africa and China has attracted a lot of interest from global players, analysts, and researchers who are asking rhetorical questions, such as, what does China want from Africa?, and what does Africa want from China? Is it the case that China is using its soft power to exploit Africa's natural resources, or is China genuinely interested in building a sustainable partnership for mutual benefit? One even more critical question that keeps emerging without any straightforward answer is: is China's growing influence in Africa hindering Africa's ability to follow a manufacturing-led growth path to industrialize or it is promoting it?

On one hand, some analysts have pointed out that China's growing influence in Africa has dented Africa's efforts at industrialization, particularly through unfair import competition and acts that perpetuate Africa's dependence on natural resources. For example, Ancharaz (2013) points out that the influx of cheap Chinese imports into Africa has caused significant injury to local industry, with the impact varying in intensity across countries. Trade unions in Zambia, Ghana, South Africa, Kenya, and many other countries on the African continent have at one time or the other blamed Chinese cheap imports for undermining the textiles, clothing, electrical and other light manufacturing products. In Ethiopia, according to Ancharaz (2013), while competition from Chinese shoe imports has forced the local footwear industry to innovate and upgrade, several producers have been squeezed out while surviving firms have contracted. Similarly, in Ghana, many clothing and textile industries that were set up in the early 2000s have collapsed, largely due to cheap imports from China (Ibrahim, 2017). Evidence from a survey from Mauritius shows that small and medium-sized enterprises (SMEs) in the clothing, footwear, and furniture sectors have borne the brunt of Chinese competition, being unable to match the price-quality ratio offered by Chinese products (Edinger & Sandrey, 2013).

On the face of it, there probably are good reasons to be concerned about whether African interests are being well served because of many reported cases of opaque deals; large-scale corruption and mismanagement; doubts about project feasibility; large trade imbalance; low quality infrastructure projects; wanton violation of environmental regulations, and abuse of workers and labor regulations.

On the other hand, other analysts have argued that sustained Chinese interest in Africa has resulted in a productive infrastructural boom and, in some cases, Chinese-funded special economic zones (SEZs) have attracted a critical mass of investors from China which has stimulated higher value-added manufacturing activities and generated significant productivity spillovers and technology transfers that have developed links with the domestic economy (Ancharaz, 2013; Chen et al., 2016; McKinsey, 2017).[1] This, according to such a viewpoint, has triggered manufacturing-led growth in many countries in the region, such as Ethiopia, Nigeria, South Africa, and Kenya, producing goods, such as automobile assembly, electronic products, cement, steel, garments, and shoes. These, no doubt, should serve as a key contributor to unlocking Africa's potential for diversification and to boost their value-added manufacturing industries and exports.

However, despite China's investments and foreign direct investment (FDI) flows to Africa, available data from the World Bank's World Development Indicators (2018) indicate that the value-added manufacturing to GDP ratio has declined from about 14 percent in 2000 to 9.8 percent in 2017 (and this has stagnated over the last seven years), while the overall industrial performance has declined from 26 percent in 2010 to 23 percent of GDP in 2017. Over the same period, African manufactured exports contributed the lowest amount, of about 2 percent, to global manufactured exports. While it is not straightforward to gauge what accounts for this decline in the pace of industrialization in Africa, it will be interesting to know the role China's engagement has played, besides the well-known factors such as a lack of enabling policy environment, deficiency in skills, capital, and productive infrastructure.

Moreover, Edinger and Sandrey (2013) have argued that any positive impact from China's activities in Africa will be largely dependent on a country-specific institutional and political context. This is because weakness in these variables has fuelled concerns about corruption and the rent-seeking behavior of African leaders, stakeholders, and Chinese investors, which tend to distract from diversification opportunities and sustained industrialization efforts. This viewpoint is also consistent with a World Bank report, "Assessing Aid" (World Bank, 1998) that argued that aid only works when the policy environment is right.

Given this background and given the fact that there is limited evidence on the exact impact of Chinese engagement in Africa, particularly on the survival rates and development of industries, this study seeks to investigate, on balance, the effect of Chinese activities on Africa's industrialization drive. More specifically, the study investigates, first, the effects of China's investments, trade, loans, and financing of infrastructure in Africa on the value-added manufacturing and on overall industrial sector growth in Africa. Second, the study examines the potency or effectiveness of Chinese activities on industries within a different enabling policy and institutional context (such as political stability, government effectiveness, control of corruption, or rule of law).

There are three main contributions from this chapter. First, it will outline a statistically significant set of drivers that policymakers in countries in Africa who are interested in speeding up industrialization can leverage to create the desired outcomes. Second, using a Pooled Mean Group (PMG) estimator, which allows the short-term parameters to differ between groups while imposing equality of the long-term coefficients between countries, the findings indicate estimates of the net effect of Chinese engagements, in particular, trade and investments on the African industrialization drive, both on the short- and long-term basis. Third, the chapter will help gauge the kind of institutional and governance structures necessary to optimize the gains from these growing Sino-African trade and investment ties for the continent's industrialization drive. These findings are particularly necessary as it will equip policymakers in Africa to devise strategies to make the most of the Chinese government's recent announcement to scale up its engagement with Africa and deepen economic cooperation with the continent. At the September 2018 Forum on China-Africa Co-operation (FOCAC) summit, President Xi Jinping reiterated his pledge to invest US$60 billion in Africa by the end of 2019. This will provide support to Africa by way of grants, interest-free loans, concessional loans, credit lines, and development financing. This is as well as what is being offered under the Belt and Road initiative.[2] While it is presently not known how much of this will actually translate into capital and investment in Africa, it nevertheless demonstrates a sustained and ever-growing interest in Africa and therefore the continent's leaders should strategically position themselves to ensure a win-win relationship. Finally, the findings of this chapter (in particular the net impact) will contribute to the emerging literature on the impact of the Chinese influence on African industrialization specifically and more generally on its development agenda.

The rest of the chapter is structured as follows: Section 15.2 briefly reviews the empirical literature on the role of China in Africa and the impact it has had on African economies. Sections 15.3 and 15.4 describe the methodology, empirical design, and data sources, while Section 15.5 discusses the estimation results. Section 15.6 concludes with policy implications.

15.2 Overview of scale and scope of Sino-African economic relations

China and Africa enjoy several levels of relations that range from historical, political, diplomatic, economic, military, social to cultural connections. The economic relationship between China and Africa heightened at the dawn of the twenty-first century, albeit the political relationship dates back to the early 1970s. Essentially, China gained its seat in the United Nations in 1971 predominantly due to the strong vote received from the African countries. China's relations with Africa remained political until the late 1990s as China underwent comprehensive economic reforms to open up its economy to the rest of the world. With the remarkable growth in performance achieved, it became evident that the country needed to ensure a constant supply of natural resources to sustain the high growth. This initiative placed Africa as an important region for Chinese economic activities (Busse et al., 2016).

While these relations are varied and date back several centuries, our interest in this chapter is on the contemporary economic relationship that has been built and has been intensifying since the turn of the millennium (the twenty-first century). In just two decades or so, China has become Africa's largest economic partner and has built increasingly strong economic ties with the continent. A recent study by McKinsey (McKinsey, 2017) observes that across trade, investment, infrastructure financing, and aid, no other country has such depth or breadth and is entrenched in today's Africa than China. According to this study, more than 10,000 Chinese-owned firms are currently operating in Africa, worth over US$500 billion and foreign direct investment (FDI), for example, has grown by 40 percent per year from US$1bn in 2004 to over US$35bn in 2015. In what follows, we show snapshots of trends in trade, investments, loan infrastructure financing or contract services and labor using data from the China Africa Research Institute (CARI) at Johns Hopkins University.[3]

15.2.1 *Chinese loans to Africa*

Since 2000, Chinese loans to African countries have steeply increased, some of which can be described as official development assistance (ODA), suppliers' or export credit, commercial or non-concessional in nature. While not all African countries have received loans from China, the available data show that from 2000 to 2017, the Chinese government, banks, and contractors extended US$143 billion in loans to African governments and their state-owned enterprises (SOEs). According to CARI, Angola is the top recipient of Chinese loans, with $42.8 billion disbursed over 17 years.

A unique dimension of this is how some of these loans are either described as tied or resource-backed loans. Although resource-backed loans (also known as resource for infrastructure (RFI)) represents a relatively small share of the number of loans made by Chinese policy banks in Africa, these loans are often huge, they make up a substantial share of its portfolio (Landry, 2017). The key difference between RFI deals—which have been largely employed by China's policy banks, including Eximbank and the China Development Bank—and other resource-backed loans is that, according to Halland et al.'s (2014)[4] definition, the money from RFI arrangements is spent exclusively on infrastructure projects.

There is, however, a growing concern over China's lending practices, as critics have argued that although the terms and conditions are often more favorable than those of the West, it presents a giant "debt trap" akin to "neocolonialism." According to Chin (2012), while China has been responsive to some of the recent criticisms of its lending policies, its approach to development finance still differs significantly from that of the Bretton Woods Institutions, such as the International Monetary Fund and the World Bank.

15.2.2 *China-Africa trade*

On the trade front, China-Africa trade is the strongest link of the engagements and the former remains Africa's largest trading partner. Figure 15.1 shows that the value of trade has increased from less than US$10 billion in 2002 to US128

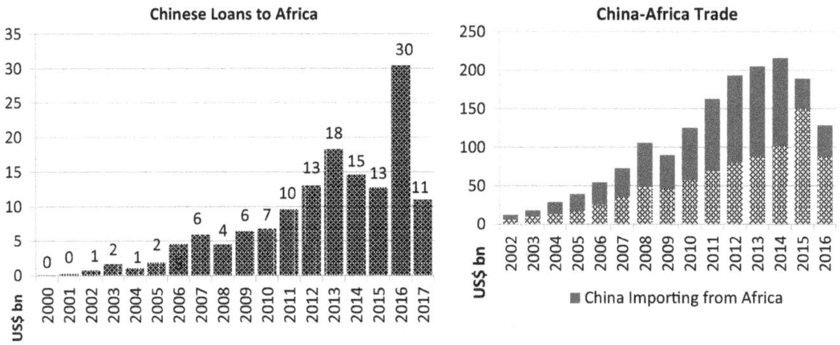

Figure 15.1 Chinese trade and loans to Africa, 2000–2017

Source: Data from the China-African Research Initiative (CARI) of Johns Hopkins University.

billion in 2016 down from a high of US$215 billion in 2014. Chinese imports from Africa consist largely of mineral ores, petroleum, and agricultural products while Chinese exports to Africa are largely made up of light manufactured goods. There is, however, criticism that African markets are being harmed by unbridled imports of low-cost Chinese-made products because they are putting great competitive pressure on local industries and businesses.

15.2.3 Chinese FDI flows to Africa

Over the last two decades or so, the number of Chinese FDIs in Africa have been growing not only in the natural resource sectors but also increasing the diversification of investments to the non-resource sectors of the economy, including banking, ICT, real estate, manufacturing, power generation, and general services. Over the 2002–2016 period, flows of Chinese FDI into Africa increased significantly, peaking in 2008 (this was also the only year in the past decade when Chinese FDI flows to Africa exceeded those from the U.S.) and stabilizing over the 2011–2015 period (Figure 15.2). During this time, China's FDI stock in Africa rose from US$491 million to US$32.4 billion and grew at an annual rate of 20.5 percent between 2009 and 2012. According to the China Africa Research Institute database (CARI, 2017), the top five African destinations for Chinese FDI in 2014 were Algeria, Zambia, Kenya, Republic of Congo, and Nigeria, with Algeria accounting for more than 20 percent of all Chinese FDI flows to Africa in 2014.

15.2.4 Chinese infrastructure contracts in Africa

According to the China Africa Research Institute database (CARI, 2017), in 2016, the gross annual revenues of Chinese companies' engineering and construction projects in Africa totaled US$50 billion, a slight decrease from 2015

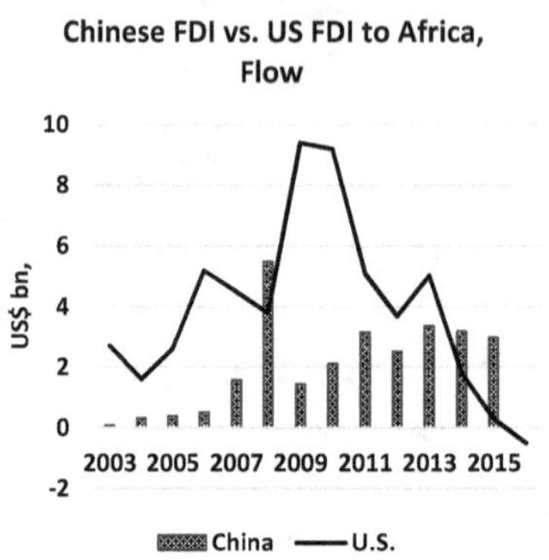

Major sources of FDIs in Africa's manufacturing sector in 2016

Country	Size of investment ($US billion)	Market share in Africa (%)	Number of investment projects in 2016
China	36.1	38.4	66
UAE	11.0	11.7	35
Italy	4.0	4.3	20
USA	3.6	3.9	91
Japan	3.1	3.3	27
UK	2.4	2.5	41
France	2.1	2.2	81

Figure 15.2 Chinese FDI flows to Africa
Source: Data from CARI.

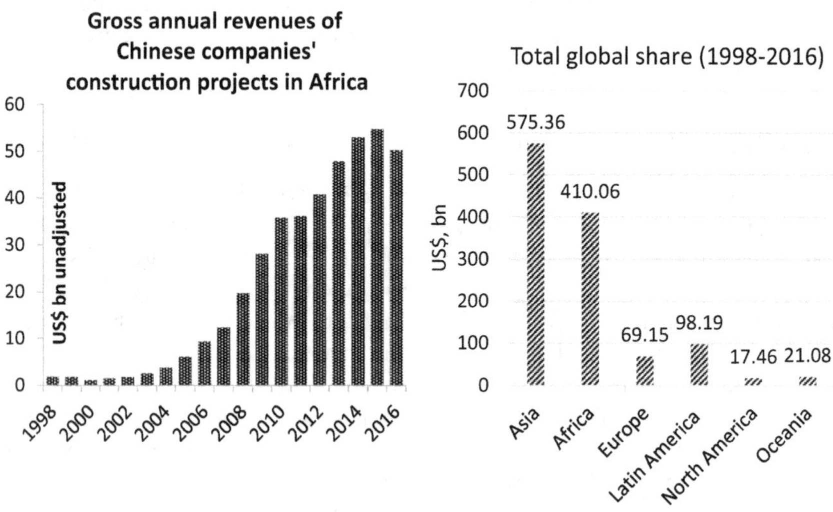

Figure 15.3 Gross revenues of Chinese construction projects in Africa
Source: Data from CARI.

(Figure 15.3). Between 1998 and 2016, Africa was the second highest recipient of the total global share of Chinese infrastructure projects (valued at US$410.06 billion), second only to Asia (Figure 15.3). The top five countries are Algeria, Ethiopia, Kenya, Angola, and Nigeria, which account for 49 percent of all

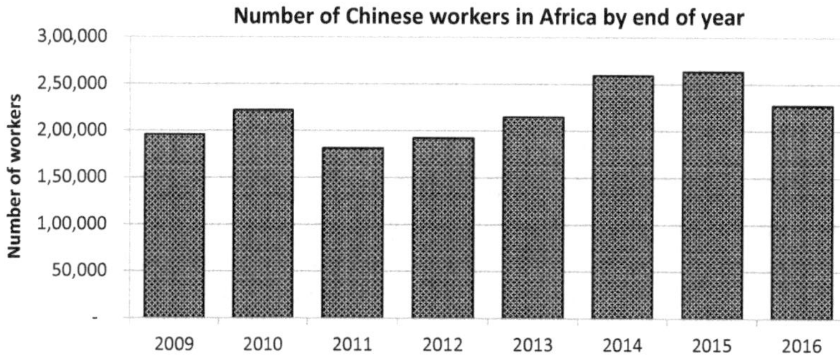

Figure 15.4 Chinese workers in Africa, 2009–2016
Source: Data from CARI.

Chinese companies' 2016 construction project gross annual revenues in Africa. Research conducted by Hanauer and Morris (2014) points out that African officials overwhelmingly view China's role in Africa positively, welcoming China's heavy emphasis on government-to-government contracts with few, if any, strings attached. According to the study, African leaders praise China's contributions to their nations' infrastructure, highlighting visible improvements that contribute to expanded economic activity, job creation for local workers, and tangible improvements to roads, rails, bridges, and other transportation networks.

15.2.5 Chinese workers in Africa

While official Chinese sources indicate that the number of Chinese workers in Africa by the end of 2016 was 227,407 (see Figure 15.4), a 2013 report by *The Economist* estimated one million Chinese citizens reside and work in Africa. It further estimated that 200,000 Africans are working in China. In 2016, the top five countries with Chinese workers are Algeria, Angola, Ethiopia, Nigeria, and Kenya, and this, according to the China Africa Research Institute database (CARI, 2017), accounted for 65 percent of all Chinese workers in Africa.

15.3 Literature review

Theoretical literature that underpins industrial policy and trade is mainly centered around two theories: the notion of comparative advantage that was first developed by the classical economist, David Ricardo (1817), and the theory of infant industry that was first developed by Alexander Hamilton (1791). While both theories are relevant for this study, the theoretical foundation of this study is tilted toward the theory of infant industry. This is due to the fact that most industries in Africa are infant, small, and burgeoning, which have to compete with large and well-established industries' products from countries like China or elsewhere and might have to be protected or supported to build their productive capabilities to compete effectively, which they often are lacking. The infant industries theory postulates that for domestic industries to thrive, developing countries need to protect and nurture their industries in their infancy through deliberate industrial policy measures until they mature and can compete with superior producers from abroad.

According to this viewpoint, even in the industries in which they are supposed to have a comparative advantage (such as garment, textile, and shoes); industries in developing countries struggle to establish themselves because they lack the necessary technological and organizational capabilities to organize the production and sell the products (especially in export markets) in an effective way (Signé 2018). In this regard, the main challenge for developing countries is to find a way to deliberately change those capabilities through an appropriate combination of private sector efforts or by obtaining support from development partners like China (to increase productive capabilities through investments in physical equipment, worker training, the development of management skills, R&D, etc.) and public policy intervention, particularly rolling out a deliberate industrial policy and initiatives/public investments that improve physical infrastructure, economic institutions, human capital, basic R&D, and the general business enabling environment.

15.3.1 Empirical literature

Empirical studies on the impact of Chinese economic activities in Africa have yielded mixed results (Cheng, 2016; Donou-Adonsou & Lim, 2018; Dreher Fuchs, Parks, Strange, & Tierney, 2017). While some studies found Chinese activities do impact economic growth of African economies positively, others conclude that such activities adversely impact or had no effect on the economic growth of these economies. For instance, Donou-Adonsou and Lim (2018) investigated the impact of Chinese and US FDI as well as trade openness on the growth of African economies. Using fixed effects panel regression and instrumental variable techniques, the study found Chinese FDI to positively impact on incomes in Africa. The study also found strong evidence of Chinese investment crowding out US investment in Africa.

Isaksson and Kotsadam (2017) examined the effect of Chinese development finance on trade union involvement in Africa. By applying the ordinary least squares (OLS) and linear probability models to the Afrobarometer survey between 2000 and 2012, the study found Chinese development projects discouraged trade union involvement in the local area where these projects were undertaken, unlike other development partners like the US and World Bank. Dreher et al. (2017) further studied the impact of Chinese ODA on the growth of African economies. The authors found an additional Chinese ODA project to increase economic growth by 0.7 percentage points in recipient African countries.

In a related study, Liu and Tang (2017) studied the impact of Chinese ODA on trade flows. The results obtained from a log-linear gravity model revealed a negative relationship between current flows of foreign aid and trade between China and Africa. Busse, Erdogan, and Muhlen (2016) examined the effect of Chinese FDI and trade on the GDP per capita of African economies. The results obtained from a Generalized Method of Moments (GMM) model found evidence of a displacement effect on African firms due to competition from China. Chinese FDI and aid were also found to have no significant impact on the growth of African economies. There was also strong evidence to suggest that African countries that export natural resources to China have benefitted from positive terms-of-trade effects.

On issues of corruption, Isaksson and Kotsadam (2016) investigated the effect of Chinese aid on corruption of African economies. OLS and linear probability models were applied to the Afrobarometer survey data between 2000 and 2012. The results obtained suggest that projects sponsored with aid from China fuelled local corruption in African economies with no observable impact on economic activity. Cheng (2016) examined the impact of Chinese aid on the economic growth of Africa. Results from the two-stage least squares model found no significant relationship between Chinese aid and economic growth of African countries. This finding tends to corroborate the results obtained by Busse et al. (2016).

The African Development Bank Group (ADB, 2011) studied the effect of Chinese FDI and diplomatic ties on the turnover of economic cooperation of African countries. The results of a probit regression technique revealed a statistically significant positive effect of Chinese stock of FDI on the turnover of economic cooperation of African countries.

Chen, Dollar, and Tang (2015) employed the tobit model to study the impact of political stability, capital intensity, rule of law, and natural resource rents on Chinese Outward Direct Investment (ODI) in African economies. The results obtained show that Chinese firms were likely to invest in capital-intensive sectors of African economies. The study also found that the level of rule of law does not matter in Chinese investment in Africa, however, political stability was critical. Also, Chinese firms were more likely to invest in resource-rich but institutionally poor African countries.

Mourao (2018) examined the traditional dimensions that affect the distribution of FDI in African countries by employing stochastic frontier models. The study concluded that dynamic national markets with large populations and significant forest area were the most preferred destinations for the allocation of Chinese FDI. The paper also finds strong evidence to suggest that Chinese investors are attracted to the political and institutional particularities of each African country.

On country-specific studies, Tang (2016) explored the extent to which Chinese manufacturing firms have driven manufacturing in Ghana. The author finds evidence of increased investment by Chinese firms over the past decade. However, a few of these investment projects have been abandoned or not implemented due to the hostile investment environment. A similar study by Ibrahim (2017) on the Ghanaian economy focused on the impact of Sino-Africa trade relations on the textile industry. The paper finds strong evidence to suggest that trade relations between the two countries had negatively impacted on the Ghanaian textile industry. The adverse implications of the trade relations were mostly evident in employment generation. The study, however, found some positive benefits to accrue for consumers through cheaper prices.

Furthermore, Cook, Lu, and Tugendendhat (2016) explored the role of Chinese migrants to Africa in the agri-food sector in Ghana and Ethiopia. While the impacts of the Chinese presence on local development were modest, they appear to be positive in the sense that they continue to create economic opportunities for both themselves and the local people. Bräutigam and Tang (2012) explored China's engagement in rural Ethiopia in historical perspective by focusing on foreign aid and investment by Chinese firms between 1970 and 2011. The paper finds Chinese engagement in agriculture and rural development to be longstanding, but has dwindled over the years.

Chen et al. (2016) examined trends of Chinese FDI and technology transfer in Nigeria's manufacturing sector. The paper finds evidence of technology transfer, albeit with negative perceptions by the local people toward Chinese investment. While Nigerian economic policies have served to enhance Chinese investment and skills promotion in Nigeria, a more coherent strategy is required to leverage the potential resources it brings.

15.4 Methodology

An autoregressive distributed lag (ARDL) model is employed to estimate the effect of Chinese activities in Africa, such as stock of FDIs, exports to Africa, and infrastructure contracts on manufacturing and industry GDP growth for African countries. The model is estimated with the help of a pooled mean group (PMG) estimator. The estimator allows the short-term parameters to differ between groups while imposing equality of the long-term coefficients between countries. The model also assumes that the error terms are independently and normally distributed across time and cross-sections with zero means and constant variances. The PMG estimator highlights the dynamic adjustment between the short run and the long run. Following Pesaran et al. (1999), Demetriades and Law (2006), and ADB (2018), the models are specified as follows:

$$\Delta M\_GDP_{it} = (\alpha_1 - 1)M\_GDP_{it-1} + \sum_{j=1}^{m-1} \beta_j \Delta InCA_{it-j} + \sum_{j=1}^{k} \alpha_j M\_GDP_{it-1} + \sum_{j=0}^{m} \beta_j InCA_{i+t-j} + f_i + f_t + \varepsilon_{it}$$

$$\Delta I\_GDP_{it} = (\alpha_1 - 1)M\_GDP_{it-1} + \sum_{j=1}^{m-1} \beta_j \Delta InCA_{it-j} + \sum_{j=1}^{k} \alpha_j M\_GDP_{it-1} + \sum_{j=0}^{m} \beta_j InCA_{i+t-j} + f_i + f_t + \varepsilon_{it}$$

where *M_GDP* denotes manufacturing value-added growth (or percentage of GDP); *I_GDP* denotes industry value-added growth (or percentage of GDP); *In CA* is the natural logarithm of Chinese activities in Africa (these include the stock of foreign direct investment (FDI), Chinese exports to Africa and Chinese contracts); Δ is the change operator; f_i and f_t indicate the country fixed-effects and time effects respectively; and ε_i is a white noise error term. Also, the half-life of the adjustment to long-run equilibrium is approximated by $-In(2)/In(1+\beta)$ which denotes the time necessary for a disturbance from the long-run equilibrium to be halved.

The next issue we considered is the efficiency or potency of Chinese activities (trade, infrastructure contract, etc.) in a good institutional and policy environment. This analysis is based on the findings by the World Bank (1998) which in a growth regression finds aid not significant but the interactive variable, aid times policy, significant. In this respect, we introduced an interactive term which seeks to measure the effectiveness of the variable of interest in the context of a country's specific level of governance and institutional environment, such as government effectiveness, control of corruption, political stability, regulatory quality, and the rule of law. The model is specified as follows:

$$\Delta M\_GDP_{it} = (\alpha_1 - 1)M\_GDP_{it-1} + \sum_{j=1}^{m-1} \beta_j \Delta InX_{it-j} * IV_{it-j} + \sum_{j=1}^{k} \alpha_j M\_GDP_{it-1} + \sum_{j=0}^{m} \beta_j InX_{i+t-j} * IV_{i+t-j} + f_i + f_t + \varepsilon_{it}$$

$$\Delta I\_GDP_{it} = (\alpha_1 - 1)I\_GDP_{it-1} + \sum_{j=1}^{m-1} \beta_j \Delta InX_{it-j} * IV_{it-j} + \sum_{j=1}^{k} \alpha_j I\_GDP_{it-1} + \sum_{j=0}^{m} \beta_j InX_{i+t-j} * IV_{i+t-j} + f_i + f_t + \varepsilon_{it}$$

where *IV* denotes a vector of institutional variables (government effectiveness, political stability, control of corruption, regulatory quality, and rule of law) (Table 15.1).

15.4.1 Data type and source

The study employed secondary data on 40 African countries from 2003 to 2016 for the analyses. The data on manufacturing and industry GDP growth were sourced from the World Bank's World Development Indicators (WDI) while government effectiveness, political stability, control of corruption, regulatory quality, and the rule of law were sourced from the World Governance Indicators (WGI) 2018 edition. Moreover, data on the stock of Chinese foreign direct investment,

Table 15.1 Definition and description of variables

Variable	*Description*	*Measurement*	*Expected sign*
Manufacturing GDP growth	This is a continuous variable which measures the value-added (net output after adding up all outputs and subtracting intermediate inputs) of the manufacturing sector	It is expressed as a percentage change of manufacturing GDP. Or value-added manufacturing to GDP growth.	
Industry GDP growth	This is a continuous variable which measures the value-added (net output after adding up all outputs and subtracting intermediate inputs) of the manufacturing sector	It is expressed as a percentage change of industry GDP. And also as a percentage of GDP.	
Exports to Africa	This measures the value of Chinese exports of goods to African countries		-
Foreign direct investment (FDI)	This measures the stock of Chinese FDI in African countries	In stock	+
Contracts	This is a continuous variable measures the gross annual revenues of Chinese companies' construction projects in Africa	It is the turnover of contracted projects in African countries	-/+
Political stability	Political stability and absence of violence/terrorism measures perceptions of the likelihood of political instability and/or a politically-motivated violence, including terrorism	This ranges from approximately -2.5 (weak) to 2.5 (strong) governance performance	+
Government effectiveness	This variable reflects perceptions of the quality of public services, the quality of the civil service and the degree of its independence from political pressures, the quality of policy formulation and implementation, and the credibility of the government's commitment to such policies	This ranges from approximately -2.5 (weak) to 2.5 (strong) governance performance	+
Regulatory quality	This variable mirrors perceptions of the ability of the government to formulate and implement sound policies and regulations that permit and promote private sector development	This ranges from approximately -2.5 (weak) to 2.5 (strong) governance performance	+

(*continued*)

Table 15.1 Cont.

Variable	*Description*	*Measurement*	*Expected sign*
Rule of law	This variable mirrors perceptions of the extent to which agents have confidence in and abide by the rules of society, and in particular the quality of contract enforcement, property rights, the police, and the courts, as well as the likelihood of crime and violence	This ranges from approximately -2.5 (weak) to 2.5 (strong) governance performance	+
Control of corruption	This variable reflects perceptions of the extent to which public power is exercised for private gain, including both petty and grand forms of corruption, as well as "capture" of the state by elites and private interests	This ranges from approximately -2.5 (weak) to 2.5 (strong) governance performance.	-

Chinese exports to Africa, and Chinese contracts were sourced from the China Africa Research Institute (CARI). The countries involved include; Benin, Botswana, Burundi, Cameroon, Cape Verde, Central African Republic, Chad, Comoros, the Democratic Republic of Congo, Congo, Côte d'Ivoire, Egypt, Ethiopia, Gabon, Gambia, Ghana, Guinea, Guinea-Bissau, Kenya, Lesotho, Liberia, Malawi, Mauritania, Mauritius, Morocco, Mozambique, Namibia, Niger, Nigeria, Rwanda, Senegal, Seychelles, Sierra Leone, South Africa, Tanzania, Togo, Tunisia, Uganda, Zambia and Zimbabwe.

15.5 Estimation results

15.5.1 Summary statistics

This section presents the summary statistics of the variables used in the study. The descriptive measures presented include the mean, standard deviation, minimum and maximum values of the variables from 2003 to 2016 as summarized in Table 15.2. Manufacturing and industry GDP growth for the African economies averaged 3.86 percent and 4.2 percent respectively while their share in GDP is 9.69 percent and 24.20 percent with standard deviations of 4.62 percent and 12.50 percent respectively. Moreover, foreign direct investment, exports to Africa and Chinese contracts averaged US$258.80 million, US$1,197.30 million and US$371.82 million respectively.

With regards to the institutional variables, the mean estimate for government effectiveness, control of corruption, political stability, regulatory quality, and

Table 15.2 Summary statistics

Variable	*Mean*	*Std. Dev.*	*Minimum*	*Maximum*
Manufacturing % of GDP growth (%)	9.6927 (3.86)	4.6247 (2.96)	0.2326 (–2.6)	23.0282 (7.8)
Industry % of GDP growth (%)	24.19780 (4.2)	12.4959 (2.11)	4.1480 (–1.9)	77.4162 (7.5)
Foreign Direct Investment (US$, 000)	258.8016	655.0122	0	5954.02
Exports to Africa	1197.296	3195.596	0.6939	47834.31
Contracts	371.8215	747.1482	0	6832.03
Government effectiveness	–0.6570	0.6302	–1.8483	1.0494
Control of corruption	–0.5783	0.6160	–1.5385	1.2167
Political stability	–0.4978	0.8818	–2.2992	1.2002
Regulatory quality	–0.6001	0.5775	–2.2362	1.1273
Rule of law	–0.6124	0.6389	–1.8523	1.0771

Source: Author's computation with data from CARI and WDI.

rule of law stood at -0.66, -0.56, -0.50, -0.60, and -0.61 respectively. Thus, on average, Table 15.2 shows a weak governance performance in all the institutional variables used in the study.

15.5.1.1 Effect of Chinese exports to Africa on manufacturing and industry GDP growth of African countries

The estimation results of the pooled model as shown in Table 15.3 reveal that Chinese exports to Africa have a significant impact on manufacturing and industry GDP growth of African countries. Specifically, a percentage increase in Chinese exports to Africa is likely to increase industry growth by 2.58 percent in the short run. However, in the long run, a 1 percent increase in Chinese exports to Africa is likely to decrease manufacturing and industry GDP by 0.31 percent and 0.35 percent respectively. The latter result is not surprising as it is consistent with findings of the McKinsey Report (2017) study, entitled, "Dance of the Lions and Dragons," which surveyed more than 1,500 Chinese firms across 16 African countries and reported in one of its findings that, in some cases, Chinese firms and imports from China have lowered prices for existing products by as much as 40 percent through improved technology and efficiencies of scale. This has led to several manufacturing firms, including clothing and textile factories, collapsing in almost all Africa countries.

Furthermore, interacting Chinese exports with institutional variables prevalent in African economies presents a different perspective in terms of their effect on manufacturing and industry GDP growth. The results obtained show that, in the context of weak government effectiveness, political stability, control of corruption, regulatory quality, and the rule of law, a percentage increase in

Table 15.3 Effect of Chinese exports on manufacturing and industry GDP growth

	Manufacturing GDP growth			*Industry GDP growth*		
	Short-run impact	*Long-run impact*	*Speed of adjustment (years)*	*Short-run impact*	*Long-run impact*	*Speed of adjustment (years)*
Chinese exports	0.0772	–0.3123***	1.59	2.5822**	–0.3504***	1.23
Export*gov't effectiveness	0.0608	–0.8621***	2.62	–0.3495*	0.0916	1.34
Export*political stability	0.0091	–0.1790***	2.08	0.1426	0.3178***	1.45
Export*control of corruption	–0.0187	–1.0117***	3.19	–0.3034	0.0034	1.33
Export * regulatory quality	–0.0793	–0.1838***	1.85	–0.3086	0.4755***	1.29
Export*rule of law	–0.0369	–0.0954***	1.90	–0.2047	–0.0630	1.27

Note: *** $p<0.01$, ** $p<0.05$, * $p<0.1$.
Source: Author's estimation.

Chinese exports to Africa would have an adverse impact on manufacturing GDP growth in the long run. For example, Table 15.3 shows that in the face of weak governance effectiveness, a 1 percent increase in Chinese exports to Africa is likely to decrease industry GDP by 0.34 percent in the short run. This therefore suggests that institutional quality is vital for firms in Africa to have the ability to compete with imported products from China.

15.5.5.2 Effect of Chinese foreign direct investment to Africa on manufacturing and industry GDP growth of African countries

This section discusses the influence of Chinese FDI on manufacturing and industry GDP growth of African economies. The estimation results as shown in Table 15.4 reveal that a 1 percent increase in Chinese FDI would reduce manufacturing GDP growth by 0.27 percent and 0.15 percent in the short run and long run respectively. However, in terms of its effect on industry GDP growth, a 1 percent increase in FDI would increase growth by 0.5 percent and 1.13 percent in the short run and long run respectively. Moreover, in the face of weak government effectiveness, political stability, regulatory quality, and the rule of law, an increase in Chinese FDI would have adverse consequences on manufacturing GDP growth of African economies. This finding is similar to the one found by Mourao (2018), which finds evidence to suggest that Chinese investors are attracted to the political and institutional particularities of each African country.

Table 15.4 Chinese FDI and manufacturing and industry GDP growth of African economies

	Manufacturing GDP growth			*Industry GDP growth*		
	Short-run impact	*Long-run impact*	*Speed of adjustment (years)*	*Short-run impact*	*Long-run impact*	*Speed of adjustment (years)*
FDI	–0.2713*	–0.1489**	1.67	0.5036*	1.1306***	1.65
FDI*gov't effectiveness	–0.1327	–0.1320**	1.64	–0.3083	–0.8894***	1.49
FDI*political stability	–0.0307	–0.1402***	2.13	0.3228**	–0.4574***	1.18
FDI*control of corruption	–0.0854	–0.0416	1.84	–0.2510	–0.8856***	1.65
FDI*regulatory quality	–0.0719	–0.1137*	1.70	–0.2618	0.3515***	1.12
FDI*rule of law	–0.0366	–0.1516**	1.94	–0.2061	–0.6280***	1.19

Note: *** $p<0.01$, ** $p<0.05$, * $p<0.1$.
Source: Author's estimation.

15.5.5.3 Effect of Chinese contracts on manufacturing and industry GDP growth of African countries

Here, we present the estimation results of the influence of Chinese contracts in infrastructure projects/investments on value-added manufacturing and industrial output in African countries. Table 15.5 shows that a 1 percent increase in Chinese contracts would reduce manufacturing and industry GDP growth by 0.74 percent and 0.27 percent respectively in the long run. Further, the estimation results show that in the context of weak corruption control, infrastructure contracts have an adverse effect on both manufacturing and industrial growth. Specifically, in the face of weak control of corruption, a 1 percent increase in Chinese contracts would decrease manufacturing and industry GDP growth by 1.48 percent and 2.01 percent respectively. Considering the mounting criticisms concerning Chinese infrastructure projects and contract execution practices and the issue of transparency, project quality, and value for money, this finding is not too surprising. Isaksson and Kotsadam (2017), investigating Chinese aid and local corruption, found that the empirical results consistently indicate more widespread local corruption around active Chinese project sites. According to these authors, the effect is seemingly not driven by an increase in economic activity, but rather seems to signify that the Chinese presence impacts norms.

15.6 Conclusion

The chapter has sought to investigate the effect of Chinese growing interest and engagements in Africa on value-added manufacturing and industrial growth in Africa. More specifically, the study investigates, first, the effects of China's

Table 15.5 Chinese contracts and manufacturing and industry GDP

	Manufacturing GDP growth			*Industry GDP growth*		
	Short-run impact	*Long-run impact*	*Speed of adjustment (years)*	*Short-run impact*	*Long-run impact*	*Speed of adjustment (years)*
Contracts	0.0830	−0.7443***	1.92	0.3012	−0.2713***	1.35
Contracts*gov't effectiveness	−0.1830	0.3085***	1.82	−0.4194*	0.1748**	1.38
Contracts*political stability	−0.0171	−0.1151**	2.25	0.1618	0.1670**	1.50
Contracts*control of corruption	0.0826	−1.4822***	4.22	0.1264	−2.0100***	3.24
Contracts * regulatory quality	−0.0313	−0.0463	2.03	−0.3191*	0.5961***	1.39
Contracts*rule of law	−0.0337	0.2899***	1.91	−0.1563	0.0202	1.37

Note: *** $p<0.01$, ** $p<0.05$, * $p<0.1$.
Source: Author's estimation.

investments, trade, loans, and financing of infrastructure in Africa on the value-added manufacturing and on overall industrial sector growth in Africa. Second, the study examines the potency or effectiveness of Chinese activities on industries in the different enabling policy and institutional contexts (such as political stability, government effectiveness, control of corruption, or rule of law).

Using data from 40 African countries that span from 2003 to 2016 and applying an autoregressive distributed lag (ARDL) model with the help of a pooled mean group (PMG) estimator, the study reveals a range of interesting findings. The study finds that Chinese exports to Africa are likely to increase industry growth by 2.58 percent in the short run. However, in the long run, a 1 percent increase in Chinese exports to Africa is likely to decrease manufacturing and industry GDP by 0.31 percent and 0.35 percent respectively. This suggests that while Chinese exports to Africa may have a positive influence on the African industrialization drive, the benefit will only accrue in the short term. In the long term, increasing Chinese exports to Africa is likely to stifle the industrialization efforts of African leaders. The plausible reason for this long-term negative impact may be explained by a survey study finding (McKinsey, 2017). The study finds that Chinese firms and imports from China have lowered prices for existing products in Africa by as much as 40 percent through improved technology and efficiencies of scale. This has led to several clothing and textile factories collapsing in almost all Africa countries. Moreover, the negative impact even becomes more pronounced, in the face of weak institutions. An increase in Chinese exports to Africa is likely to generally decrease both manufacturing and industry GDP in Africa.

Regarding the effect of Chinese FDI flows, the study finds that an increase in Chinese FDI reduces manufacturing GDP growth in the short run and long run respectively. However, its effect on industry growth is positively significant on the horizon. In the face of weak government effectiveness, corruption, regulatory quality, and the rule of law, an increase in Chinese FDI would have adverse consequences on both manufacturing and industrial growth in African economies.

The findings on Chinese contracts in infrastructure suggest that an increase in Chinese contracts would lead to a reduction in value-added manufacturing and industry GDP growth. However, in the midst of strong government effectiveness and rule of law, service contracts have a positive effect on manufacturing in the long run, while in the face of weak corruption control, contracts have an adverse effect on both manufacturing and industrial growth in the short run.

In sum, the findings point to the fact that the gains from the Chinese influence in Africa can only be realized if the Africans strengthen their governance and institutional environment. That is to say, the efficiency and potency of Chinese activities in Africa on industrialization efforts can be maximized by strengthening political stability, control of corruption, and regulatory quality, with government effectiveness being an additional factor required. Building new institutions and strengthening existing ones will mean that the African economic environment will not only reduce the incentives for rent-seeking activities that result in corruption, low quality infrastructure projects, wanton violation of environmental and labor regulations, but also create the necessary business environment that enhances the productive capability and competitiveness of domestic industries to compete effectively with Chinese imports. It will also mean Africans build their own strategy of engagement with China and clearly link the China strategy to national industrial policy, including incentives for Chinese FDI that go to the priority sectors of the economy, ensuring technological/skill transfer and local content.

Notes

1 According to Chen et al. (2016), this is also happening because the boom in China that boosted domestic growth and income has resulted in higher wage costs which are moving an increasing number of Chinese firms to many places in Africa in search of lower labor cost and inputs. This therefore presents a favorable opportunity for the African continent to boost their export and manufacturing sectors, as well as offering opportunities to absorb Chinese industries seeking to reduce costs offshore.

2 The Belt and Road initiative (which was previously known as One Belt, One Road), is a development strategy adopted by the Chinese government involving infrastructure development and investments in countries in Europe, Asia, and Africa in 2014, in "a bid to enhance regional connectivity and embrace a brighter future." About a trillion-dollar investment is envisaged in this initiative and already countries on the African continent such as South Africa and Botswana have signed up to it.

3 Available at www.sais-cari.org/data-china-africa-trade.

4 Also cited in Landry (2017).

References

ADB (African Development Bank Group). (2011). China and Africa: An emerging partnership for development? Available at: www.afdb.org/

ADB (African Development Bank). (2018). The African Economic Outlook (AEO). Available at: www.afdb.org/fileadmin/uploads/afdb/Documents/Publications/African_Economic_Outlook_2018_-_EN.pdf

Ancharaz, V. (2013). Can Chinese SEZs spur industrial development in Africa? *Bridges Africa Magazine*, 2(6). Available at: www.ictsd.org/bridges-news/bridges-africa/news/is-china-bad-for-africa%E2%80%99s-industrialisation

Bräutigam, D., & Tang, X. (2012). An overview of Chinese agricultural and rural engagement in Ethiopia. IFPRI Discussion Paper 01185. Available at: https://landmatrix.org/media/uploads/china-in-ethiopia_ifpri.pdf

Busse, M., Erdogan, C., & Muhlen, H. (2016). China's impact on Africa: The role of trade, FDI and aid. *KYKLOS*, 69(2), 228–262.

CARI (China Africa Research Institute). (2017). Database. Available at: www.sais-cari.org

Chen, W., Dollar, D., & Tang, H. (2015). Why is China investing in Africa? Evidence from the firm level. CARI Working Paper, Johns Hopkins University.

Chen, Y., Yuan, I., Ukaejiofo, R., Xiaoyang, T., & Brautigam, D. (2016). Learning from China? Manufacturing, investment, and technology transfer in Africa. CARI Working Paper 2, Johns Hopkins University.

Cheng, M. (2016). *Has Chinese foreign aid contributed to economic growth in Africa?* Washington, DC: Georgetown University Press.

Chin, G. (2012). Two-way socialization: China, the World Bank, and hegemonic weakening. *The Brown Journal of World Affairs*, 19(1), 211–230. Available at: www.jstor.org/stable/24590939?seq=1#metadata_info_tab_contents

Cook, S., Lu, J., & Tugendendhat, H. (2016). Chinese migrants in Africa: Facts and fictions from the agri-food sector in Ethiopia and Ghana. *World Development*, 81, 61–70.

Demetriades, P., & Law, S. H. (2006). Finance, institutions and economic development, International Journal of Finance & Economics, 11(3), 245–260.

Donou-Adonsou, F., & Lim, S. (2018). On the importance of Chinese investment in Africa. *Review of Development Finance*, 5, 1–11.

Dreher, A., Fuchs, A., Parks, B. Strange, A., & Tierney, M. (2017). Aid, China, and growth: Evidence from a new global development finance dataset. AIDDATA, A Research Lab at William & Mary, Working Paper no. 46.

Edinger, H., & Sandrey, R. (2013). Is China bad for Africa's industrialisation? *Bridges Africa Magazine*, 2(6). Available at: www.ictsd.org/bridges-news/bridges-africa/news/is-china-bad-for-africa%E2%80%99s-industrialisation

Halland, H., Beardsworth, J., Bryan, C. L., & Schmidt, J. (2014). Resource financed infrastructure: A discussion on a new form of infrastructure financing. Washington, DC: World Bank Group. Available at: http://documents.worldbank.org/curated/en/394371468154490931/Resource-financed-infrastructure-a-discussion-on-a-new-form-of-infrastructure-financing

Hanauer, L., & Morris, L. J. (2014). Chinese engagement in Africa: Drivers, reactions, and implications for U.S. policy. Santa Monica, CA: RAND Corporation. Available at: www.rand.org/pubs/research_reports/RR521.html

Ibrahim, I. (2017). Impact of Sino-Africa economic relations on the Ghanaian economy: The case of textiles. *International Journal of Innovation and Economic Development*, 3(1), 7–27,

Isaksson, A-S., & Kotsadam, A. (2016). Chinese aid and local corruption. University of Gothenburg, Working Paper in Economics, No. 667.

Isaksson, A., & Kotsadam, A. (2017). Racing to the bottom? Chinese development projects and trade union involvement in Africa. University of Gothenburg, Working Paper in Economics No. 699.

Landry, G. D. (2017). Sicomines: A resource-for-infrastructure case study. Research Sponsored by the China Africa Research Institute, Johns Hopkins University, School of Advanced International Studies. Available at: https://static1.squarespace.com/static/526eec2ce4b0178a935d2104/t/58bddf5e9f745699f218aa48/1488838500718/NRGI+Blog+-+Sicomines+A+Resource+for+Infrastructure+Case+Study+(David+G.+Landry).pdf

Liu, A., & Tang, B. (2017). US and China aid to Africa: Impact on the donor-recipient trade relations. Munich Personal RePEc Archive (MPRA). Available at: https://mpra.ub.uni-muenchen.de/82276/

McKinsey. (2017). Dance of the lions and dragons: How are Africa and China engaging and how will the partnership evolve? Available at: www.mckinsey.com/featured-insights/middle-east-and-africa/the-closest-look-yet-at-chinese-economic-engagement-in-africa

Mourao, P. (2018). What is China seeking from Africa? An analysis of the economic and political determinants of Chinese Outward Foreign Direct Investment based on Stochastic Frontier Models. *China Economic Review*, 48, 258–268.

Pesaran, M. H., Shin, Y., & Smith, R. P. (1999). Pooled mean group estimation of dynamic heterogeneous panels. Journal of the American Statistical Association, 94(446), 621–634.

Signé, L. (2018) The potential of manufacturing and industrialization in Africa: Trends, opportunities, and strategies. Africa Growth Initiative, Brookings Institute. Available at: www.brookings.edu/experts/landry-signé

Tang, X. (2016). Chinese investment in Ghana's manufacturing sector. China-Africa Research Initiative, School of Advanced International Studies, Johns Hopkins University, Working Paper No. 2016/8. Available at: www.sais-cari.org/publications

The Economist. (2018). Chinese workers and traders in Africa. May 17. Available at: www.economist.com/special-report/2018/05/17/chinese-workers-and-traders-in-africa

World Bank. (1998). Assessing aid: What works, what doesn't, and why. World Bank policy research report Washington, DC: World Bank Group. Available at http://documents.worldbank.org/curated/en/612481468764422935/Assessing-aid-what-works-what-doesnt-and-why

World Development Indicators. (2018). Database. The World Bank Group. Available at: https://databank.worldbank.org/source/world-development-indicators

16 A new partnership between business and development

A case study of Ethiopia's industrial development

Izumi Ohno and Sayoko Uesu

16.1 Introduction

With accelerating globalization, private financial flows to developing countries have dramatically increased, exceeding the volume of Official Development Assistance (ODA). In 2016, private finance accounted for roughly 50 percent of the total financial flows[1] to developing countries from the Organization for Economic Co-operation and Development (OECD) Development Assistance Committee (DAC) countries, while ODA constituted only 15 percent (Figure 16.1). Collaboration between DAC donors and the private sector is increasing, along with the evolution of the global development agenda, such as the Millennium Development Goals (MDGs) and the Sustainable Development Goals (SDGs), which were adopted by the United Nations (UN) in 2000 and 2015 respectively. Notably, Germany and the United States (US) have launched their respective development partnerships with the private sector, followed by the United Kingdom (UK), the Netherlands, Sweden, Australia, and other donors including Japan.

The private sector also seized the opportunity presented by globalization; a new business model was initiated, as noted in Prahalad's (2004) "Base of the Pyramid (BOP)" and Hammond's (2007) "inclusive business." This is a new development partnership model in the sense that core business operations aim to directly address the social and development challenges faced by low-income consumers in developing and emerging economies.

After the 2008 financial crisis, multinational corporations (MNCs) actively expanded their business operations in low- and middle-income countries, shifting their investments from stagnant advanced countries. Moreover, the international business and financial communities faced growing calls to pay due attention to societal progress as a core business strategy, not just short-term profit maximization (Porter & Kramer, 2011).[2] The crisis also prompted a number of donor countries to seek potential synergies between development aid and domestic commercial interests (Große-Puppendahl, Byiers, & Bilal, 2016).

Furthermore, due to technological progress and the reduced costs of transport and telecommunication, production processes are becoming increasingly fragmented, arranged in global networks spanning many countries (the global

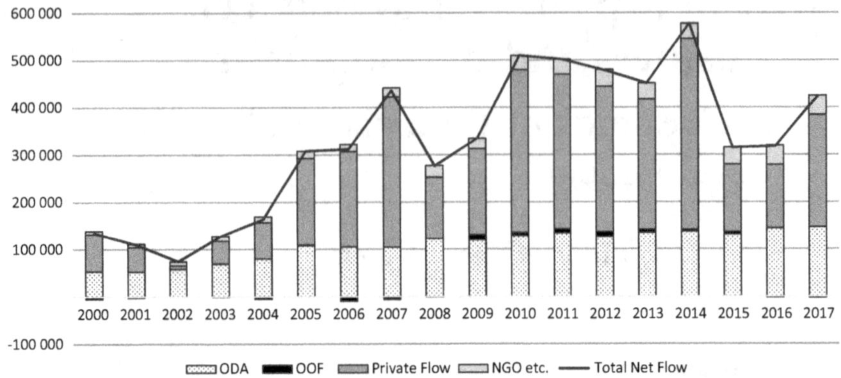

Figure 16.1 Financial flows from OECD-DAC countries to developing countries

value chains (GVCs)) (Barrientos, Gereffi, & Rossi, 2011). Against this backdrop, many developing countries are determined to join GVCs in the interests of job creation and technological upgrading. With the expansion of GVCs in low-income countries, MNCs have been undertaking an increasingly wide range of corporate social responsibility (CSR) activities, such as the promotion of decent work, and social and environmental compliance. This trend corresponds to the vision embraced by the 2030 Agenda for Sustainable Development or the SDGs, adopted at the UN in 2015. A global coalition for sustainable production and manufacturing is emerging, bringing together businesses, donor agencies, and civil society organizations to promote the setting of standards for CSR and also to monitor MNC supply chain management.

There is another new phenomenon related to public-private partnership (PPP): some emerging economies, such as China, India, and Turkey, have been increasingly active in aiding the economic upgrading of low- and middle-income countries. In particular, we are seeing the massive involvement of Chinese public and private entities in the production sector in low-income countries (especially in Sub-Saharan Africa), though little is known about those operations. Kragelund (2015) observes that they contribute to the creation of "developmental space" in policymaking in Africa, and that traditional alliances (between DAC donors and African countries) are being replaced by this new phenomenon. In general, the values and practices of such emerging economies are different from those of the traditional donors, yet some of the activities of emerging economies seem to complement those of traditional donors in terms of support for upgrading, particularly when the recipient government has a clear policy and strong commitment.

Therefore, it is worth identifying the various types of development partnerships with the private sector, to understand their different characteristics with a focus on individual stakeholders, and draw their implications for the industrialization of today's developing countries.

The chapter is divided into six sections. Following this introductory section, Sections 16.2 – 16.4 review recent trends in and various models of development partnerships with the private sector and identify the key features of those partnerships. In particular, we examine: (1) new partnership models involving traditional donors and the private sector; (2) the evolution of the Japanese development partnership with the private sector, and (3) PPP models of emerging economies. Section 16.5 presents a case study of Ethiopia and analyzes the practices of major donors (both traditional donors and non-traditional donors, such as China and Turkey) and MNCs on the ground. Ethiopia is an interesting case to analyze how new and diverse partnership models are evolving. The country is beginning to join the global garment supply chains and is attracting foreign direct investment (FDI) from both advanced and emerging economies. Furthermore, many donors are actively engaged in development partnerships with the private sector to support the government's industrialization drive. Section 16.6 summarizes the main findings and derives implications for today's latecomer countries, as well as for donors, including Japan.

It should be noted that because of the multitude of frameworks and tools provided by the diverse stakeholders, and in light of the difficulty of achieving a clear and comprehensive picture of and accurate data for most of the new donors, our analysis is limited to selected cases of social and economic upgrading in the textile and garment industry and the establishment of industrial parks in Ethiopia and some Asian countries.

16.2 New partnership models involving traditional donors and the private sector

Since the early 2000s, traditional donor agencies and international organizations have introduced a great number of new measures to promote partnerships with the private sector within their ODA activities, as illustrated by Große-Puppendahl et al. (2016). In this section, we examine three types of new development partnership which have been initiated by the private sector and supported by traditional donors and international organizations. These include: (1) the "Base of the Pyramid" (BOP) business, alternatively called "inclusive business," which targets the poor as consumers, suppliers, or distributors; (2) the SDGs' business, or "sustainable development business," which provides business solutions for broader global development challenges; and (3) corporate social responsibility (CSR) in value chain management, which addresses a wide range of issues, with a substantial focus on aspects such as decent work, safety, environment, or procurement practices.

16.2.1 BOP business

As mentioned in the introductory section, BOP business is a private sector approach to providing goods, services, and livelihoods to the low-income group on a commercially viable basis. According to the International Financial

Corporation (IFC), the BOP comprises four billion people who earn less than US$8 per day in purchasing power parity (Hammond, Kramer, Katz, & Tran, 2007). The concept of BOP business was originated by Hart and Prahalad in late 1990s, presented as "the Strategy for the Bottom of the Pyramid" (Prahalad & Hart, 1999). Corresponding to the international commitment to achieving the MDGs by 2015, BOP business came to attract attention as an innovative, market-based approach to poverty alleviation, avoiding aid dependency.

A classic example of this type is Hindustan Unilever, a subsidiary of a British-Dutch corporation which sells consumer products (e.g., soap, shampoo, water purifiers) in small packages at affordable prices, contributing to the improvement of health and sanitation in rural India. By engaging rural women as door-to-door sellers or managers of petty shops, Hindustan Unilever supports the empowerment of women. It also collaborates with donors (e.g., United States Agency for International Development (USAID), the World Bank, United Nations Children's Fund (UNICEF)) to raise awareness of health and hygiene issues (e.g., "Global Public-Private Partnership for Hand Washing with Soap").

The BOP business has inspired numerous new projects supported by donors and the private sector, although many early attempts to target the BOP market have failed (Jager & Sathe, 2016). In its early stages, the BOP business model was criticized for being too commercially driven, since its commitment to upgrading local industry/economic activities and the promotion of skill transfer to the poor were weak. The subsequent BOP 2.0 tried to address this issue by incorporating the BOP into broader development-oriented instruments. According to Ghosh and Rajan (2019), that helped to strengthen the supply chain for businesses and thus engaged the local population not just as consumers, but also as producers, distributors, and suppliers.

Jagar and Sathe (2016) suggest a revision of some early assumptions, particularly: (1) MNCs can predict the needs of poor consumers; (2) poor consumers can afford products when the prices are dramatically reduced; and (3) the cost and difficulty of reaching the poor are manageable. More recently, Caneque and Hart (2016) proposes BOP 3.0, by placing considerable focus on the marketing aspect.

It is important to note that the notion of poverty (or poor people) was redefined with the evolution of BOP, and currently we see the emergence of innovative attempts by local entrepreneurs, as in the digital sector in Kenya, supported by new financing tools (e.g., impact investing).

16.2.2 PPPs for sustainable development

The second new type of development partnership is broader business engagement aimed at sustainable development, reaching beyond poverty reduction. The UN Global Compact, launched in 1999, created the initial momentum toward mobilizing the private sector for the achievement of development outcomes.[3] This approach has attracted much attention from both business and aid communities especially after the 2008 financial crisis—in response to global calls

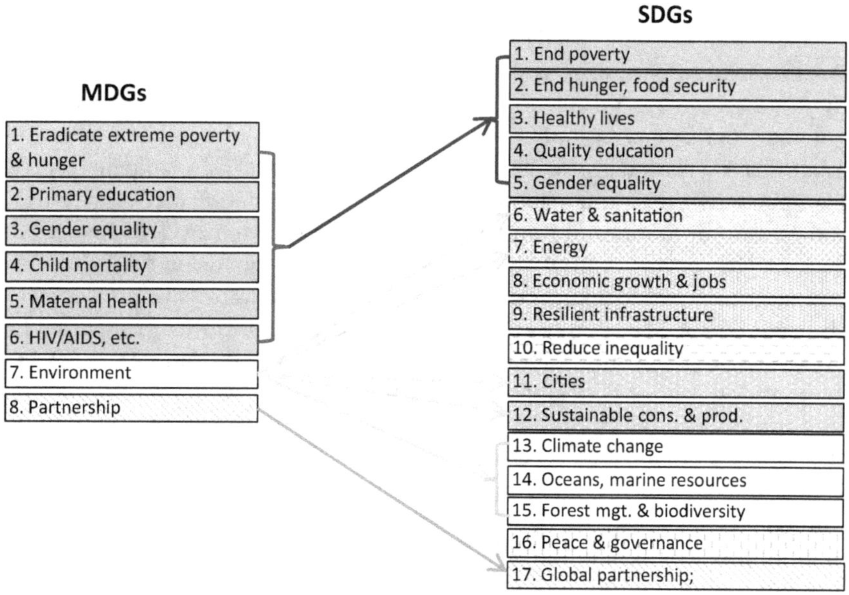

Figure 16.2 Evolution of MDGs to SDGs

for responsible and sustainable business. The adoption of the SDGs by world leaders at the UN in 2015 has further contributed to promoting PPPs for sustainable business. The SDGs mark a departure from the MDGs in that business is explicitly called on to apply their creativity and innovation to solve sustainable development challenges (Figure 16.2). Being comprehensive, the SDGs present an opportunity for business-led solutions and technologies to be developed and implemented to address a wide range of development challenges (GRI, UNGC, WBSCD, 2015; Ohno, Konya, Shiga, Murillo, & Charvet, 2019).

Since 1999, the German government (Federal Ministry for Economic Development and Cooperation (BMZ)) has been supporting develoPPP.de, a development partnership program with the private sector, involving three agencies, including the German Agency for International Cooperation (GIZ). DeveloPPP.de provides German and European companies, and their subsidiaries in developing countries and emerging economies, with financial and professional support (cost-sharing, to a maximum of 200,000 million Euro). The priority areas include food security, decent production and working conditions, employment, vocational training, environmental protection, conservation of natural resources, mitigating the impact of climate change, and technology transfer.

USAID also has had a long-standing partnership program, the Global Development Alliance (GDA), with the private sector (not limited to Americans). Launched in 2001, GDA co-invests resources based on the principle of shared value. More recently, GDA established Development Innovation Ventures (DIV) to test new ideas, to quickly and cheaply gather evidence of what works and does not, and to provide ongoing support for proven solutions.

These bilateral donor initiatives have developed into multilateral platforms. For instance, to encourage companies to develop inclusive business models in BOP markets, the UN launched Business Call to Action (BCtA) in 2008, with funding from several bilateral donors (the Department of Foreign Affairs and Trade (DFAT, Australia), the Department for International Development (DFID, the UK), the Swedish International Development Cooperation (SIDA), USAID) and directed by the United Nations Development Programme (UNDP) as a secretariat. The concept of BOP business has been fully integrated in the BCtA process and broadened to address the more comprehensive sustainable development challenges in the SDG era. As of 2019, this multilateral platform is supported by over 200 companies from various sectors in more than 70 countries. BCtA has been evaluated as a successful program (Ghosh & Rajan, 2019).

A report produced by the Business and Sustainable Development Commission (BSDC, 2017) estimates that achievement of the SDGs by 2030 will create at least US$12 trillion in market opportunities in four economic systems: food and agriculture; cities, energy; and materials; and health and well-being. More than half of those SDG-related business opportunities will emerge in developing countries. The BSDC report also projects the creation of 380 million new jobs by 2030, 90 percent of which would be located in developing countries. Increasingly, in general, both corporations and small and medium-sized enterprises (SMEs) are interested in using their technologies, know-how, and entrepreneurial spirit to address social and environmental challenges (in areas such as clean energy, smart cities, and affordable housing), and to provide business solutions to resolve global issues and the meeting of various development challenges.

16.2.3 CSR in value chain management

The third new type of development partnership emphasizes responsible business and involves donor agencies collaborating with the private sector to ensure CSR in GVCs, particularly regarding social and environmental compliance. As MNCs increasingly invest in developing countries which face weak governance and enforcement capacity, there is growing recognition among companies of the need to assume CSR in value chain management—in partnership with donor agencies and non-profit organizations (NPOs), as necessary.

Historically, the concept of CSR itself has long been a design element of business practice in developing countries, not limited to social and environmental issues. In Bangladesh, philanthropic activities have been in place since the colonial era, and the current notion of CSR emerged with the introduction of the 1992 Hawkins Bill in the US; buyers in the US and the European Union (EU) became more cautious about products involving child labor in their engagement in the export processing sectors (garments and shrimps) (Nasrullah & Rahim, 2014). Soon application of the bill was extended to other industrial sectors (e.g., leather and footwear, agribusiness, electronics).

The recent expansion of GVCs provides opportunities for developing countries to participate in global markets and acquire knowledge and technology from FDI companies. In the industrial sector, such participation occurs mostly at the entry level of the garment sector, which requires abundant low-wage workforce with relatively low skills. Despite the efforts of the companies, some academics are skeptical about CSR, pointing out that "many developmental issues cannot be tackled through a business rationale or be converted into business issues" (Mueller-Hirth, 2016; Amaeshi & Idemudia, 2018).

In this regard, partnership with donor agencies can compensate to some extent for such deficiencies. In fact, when the grim condition of those "sweatshops" was made public, Western donors and civil society organizations (CSOs) moved to enhance development partnerships to promote sustainable production and manufacturing. For instance, the International Labour Organization (ILO), together with IFC, introduced the Decent Work Programme in 2006 to improve labor standards and competitiveness in global supply chains, especially related to labor-intensive industries in developing countries (ILO, 2016). The program assists companies in improving practices through the application of core ILO labor standards and national labor laws, providing technical assistance in such areas as worker-management cooperation, working conditions, and social dialogue. The program is supported by bilateral donors (e.g., Australia, GIZ, the US, the Netherlands, and the Danish International Development Agency (DANIDA)), major apparel brands, CSOs, and the governments of developing countries. Regarding cotton production, there are multi-stakeholder platforms such as the "Better Cotton Initiative" (initiated by the World Wildlife Fund in 2005) and "Cotton made in Africa" (started by the Aid by Trade Foundation in 2005), which set criteria for environmental, economic, and social sustainability, train farmers in cultivation methods, and implement third-party verification. These actions were initiated by NPOs and have subsequently been expanded with funding from donor agencies, MNCs, other businesses, and producer organizations. Among traditional donors, USAID, Germany (BMZ, GIZ)), SIDA, and Switzerland are strongly engaged in such platforms.

The Accountable Garment Sector Challenge Fund, supported by the UK DFID during 2010–2013, went one step further; it aimed to make responsible and ethical production the norm in the garment manufacturing sector supplying the UK. Competitive grants were given to companies, non-governmental organizations (NGOs), and trade unions committed to demonstrating sustainable improvements in the working conditions of garment workers in Bangladesh, India, Nepal, and Lesotho.

However, despite an array of support, Bangladesh experienced the Tazreen tragedy in 2012 and the Rana Plaza collapse in 2013 (which killed over 1,000 local workers). Those incidents dramatically heightened consumer awareness of working conditions in developing countries. In response, the German government invited business representatives to the collaborative launch of Partnership for Sustainable Textiles in 2014, a multi-stakeholder platform to foster the continuous improvement of social, environmental, and economic sustainability along the entire textile value chains. With GIZ serving as a secretariat, the Partnership for Sustainable Textiles developed its Plan of Action, which laid down binding partnership standards for the production of raw material and of textiles and clothing. Companies may also consider applying for develoPPP.de (described earlier) to receive support to study and pilot necessary measures in their operations in developing countries.

The above examples demonstrate that development partnerships with the private sector have expanded significantly through bilateral and multilateral efforts, and are now producing synergies in the form of multi-stakeholder global platforms. The scope of partnership has also broadened from the initial narrow focus on poverty reduction (typically, BOP business in the MDG era) to cover economic upgrading and the sustainability agenda, including environmental and social compliance (corresponding to the SDG era). However, some critics argue that there is too much focus on "imposed and externally driven" social and environmental compliance (Nasrullah & Rahim, 2014). In response, Sitnikov and Bocean (2016) suggest that CSR focus on the core issues (e.g., organizational governance, human rights, labor practices, the environment) could be useful for addressing the specific problems of economies with weak governance, and hence contribute to the institutional development of such countries.

16.3 Evolution of Japanese development partnership with the private sector

16.3.1 Traditional Japanese PPPs for industrial upgrading

For decades, Japanese ODA has been engaged in PPPs in East Asian countries. Such partnerships, by linking FDI, trade and aid (the so-called "Trinity Model" of development cooperation; Shimomura, 2013), helped to develop a strong infrastructure and a skilled labor force, supplementing the Flying Geese pattern of production networks in East Asia. It should be noted that this model became a guiding principle (or core belief) of Japanese ODA and attracted strong interest among the other developing regions, including Africa. Since then, Japan has been endeavoring to introduce this model in other developing regions so as to foster a better investment climate and industrial upgrading; but it must be said that this has proved difficult outside Japan's economic sphere, especially in areas where the business climate was fragile.

Japanese ODA in partnership with the private sector can be classified into five types: (1) the development of industrial human resources; (2) the development of FDI-local business links; (3) the capacity development of the national and local governments for enterprise support; (4) the improvement of the investment climate; and (5) support for industrial park development/Special Economic Zones (SEZs) (JICA, 2012). ODA is involved in such matters as off-site infrastructure and advisory services for strategic FDI attraction, skill development at educational institutions, and on-the-job training (OJT), which may be implemented separately or in combination. Although the World Bank and other Western donors also support private sector development, they are primarily interested in establishing the regulatory framework for business operations and improving the investment climate. In relative terms, Japan is more interested in the real economy issues, such as industrial human resource development, FDI-local links, and industrial parks/SEZs (Ohno, 2013).

For example, JICA and the Association for Overseas Technical Cooperation for Sustainable Partnership (AOTS, a public-private body set up in 1959 for human resource development in developing countries) for decades have been supporting the training and education of skilled workers, technicians, and engineers in Asia, so that local workers and professionals could familiarize themselves and be equipped with Japanese-style production and management (see point (1) above), which emphasizes quality and productivity. That training can be undertaken through either OJT or formal education. Typical examples include support to Technical and Vocational Education and Training (TVET) and universities such as the King Mongkut University of Technology (in Thailand), the Thai-Nichi Institute of Technology (in Thailand), and the Hanoi University of Industry (in Vietnam). In addition, Japanese public and private institutions have been supporting the introduction and diffusion of Kaizen (a Japanese system for continuous improvement of productivity and product quality) in factories and fostering Kaizen trainers in the public and private sectors. Starting with Singapore in 1983, JICA has implemented various projects to promote the Kaizen method, not only in Asia but also in Africa and Latin America (Ueda, 2009).

Another example of Japanese ODA in partnership with the private sector is support for the development of industrial parks and SEZs (see point (5) above). The history of SEZs' development dates back to the late 1970s. Their development can be public, private, or via PPP, and since the 1990s, the use of PPPs has been on the rise. More recently, SEZs have been playing an instrumental role in the development of GVCs and in boosting developing countries' participation in GVCs. The number of SEZs has grown rapidly around the world during the recent decade. At present, there are at least 5,383 SEZs set up in 147 economies (UNCTAD, 2019).

Japan is one of the original donors which have supported industrial parks and SEZs in East Asia. The Eastern Seaboard Development in Thailand and the Than Long Industrial Parks in Vietnam (where massive ODA loans were provided in the mid-1980s to the 1990s, and the 1990s, respectively) are well-known examples of PPPs aimed at industrial upgrading of developing countries, where Japanese ODA supported off-site infrastructure development of industrial parks (such as roads, water supply, power), preparing the enabling environment for investors, including private zone developers. More recently, since around 2012, the financial instruments of Japanese ODA have diversified to include private-sector investment finance, which offers ODA loans and equity investment to business projects in developing countries, often in partnership with major Japanese developers (typically, major trading companies called *sogo shosha*).[4] A typical example is the Thilawa SEZ in Myanmar, inaugurated in 2011, and developed through a joint venture between the two governments and private consortiums from Myanmar and Japan (Myanmar Japan Thilawa Development, Ltd., MJTD).[5] Here, JICA provides private-sector investment finance to MJTD to support industrial complex development and operations, as well as providing technical cooperation to the Thilawa SEZ Management Committee in introducing One-Stop Services. Furthermore, recipient countries have become more diverse, and currently, ODA projects are underway in support of industrial parks/SEZ development in Bangladesh, India, and Kenya.

As explained earlier, the traditional Japanese PPP model has emphasized economic upgrading to enable local suppliers to meet Japanese companies' high quality-cost-delivery (QCD) requirements and hence become long-term manufacturing partners with Japanese FDI. Labor-intensive manufacturing processes (as in the garment industry) require massive amounts of cheap labor and thus contribute to job creation in host countries. But this is only the first stage of the industrialization ladder of GVCs. While the establishment of SEZs greatly contributes to job creation, there is also a need to foster disciplined and skilled workers, as well as develop parts and components and related service industries so that host countries can move up the GVC ladder for higher value-added activity.

16.3.2 A new form of PPP for SDGs

In addition to the above-mentioned traditional PPP, the Japanese government, together with JICA and the Japan External Trade Organization (JETRO), began to use the ODA budget to promote BOP business from around 2010 and later the broader sustainable businesses, to encourage the Japanese private sector (both large companies and SMEs) to engage in overseas business by using their technologies to solve development challenges. This is largely in line with the new partnership models introduced by other traditional donors since the early 2000s (see Sections 16.2.1 and 16.2.2).

In September 2016 (one year after the UN adoption of the SDGs), JICA formulated a position paper on the SDGs (JICA, 2016) and in February 2017 launched the SDGs' Business Supporting Survey (BSS), a scheme for matching Japanese companies (mainly large companies) and developing countries which seek knowledge and technology upgrading to meet development challenges. The new matching scheme highlights the work to help establish partnerships for further industrial and economic development (Kobukura, 2018); from the time of the launch of the BSS launch in February 2017 to the end of December 2018, 15 proposals from the private sector have been adopted by JICA.

Figure 16.3 presents an example of SDG business in Senegal, undertaken by Kagome, a major Japanese agro-processing company, specializing in tomato production and processed products (JICA, 2019). Processed tomatoes (canned) are widely used in West African cuisine, yet the region has been heavily dependent on imported products. After three years of research and experimentation, Kagome established its local company, Senegal Sarl in 2017, with support from JICA and JETRO. Currently Kagome is working to create its tomato value chain (including the establishment of a local processing facility), aiming to contribute to the

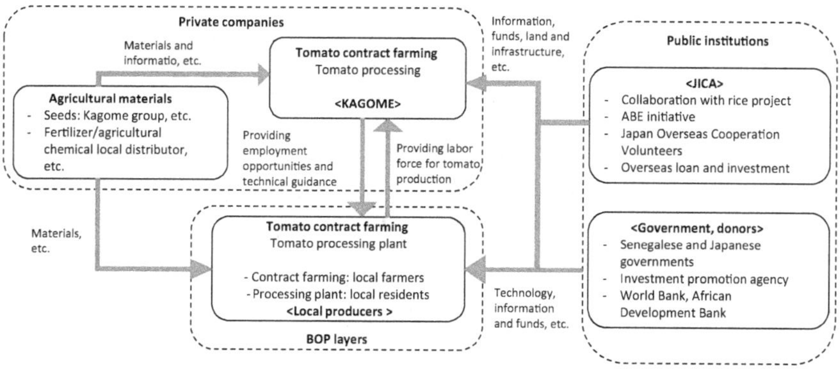

Figure 16.3 The case of SDG business in Senegal

achievement of goal 2 (sustainable agricultural development), goal 1 (poverty reduction), and goal 3 (promotion of health) of the SDGs (IDCJ, 2018). Kagome's business model was initially designed with the support of JICA's BOP business promotion survey in 2015–2017, and subsequently developed into the SDG business from 2017 as the new scheme was put in place. JICA's support primarily focused on tomato production and agro-processing, as well as the incorporation of small farmers (BOP people) into these processes. In parallel, JETRO provided complementary support to Kagome, focusing on business operations in Africa.

Another PPP instrument was launched in 2012, which focuses on utilization of the knowledge and technologies of Japanese SMEs in solving development challenges. Compared to the BOP and SDG business schemes which follow other donor practices, this is a unique initiative targeting Japanese SMEs. It reflects Japan-specific factors: Following the 2008 financial crisis, traditional Japanese-style *keiretsu* production relations crumbled, and an increasing number of SMEs began to seek new opportunities overseas, making management decisions and taking risks to establish overseas production bases independent of their large parent companies (Ohno, 2016). The Ministry of Economy, Trade and Industry (METI) and its related agencies, such as JETRO, AOTS, and the Organization for Small and Medium Enterprises and Regional Innovation (SMRJ), have long supported Japanese businesses across the board. Now, notably even the Ministry of Foreign Affairs (MOFA) and JICA have started to use the ODA budget to support the overseas expansion of SMEs (Ohno, 2016). Since its introduction, a total of 784 proposals have been adopted, 20–30 percent of which target TVET and industrial support (JICA, 2019).

These cases can be regarded as the first two instances of the above-mentioned development partnerships and are in line with the traditional focus on industrial upgrading. On the other hand, Japanese ODA's engagement in multi-stakeholder platforms for CSR (the third type) has been somewhat limited compared to that of other donors.

16.3.2.1 Balancing commercial interests and development outcomes

It is important to note that the recent emphasis on PPPs aimed at promoting Japanese private sector involvement in developing countries is in accord with the policy direction of the Abe administration (i.e., the Growth Strategy announced in 2010). That policy direction is also reflected in the outcomes of the seventh Tokyo International Conference of African Development (TICAD 7), held in Japan in August 2019, which proposed that the Japanese private sector be given a central role in the promotion of African development. In the background is a growing concern that Japan has now been left far behind regarding the emerging economies in the African market. Despite the strong interest and commitment from governmental bodies (such as MOFA, METI, JICA, or JETRO) and top management in the private sector, the PPP instruments now in place and some good practices that have already emerged (such as the Africa Kaizen Initiative, launched at the TICAD 6 in 2016, in partnership with the New Partnership for Africa's Development, NEPAD)[6], a number of private representatives point to the numerous related challenges, such as a lack of knowledge and experience, faced by the African continent. To meet those challenges, the government and the private sector have committed to sustaining public-private dialogue. Under such circumstances, it is essential to strengthen partnerships with other stakeholders (especially those familiar with the local context), and in that process, it is also important to strengthen mutual understanding with each partner in terms of the characteristics.

16.4 The rise of emerging economies and partnerships for industrial upgrading

Much has been written about the role of public and private financing from emerging economies (e.g., China, India, Turkey), and their impact. While we cannot simply generalize their models, some scholars note the aid model of these countries is driven by commercial and strategic concerns (Wan, 2014). We will restrict discussion here to a presentation of some basic characteristics of those partnerships, with particular focus on apparel/textile GVCs and SEZs/industrial parks. (More detailed analysis will be provided in the case study of Ethiopia in Section 16.5.)

16.4.1 China's public and private partnership model

China's eleventh Five-Year Plan, released in 2006, announced the overseas expansion of the development of Chinese SEZs, which played a key role in realizing the rapid growth of coastal areas in the 1970 and 1980s. This new policy direction is intended to encourage Chinese companies to target new markets, build global brands, and invest abroad. This is a state-led initiative, supported by the Ministry of Commerce of People's Republic of China (MOFCOM) and public banks, with the actual implementation done by specially created companies (Tang, X.,

2015). The MOFCOM is supporting the Chinese companies by providing a set of incentives, grants, loans, and interest rebates, as well as subsidies covering up to 30 percent of pre-construction and implementation costs (Nicolas, 2017). The companies receive logistical support in matters such as negotiation with the host government regarding land, tax incentives, and work permits—with the host government typically providing land and external infrastructure for the zone (Tyson, 2018).

The export of the Chinese SEZs model was also announced at the third Forum on China-Africa Cooperation (FOCAC) Summit in 2006, showing China's willingness to share its development experiences of FDI attraction with Africa. Seven African countries were selected, and each zone received a subsidy of up to 200 million RMB (US$33 million) (Nicolas, 2017). In fact, Algeria, Angola, Ethiopia, Kenya, Mauritius, Nigeria, Rwanda, and Zambia now have SEZs with the assistance of China, and in 2018, Djibouti joined the ranks, as a part of the Belt and Road Initiative (BRI) (UNCTAD, 2019). While it is too early to assess their impact on local economies, it is interesting to note the job creation effect of SEZs at the local level: Chinese projects have been generally criticized for being isolationist, bringing Chinese nationals in as workers. In other words, Chinese companies may have simply hired local workers whose wages are lower than those in China.[7]

16.4.2 The case of Turkey in Africa

Somewhat overshadowed by investment by China and India, Turkish investment is on the rise in Africa. The current Turkish government, led by the Justice and Development Party (in Turkish: Adaletve Kalkınma Partisi AKP), in power since 2003, attaches great importance to promoting the involvement of Turkish enterprises (with a focus on SMEs) in the African market, as announced in its policy direction paper, "Strategy Development of Economic Relationships with Africa." According to Habiyaremye and Oĝuzlu (2014), Turkey followed the example of Chinese involvement, became an observer in the African Union (AU) in 2003, and declared itself to be a strategic partner of the AU in 2008. In addition to the remarkable expansion of the Turkish Airlines network, the Turkish Confederation of Businessmen and Industrialists (TUSKON) has been holding the Turkey-Africa Trade Bridge Summit every year since 2005. Another private initiative is the funding of Turkish schools in Africa since 1990s, so as to foster the development of future business partners who have a good understanding of the Turkish language and culture. The Turkish International Cooperation and Development Agency (TIKA) is also involved in strengthening Turkey's ties with African countries.

Those partnerships are strengthened by the high-level political commitment of the AKP. In fact, the tactical alliance between the AKP and business associations, called "the Anatolian Tigers," is benefitting from the new African market, which also strengthens the domestic political base of the AKP (Habiyaremye & Oĝuzlu, 2014).

16.5 Case study: Multiple partnerships for industrial development in Ethiopia

Ethiopia deserves special attention because the country is beginning to join the global garment supply chains, and various types of development partnerships with the private sector are taking place in their latest forms. In this section, we first review Ethiopia's endeavor to industrialize and the recent FDI trends, and then analyze the way these new partnerships are taking place in Ethiopia, with reference to traditional donors, Japanese ODA, and emerging economies. It also shows how such diverse partnerships intend to support the country's participation in the apparel and textile GVCs.

More specifically, Ethiopia has been chosen for a case study for three reasons. First, the Ethiopian government stands out among the Sub-Saharan African countries for its serious commitment to industrial development and for the high-growth since 2000s. The current five-year plan sets a new aim to "render the country a leader in light manufacturing in Africa and one of the leaders in overall manufacturing globally" (FDRE, 2016), with the aim of massive job creation, technology transfer, and industrial development. Second, Ethiopia is taking advantage of its abundant low-cost labor pool to attract a large volume of labor-intensive, light manufacturing FDI—not only from emerging economies but also from Western apparel giants. Third, active development partnerships are unfolding, involving government, donors, MNCs, and major apparel buyers.

16.5.1 Ethiopia's endeavor to industrialize and recent FDI trends

Ethiopia is unique among Sub-Saharan African countries in its bold and determined approach to economic transformation. With strong policy ownership, since 1991, the country has established the proactive development orientation expressed in the concepts of a Democratic Developmental State and Agricultural Development Led Industrialization (ADLI). This unique policy direction was driven by the strong leadership of former Prime Minister (PM) Meles Zenawi (1991–2012) and his successor Hailemariam (2012–2018). PM Meles's strong interest in East Asian development model—he and his colleagues studied at the Open University in the UK—has yielded a series of policy initiatives, starting with the ADLI (1992–1993 and onward), the three-year Sustainable Development and Poverty Reduction Program (SDPRP, 2002–2005) and A Plan for Accelerated and Sustained Development to End Poverty (PASDEP, 2005/06–2009/10). It was PM Meles who asked the Japanese government and JICA for two pillars of industrial development cooperation: (1) industrial policy dialogue with Japanese researchers to learn the East Asian development experiences; and (2) the Kaizen project, guided by Japanese experts, to acquire a Japanese way of participatory production management to improve efficiency and productivity on the factory floor.

More recently, the Ethiopian government has made clear its commitment to industrialization, with the launch of the five-year plan, Growth and Transformation

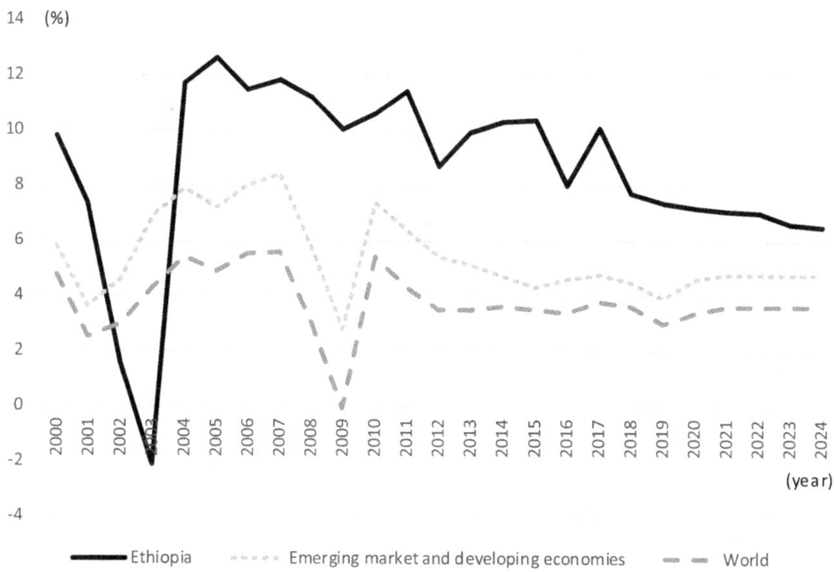

Figure 16.4 GDP growth and forecasts, 2000–2024 (%)

Plan (GTP) I (2010/11–2014/15) and the current GTP II (2015/16–2019/20). In a practical sense, transformation means industrialization. The objective of GTP I and II is to enhance the productivity of the agriculture and manufacturing sectors and set conditions for industrialization so that the main engine of growth could shift from agriculture to industry. In 2015, the Ethiopian government announced its ten-year strategy and national goal of becoming a lower-middle-income country by 2025. Covering the first five years of this period, GTP II articulated a national vision of becoming a leading nation in light manufacturing in Africa in particular and in manufacturing in general (FDRE, 2016). GTP II sets ambitious targets for 2020, including 11 percent annual average growth rate; 8 percent share of manufacturing in Gross Domestic Product (GDP) (currently 4.6 percent); and manufacturing employment of 750,000 (currently 380,000).

Ethiopia has sustained economic growth since 2004, with the highest level of growth recorded over the past decade (Figure 16.4). The country's average growth rate during 2006–2014 was 10.5 percent (World Bank database), and the poverty ratio dropped from 38.7 percent (2004–2005) to 23.4 percent (2014–2015). External financial flows to Ethiopia dramatically increased with the introduction of proactive development policies, and in particular after 2013 (Figure 16.5, Figure 16.6).

To seize this historical opportunity, the government introduced a set of additional policy initiatives: the FDI proclamation and regulation were revised; the FDI administration was centralized and strengthened in the Ethiopian Investment Commission (EIC), now directly under the PM; and industrial parks and their

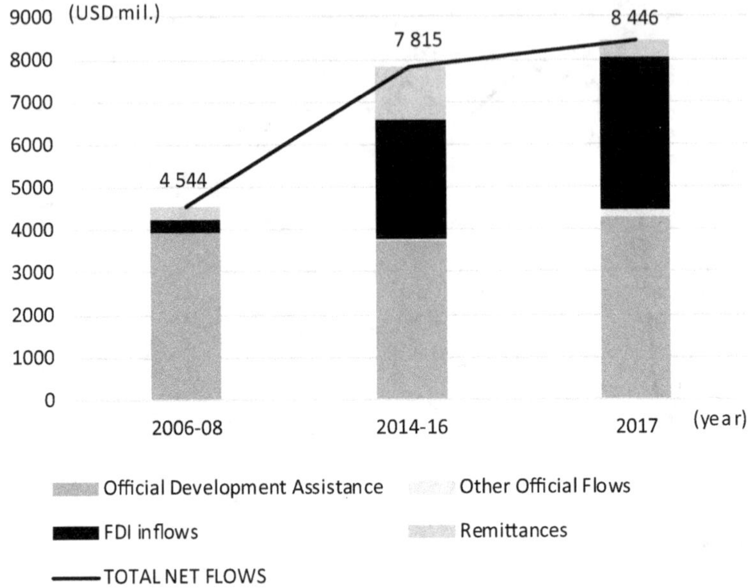

Figure 16.5 External financial flows to Ethiopia (US$ million)

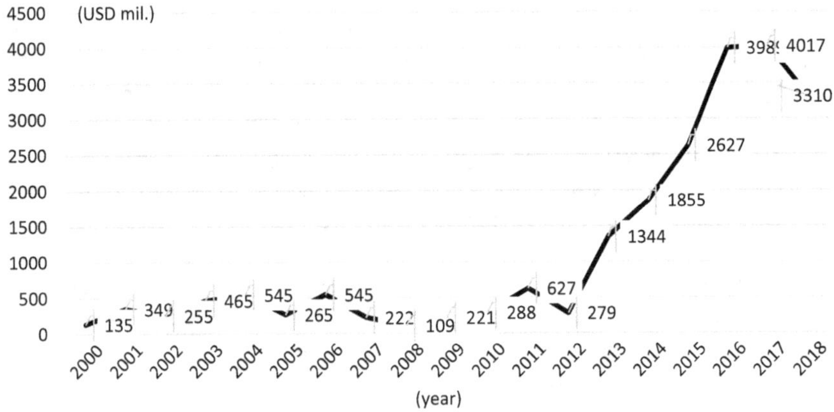

Figure 16.6 FDI inflows to Ethiopia, 2000–2018 (US$ million)

managing authority, the Industrial Parks Development Corporation (IPDC), were created, modeled on Singapore's Jurong Town Corporation. Dr. Arkebe Oqubay, Minister and Special Adviser to the PM—a key figure in the promotion of the concept of industrial parks (IPs)—wrote that "Hawassa Industrial Park (HIP) has become the flagship industrial estate whose successes and lessons are to be replicated in a dozen-or-so proposed state-run industrial parks" (Oqubay, 2015) (see Box 16.1 for HIP). Separate parks are also planned for agro-processing and for SMEs, and big projects, integrated steel production and a petrochemical complex, are being studied. The quality of industrial workers, and compliance with international labor and environmental standards, have become critical issues (see Table 16.1 for the status of IPs).

The proactive, trial and error attitude of Ethiopian industrial policy direction was crucial to attracting labor-intensive manufacturing FDI, especially for the apparel sector. Balchin and Calabrese (2019) identified three phases in the increase of such FDI. The first wave, dating from the early 2000s, consisted of small-scale investments, mostly from individual Indian and Pakistani entrepreneurs—and since 2004, the Ethiopian government has targeted Turkey, India, and China as sources of FDI in manufacturing (Oqubay, 2015; Tiwari, 2015). The second wave was triggered in 2008 by the increase in Turkish investment. Since mid-2010, significant investment flew in from Asian countries, largely for the industrial parks. Many studies have noted that the second and third waves have been central to the acceleration of garment production in Ethiopia (Staritz & Whitfield, 2017).

In this process, "The government realized that the focus on local investment took place without a full understanding of GVCs in the garment sector" (Balchin & Calabrese, 2019, p. 23). It should also be noted that the roles of former PM Meles and his economic advisor, Dr. Oqubay, were again decisive in attracting FDI suitable for Ethiopian needs. As in the case of Kaizen from Japan, PM Meles extended direct invitations to foreign public and private partners to come and invest in Ethiopia. For instance, the president of the Turkish apparel maker, Ayka, and the former vice-president of the Chinese shoemaking firm, the Huajian Group, recall personal invitations from PM Meles (Tiwari, 2015). European and American apparel buyers, such as Hennes and Mauritz (H&M) and Philip-Van Heusen (PVH), were also impressed by the strong commitment of senior governmental officials, notable in the swift reactions and high availability of Dr. Oqubay, a strong promoter of IPs in Ethiopia (Mihretu & Llobet, 2017). As shown below, HIP is a good example of how the government's efforts have resulted in attracting apparel giant PVH and its Asian suppliers to Ethiopia, and also how PVH emphasizes CSR in its supply chain management.

16.5.2 Growth of development partnerships in support of Ethiopia's industrialization

In the early 2000s, only a few donors (UNIDO, USAID, Italy, Germany, and Japan) were helping the industrial development of Ethiopia; at that time the overall focus of the aid community was poverty reduction and governance. But, since around 2010, together with the global business trends and in alignment with the Ethiopian government's GTP I and II, an increasing number of donors have joined to support the economic transformation agenda (DFID, EU, SIDA, etc.). The existing donors, who were already interested in industrial development, expanded the scope of their support as well. The financial flow of trade-related

Table 16.1 Status of selected industrial parks in Ethiopia

	Name of parks	*Region*	*Land in ha*	*Major eligible manufacturing sectors*
I. Government-developed IPs				
1	Addis Industry Village	Addis Ababa	8.7	Apparel
2	Bole Lemi I	Addis Ababa	157	Apparel & Textile
	Bole Lemi II	Addis Ababa	170	Apparel & textile
3	Kilinto	Addis Ababa	279	Pharmaceutical hub
4	Hawassa	South	300 (140 in phase I)	Apparel & textile
5	Adama	South–East	2000 (120 in phase I)	Assembling, garments, food
6	Diredawa	East	4000 (150 in phase I)	Apparel, garments, and machinery
7	Mekelle	North–East	1000 (75 in phase I)	Apparel & textile
8	Kombolcha	North–East	700 (75 in phase I)	Apparel & textile
9	Jimma	South–West	1000 (75 in phase I)	Apparel & textile
10	Bahir–Dar	North–West	1000 (75 in phase I	Apparel & garment
11	Debre–Birhan	North–East	100 (75 in phase I)	Apparel, agroindustry

Investors (country of origin)	*Export (US$) (target/actual)*	*Job creation (target/actual)*	*Construction completion period*	*Occupancy rate (%)*
–	–	–	Operational since the 1980s	100
11 investors (Taiwan, South Korea, India, China, etc.)	1 billion (annual)/ 2 millions (month)	35,000/ 14,200 (Feb. 2019)	Operational since 2014	100
China	–	15,000	Construction completed in Summer 2019	–
10 global investors (China, etc.) signed the MOU	–	15,000	Construction completed in Summer 2019	–
25 investors (US, China & Hong Kong, Indonesia, Taiwan, Spain, France, the UK, Belgium, India, Sri Lanka, etc.)	1 billion (annual)/ 3 millions (month)	60,000/ 16,000 (Feb. 2019)	Operational since Jan. 2017	100
China, South Korea	38 million (annual)	25,000/ 1,500 (2018)	Operational since Aug. 2017	75
China	–	40,000	Operational since Sep. 2017	26
India, Sri Lanka, Bangladesh	–	20,000/3,800 (2018)	Operational since June 2017	80
Italy, US, South Korea	–	20,000/3,800 (2018)	Operational since June 2017	100
China	–	25,000	Operational since Feb. 2018	100
Hong Kong	–	20,000	Operational since May 2018	100
Belgium	–	13,000	Inaugrated in Mar. 2019	50

Table 16.1 Cont.

	Name of parks	*Region*	*Land in ha*	*Major eligible manufacturing sectors*
12	Arerti	North–East	804 (75 in Phase I)	Construction products, home appliance
13	Aysha	Somalia (East)	100 (75 in phase I)	Apparel & textile
II. Private IPs				
1	Eastern Industrial Zone	South	500	Various
2	Huajian Light Industry City	Addis Ababa	138	Shoe garment
3	Modjo George Shoe IP	South	50	Leather
4	DBL	North–East	78.5	Apparel & textile
5	Velocity	North–East	176.7	Apparel & textile
6	Kingdom Linen Industry Zone	East	32	Linen
III. Regional developed IPs (Integrated Agro-Industrial Parks)				
Bure (Amhara), Bulbura (Oromia), Yirgarem (SNNPR), Baeker (Tigray)				

Sources: Gebremariam & Feyisa (2019), IPDC (n.d.), UNIDO (2018), Mihretu & Llobet (2017), Nicolas (2017), Schaefer & Oya (2019).

ODA doubled between 2006/08 and 2017 (Figure 16.7). Figure 16.8 illustrates the major components of industrial support by official donors and its evolution over the same period.

As indicated earlier, former PM Meles, PM Hailemariam, and their teams were very interested in learning from the East Asian development experience and actively sought policy advice and technical and economic cooperation from Asian and emerging economies (e.g., China, South Korea, Japan, Turkey, India). In some cases, learning and the exchange of ideas were realized outside the traditional development cooperation channels.

Ethiopia's partnership with China is the longest and most influential (at least in volume) among its partnerships with Asian partners. A number of studies have observed that Ethiopia is emulating the Chinese model (Gelan, 2018; Hackenesch,

Investors (country of origin)	*Export (US$) (target/actual)*	*Job creation (target/actual)*	*Construction completion period*	*Occupancy rate (%)*
–	–	–	Planning stage	–
–	–	–	Planning stage	–
Qiyuan group (China), 83 companies (56 operational in 2019)	3 billions (annual)/ 4.5 millions (month)	100,000/ 23,412 (Feb. 2019)	Operational since 2006	–
Huajian Group (China)	–/30 millions (annual)	–/ 4,600 (2018)	Partly operational	–
George Shoe group (Taiwan)	–	–	–	–
DBL (Bangladesh) is H&M's supplier	–	4,000/ –	–	–
Vogue group (India)	–	–	–	–
Kingdom group (China)	–	–	Signed the MOU	–

2018). PM Meles repeatedly referred to the role of China in his official speeches and intra-party discussion (Tiwari, 2015). Hackenesch (2018:135) mentions that "the learning process is facilitated by close cooperation between Chinese and Ethiopian governments and ruling parties" since 2006, as China offered training programs (10 days to one month) to various segments of national and regional administrations, including newly appointed senior officials after a governmental reshuffle. From 2006 to 2010, about 200 officials participated in study tours, and that number is still increasing, as the MOFCOM also offers short- and long-term scholarship to study at Chinese universities. However, Hackenesch notes that the impact of those training programs is unknown, given the lack of systematic assessment due to the opacity of Chinese assistance.

Nevertheless, it is clear that the Ethiopian government has been applying the Chinese SEZs model in the country; Ethiopia's experience with SEZs (in Ethiopia the term "IP" is used) began with the Eastern Industrial Zone, established in

Box 16.1 Hawassa Industrial Park (HIP)

HIP, a flagship IP developed and supported by the Ethiopian government, specializes in textile and garment production. It is built on 300 ha of land located 275 km south of Addis Ababa, and the government invested US$250 million. HIP is the second IP developed by the government, after Bole Lemil I in Addis Ababa. HIP is impressive for (1) its efforts to integrate and reorganize all industrial policy tools around the IP strategy; (2) its efforts to attract foreign manufacturing investors and its prompt and careful responses to their requests; (2) a large number of new measures related to HIP, including recruitment, housing and training of the workforce, prompt construction of a new airport, and a plan to extend the existing railroad line; (4) adjustments in industrial park policy based on errors identified in the establishment of Bole Lemi I, the first state-run IP of Ethiopia; (5) innovative HIP policies, notably one-stop service and zero liquid emissions; (6) the creation and active use of the HIP tenant association and frequent discussion among key policymakers and the association.

The first phase of HIP became operational in July 2016, after just nine months of construction (to build 37 giant factory sheds). HIP was constructed by Chinese private companies, with the support of Chinese loans. In parallel, Ethiopian IP managers were offered the opportunity to participate in two study tours to China to learn about IP management and design. The tours were organized by MOFCOM in 2017 and the Ethiopian participants (including officials, engineers, workers) noted that there were technology and skill transfers in the process (Tang, K., 2019).

One of the aims of HIP is to invite world-class investors. Attracted by HIP's competitiveness, Philip-Van Heusen (PVH), a leading firm in a GVC, began investing in HIP and mobilizing its Asian suppliers (from locations including Sri Lanka, Hong Kong, and China, etc.). PVH regarded Ethiopia as a strategic hub for their global apparel and textile production networks, largely because of the country's numerous competitive advantages. According to Mihretu and Llobet (2017), Ethiopia's main advantages are: (1) low labor costs (for skilled and unskilled workers); (2) a large and trainable workforce; (3) accessible and sustainable hydraulic energy; (4) the lowest electricity costs in Africa; (5) its relative proximity to Europe; (6) preferential market access (e.g., African Growth and Opportunity Act (AGOA) in the US, Everything But Arms (EBA) in the EU, Common Market for Eastern and Southern Africa (COMESA)); (7) significant state support/incentive programs; (8) availability of quality raw materials; and (9) political stability and macroeconomic growth. For PVH, since HIP was their first major effort at large-scale relocation in Sub-Saharan Africa, they are keen to comply with CSR and have taken initiatives, in partnership with Western donors and international organizations, to enhance the environmental and social sustainability of their business operations in Ethiopia. Such corporate behavior is closely related to the consumer preferences of European and US markets.

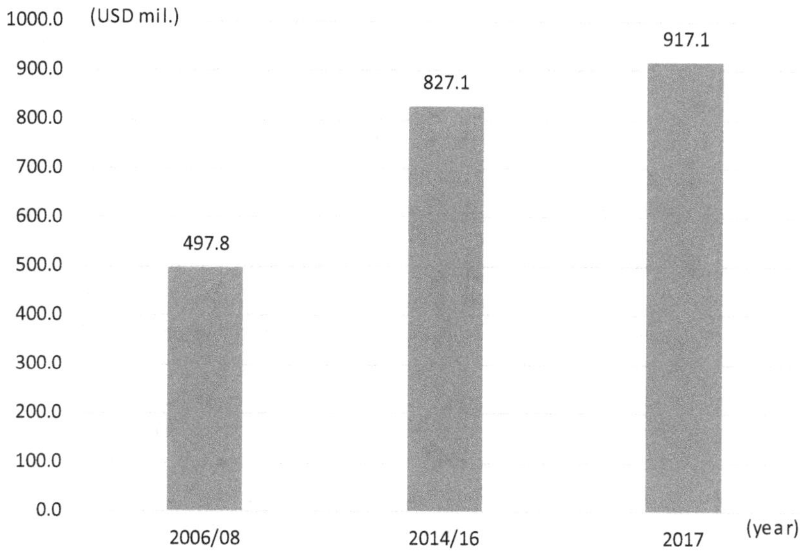

Figure 16.7 Trade-related ODA to Ethiopia (2006/2008–2017)

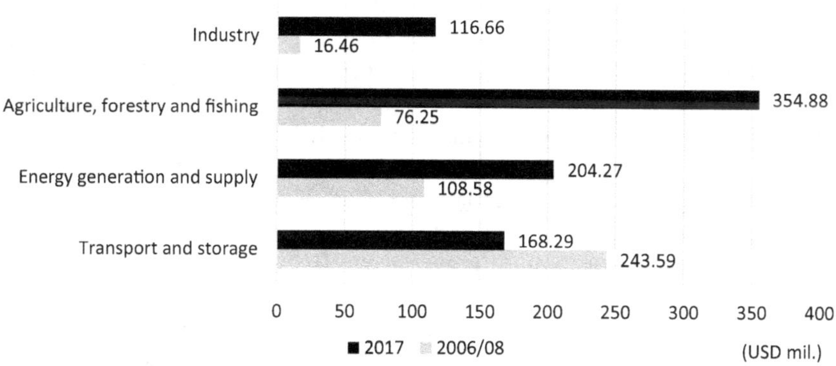

Figure 16.8 Major components of industrial support (2006/2008–2017)

2007 as a Chinese-private IP. While China went on to construct another private IP in Ethiopia, and there were some technology transfers in construction and IP management, the Ethiopian government opted to construct government-led IPs so as to ensure long-term sustainability (Tang, K., 2019).[8] Fifteen IPs have been constructed by 2019, and more are in the pipeline (according to the Ethiopian government, a total of 30 IPs will be established by 2025). In addition, it is important to note that cooperation between the ruling parties (the Chinese Communist Party, CCP and the Ethiopian People's Revolutionary Democratic

Front, EPRDF) has also served as a strong channel for discussion of the development experience and the management of the ruling party. Such close party-to-party relationships have helped to strengthen economic and political cooperation between the two countries (Hackenesch, 2018, pp. 136–137).

The case of Turkey offers another interesting perspective on the deepening of industrial cooperation. Besides the government-to-government cooperation discussed above, a transnational migratory network of textile labor between Ethiopia and Turkey has been in place since the 1990s. Turkey is one of the major importers of Ethiopian garments, due to significant investments by Turkish firms (notably Ayka),[9] who are integrating Ethiopian textile production into their GVCs. Another example is collaboration with the Ethiopian Textile Industry Development Institute (ETIDI), supported by India's National Institute of Fashion Technology (NIFT).

Japanese sharing of East Asian experiences was achieved via academic cooperation at first; it then developed into a wide range of Japanese ODA programs. At the request of the then PM of Ethiopia, in 2009, Japan began supporting Ethiopia's industrial development through two programs: (1) industrial policy dialogue (by a team from JICA and the National Graduate Institute for Policy Studies (GRIPS) including the authors) to share the East Asian development experience and to discuss with the country's policymakers pragmatic policies based on the Ethiopian reality; and (2) a Kaizen project aimed at training local Kaizen consultants, building an institutional foundation, and improving quality and productivity at the factory level (Ohno & Ohno, 2019). The Kaizen project is notable in that it paved the way to the establishment of the Ethiopia Kaizen Institute (EKI) in 2013. The EKI, aiming to serve as a national and regional hub for quality improvement, collaborates with a wide range of organizations that support industrial upgrading. For instance, the EKI supports the world's first PhD program in Kaizen Management (Quality and Productivity Management), offered at Mekele University. As of January 2020, these two programs (industrial policy dialogue and the Kaizen project) have entered the third phase of implementation. Over the past decade, the portfolio of JICA's industrial cooperation to Ethiopia has expanded to include additional programs such as: export promotion through the creation of Ethiopian unique and high-quality products ("Champion Products"); and capacity development of IPDC to improve the quality of IPs and promote strategic FDI attraction. As part of the PPP for SDGs, a Japanese SME is also engaged in the quality management and inspection business for original equipment manufacture (OEM) production of Japanese apparel companies.

In addition to JICA support, METI, JETRO, and AOTS are working with Japanese companies interested in doing business in Ethiopia. For example, Itochu, a Japanese trading company which has longstanding expertise in the apparel and garment sector, signed a Memorandum of Understanding (MOU) with the EIC and the ETIDI in August 2019 to support quality and productivity control in the Ethiopian textile materials and garment industry and setting out the Japanese quality assurance system. The company sent its own experts to garment factories in Ethiopia, which is complemented by METI's support for additional external experts. Overall, most of the above activities are related to economic upgrading of Ethiopian local companies.

The World Bank, which previously had a modest engagement in private-sector capacity building through a matching fund, now offers a broader range of large-scale assistance to Ethiopia. These include industrial parks, female entrepreneurs, and job creation for refugees (in tandem with the UK and the EU).[10] The ILO is actively developing "decent work"-related projects, in partnership with European donors and FDI firms. UNIDO, based on its long-term engagement, has designated Ethiopia a model partner country for inclusive and sustainable industrial development.

16.5.3 Development partnerships in apparel and textile GVCs

In the apparel and garment sector of Ethiopia, various types of PPPs are being supported by donor agencies, international organizations, and MNCs in the latest forms, such as the Partnership for Sustainable Textiles, explained in Section 16.2.3. In Ethiopia, H&M, a Swedish multinational clothing retail giant, SIDA, ILO, and more recently, a German development cooperation (BMZ and GIZ) are key members of the partnership.

H&M began its operations in Ethiopia in 2013. Currently, it works with 10 suppliers (Indian and Sri Lankan companies and one Ethiopian). Similar to PVH, H&M intends to make Ethiopia an African hub for socially responsible production of garments for both the global and domestic markets. This also presents an opportunity for Ethiopia to be seen by major multinational brands as a potential sourcing country with an explicit commitment to fair global supply chains, fully respecting universal human rights, ILO principles, and the development goals of the sourcing countries. Driven by those motives, H&M and SIDA launched a three-year industrial relations project in 2014, running from September 2015 to August 2018, with a total investment of US$3,095,000. The project is funded by SIDA and H&M and implemented by the ILO in collaboration with the Ethiopian Ministry of Labour and Social Affairs, the Ministry of Industry, the Confederation of Ethiopian Trade Unions, and the Ethiopian Employers Federation. The project aims to contribute to the development of a socially sustainable textile and garment industry in line with Ethiopia's GTP II. H&M also signed the agreement with the ILO in September 2014, with the aim of establishing a positive, innovative model for other brands and creating a global alliance to promote the ILO's Decent Work Agenda in the supply chains of the global garment industry.[11]

Bangladesh-based ready-made garment and textile giant DBL Group is making progress with its plans to establish a factory in Ethiopia, supported by long-time customer H&M, that will provide some 4,000 jobs. A Mekele-based integrated knitting, dyeing, and garment facility will be solely owned by DBL Group, with Swedish state-owned investment firm Swedfund lending US$15 million in the form of a loan for the facility. Fast fashion retailer H&M is committed as a long-time buyer and will support the factory with expert knowledge in sustainable textile production. Decent work conditions, job creation for women, and environmental considerations are some of the key goals for the project, which is aimed at advancing one of Ethiopia's prioritized industry sectors.

The German government (through BMZ) will contribute one million euros to help fund a vocational training center; two companies will contribute a total of one million euros. The aim is to firmly establish high social and environmental standards in the growing textile export industry in Ethiopia from the ground up. In future, appropriate training of skilled workers and managers will create a foundation for working toward those standards.

Germany is also involved in development cooperation activities to make the Ethiopian textiles and garment industry sustainable. For instance, BMZ is supporting measures to train labor inspectors, expand environmental management systems in industrial parks, and promote dialogue between management and workers.

Further to the above, emerging economies are actively engaged in industrial upgrading of Ethiopia's apparel and textile sector: Chinese and Turkish investors have been providing skill upgrading through partnerships with Ethiopian institutions, such as Dire Dawa University, which has a specialized department of garment industry and technology.

India has been also involved in the ETIDI Project, a five-year capacity building program launched in July 2013 between the two governments. In partnership with the National Institute of Fashion Technology (NIFT) in India, the project aims to create a Center of Excellence through a twinning arrangement with NIFT to support various training programs in Ethiopia and higher education programs in India for ETIDI officers/experts. The domains chosen in the first phase aimed at strengthening the capabilities of ETIDI in training, consulting, research, and marketing support services for the Ethiopian apparel industry. Reflecting the assessment of Phase I of the ETIDI-NIFT project, and in order to bridge the gap between the sector's performance and that in international scenarios, a MOU for the second phase of the NIFT–ETIDI twinning arrangement was signed in April 2018. The duration of the second phase of the project will be three years, with a focus on factory interventions in apparel export merchandising/marketing and garment technology.

Despite a number of efforts by external actors (donors and MNCs), Ethiopian working conditions—low wages and some labor practices—have been pointed out by academics (Barrett & Baumann-Pauly, 2019; Gelan, 2018; Hardy & Hauge, 2019; Schaefer & Oya, 2019) and criticized by the workers association (WRC, 2018).[12] In response, the Ethiopian government has decided to explore the setting of a minimum wage.[13] At the time of writing, the state of those explorations is not clear—but it is acknowledged globally that the improvement of working conditions motivates workers, leading to enhanced productivity in the end. Another setback is the political turmoil that occurred in Hawassa City in July 2019, disturbing HIP operations for some time. The Ethiopian press quoted PM Abiy as saying that the government faced huge pressure from foreign investors to terminate HIP operations if the situation did not change.

16.6 Conclusion and implications for industrialization of today's developing countries

We have briefly reviewed new and diversified models of development partnerships with the private sector and shown how they have been applied in Ethiopia. Although the list of actors and instruments presented here is not exhaustive, we consider it useful to summarize key features and lessons learned from the experiences over the past 10 years.

First, with the advance of the SDGs' agenda and the deepening of economic links through GVCs, various stakeholders have come to support the industrialization of developing countries through partnerships with the private sector. In one sense, Japan was the pioneer of development cooperation in partnership with the private sector: The Trinity Model (FDI, trade, and aid) of development cooperation has been widely practiced in East Asia since the mid-1980s, contributing to the development of regional production networks. However, along with the evolution of the global development agenda, such as the MDGs and the SDGs, and global calls for CSR in value chain management, particularly after the 2008 financial crisis, new models of development partnerships with business have emerged, initiated by Western donors and scholars, and joined by CSOs and NPOs. These new models envisage the role of business in providing innovative solutions for sustainable development and ensuring social and environmental compliance in GVCs (particularly, operations concerned with developing countries). Now, JICA is also engaged in PPPs for sustainable business. Moreover, as emerging economies (such as China, India, Turkey) have expanded FDI into developing countries, they are exploring various types of cooperation arrangements with host countries.

Second, there exist clear differences between Western donors and Japan (and to some extent, emerging donors) in the orientation of development partnerships with the private sector—particularly over social vs. economic upgrading. As discussed earlier, Western donors and MNCs are strongly interested in meeting social and environmental standards as a central concern for promoting apparel and garment sector competitiveness in developing countries. This is closely related to consumers' trends in European and American markets, which are ethically conscious. On the other hand, Japanese agencies and companies are more interested in productivity and quality improvement of the production and service delivery processes, such as meeting QCD requirements. As a general tendency, Japanese stakeholders consider that skill upgrading and quality improvement are the first stages of work to strengthen the apparel and garment GVCs—or they should go hand in hand with social upgrading. This is why JICA is implementing Kaizen support in many developing countries, including Ethiopia. But the Ethiopian case study shows that there is much emphasis on, and support for, labor and environment issues by Western donors and MNCs.

Other latecomer countries, such as Myanmar, have been struggling to meet the higher quality standards required by the Japanese market, and the need to satisfy social standards reflecting the interests of consumers in the main export market (the EU). Many developing countries involved in (or with interests in) participating in apparel GVCs will face such difficult dilemmas, but the importance of skill upgrading should not be neglected in this sector. In sum, today's developing countries must tackle the dual challenges of social and economic upgrading in GVCs. Donors and MNCs should provide support programs for value chain inclusion of local companies and the capacity development of host country governments to improve their business environments, as well as policies, and the capabilities, both of humans and of enterprises.

Third, recipient views have been absent from the discussion so far, even though the host country government and local stakeholders are likely to be associated with the identification and formation of partnerships driven by MNCs or bilateral donors' programs, reflecting a commercial interest. In this regard, the determination of national leaders to achieve industrial upgrading is critically important, and the governments should make serious efforts to strategically target FDI to invite qualified partners and ensure technology transfer to local companies. The Ethiopian case study suggests the vital role played by political leadership in attracting foreign investors, developing IPs (including HIP), and initiating Kaizen and other industrial development cooperation. These are laudable achievements, considering that the country lacks general prerequisites for FDI attraction (factors such as experience with domestic and external conflicts, a landlocked and resource-poor country). The Ethiopian model will not be easy to emulate, yet it does offer a different perspective and new policy choices for other latecomers. Nevertheless, we need to closely watch the leadership model of the current PM Abiy.

PM Abiy, newly appointed in 2018, only recently announced a clear economic policy. His new policy direction, the "Homegrown Economic Reform Agenda," announced in October 2019, seems to be distancing itself from the developmental state model adopted by the former PM Meles and PM Hailemariam, and signaling his intention to build a closer partnership with the World Bank and the International Monetary Fund (IMF), which emphasize traditional liberalization and privatization. While it is too early to predict the impact of such policy changes, it is important that PM Abiy follows his predecessors in diversifying economic partnerships so as to sustain growth in key sectors and achieve both social and economic upgrading of GVCs. There is also a possibility that more emerging or non-traditional donors (for instance, the Gulf states) may come forward, bringing a different kind of development partnership with the private sector.

Notes

1 ODA, non-ODA flows (other official flows (OOF), foreign direct investment (FDI) etc.) and personal remittances are included, based on OECD-DAC definition.

2 Porter and Kramer (2011) argue that the principle of shared value involves creating economic value in a way that *also* creates value for society by addressing its needs and

challenges. Shared value goes beyond social responsibility and philanthropy, and is a new way to achieve economic success.

3 The UN Global Compact is a voluntary initiative based on CEO commitments to implement universal sustainability principles (such as human rights, labor, environment and anti-corruption policies) and take actions that advance societal goals. It is funded by contributions from governments to the UN Global Compact Trust Fund and from business to the Foundation for the Global Compact.

4 The Overseas Economic Cooperation Fund of Japan (OECF) (the predecessor of today's JICA ODA loan operations) used to provide private-sector investment finance, but on a limited scale. Furthermore, when the new JICA was established by integrating ODA loans, technical cooperation, and grants in 2008, there was a period when private-sector investment finance was put on hold. After several years of hiatus, in 2012, the Japanese government decided to reactivate private-sector investment finance to companies in developing countries.

5 JICA signed a joint venture agreement with its Myanmar partners on the Thilawa SEZ Development Project in April 2014 to extend private sector investment finance to MJTD (equity participation). MJTD's shareholder composition is 51 percent for Myanmar and 49 percent for Japan (three trading companies (Mitsubishi, Marubeni, and Sumitomo), several banks, and JICA). JICA is also providing comprehensive financial packages to the Bangladesh government to develop the Bangladesh Economic Zones Authority (BEZA) in introducing a one-stop service. It also supports Mombasa SEZ development in Kenya.

6 JICA has been supporting Kaizen in various countries in Africa (e.g., Ethiopia, Ghana, Tanzania, Tunisia, and Zambia). To further contribute quality and productivity improvement in Africa, JICA launched the Africa Kaizen Initiative at TICAD 6, held in Kenya in 2016, which became a joint initiative with the NEPAD in 2017. Since 2015, annual Kaizen conferences have been organized in Africa, aimed at mutual learning of know-how and practical experiences with Kaizen and promoting networks.

7 According to the NYU Stern Center research, Ethiopia ranks among the lowest pay in the global garment supply chain. The study compares the monthly minimum wage in selected countries, such as Turkey (US$340), China (US$326), Bangladesh and Myanmar (both US$95), and Ethiopia (US$26) (Barrett & Baumann-Pauly, 2019).

8 K. Tang (2019) explained that Ethiopian researchers, who took part in the study of industrial parks, believed that private parks would only pursue short-run profits, thus were not suitable for Ethiopia.

9 Established in 2006, Ayka Addis built its factory in Ethiopia at a cost of US$140 million at Alemgena, located some 20 kilometers west of Addis Ababa. Operational since 2010, Ayka has created more than 10,000 jobs and contributed to about half of the textile export in 2014 (Anadolu Agency, 2014). Yet, Ayka started to claim a loss and went bankrupt in 2019, as the company could not pay back the 1.3 billion birr loan from the Development Bank in Ethiopia. (*Capital*, 2019).

10 The World Bank's portfolio in industrial development in Ethiopia has grown rapidly. Major projects include: Competitiveness and Job Creation Project for selected IPs, such as Bole Lemi II & Kilinto (US$250 million, approved in 2014), SME Finance Project (US$200 million, approved in 2016), Economic Opportunities Program (for Ethiopians and refugees US$202 million, approved in 2018), and the Growth and Competitiveness Program (development policy finance/ US$1200 million, approved in 2018).

11 The agreement covers the improvement of industrial relations, working conditions, and productivity at the national, regional, and factory levels (ILO, 2016). At the

national level, the agreement assists actors to develop and improve comprehensive approaches to: (1) socially sustainable management of global supply; (2) improvement of productivity and competitiveness of the textile and garment industry; and (3) improvement of labor market governance (labor law, wage policy, labor inspection, social dialogue, collective bargaining, dispute settlement) toward better wages and working conditions, and respect for workers' rights in the industry. At the regional and sectoral levels, the project will assist the labor administration in strengthening labor inspection capacity, social dialogue and dispute settlement for improved industrial relations. It will also build capacity of employers, workers, and their organizations at the sectoral and enterprise levels, in terms of strengthening organizational capacity, developing sound industrial relations and social dialogue practices, so as to improve wages and working conditions in tandem with work to enhance productivity. At the factory level, the agreement will provide demand-driven capacity building support, informed by a baseline survey, to improve productivity and strengthen labor relations in full compliance with ILO principles.

12 In addition to low wages (monthly base wage for apparel workers is set at 750 birr (US$26) by the government), cultural clashes between foreign middle managers and Ethiopian workers (aggressive attitude by the expatriate supervisors from South and East Asia), lack of dormitory facilities, and weak opportunity for workers' collective action are pointed out as the main reasons for low productivity and the high attrition rate of workers.

13 In this regard, H&M supported the ILO's call for the Ethiopian government to introduce a national wage-setting mechanism (Banerji, Earley, & MacAllister, 2018).

Bibliography

Amaeshi, K., & Idemudia, U. (2018). Africapitalism: A management idea for business in Africa? In K. Amaeshi, A. Okupe, & U. Idemudia (Eds.), *Africapitalism: Rethinking the role of business in Africa* (pp. 19–41). Cambridge: Cambridge University Press.

Anadolu Agency. (2014). Turkish firm declared top textile exporter in Ethiopia. *Hurriyet Daily*, September 14. Available at: www.hurriyetdailynews.com/turkish-firm-declared-top-textile-exporter-in-ethiopia------71951 (accessed January, 7, 2020).

Balchin, N., & Calabrese, N. (2019). *Comparative country study of the development of textile and garment sectors: Lessons for Tanzania*. London: ODI Report. Available at: www.odi.org/publications/11343-comparative-country-study-development-textile-and-garment-sectors-lessons-tanzania (accessed January 2, 2020).

Banerji, S., Earley, K., & MacAllister, P. (2018). Review of H&M group's roadmap to fair living wage. Ethical Trading Initiative. Available at: www.ethicaltrade.org/resources/review-hm-groups-roadmap-to-fair-living-wage (accessed January 2, 2020).

Barrett, P.M., & Baumann-Pauly, D. (2019) *Made in Ethiopia: Challenges in the garment industry's new frontier*. New York: NYU STERN Center for Business and Human Rights. Available at: www.stern.nyu.edu/experience-stern/faculty-research/made-ethiopia-challenges-garment-industry-s-new-frontier (accessed January 2, 2020).

Barrientos, S., Gereffi, G., & Rossi, A. (2011). Economic and social upgrading in global production networks: A new paradigm for a changing world. *International Labour Review*, 150, (3–4), 319–340. Available at: www.researchgate.net/publication/228278108_Economic_and_Social_Upgrading_in_Global_Production_Networks_A_New_Paradigm_for_a_Changing_World (accessed January 2, 2020).

BSDC. (2017). Better business, better world. Available at: http://report.businesscommission.org/report (accessed January 2, 2020).

Caneque, F. C., & Hart, S. L. (Eds.) (2016). *Base of the pyramid 3.0: Sustainable development through innovation & entrepreneurship*. Oxford: Greenleaf Publishing.

Capital. (2019). DBE floats Ayka Addis for record foreclosure. July, 1. Available at: www.capitalethiopia.com/featured/dbe-floats-ayka-addis-for-record-foreclosure/ (accessed January, 7, 2020).

FDRE. (2016). Growth and Transformation Plan II (GTP II) 2015/16–2019/20. Vol. I: Main text. National Planning Commission. May 2016 (English trans.).

Gebremariam, F. M., & Feyisa, B. D. (2019). Assessing the performance of industrial parks in Ethiopia: The case of Bole Lemi 1, Eastern Industry Zone and Hawassa Industrial Parks. *Social Sciences and Education Research Review*, 6(1), 72–111. Available at: https://sserr.ro/wp-content/uploads/2019/07/SSERR_2019_6_1_72_111.pdf (accessed January 2, 2020).

Gelan, A. (2018). *Chronicles: On the political economy of plunder in Ethiopia (1991–2018)*. Kindle Direct Publishing.

Ghosh, S., & Rajan, J. (2019). The business case for SDGs: An analysis of inclusive business models in emerging economies. *International Journal of Sustainable Development and World Ecology*, 26(4), 344–353.

GRI, UNGC, WBSCD (Global Reporting Initiative, United Nations Global Compact, World Business Council for Sustainable Development). (2015). SDG compass: The guide for business action on the SDGs. Available at: https://sdgcompass.org/wp-content/uploads/2015/12/019104_SDG_Compass_Guide_2015.pdf (accessed September 10, 2020).

Große-Puppendahl, S., Byiers, B., & Bilal, S. (2016). Beyond aid in private sector engagement: A mapping of the opportunities and challenges of development and commercially-oriented public support to private sector engagement. ECDPM Discussion Paper No. 187, Brussels: European Centre for Development Policy Management (ECDPM). Available at: https://ecdpm.org/publications/beyond-aid-private-sector-engagement/ (accessed January 2, 2020).

Habiyaremye, A., & Oĝuzlu, T. (2014). Engagement with Africa: Making sense of Turkey's approach in the context of growing East-West rivalry. *Uluslararasi Ilişkiler*, 11(41), 65–85. Available at www.uidergisi.com.tr/wp-content/uploads/2016/06/41_2.pdf (accessed January 2, 2020).

Hackenesch, C. (2018). *The EU and China in African authoritatian regimes: Domestic politics and governance reforms*. Cham, Switzerland: Palgrave Macmillan.

Hammond, A. L., Kramer, W. J., Katz, R. S., & Tran, J. T. (2007). The next 4 billion: market size and business strategy at the base of the pyramid. Washington, DC: World Bank. Available at: http://documents.worldbank.org/curated/en/779321468175731439/The-next-4-billion-market-size-and-business-strategy-at-the-base-of-the-pyramid (accessed January 2, 2020).

Hardy, V., & Hauge, J. (2019). Labour challenges in Ethiopia's textile and leather industries: No voice, no loyalty, no exit? *African Affairs*, 118, 1–25.

IDCJ (International Development Center of Japan). (2018). SDGs business company example, Kagome, Inc. [in Japanese]. Available at: https://idcj.jp/sdgs/img/SDGs_Company_Example_02.pdf (accessed January 2, 2020).

ILO. (2016). Decent work and sustainable development in the textile and garment industry in Ethiopia. Press release, February 4. Available at: www.ilo.org/africa/media-centre/pr/WCMS_448711/lang--en/index.htm (accessed January 2, 2020).

IPDC. (n.d.) Industrial parks developed and under construction by Industrial Parks Development Corporation (IPDC). Available at: http://www.ipdc.gov.et/index.php/en/industrial-parks (accessed January 2, 2020).

Jager, U., & Sathe, V. (2016). The importance of vision and purpose for BoP business development. In F. C. Caneque, & S. L. Hart (Eds.), *Base of the pyramid 3.0: Sustainable development through innovation & entrepreneurship.* Oxford: Greenleaf Publishing.

JICA. (2012). Implementation system: Public-private partnerships—new partnerships that support economic growth, Annual Report 2012. Available at: www.jica.go.jp/english/publications/reports/annual/2012/c8h0vm00002qe6vj-att/38.pdf (accessed January 9, 2020).

JICA. (2016). Toward achieving Sustainable Development Goals (SDGs), JICA's Position Paper on the SDGs. September 8. Available at: www.jica.go.jp/aboutoda/sdgs/ku57pq00002e2b2a-att/JICA_torikumi_e.pdf (accessed January 2, 2020).

JICA. (2019). Presentation on PPPs and private sector development programs, September 3, 2019. Available at: www.jica.go.jp/priv_partner/information/2019/ku57pq00002jvxcpatt/20190830_06.pdf (accessed January 2, 2020).

Kobukura, K. (2018). Strengthening partnerships and collaboration with all stakeholders is key to achieve all SDGs: Agenda 2030 and public private partnership. Discussion paper, Brussels: Friends of Europe. Available at: www.friendsofeurope.org/insights/agenda-2030-public-private-partnership/ (accessed January 2, 2020).

Kragelund, P. (2015). Towards convergence and cooperation in the global development finance regime: closing Africa's policy space? *Cambridge Review of International Affairs*, 28(2): 246–262. DOI:10.1080/09557571.2014.974141.

Mihretu, M., & Llobet, G. (2017). Looking beyond the horizon: A case study of PVH's commitment to Ethiopia's Hawassa Industrial Park. World Bank Group. Available at: http://documents.worldbank.org/curated/en/163511499673766520/A-case-study-of-PVH-s-commitment-to-Ethiopia-s-Hawassa-industrial-park (accessed January 2, 2020).

Mueller-Hirth, N. (2016). Business and social peace processes: How can insights from post-conflict studies help CSR to address peace and reconciliation? In S. Vertigans, & S. O. Idowu (Eds.), *Corporate social responsibility: Academic insights and impacts* (pp. 137–153). Cham, Switzerland, Springer.

Nasrullah, N. M. & Rahim, M. M. (2014). *CSR in private enterprises in developing countries: Evidences from the ready-made garments industry in Bangladesh*, Cham, Switzerland: Springer.

Nicolas, F. (2017). *Chinese investors in Ethiopia: The perfect match?* Paris: IFRI.

OECD. (2015). Participation of developing countries in global value chains: Implications for trade and trade-related policies. Summary Paper. OECD.

OECD and WTO. (2019). Aid for trade at a glance 2019: Economic diversification and empowerment. OECD/WTO. Available at: www.oecd.org/dac/aft/aid-for-trade-at-a-glance-22234411.htm (accessed January 2, 2020).

Ohno, I. (2013). The Japanese approach to growth support in developing countries: Supporting dynamic capacity development. In K. Ohno, & I. Ohno (Eds.), *Eastern and western ways for African growth: Diversity and complementarity in development aid* (pp. 144–169). London: Routledge.

Ohno, I. (2016). Network-based development cooperation as a way forward for Japan. In A. Asplund, & M. Söderberg (Eds.), *Japanese Development Cooperation: The making of an aid architecture pivoting to Asia* (pp. 159–176). London: Routledge.

Ohno, I., Konya, K., Shiga, H., Murillo, F., & Charvet, E. (2019). Scaling up business impact on the SDGs. Policy Brief for T20 Japan 2019, Task Force on 2030 Agenda for Sustainable Development. Tokyo: JICA-RI.

Ohno, K., & Ohno, I. (2019). A Japanese perspective on Ethiopia's transformation. In F. Cheru, C. Cramer, & A. Oqubay (Eds.), *The Oxford handbook of the Ethiopian economy* . Oxford: Oxford University Press.

Oqubay, A. (2015). *Made in Africa: Industrial policy in Ethiopia*. Oxford: Oxford University Press.

Porter, E. M., & Kramer, M. R. (2011). Creating shared value. *Harvard Business Review*, January–February, 2–17.

Prahalad, C. (2004). *The fortune at the bottom of the pyramid: Eradicating poverty through profits*. Philadelphia, PA: Wharton School Publishing.

Prahalad, C. K., & Hart, S. L. (1999). Strategies for the bottom of the pyramid: Creating sustainable development (draft). Available at: http://pdf.wri.org/2001summit_hartarticle.pdf (accessed January 2, 2020).

Schaefer, F., & Oya, C. (2019). Employment patterns and conditions in construction and manufacturing in Ethiopia: A comparative analysis of the road building and light manufacturing sectors. IDCEA Research Report, SOAS, University of London. Available at: www.soas.ac.uk/idcea/publications/reports/file141205.pdf (accessed January 2, 2020).

Sitnikov C., & Bocean C. (2016). Impact of CSR on economies with weak governance. In S. Vertigans, & S. O. Idowu (Eds.), *Corporate social responsibility: Academic insights and impacts* (pp. 187–202). Cham, Switzerland: Springer.

Staritz, C., & Whitfield, L. (2017). Made in Ethiopia: The emergence and evolution of the Ethiopian apparel export sector. Working Paper, Roskilde Universitet. Available at: https://forskning.ruc.dk/en/publications/made-in-ethiopia-the-emergence-and-evolution-of-the-ethiopian-app (accessed January 9, 2020).

Tang, K. (2019). Lessons from East Asia: Comparing Ethiopia and Vietnam's early stage special economic zone development. Working Paper No. 2019/26. SAIS China Africa Research Initiative, School of Advanced International Studies, Johns Hopkins University. Available at: https://static1.squarespace.com/static/5652847de4b033f56d2bdc29/t/5cdc2a848165f5c5cfd8ba68/1557932677135/WP-2019-05-Tang-Ethiopia-and-Vietnam-SEZ.pdf (accessed January 2, 2020).

Tang, X. (2015). How do Chinese special economic zones support economic transformation in Africa? Policy brief, Supporting Economic Transformation (SET), London: ODI. Available at: https://set.odi.org/wp-content/uploads/2015/07/How-Chinese-SEZs-support-economic-transformation-in-Africa.pdf (accessed January 2, 2020).

Tang, X. (2019). Export, employment, or productivity? Chinese investments in Ethiopia's leather and leather product sectors. Policy brief No. 39, SAIS China-Africa Research Initiative, School of Advanced International Studies, Johns Hopkins University. Available at: https://static1.squarespace.com/static/5652847de4b033f56d2bdc29/t/d 500a367c1580af35711dc/1570046115863/PB+39+-+Tang-+Leather+Ethiopia.pdf (accessed January 2, 2020).

Tiwari, P. (2015). Indian and Chinese FDI in Ethiopia: Nature, impact and challenges. *DU Journal of Undergraduate Research and Innovation*, 1(3), 124–143.

Tyson, J. E. (2018). Financing special economic zones: Different models of financing and public policy support. Supporting Economic Transformation (SET), London: ODI. Available at: https://set.odi.org/financing-special-economic-zones-different-models-of-financing-and-public-policy-support/ (accessed January 2, 2020).

Ueda, T. (2009). Productivity and quality improvement: JICA's assistance in Kaizen. In GRIPS Development Forum (Ed.), *Introducing KAIZEN in Africa*. Tokyo: GRIPS Development Forum.

UNCTAD. (2019). World investment report 2019: Special economic zones. New York: United Nations. Available at: https://worldinvestmentreport.unctad.org/world-investment-report-2019/ (accessed January 2, 2020).

UNIDO. (2018). Industrial park development in Ethiopia: Case study report. Inclusive and Sustainable Industrial Development Working Paper Series WP 21, Vienna: United Nations. Available at: www.unido.org/api/opentext/documents/download/10694802/unido-file-10694802 (accessed January 2, 2020).

Wan, M. (2014). *The China model and global political economy: Comparison, impact, and interaction*. London: Routledge.

Whitfield, L. (2018). *Economies after colonialism: Ghana and the struggle for power*. Cambridge: Cambridge University Press.

World Bank, IDE-JETRO, OECD, UIBE and WTO. (2017). Global value chain development report 2017: Measuring and analyzing the impact of GVCs on economic development. Washington, DC: World Bank. Available at: http://documents.worldbank.org/curated/en/440081499424129960/pdf/117290-WP- P157880-PUBLIC.pdf (accessed January 2, 2020).

WRC (Worker Right Consortium). (2018). "Ethiopia is a north star": Grim conditions and miserable wages guide apparel brands in their race to the bottom. Washington, DC: Worker Right Consortium (WTC). Available at: www.stern.nyu.edu/experience-stern/faculty-research/made-ethiopia-challenges-garment-industry-s-new-frontier (accessed January 2, 2020).

PART IV
Designing integrated industrial policies in sub- and super-national regions

17 Taking part in RCEP

CGE analysis focusing on industrial impact

Ken Itakura

17.1 Introduction

As the barriers to international flow of trade and investment have lowered in the past few decades, coupled with technological advances, the world economy has become more interdependent. It is even more apparent in production activities so that international production networks have been spreading to cover the world with global value chains (GVCs). According to the World Development Report 2020 (World Bank, 2019), "a global value chain breaks up the production process across countries," and "firms specialize in a specific task and do not produce the whole product." This international fragmentation of the production process has led to the rise in trade of intermediate inputs, and accounts for more than half of the world trade.

Regional trade agreements (RTAs) have also fostered the growth of trade in intermediate inputs, assuring producers freer market access within the member countries. The World Trade Organization reports that there were more than 300 RTAs in force by the beginning of 2020 (World Trade Organization, 2020). In recent years, mega-regional trade agreements (MRTA) have emerged, for example, the Trans-Pacific Partnership (TPP), the Transatlantic Trade and Investment Partnership (TTIP), and the Regional Comprehensive Economic Partnership (RCEP). These MRTAs aimed to establish a deeper integration which features not only liberalization of trade and investment but also a reduction in non-tariff barriers, regulatory harmonization, and protection measures for labor and environment. Under the MRTAs' new provisions, firms in a global value chain can expect aligned operations along the production process, thereby generating more trade in intermediate and final goods.

The industrial policy of a country needs to cope with the GVCs and the RTAs because of their interdependence. Intermediate inputs are sourced across countries from different industries, such as agriculture, natural resources, manufacturing, and services, by passing through the GVCs. Preferential market access is granted by the RTAs for both intermediate and final goods. In other words, all industries in countries of the source and the destination of the traded goods are directly or indirectly affected by the GVCs and the RTAs. Therefore, inter-industry relationships play an important role for a country to shape its industrial policy or strategy to develop targeted industries.

To quantitatively grasp the GVCs and the effect of RTAs for industrial policy consideration, we can use input-output (IO) tables which describe inter-industry relationships for one country or for the world, and then we can develop computable general equilibrium (CGE) models which are built on the IO tables. National statistical agencies around the world have published their country's IO tables. For example, the oldest IO table in Japan is for 1955, see the Appendix in Director-General for Policy Planning (2009) and the latest is based on 2015 for the reference year. For the world, multi-regional IO (MRIO) tables have been compiled, and the Institute of Developing Economies, Japan External Trade Organization pioneered the construction of internationally linked IO tables (IDE-JETRO, 1975). More recent MRIO tables have been made publicly available by Timmer et al. (2015) and the Organization for Economic Co-operation and Development (OECD, 2018), and Inomata (2018) surveys other MRIO tables.

Multi-industry CGE models have been developed as single-country models and global models, and Dixon and Jorgenson (2013) offer a collection of leading CGE models. To incorporate the MRIO tables into a CGE model, Walmsley, Hertel, and Hummels (2014) and Carrico (2017) extend the multi-country, multi-industry CGE model of the global trade and its database, known as the GTAP model and database (Aguiar, Narayanan, & McDougall, 2016; Hertel, 1997). Accounting for the structure of GVCs, Itakura and Oyamada (2015) introduce agent-specific import demands by extending the GTAP model and database. To assess the impact of MRTAs, Lee and Itakura (2018) estimate welfare and industrial output adjustment effects of sequencing of TPP, RCEP, and a free trade area of the Asia-Pacific (FTAAP) by using the dynamic GTAP model (Ianchovichina & McDougall, 2001; Ianchovichina & Walmsley, 2012). Disruption in international trade was caused by political shifts to protectionism as the US-China trade war escalated in 2018, and negative impacts were passed onto the GVCs. Itakura (2020) explores the role of GVCs in the US–China trade war, and finds that the negative impact on the world economy becomes greater if the GVCs are taken into consideration. Walmsley and Minor (2018) also estimate the impact of the trade war, focusing on global supply chains.

In this chapter, we illustrate the GVCs in the framework of MRIO analysis and provide CGE simulation results of a MRTA. Section 17.2 overviews the basic structure of IO tables, and Section 17.3 looks at GVCs for trade in value-added, and forward and backward participation in the GVCs. Key features of the CGE model incorporating the GVC structure are introduced in Section 17.4. A MRTA scenario of the RCEP is simulated in Section 17.5 and the simulation results are reported. In summary, implications for industrial policy are discussed.

17.2 Basic structure of the MRIO table

In this section, we begin with an IO table for one country, and then show how to embed the single country's IO table within a multi-region (or multi-country) IO table. Take Viet Nam in 2015, for example, the data are extracted from the

Table 17.1 Input-output table for Viet Nam

	A	*M*	*S*	*C+G+I*	*EXP*	*IMP*	*X*
A	20312	50073	5766	26518	12683	−9735	105617
M	30972	137050	50133	55810	121612	−110512	285065
S	13255	34476	41436	103308	17299	−30397	179377
VA	41078	63467	82041				
X'	105617	285066	179376				

Note*:* Figures are in million US$.
Source*:* Author's calculation based on OECD (2018).

OECD's Inter-Country Input-Output (ICIO) Tables (OECD, 2018). For our simple illustration, the 36 industries in the ICIO tables are aggregated into the following three industries: A for agriculture and natural resources, M for manufacturing, and S for services industries.

In Table 17.1, ***X*** denotes a vector of industrial production (or gross output). The gross output of manufacturing (M) is about US$285 billion, followed by services (S) and agriculture and natural resources (A), US$179 billion and US$106 billion respectively. In the IO table, gross output equals the sum of intermediate input and value-added (*VA*) for industry's cost structure, and it also equals the sum of intermediate demand and final demand for industry's sales structure.

Looking at the cost structure, each industry demands intermediate inputs supplied by all industries. For manufacturing (M) in the third column in Table 17.1, intermediate input from industry A is about US$50 billion, and the one from industry S is around US$34 billion. Intra-industry demand and supply of intermediate input in the industry M are US$137 billion. Thus, the industry M bears the cost of intermediate inputs which amount to US$221 billion in total. The difference between the gross output and the cost of intermediate inputs is the value that each industry adds to the economy (*VA*). In 2015, Vietnamese manufacturing industry added value by US$63 billion. By taking the ratio of value-added to gross output, manufacturing has the smallest ratio (22 percent = 63/285*100) compared to agriculture and natural resources (39 percent) and services (46 percent). This indicates that for manufacturing to produce one unit of gross output, the cost share of intermediate inputs is higher than other industries.

For the sales structure, Vietnamese industrial gross outputs meet the demands from economic agents who are producers, consumers, investors, and governments in home and foreign countries. Industries (A, M, and S) in Viet Nam (home) generate intermediate demand. Domestic (home) consumer (C), investor (I), and government (G) constitute a part of the final demand, while foreign economic agents are served by exports (EXP) from Viet Nam. On the other hand, foreign producers supply goods to Viet Nam, so the imports (IMP) are subtracted from the final demand.

Summing the value-added (VA) across industry, we can calculate total value-added in Viet Nam for 2015, and which amounts to US$186 billion (= 41 + 63 + 82).

This total value-added corresponds to the gross domestic product (GDP). The accounting identity of GDP holds for the sum of consumption (C), investment (I), government spending (G), and exports (EXP), minus imports (IMP). These expenditures on goods and services constitute the final demand.

What if the final demand for Vietnamese manufacturing changes for any reason, and what will be the impact on gross output in other industries? With the IO table to hand, we can answer with a number. First, for each industry, dividing intermediate input by gross output gives us input coefficients, which indicate how many inputs are needed to produce one unit of output. Let $\boldsymbol{A}$ be the matrix of input coefficients, $a_{ij} = x_{ij} / X_j$, where x_{ij} is intermediate input i in industry j. Second, the Leontief's inverse matrix, $\boldsymbol{L}$, is computed by $\boldsymbol{L} = (\boldsymbol{I} - \boldsymbol{A})^{-1}$, taking the inverse of identity matrix, $\boldsymbol{I}$, minus the input coefficient matrix. Finally, express the change in final demand for Vietnamese manufacturing in terms of a vector, $\Delta\boldsymbol{F} = (0,1000,0)$, which means US$1 billion increase in the final demand for manufacturing. By multiplying the Leontief inverse matrix by the change in final demand, $\boldsymbol{L}\Delta\boldsymbol{F}$, we obtain the result (564, 2506, 486). The increase in final demand for manufacturing by US$1 billion generates US$3.6 billion worth of total gross outputs in Viet Nam. Thus, the manufacturing industry gains directly and indirectly from the increase by US$2.5 billion, while the inter-industrial relationships indirectly benefit the agricultural and natural resource industry by US$564 million and the services industry by US$486 million.

The result on gross outputs can be translated into the change in value-added by industry. For this conversion, the ratios of value-added to gross output, $v_j = VA_j / X_j$, are put into a diagonal matrix, and then multiplied by the result on gross outputs. Then, we obtain the impact on value-added by industry (220, 558, 222). The increase in value-added mostly accrues to the manufacturing with US$558 million, but other industries indirectly benefit by more than US$200 million. It should be noted that the sum of the changes in value-added is exactly US$1 billion, the amount which we assumed to increase in the final demand. This is because of the accounting identity in which the change in total final demand must be reflected in the change in the value-added total.

Since Vietnamese industries use a lot of imported intermediate inputs, the impact on value-added spreads through the global value chains (GVCs) to affect foreign countries. To see this, we extend the single country IO table (Table 17.1) to the multi-region IO (MRIO) table as shown in Table 17.2. The MRIO adds Japan and rest of the world (ROW), retaining the same three industries and the same reference year of 2015.

Reflecting the three industries in three regions, the gross output vector $(\boldsymbol{X})$ has nine components. Note that the gross outputs and the value-added for Viet Nam are the same as in Table 17.1, and the difference in the last digit of data is due to a rounding error. Recall the imports of Viet Nam are (-9.7, -110.5, -30.3) billion US$. These imports are split into two parts: imports for intermediate inputs and ones for final demand. In Table 17.2, two blocks in dark-gray correspond to them. Imported intermediate inputs are distinguished by the source of country and industry. For example, the Vietnamese manufacturing industry

Table 17.2 Multiregional input-output table for three regions in 2015

		Viet Nam			*Japan*			*ROW*			*Viet Nam*	*Japan*	*ROW*
		A	*M*	*S*	*A*	*M*	*S*	*A*	*M*	*S*			
Viet Nam	A	18499	44915	5173	22	854	284	1128	6435	1335	24347	93	2532
	M	20158	75230	31035	128	3925	3358	3120	33194	20367	37030	5720	51800
	S	9643	24129	33853	9	267	374	408	2853	4426	94453	655	8307
Japan	A	3	11	3	8996	53798	16904	257	491	182	3	30080	400
	M	718	4001	1311	21617	901884	527885	9652	190392	74379	1545	662275	220874
	S	329	1051	797	22715	492865	1397128	5519	51929	83951	576	3379354	85444
ROW	A	1810	5147	590	1663	94180	27423	2027091	4620031	1172363	2168	6494	2595924
	M	10096	57819	17787	3206	115334	76864	1273123	14792197	8421111	17235	178552	14694595
	S	3283	9296	6786	1534	42214	82237	1345169	7789099	26343325	8279	104205	49487472
	VA	41078	63467	82041	51238	911209	3389204	5889418	12171297	49101459			
	X'	105618	285066	179377	111128	2616530	5521660	10554884	39657919	85222898			

Source: Author's calculation based on OECD (2018).

imports intermediate input from Japanese manufacturing (US$4 billion) and from ROW's manufacturing (US$57.8 billion), along with other industries. And the final demand (FD) in Viet Nam imports manufacturing products is from Japan (US$1.5 billion) and from ROW (US$17 billion). Exports from Viet Nam of Agricultural goods are (13 billion US$), of manufacturing goods (122 billion US$), and of services (17 billion US$) in Table 17.1. Similar to the imports, the exports are split into two parts: exports for intermediate demand and exports for final demand in Japan and ROW. They are shown in light-gray shaded blocks in Table 17.2. Thus, the exports and the imports in the single country IO table (Table 17.1) are decomposed and relocated in the MRIO table (Table 17.2) to enrich the information on trade flows of goods and services.

Returning to the previous question which asked the impact of US$1 billion increase in the final demand on Vietnamese manufacturing, the vector of change in final demand ($\Delta \boldsymbol{F}$) has now 9 components of zeros, except for the second component as 1000. The input coefficient matrix ($\boldsymbol{A}$) with size of 9×9 and the same size of identity matrix give us the Leontief inverse matrix, $\boldsymbol{L} = (\boldsymbol{I} - \boldsymbol{A})^{-1}$. The impact on gross output can be computed by $\boldsymbol{L}\Delta\boldsymbol{F}$, and the result is (289, 1478, 187, 1, 46, 23, 138, 629, 299). The first three components are for Viet Nam, and the total impact on Vietnamese gross outputs is about US$2 billion which is less than the previous result (US$3.6 billion) when the single country IO table is used. Because of the inter-industry links across countries, the impact on gross outputs spreads to Japan and the ROW (US$1.1 billion).

The impact on value-added is obtained by multiplying the diagonal matrix of the ratios of value-added to gross output by the Leontief inverse matrix, and by the vector of change in final demand, $\boldsymbol{VL}\Delta\boldsymbol{F}$. The results on value-added are (112, 329, 85, 1, 16, 14, 77, 193, 172). The US$1 billion increase in final demand for Vietnamese manufacturing generates US$526 million value-added in Viet Nam (sum of the first three components) and US$473 million in Japan and the ROW in total. The accounting identity holds at the world level, and the increase in final demand is absorbed in the increase in value-added.

17.3 Trade in value-added and the global value chains

Exports from one country serve to aid foreign countries' intermediate and final demands. For example, exports from Viet Nam are about (13, 122, 17) billion US$ by industry, as reported in Table 17.1, and of which (3, 58, 9) billion US$ are exported for the foreign final demands in Japan and ROW, calculated from Table 17.2. Taking the difference between them (i.e., subtracting, 13 – 3, 122 – 58, 17 – 9), more than half of the Vietnamese exports are for intermediate demands in Japan and the ROW. Although the exports are used in large amounts as intermediate inputs in foreign markets, they eventually become a part of the final demand to be sold in all countries. As we observed in Section 17.2, the final demands are linked to the value-added across the industry and the country, which are the source of a country's income. This is the reason why we are interested in linking the final demand to the value-added.

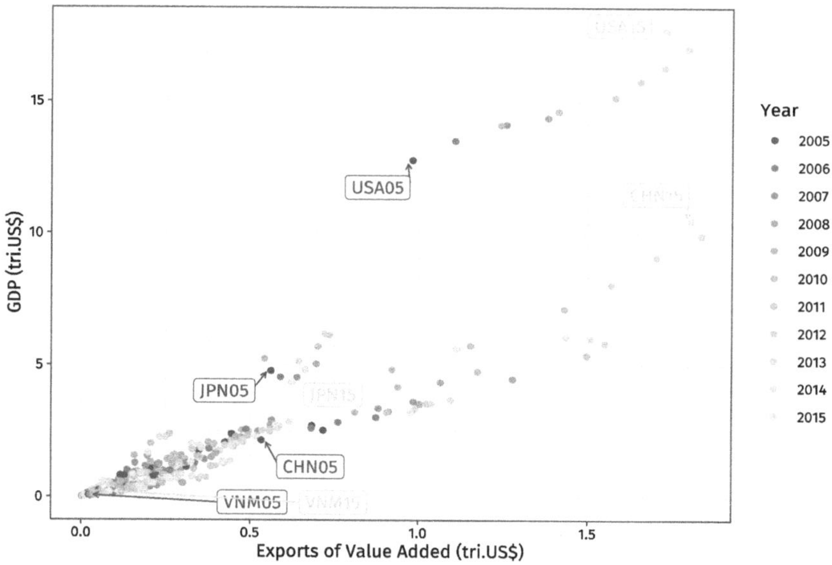

Figure 17.1 Exports of value-added and GDP for 2005–2015

Note: Nominal US$ in trillion.

Source: Author's calculation based on OECD (2018).

To tie the links between foreign final demand and the domestic value-added, we can compute indices for trade in value-added. For this purpose, we look at exports of value-added which measures domestic value-added embodied in foreign final demand (OECD, 2019). The exports of value-added are computed by multiplying by the diagonal matrix of the value-added ratio, the Leontief inverse matrix, and the vector of foreign final demand, $\boldsymbol{V}\boldsymbol{L}\boldsymbol{F}^{f}$. The vector of foreign final demand consists of row-sums of the final demands less domestic final demands, but a matrix form can be used for decomposition (Table 17.2).

Figure 17.1 plots the exports of value-added and the value-added total which is defined as GDP, for the 65 countries in the OECD's ICIO tables from 2005 to 2015. The US has the largest exports of value-added and GDP in 2005, and its exceptionally large position continues to 2015 when the Chinese exports of value-added become slightly bigger than the US. Unlike the expansion in both the exports of value-added and the GDP in the US and China, the Japanese GDP shrinks from 2005 to 2015 while the exports of value-added increase to a small degree. Exports of value-added from Viet Nam have grown considerably, but the absolute size in Figure 17.1 masks their expansion. To show this more clearly, Viet Nam's exports of value-added by industry are presented in Figure 17.2. The exports of value-added in manufacturing are more than four times larger for the decade since 2005. Agriculture and natural resources and services industries have also expanded so that their exports of value-added have doubled over the

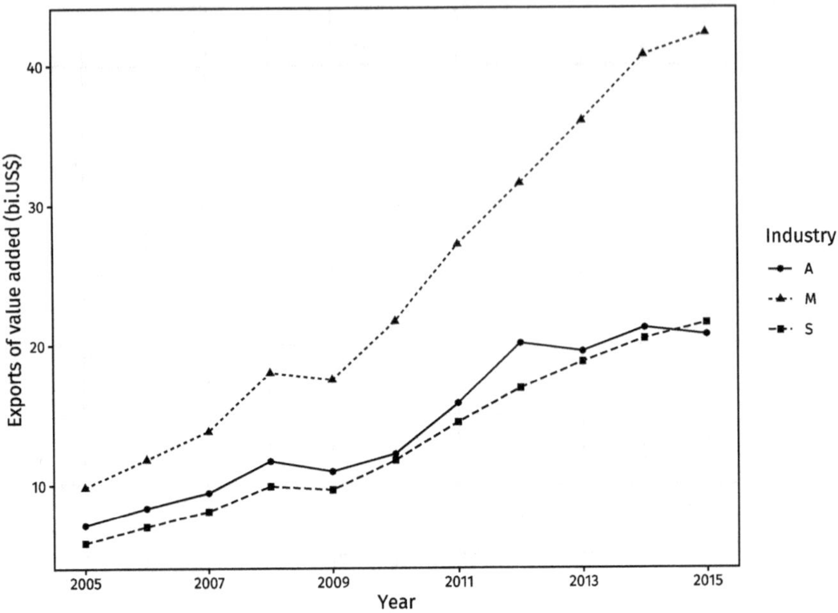

Figure 17.2 Viet Nam's exports of value-added for 2005–2015

Note*:* A for agriculture and natural resources, M for manufacturing, and S for services.

Source: Author's calculation based on OECD (2018).

same period. The growth in exports of value-added indicates that the industries in Viet Nam have become more connected to foreign final demands.

Connection to the foreign markets can be expressed in another way as forward and backward participation in the global value chains (GVCs). The two participation indices are obtained from the matrix of value-added embodied in trade, which is computed as $\boldsymbol{V}\boldsymbol{L}\boldsymbol{E}$, where $\boldsymbol{E}$ is a diagonal matrix of exports. The result is a square matrix with the size of industry times country. For example, when computed from Table 17.2, the matrix of value-added embodied in trade is 9 × 9. The sources of value-added by industry and country are in rows of the matrix, and the exports by industry and country are in columns. Note that the column sums equal the exports. Diagonal blocks of the matrix show how much the exports from home country contribute to add value to its own industries.

Forward participation in the GVCs measures domestic value-added embodied in foreign exports by industry. Thus, the foreign exports of each industry can be linked to the total value-added in home country. On the other hand, backward participation in the GVCs evaluates foreign value-added embodied in home exports. It means that imported intermediate inputs used in home industries are traced back to the foreign source of value-added. Computed from the OECD's ICIO tables, Figure 17.3 shows the forward participation and the backward

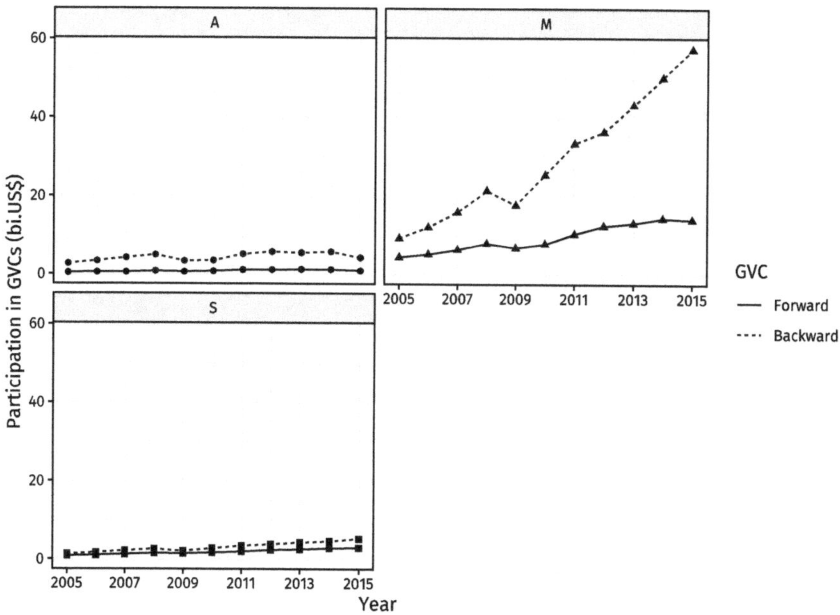

Figure 17.3 Viet Nam's participation in global value chains for 2005–2015
Note: A for agriculture and natural resources, M for manufacturing, and S for services.

participation in the GVCs for Viet Nam. The forward and backward participations have remained low for the agriculture and natural resources (A) and the services (S), and it reflects the fact that Vietnamese exports from these industries are relatively small compared to the manufacturing (M). The forward participation in manufacturing has moderately grown over the period, implying that foreign exports of manufacturing have used more intermediate inputs from Viet Nam so as to increment the value-added in Viet Nam. More significantly, in Figure 17.3, the backward participation in manufacturing has rapidly expanded. As the Vietnamese manufacturing exports have risen considerably, Viet Nam has increasingly imported the intermediate inputs from abroad, causing the foreign value-added to increase.

Industrial variation can be seen more clearly for the forward participation rate and the backward participation rate in the GVCs in Figure 17.4. The two rates are calculated by dividing the participation indices by each country's exports. For agriculture and natural resources, the forward participation rates are very small, while the backward participation rates are widely spread. The cluster of services lies over the backward participation rate of the agriculture and natural resources in Figure 17.4. This indicates that the foreign exports in services are adding more value to the home country than the agricultural and natural resources, and that the home country's exports are due to the wide range of imported intermediate

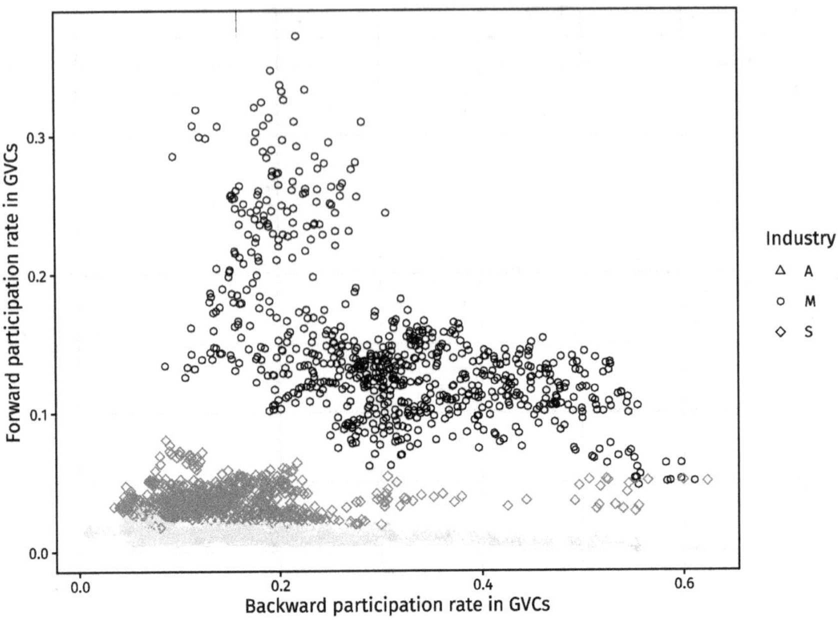

Figure 17.4 GVC participation rates for 2005–2015

Note: A for agriculture and natural resources, M for manufacturing, and S for services.

Source: Author's calculation based on OECD (2018).

shares. Manufacturing dominates both the forward and the backward participation rates in the GVCs. As the foreign value-added embodied in the home country's exports (the backward participation) becomes smaller than 0.3, the domestic value-added embodied in foreign exports (the forward participation) tends to exceed 0.2. Although the degree of data aggregation in the ICIO tables may affect the results, it seems that in manufacturing, there is a negative correlation between the forward and the backward participation rate in the GVCs.

17.4 Global value chains in the CGE model

Global value chains (GVCs) can be numerically grasped in a multi-region input-output (MRIO) table, as discussed in the previous sections. In turn, the GVCs can be introduced into a computable general equilibrium (CGE) model because the MRIO table forms the underlying foundation of the model. Thus, by construction with the MRIO table, the CGE model with the GVCs features the exhaustive accounting identities holding at the world level and the inter-country and inter-industry relationships of goods and services. Economic agents in the CGE model used in this chapter are producers, consumers, investors, and governments in home and foreign countries. Each economic agent states the demand for goods

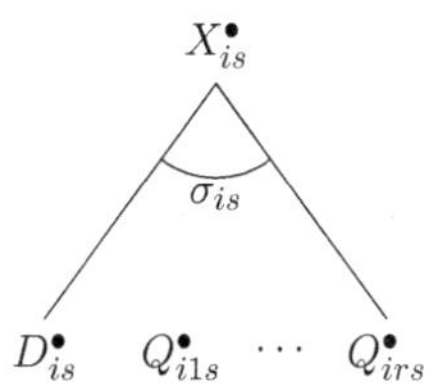

Figure 17.5 Import sourcing by agent

Note: A s composite good D_{is} in region Q_{irs}, r domestically produced good, X_{is} import from region σ_{is}, region X_{is} specific substitution elasticity.

and services in the constant elasticity of substitution (CES) function, illustrated in Figure 17.5. In the model, we assume that goods and services are differentiated by the place they are produced (Armington, 1969). Armington's assumption has been extensively adopted by many CGE models.

In country s, a domestically produced good, D_{is}, and an imported good, Q_{irs}, from country r are aggregated by the CES function to form a composite good, X_{is}. In Figure 17.5, the dod, •, refers to an economic agent. It should be noted that economic agents share the substitution elasticity, σ_{is}, so the substitution parameter is region generic due to data limitation. However, the demand itself is agent-specific, capturing the GVC's structure in the MRIO table. This is the uniqueness of the model used in this chapter, compared with the import demand function in conventional CGE models, for example, Hertel (1997) and McDougall (2003).

Producers combine the composite goods (X_{is}) and value-added to produce output, by using the Leontief function. The value-added in the model comprises five factor inputs, such as skilled and unskilled labor, capital, land, and natural resources, and their endowments are fixed for a period. The land and natural resources are specific production factors for some industries. Producers are competing in perfectly competitive markets of output and factor inputs. In the latter market, factor inputs move across industries at assumed sluggishness. Due to the competition over the limited supply of factor inputs in a period, some industries expand while others contract. Outputs are sold to meet the intermediate demands and the final demands at home and abroad, subject to taxes and subsidies as well as international transportation costs.

Consumer and government are a part of the final demand in a country, deciding the amount of domestic and foreign goods and services to consume. The final demand of the consumer is modeled by a constant difference of elasticities (CDE) function to take the non-homothetic preference into consideration. the final demand of the government is defined in a constant elasticity of substitution (CES) function. Economic welfare at the country level is determined by equivalent variation on aggregate income based on the consumer, the government, and the savings which take a fixed portion of the national income. Investment is for fixed capital formation, financed by savings. International capital mobility and capital accumulation are assumed in the model, following Ianchovichina and McDougall (2001), and Ianchovichina and Walmsley (2012). This investment dynamics is built into the comparative static model (Hertel, 1997; McDougall, 2003).

To incorporate the GVCs into the dynamic CGE model, we combine the OECD's ICIO tables (OECD, 2018) with the GTAP Data Base version 9 (Aguiar et al., 2016). Applying the modeling strategy in Itakura and Oyamada (2015), the import demand is formulated as agent-specific. After merging the GVC structure into the GTAP database, we aggregate the database for 14 industries and 19 regions.

17.5 A mega-regional trade agreement scenario of RCEP

Any industrial policies affecting final demand and trade will cause changes in value-added in both the home and foreign countries. In the previous sections, we illustrated with simple examples of the links from final demand and trade to value-added in the framework of the MRIO analysis. This section provides a dynamic CGE analysis on a mega-regional trade agreement (MRTA), and the MRTA undoubtedly affects trade, final demand, and value-added. In the CGE analysis, substitution among the source countries plays a key role when the MRTA brings preferential market access to the member countries.

We take the Regional Comprehensive Economic Partnership (RCEP) as our MRTA scenario. The RCEP is a regional agreement involving the ten countries of the Association of Southeast Asian Nations (ASEAN) and its six neighboring countries, Japan, China, South Korea, Australia, New Zealand, and India. The RCEP agreement has been negotiated since 2012 and aimed to be concluded by the end of 2019. As the negotiation continues, however, we assume that the RCEP would conclude in 2020 and take effect in 2021. Although India expressed possible withdrawal from the agreement in November 2019, the RCEP scenario assumes India will continue to take part in the accord. To quantify the potential economic impact of the RCEP, we need to create a baseline scenario which represents a hypothetical future state of the world economy absent from the RCEP. Then, the policy scenario which implements the RCEP can be compared against the baseline scenario, thereby generating deviations from the baseline scenario as the impact caused by the policy change.

The baseline scenario is set up with the GTAP Data Base version 9 (Aguiar et al. 2016), and the projections from the United Nations (2017) of total and working-age populations and ones from the International Monetary Fund (2018) for real GDP and gross investment. We include the regional trade agreements in the baseline scenario which has been implemented, and they are ASEAN FTA, ASEAN-China, ASEAN-Korea, ASEAN- Japan, ASEAN-Australia-New Zealand, ASEAN-India, EU-Korea, Korea-US, China- Korea, Australia-Japan, Australia-Korea, Australia-China, and TPP without the US.

The policy scenario of the RCEP includes the removal of the bilateral tariffs except for a few sensitive products among the member countries, a reduction in tariff equivalents of barriers in services trade, and improvements in logistics

Table 17.3 Impact of RCEP on bilateral trade volume, 2035

	Japan	*China*	*Viet Nam*	*RoASEAN*	*RoRCEP*	*USA*	*EU28*	*ROW*
Japan	..	71.1	9.4	11.5	22.8	−1.7	−2.0	−1.5
China	9.2	..	8.3	6.6	26.0	−2.5	−2.8	−3.1
Viet Nam	−0.7	17.1	..	17.1	18.4	11.0	9.7	5.5
RoASEAN	6.9	8.6	3.9	7.9	23.5	−2.7	−1.7	−2.9
RoRCEP	5.5	21.1	43.3	23.5	4.7	3.2	3.2	3.9
USA	−0.7	1.4	−4.3	−1.4	−2.4	..	−0.4	−0.7
EU28	−0.1	1.0	−4.7	−2.5	−2.5	−0.2	−0.4	−0.6
ROW	1.5	2.0	−7.5	−2.4	−3.5	−0.2	−0.3	−0.6

Note: Results are reported in percentage changes relative to the baseline. The rest of ASEAN (RoASEAN), the rest of RCEP (RoRCEP), and the rest of the world (ROW).

Source: Author's simulation results.

of merchandise goods, and they are adopted from the specifications in Lee and Itakura (2018). The policy scenario is gradually implemented over the ten-year period from 2021 to 2030, and the simulations are set up for 2011–2035. The baseline and the policy scenarios are implemented by the GEMPACK economic modeling software (Harrison & Pearson, 1996).

Table 17.3 reports the simulation results for the impact of RCEP on bilateral trade volume in 2035. The figures are measured in percentage changes relative to the baseline, and the trade volumes are evaluated in constant US dollars in 2011. Export volume from Japan to China shows a significant rise of 71 percent and it is the biggest impact on the bilateral trade volume. Because the RCEP creates a preferential trading area, it is observed that the RCEP members will increase trade volume with their partners, whereas they tend to divert trade from non-member countries. The US and the EU are not member countries but their export volumes to China increase, reflecting the GVCs in China for intermediate inputs from the US and the EU. The small negative impact on Vietnamese exports to Japan is counterintuitive for the RCEP members. This can be explained by decomposing the bilateral trade volume. Before looking at the details, there are some remarks on the results. First, the ASEAN had already enacted the trade agreements with Japan, China, South Korea, Australia, New Zealand, India, and even for the ASEAN members. This fact makes the room for tariff-related trade expansion somewhat limited unless non-tariff barriers or impediments to investment are lifted. Second, the export volumes from Viet Nam increase for all the destination countries but Japan, resulting in total export volume change as positive. Third, when a conventional CGE model without the GVC structure is used for the same policy scenario, the export volume from Viet Nam to Japan turns out to be positive. This observation comparing the CGE models with and without the GVCs may indicate the significance of GVCs in computing the impact on bilateral trade at industry level.

Table 17.4 Decomposition of the export volume from Viet Nam to Japan, 2035

	CGE with			
	GVC	*Producers*	*Consumer*	*Govt*
Total	–0.7	19.7	–20.4	0.0
Agric	–0.2	–0.2	0.0	0.0
Mining	–5.0	–5.0	0.0	0.0
FoodProd	–1.1	–1.6	0.4	0.0
TextApparel	–55.2	–13.1	–42.1	0.0
PetroChem	7.6	6.8	0.8	0.0
Metals	8.7	8.5	0.3	0.0
Machinery	7.8	7.3	0.4	0.0
ElecEquip	7.0	3.5	3.5	0.0
Auto	21.1	8.3	12.8	0.0
TransEquip	1.2	1.1	0.1	0.0
OthMnfct	3.5	2.6	0.9	0.0
ConstUtil	0.0	0.0	0.0	0.0
TradeTrans	3.1	0.6	2.4	0.0
Services	0.9	0.7	0.2	0.0

Note: Results are reported in percentage changes relative to the baseline.

Source: Author's simulation results.

The small but negative impact on Vietnamese export volumes to Japan can be decomposed into details by industry and by economic agents, as shown in Table 17.4. Looking across economic agents, the total change of -0.7 percent is a combination of a considerable rise in intermediate input demand by Japanese producers (19.7 percent) and the offsetting fall in final demand by Japanese consumers (-20.4 percent), and virtually no change in government spending in Japan. On the other hand, decomposing by industry, the largest negative impact is found in the textile and apparel industry (-55.2 percent), followed by mining, food processing, and agriculture. However, a substantial increase in manufacturing industries led by automobiles (21.1 percent) and metals (8.7 percent) makes up for the loss. Given the results in Table 17.4, a feasible industrial policy response for Viet Nam with respect to Japan would be the promotion of automobile exports targeting consumers and producers, and support for exporting manufactured intermediates except for textiles and apparel. Industrial policy measures would be prepared to mitigate the fall in textile and apparel export to Japan. As for the services export, trade and transport services for Japanese consumer can be encouraged by policy measures. It is possible to decompose this further by Japanese producers. By doing so we can identify, for example, which Japanese industry should be selected for Vietnamese export promotion of the manufactured intermediate inputs. These decomposition analyses can be done for other RCEP member countries as well.

Change in trade affects value-added, as we saw in the MRIO analysis. The impact of RCEP on trade volume has caused the changes in value-added. When

Table 17.5 Impact of RCEP on real GDP, 2035

	US$, billion	*(%)*
Japan	26	0.4
China	123	0.4
Viet Nam	29	4.8
Rest of ASEAN	147	2.1
Rest of RCEP	373	2.2
USA	–17	–0.1
EU28	–54	–0.2
ROW	–86	–0.2
World	541	0.4

Note: Results are reported in billion constant 2011 US dollar and in percentage changes relative to the baseline.

Source: Author's simulation results.

we aggregate the changes in value-added in total, we can interpret the impact in terms of real GDP. Table 17.5 reports the impact on real GDP in 2035. All the RCEP member countries gain in real GDP, and Viet Nam shows the largest increase in percentage change while the rest of RCEP results in the biggest gain in absolute term. The world as a whole increases the real GDP, but the non-member countries experience small losses.

17.6 Conclusion

In this chapter our aim is to numerically grasp the interdependence of the world economy by using world input-output (IO) tables and a computable general equilibrium (CGE) model of the global trade, and they are presented as useful tools for industrial policy consideration. The global value chains (GVCs) connect the international fragmentation of the production process to final demand and value-added by industry. These inter-industry relationships across countries are described in a multi-regional IO (MRIO) table, and we use the OECD's ICIO tables (OECD 2018) to illustrate analysis of the GVCs. Trade in value-added, forward and backward participations in the GVCs are explored in the MRIO analysis. A dynamic CGE model with GVCs structure is applied to simulate a mega-regional trade agreement (MRTA), and we take the Regional Comprehensive Economic Partnership (RCEP) as the policy scenario to be evaluated. In the results, the unique feature of the model enables us to gain insights into possible industrial policy responses to the MRTA. With the decomposition analysis, we can identify both economic agents and industries that would benefit from industrial policy support.

We review the basic structure of the MRIO table, and the data example is taken from the OECD's ICIO tables (OECD, 2018). Viet Nam in 2015 is used as an example, basically focusing on the aggregated data with three industries.

Analytical illustrations are shown in the framework of MRIO analysis, computing the linkages between change in final demand to value-added. When we explore the forward and backward participation in the GVCs, we found that the manufacturing dominates both participation indices, and that a negative correlation between them may exist.

Unlike the MRIO analysis, the change in prices and efficiencies induced by the RCEP plays a crucial role in the dynamic CGE analysis. The agent-specific demand generates substitution effects among the sourcing countries as it responds to the changes in relative prices caused by removing tariffs, reducing non-tariff barriers in services trade, and facilitating the logistics of merchandise goods. Bilateral trade volumes are determined collectively by the changes in agent-specific demands, and they are also influenced by the GVCs. The unique feature built into the CGE model as the GVCs' structure makes it possible to decompose the changes in bilateral trade volume by economic agent and by industry. Details of the results can offer useful insights into a feasible industrial policy response, and we can identify the economic agents and the industries who are most affected by the MRTA. Given the interdependence of the world economy, an industrial policy needs to cope with the GVCs and the MRTAs.

It should be noted that the results reported in this chapter are subject to the datasets, the level of data aggregation, and the assumptions involved in the MRIO analysis and the CGE model simulation. In other words, there are many ways to improve the analysis. The most obvious task to be done next is to keep updating the data inputs as well as the projections, for it seems to be a straightforward task. Given the large extent of GVCs, estimating key parameters, such as the substitution elasticities, is challenging, while the CGE model validation is desirable but seems to be a formidable task.

References

Aguiar, A., Narayanan, B., & McDougall, R. (2016). An overview of the GTAP 9 data base. *Journal of Global Economic Analysis*, 1(1), 181–208.

Armington, P. S. (1969). A theory of demand for products distinguished by place of production. *IMF Staff Papers*, 16(1), 159–178.

Carrico, C. (2017). An enhanced analytical framework for evaluating the effects of trade costs along global value chains. *Journal of Global Economic Analysis*, 2(2), 43–111.

Director-General for Policy Planning (2009). 2005 Input-output tables for Japan. Available at: www.soumu.go.jp/english/dgpp ss/data/io/io05.htm

Dixon, P. B., & Jorgenson, D. W. (Eds.) (2013). *Handbook of computable general equilibrium modeling*. Amsterdam: North Holland.

Harrison, W. J., & Pearson, K. R. (1996). Computing solutions for large general equilibrium modeling using GEMPACK. *Computational Economics*, 9, 83–127.

Hertel, T. W. (Ed.) (1997). *Global trade analysis: Modeling and applications*. New York: Cambridge University Press,

Ianchovichina, E., & McDougall, R. (2001). Theoretical structure of dynamic GTAP. GTAP technical paper, Purdue University, No. 17, 1–68.

Ianchovichina, E., & Walmsley, T. (Eds.) (2012). *Dynamic modeling and applications for global economic analysis.* New York: Cambridge University Press.

IDE-JETRO (Institute of Developing Economies, Japan External Trade Organization). (1975). ASEAN international input-output tables. Chiba, Japan: IDE-JETRO.

Inomata, S. (2018). Multi-country supply and use tables and input-output tables. In United Nations, *Handbook on supply, use and input-output tables with extensions and applications* (pp. 451–473). New York: United Nations Statistical Division,

International Monetary Fund (2018). *World economic outlook database.* Washington, DC: IMF.

Itakura, K. (2020). Evaluating the impact of the US–China trade war. *Asian Economic Policy Review*, 15(1), 77–93.

Itakura, K., & Oyamada, K. (2015). Extending GTAP data base and a CGE model with global input-output linkage. In S. T. Otsubo (Ed.), *Globalization and development: Leading issues in development with globalization* (pp. 344–363). London: Routledge.

Lee, H., & Itakura, K. (2018). The welfare and sectoral adjustment effects of mega- regional trade agreements on ASEAN countries. *Journal of Asian Economics*, 55, 20–32.

McDougall, R. (2003). A new regional household demand system for GTAP. GTAP Technical Paper, Purdue University, no. 20, 1–57.

OECD (Organization for Economic Co-operation and Development). (2018). *Inter-country input-output tables.* Paris: OECD.

OECD (Organization for Economic Co-operation and Development). (2019). *Guide to OECD's trade in value added (TiVA) indicators.* Paris: OECD.

Timmer, M. P., Dietzenbacher, E., Los, B., Stehrer, R., & de Vries, G. J. (2015). An illustrated user guide to the world input-output database: The case of global automotive production. *Review of International Economics*, 23, 575–605.

United Nations. (2017). *World population prospects: The 2017 revision.* New York: United Nations.

Walmsley, T., Hertel, T. W., & Hummels, D. (2014). Developing a GTAP-based multi-region, input-output framework for supply chain analysis. In B. Ferrarrini & D. Hummels (Eds.), *Asia and global production networks: Implications for trade, incomes and economic vulnerability* (pp. 16–80. Cheltenham: Asian Development Bank and Edward Elgar.

Walmsley, T., & Minor, P. (2018). Estimated impacts of US sections 232 and 301 trade actions on the US and global economies: A supply chain prospective 2018–2030. *ImpactEcon Report*, 1–73.

World Bank. (2019). *World development report 2020.* Washington, DC: The World Bank.

World Trade Organization. (2020). Regional trade agreements database. Geneva.: WTO. Available at: http://rtais.wto.org/UI/PublicMaintainRTAHome.aspx (accessed February 26, 2020).

18 Promoting both industrial development and regional convergence

Toward a regionally inclusive industrial policy

Carlos Mendez

18.1 Introduction

Large productivity differences across industries as well as large per-capita income differences across regions are common characteristics of many developing countries (Mitton, 2016; Timmer, De Vries, & De Vries, 2015). Historically, industrialization has been used as a development ladder by most of today's advanced economies. Regional convergence, besides being source of interpersonal inequality reduction, is a predictor of social cohesion, peace, and political stability. In this context, this chapter aims to explore the interaction between these two pillars of development. The ultimate goal of this exercise is to identify possible lessons that could guide the design and implementation of a regionally inclusive industrial policy (RIIP).

The economic rationale for the need of a RIIP is that, at least in the short run, a standard industrial policy package tends to favor some industries over others, as well as some regions over others. Thus, a RIIP is needed to facilitate the catch-up of lagging industries and regions over a medium to long-run horizon. By doing so, a RIIP is expected to ensure the sustainability and inclusivity of productivity-enhancing policies, which are initially targeted to specific industries and regions.

Modern industrial development is commonly associated with two tasks: (1) increasing productivity in current and potentially new (strategic) sectors; and (2) facilitating the smooth reallocation of workers from relatively low-productivity sectors to modern high-productivity sectors (McMillan, Rodrik, & Verduzco, 2014). Section 18.2 documents the performance of developing countries in each of these two tasks. In particular, it points out that countries in Africa and Latin America are facing difficulties with the reallocation of their workers to high-productivity sectors. Some key facts of regional convergence are also presented. Perhaps, the most noteworthy is that regional divergence is much more prevalent in Africa than in any other continent.

Industrial and regional development are not independent processes, they are continuously interacting with one another (Scott & Storper, 2005). In Section

18.3, some of these interactions are evaluated through the lens of an industry-based model of regional convergence (Fukao & Paul, 2018). In this model, the two sources of industrial development (within-sector growth and structural change growth) have their regional convergence equivalents. By applying this model to the Japanese industrialization experience, it is found that, in the pre-war period, regional convergence was mostly led by within-sector growth. In contrast, in the post-war period, it was mostly led by structural change growth.

Section 18.4 takes stock of the previous findings and outlines some additional lessons that may prove helpful for the design and implementation of regionally inclusive industrial policies (RIIPs). In particular, it emphasizes that the successful implementation of a RIIP largely depends on the strength and weaknesses of the institutional environment of a country (Acemoglu & Robinson, 2000; Laffont, 1996; Robinson, 2009). Specifically, a country needs to build up enough state capacity to solve coordination failures, both across industries and regions. It also needs to set up new vertical and horizontal policy linkages to exploit scale economies and spatial spillovers.

18.2 The facts of industrial development and regional convergence

18.2.1 Sectoral productivity gaps, structural change, and premature deindustrialization

Economic development is commonly associated with industrial development. Developed countries today are those who managed to diversify their production and move its resources from relatively low productivity sectors (typically agriculture) to modern industrial sectors (Gollin, 2014; Kirkpatrick & Barrientos, 2004; Lewis, 1954). This development process relies on two key factors: the relatively high productivity of the resource-receiving industry and the smooth reallocation of labor (and other production resources) across sectors (McMillan et al., 2014).

The recent availability of comparable cross-country and cross-industry datasets[1] allows us to evaluate cross-country patterns of industrial development in terms of within-sector productivity growth and structural change. The first and central fact in the study of industrial or sectorial development is that developing countries are characterized by larger productivity differences across sectors than those of developed countries. Figure 18.1 illustrates this fact by pointing to the negative relation between aggregate labor productivity and intersectoral productivity gaps. As suggested by Figure 18.1, highly productive countries are those who managed to reduce their labor productivity differences across industries.[2]

In principle, large productivity differences across sectors could also provide an avenue for development when workers move from low to high productivity sectors. This is the notion of development that is suggested in the famous work by Lewis (1954). Recent empirical work by McMillan et al. (2014) points out that this development avenue has been a feature of the growth experience of Asia. In contrast, Africa and Latin America are characterized by growth-reducing

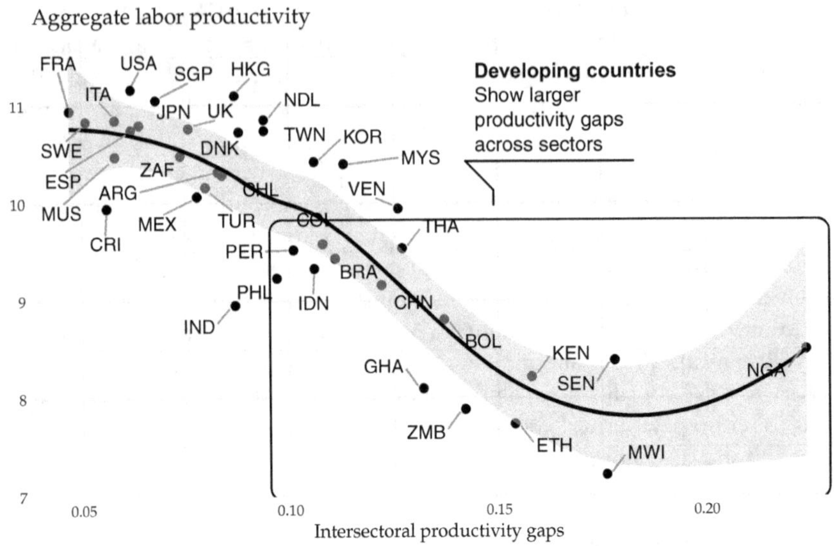

Figure 18.1 Productivity gaps across sectors in developing and developed countries

Notes: The measurement of variables is done for the year 2005. The intersectoral productivity gaps are measured using the coefficient of variation.

Source: Timmer et al. (2015).

structural change. That is, over time, workers moved from relatively low productivity sectors to even lower productivity sectors. Figure 18.2 illustrates this finding by decomposing the growth rate of each country into a within-sector growth component and a structural change component. Most Asian countries are located in the upper-right quadrant, where economies benefit from both positive within-sector and structural change growth. African and Latin American economies, on the other hand, show lower growth due their growth-reducing structural change patterns.

Persistent negative growth in structural change driven by the premature reallocation of labor out of manufacturing has potentially high socioeconomic costs. When productive resources are reallocated to lower productivity activities, the aggregate economy suffers considerable efficiency losses (Vollrath, 2009). Recent research reemphasizes that one of the reasons for underdevelopment is low aggregate productivity, which in turn is driven by resource misallocation, both across industries and firms (Restuccia & Rogerson, 2013, 2017). Also, when economies deindustrialize prematurely, the formal and human capital-intensive service sector usually does not have enough absorption capacity and scale to accommodate the migrant workers. If this is the case, there is a high probability that workers end up increasing the employment share of the informal economy, which is characterized not only by lower levels of efficiency and productivity, but also lower levels of social protection.

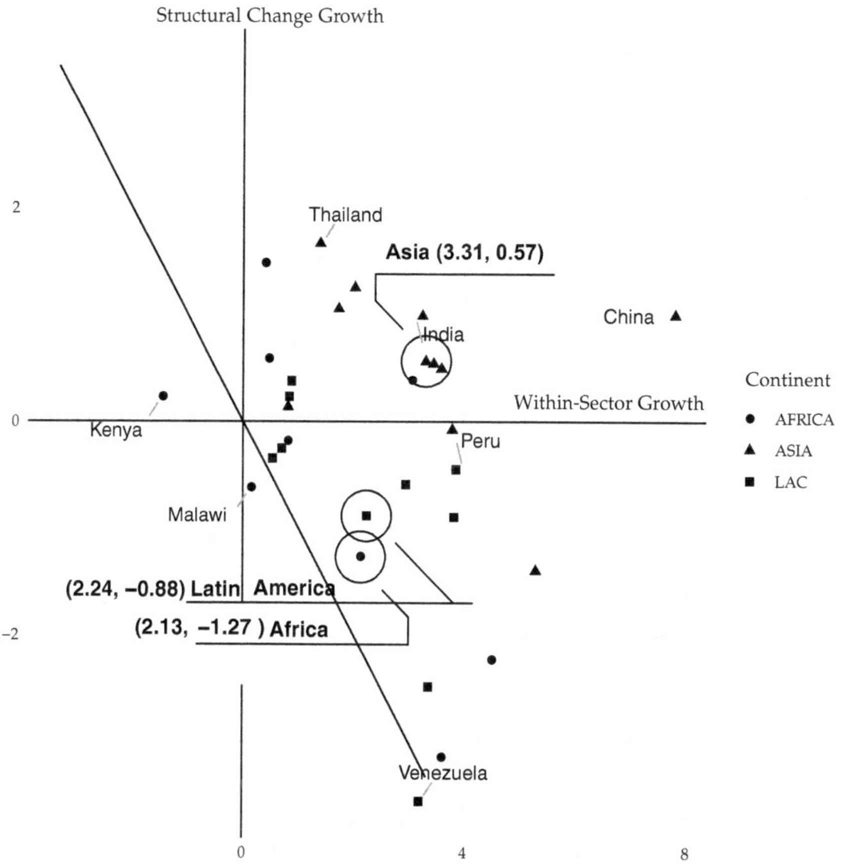

Figure 18.2 Structural change enhances growth only in Asia

Notes: Growth rates are computed for the period 1990–2005. Net growth is the sum of structural change growth and within-sector growth. Observations to the right (left) of the diagonal line indicate positive (negative) net growth.

Source: McMillan et al. (2014).

Figure 18.3 illustrates the fact that some developing countries are deindustrializing at much earlier stage when compared to industrialization levels of more developed countries (Rodrik, 2016). The vertical axis indicates the peak of the manufacturing employment share that was achieved during the 1950–2010 period. The horizontal axis indicates the level of GDP per worker (in log terms) for the year in which the manufacturing share reached its peak. A nonparametric regression between these two variables clearly indicates that the maximum share of manufacturing employment is systematically lower for the developing countries included in this sample.

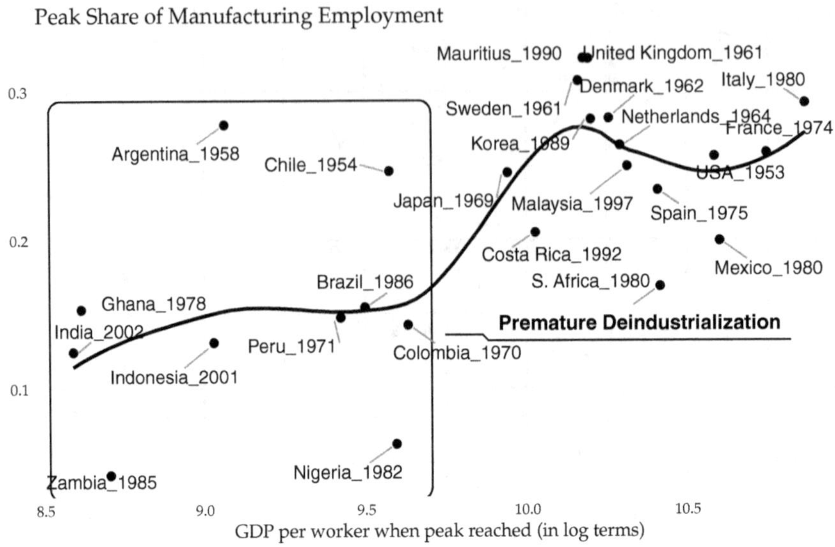

Figure 18.3 Premature deindustrialization of developing countries

Note: The list of countries is from Rodrik (2016).

Source: Timmer et al. (2015).

18.2.2 Regional income gaps and convergence

Regional income growth and regional convergence form a resurgent topic in the literature of economic growth, largely due to the availability of new data sources and the development of new statistical models for spatial analysis (Breinlich, Ottaviano, & Temple, 2014). In particular, satellite data is helping study the regional development patterns of those regions and countries where real income data in unavailable or incomparable. Comparing regional income differences across countries is often a challenging task due to the lack of regional price indices. Satellite nighttime light data offers a partial solution to this problem. For instance, Lessmann and Seidel (2017) compare measures of nominal income with those of satellite light predicted income and conclude that the latter provides a better approximation to values of real income for the regions in their sample.

One of the first insights from this literature is that regional income gaps are greater in developing countries (Figure 18.4). Moreover, these gaps have clear spatial patterns and show signs of spatial dependence (Figures 18.5 and 18.6). For instance, developed countries such as those in North American and Western Europe have the lowest levels of regional inequality. In contrast, higher inequality levels are observed in Africa, Latin America, and East Asia.

As noted by Lessmann and Seidel (2017), the results for Africa are particularly interesting and new because no systematic and comparable analysis has been

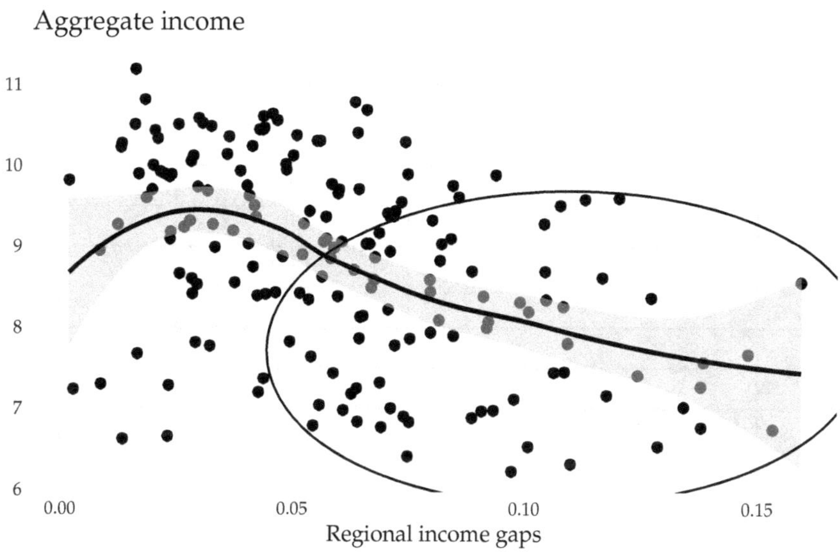

Figure 18.4 Regional incomes gaps in developing and developed countries

Notes: Both variables are measured in the year 2012. A population-weighted Gini coefficient has been used to compute regional income gaps.

Source: Lessmann and Seidel (2017).

done for such a large number of sub-national regions. In Africa, it is interesting to note that the poorest countries of the Sahel zone and the landlocked countries are characterized by both low income and low regional inequality. In contrast, countries with relatively higher income and with access to the sea, such as those in south-eastern and south-western Africa, are characterized by higher regional inequality. Moreover, relatively rich countries, such as South Africa and Namibia, are characterized by lower regional inequalities. The inverted U-shaped relationship that these income-inequality patterns suggests is consistent with the influential work of Williamson (1965), which was one of the first studies to evaluate this relationship (originally proposed by Kuznets 1955) in the regional context.

In terms of the dynamics of regional inequality, Lessmann and Seidel (2017) investigate the difference in regional inequality in the world between the 1990s and the 2000s. They conclude that 119 of 177 countries were able to reduce their regional income gaps. In other words, 67.2 percent of the countries of the world experienced some degree of regional income convergence. Figure 18.6 illustrates these changes by pointing out the spatial location of convergence (divergence) clusters. Interestingly, regional inequality decreased in high- and upper-middle-income countries, but increased in lower-middle-income and low-income countries. It is also important to note that the middle-income groups show the largest variance in the results. Such heterogeneity may suggest that a

Figure 18.5 Spatial distribution of regional income gaps
Source: Lessmann and Seidel (2017).

Figure 18.6 Regional income convergence and divergence across countries

Note: Convergence is computed by subtracting the average level of regional inequality in the 2000s from the average level of regional inequality in the 1990s. If this difference is positive, then the major subnational regions of the country under study are experiencing regional convergence.

Source: Lessmann and Seidel (2017).

simple binary classification (such as convergence vs divergence) could be masking more complex patterns. Among them, the formation of multiple convergence clubs in the middle-income range is a hypothesis that is not yet discarded.

18.3 Integrating industrial development and regional convergence

This section is based on the recent work of Fukao and Paul (2018). In their innovative work, these authors show that regional convergence can be approximated by convergence in within-sector productivity and convergence in structural change. Moreover, they apply their model to explain the regional and industrial development of Japan.

18.3.1 A simple model of industrial development and regional growth

Consider an economy with three sectors: agriculture (A), manufacturing (M), and services (S). Also, in this economy, there are two types of regions: a relatively high-productivity region (H) and a relatively low-productivity region (L). The production of A, M, and S takes place in both regions, H and L. Within each region, sectoral productivity (and wage) differences provide an incentive for labor reallocation between two points in time, t and t+1. In this context, let us denote L^t_{ji} as the labor share of sector i in region j at time t; and Y^t_{ji} as labor productivity of sector i in region j at time t.

Based on a variant of the shift-share decomposition methodology (Fabricant 1942), the change in labor productivity in region j between the time t and $t+1$ is as follows:

$$\underbrace{\Delta y_j}_{\text{Regional Growth}} = \underbrace{\sum_{i=A,M,S}\left(L^t_{ji}\right)\left(\Delta y_{ji}\right)}_{\text{Within-Sector Effect}} + \underbrace{\sum_{i=A,M,S}\left(\Delta L_{ji}\right)\left(y^t_{ji}\right) + m_{i=A,M,S}\left(\Delta L_{ji}\right)\left(\Delta y_{ji}\right)}_{\text{Structural Change Effect}}, \tag{18.1}$$

where y_{ji} is the log of labor productivity in sector i and region j. The last two terms in Equation (18.1) indicate the effect of structural change on regional productivity growth. Thus, regional growth can be decomposed as

$$\underbrace{y^{t+1}_j - y^t_j}_{\text{Regional Growth}} = \underbrace{\Phi(WS)_j}_{\text{Within-Sector Effect}} + \underbrace{\Phi(SC)_j}_{\text{Structural Change Effect}} . \tag{18.2}$$

Equation (18.2) indicates that regional productivity growth is driven by a change in within-sector productivity and a structural change effect. The former could be driven by changes in physical capital, human capital, and technology. The latter represents the reallocation of labor across sectors.

Let us now focus on the structural change effect. After some algebraic operations (see Appendix A), the structural change effect, $\Phi(SC)_j$, of region j can be decomposed into two terms:

$$\Phi(SC)_j = \left(L_{jS}^{t+1} - L_{jS}^{t}\right)\left(y_{jS}^{t+1} - y_{jA}^{t+1}\right) + \left(L_{jM}^{t+1} - L_{jM}^{t}\right)\left(y_{jM}^{t+1} - y_{jA}^{t+1}\right), \tag{18.3}$$

where the first term, $\left(L_{jS}^{t+1} - L_{jS}^{t}\right)\left(y_{jS}^{t+1} - y_{jA}^{t}\right)$, indicates the change in employment in the service sector multiplied by the productivity gap between the service and agricultural sector; and the second term, $\left(L_{jM}^{t+1} - L_{jM}^{t}\right)\left(y_{jM}^{t+1} - y_{jA}^{t}\right)$, indicates the same relation between the manufacturing and agricultural sector. In this structural change context, a low-productivity region, y_L, is able to catch up (converge) with the high-productivity region, y_H, if

$$\left[\left(L_{LS}^{t+1} - L_{LS}^{t}\right)\left(y_{LS}^{t+1} - y_{LA}^{t+1}\right) + \left(L_{LM}^{t+1} - L_{LM}^{t}\right)\left(y_{LM}^{t+1} - y_{LA}^{t+1}\right)\right] >$$

$$\left[\left(L_{HS}^{t+1} - L_{HS}^{t}\right)\left(y_{HS}^{t+1} - y_{HA}^{t+1}\right) + \left(L_{HM}^{t+1} - L_{HM}^{t}\right)\left(y_{HM}^{t+1} - y_{HA}^{t+1}\right)\right]. \tag{18.4}$$

18.3.2 An industry-based model of regional convergence

This section integrates the insights from the previously described industry growth model with a simple model of regional convergence. Consistent with the previous model, there are two sources of overall regional convergence: within-sector convergence and structural change convergence.[3] First, let us define the within-sector productivity in the period $t + 1$ as

$$y_{WS}^{t+1} = y^t + \Phi(WS), \tag{18.5}$$

where y^t is the productivity in period t, $\Phi(WS)$ is the change in productivity due to the within-sector effect. Similarly, let us define the structural change productivity in the period $t + 1$ as

$$y_{SC}^{t+1} = y^t + \Phi(SC). \tag{18.6}$$

Using these two definitions and Equation (18.2), we can write

$$y^{t+1} - y^t = y_{WS}^{t+1} - y^t + y_{SC}^{t+1} - y^t. \tag{18.7}$$

To study regional productivity differences, let us use the Gini coefficient and define it as

$$G(y) = 1 - 2\int \left[1 - F(y)\right]\frac{y}{\mu} f(y)\,dx, \tag{18.8}$$

where G is the Gini coefficient, y is labor productivity, F is a cumulative density function, μ is the mean of labor productivity, and f is a probability density function.

Using this definition, a change in regional inequality can be written as

$$\Delta G(y) = G^{t+1}\left(y^{t+1}\right) - G^{t}\left(y^{t}\right). \tag{18.9}$$

From Equation (18.7), we can write $y^{t+1} = y_{WS}^{t+1} + y_{SC}^{t+1} - y^{t}$; and from the statistical properties of the Gini coefficient (Yitzhaki, 2003), we can obtain the following approximation

$$G^{t+1}\left(y^{t+1}\right) = G^{t+1}\left(y_{WS}^{t+1}\right) + G^{t+1}\left(y_{ST}^{t+1}\right) - G\left(y^{t}\right) + \epsilon, \tag{18.10}$$

where ϵ is an approximation error. If we subtract $G^{t}\left(y^{t}\right)$ from both sides of Equation (18.10), we obtain

$$\underbrace{G^{t+1}\left(y^{t+1}\right) - G^{t}\left(y^{t}\right)}_{\text{Overall Regional Convergence}} = \underbrace{\left[G^{t+1}\left(y_{WS}^{t+1}\right) - G^{t}\left(y^{t}\right)\right]}_{\text{Within-Sector Convergence}} + \underbrace{\left[G^{t+1}\left(y_{SC}^{t+1}\right) - G^{t}\left(y^{t}\right)\right]}_{\text{Structural Change Convergence}} + \tilde{\epsilon}. \tag{18.11}$$

A decrease in the left-hand side of Equation (18.11) indicates a decrease in the Gini coefficient over time.[4] More specifically, this decrease in regional inequality is known in the economic growth literature as sigma convergence.[5] According to Equation (18.11), regional convergence has two sources: within-sector convergence and structural change convergence.

18.3.3 Some empirical evidence from the Japanese experience

Figure 18.7 shows the structural change patterns of Japan in the post-war period. The employment share shows a steady increase in services, a steady decrease in agriculture, and an inverse-U pattern in manufacturing. Over the 1953–2010 period, the employment share in agriculture declined from 42 percent to less than 5 percent. In contrast, the employment share in the service sector increased from 34 percent to 71 percent. The manufacturing share of employment grew from 24 percent in 1953 to 34 percent in 1973, and then gradually returned to 24 percent in 2010. This gradual deindustrialization is consistent with other advanced economies such as the UK, the USA, and Germany. However, it is in contrast with the fast deindustrialization experienced by developing countries in recent years (Rodrik, 2016).

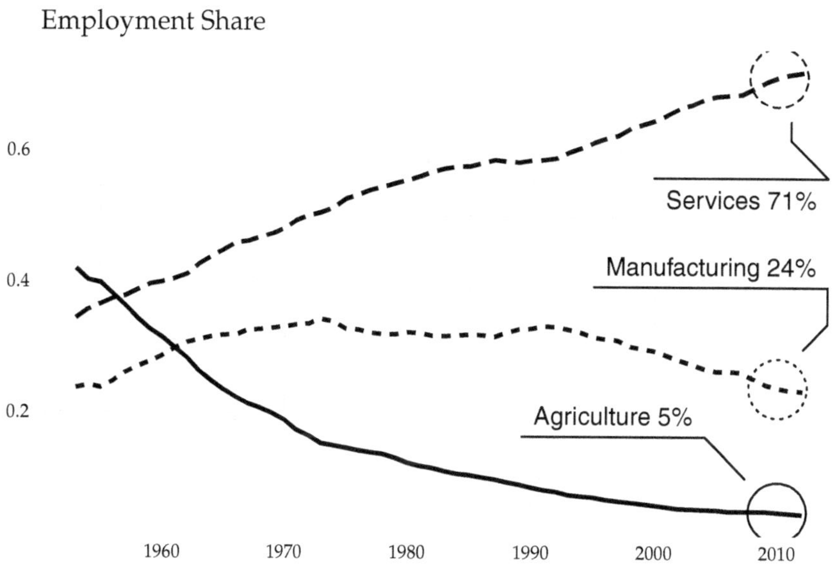

Figure 18.7 Structural change patterns of Japan
Source: Timmer et al. (2015).

Figure 18.8 shows the regional convergence process of labor productivity in Japan since the late nineteenth century. The series shows a break in 1940–1955 to indicate not only the pre-war and post-war periods, but also a difference in the set of constant prices that are used to compute real GDP (see the note to Figure 18.8 for details). According to Fukao and Paul (2018), in the pre-war period, workers moved out of agriculture and industrialization started to gain momentum. Interestingly, this initial industrialization is consistent the reduction in regional disparities shown in Figure 18.7. In the post-war period, industrialization accelerated and then, from the mid-1970s, most workers gradually moved to the service sector. A key fact associated with this process is that, in spite of such large structural changes, regional convergence continued, most noticeably at a faster rate than that of the pre-war period. Specifically, on average, the Gini coefficient decreased 10 percent in the pre-war period and almost 35 percent in the post-war period.

Table 18.1 shows the role of structural change and within-sector growth in the process of regional convergence. In particular, it highlights two different regimes of regional convergence before and after the war. In the pre-war period, the main source of convergence was within-sector growth. Between 1909 and 1925, the regional Gini coefficient decreased by 14.4 percent. The Gini decomposition of Equation (18.11) suggests that this decrease was almost entirely driven by the convergence in within-sector productivity (18.1 percent). In contrast, structural change increased regional inequality by 4.7 percent.

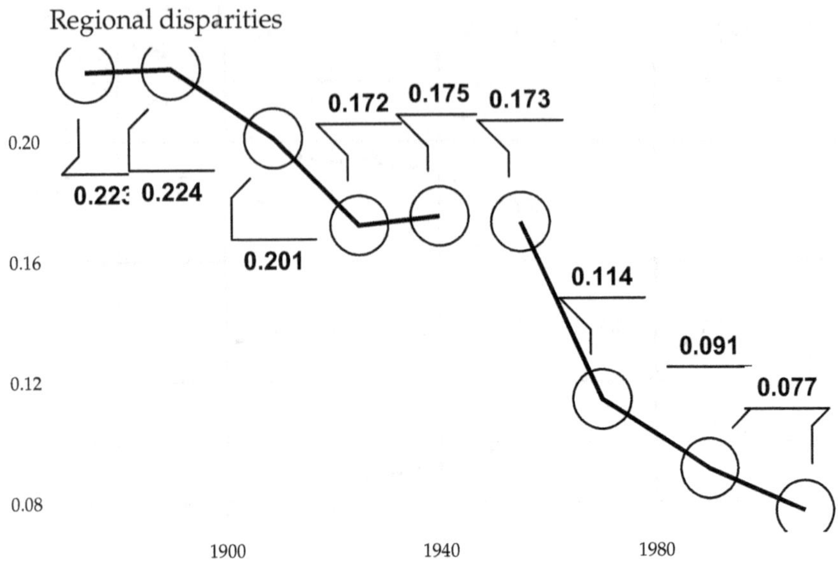

Figure 18.8 Regional convergence process of Japan

Note: Regional disparities in labor productivity are measured by the Gini coefficient. For the 1874–1940 period, real GDP is computed using constant prices of 1934–1936. For the 1955–2008 period, constant prices of the year 2000 are used.

Table 18.1 The role of structural change and within-sector growth on regional convergence

Period	*Regional convergence*	*Percentage change Gini Index*	*Within-sector convergence Effect*	*Structural change convergence Effect*	*Residual term*
Pre-war period 1874–1940					
1874–1890	No	0.5	–8	6.9	1.6
1890–1909	Yes	–11.6	–15.2	4.1	–0.5
1909–1925	Yes	–14.4	–18.1	4.7	–1
1925–1940	No	1.3	–3.2	16	–11.5
Post-war period 1955–2008					
1955–1970	Yes	–36.8	–0.1	–29.9	–6.8
1970–1990	Yes	–19.5	10	–25.9	–3.6
1990–2008	Yes	–14.1	–3.3	–15.5	4.7

Notes: Values of the table are percentage changes of the Gini coefficient in the initial year of each period. The variable under study is average labor productivity.

Source: Adapted from Fukao and Paul (2018, Table 1).

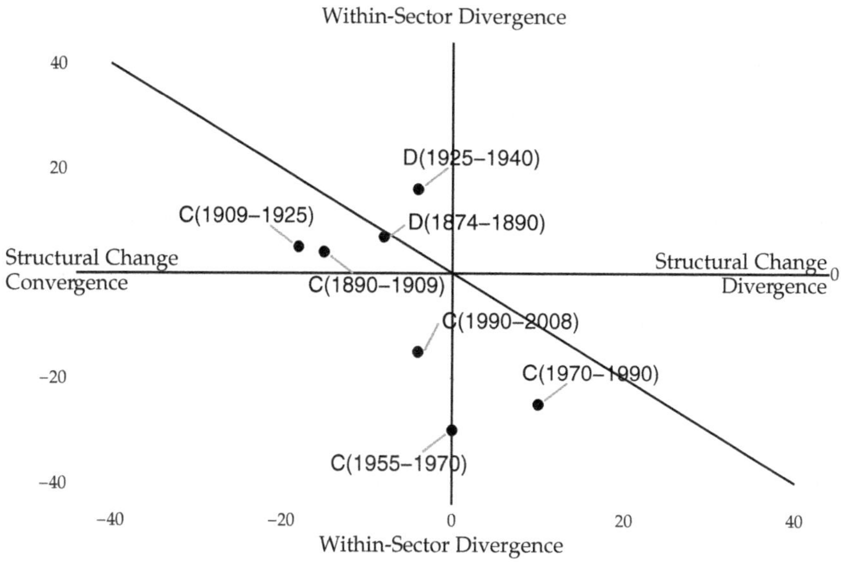

Figure 18.9 The role of structural change and within-sector growth on regional convergence
Source: Adapted from Fukao and Paul (2018, Figure 4).

In the post-war period, however, the engine of regional convergence was structural change. Between 1970 and 1990, the regional Gini coefficient decreased by 19.5 percent. This decrease was almost entirely driven by the regional convergence in structural change (29.9 percent). In contrast, within-sector growth increased regional inequality by 10 percent.[6]

From a different perspective, Figure 18.9 also shows the role of structural change and within-sector growth in regional convergence. The vertical axis indicates the percentage change of the Gini coefficient that is due to convergence in structural change. The horizontal axis indicates the percentage change of the Gini coefficient that is due to within-sector convergence. In both axes, negative values indicate convergence in each variable. The diagonal line helps identify the net convergence effect when both variables are jointly considered. For instance, when observations are located to the left (right) of the line, there is a net convergence (divergence) effect.

Figure 18.9 suggests that as most points are located to the left of the convergence line, but in different quadrants, regional convergence has been driven by both within-sector convergence and structural change convergence. However, it seems unlikely for both sources to move in the same direction. Only in the periods 1955–1970 and 1990–2008 did both sources simultaneously help reduce regional inequality. In most cases, particularly in the pre-war period, within-sector growth helped reduce regional inequality while structural change increased it.

Thus, these opposite effects on regional convergence suggest a space for a potential policy intervention, which is discussed in the next section.

Finally, it is important to note that Figure 18.9 ignores the role of the residual term of Equation (18.11). As can be seen in Figure 18.9, ignoring this term does not alter the conclusions, except between the years 1874 and 1890. During this period, the Gini coefficient increased by 0.5 percent, which indicates overall divergence. If we only consider the within-sector convergence effect (-8 percent) and the structural change convergence effect (6.9 percent), then the net effect on the Gini coefficient should be negative (-1.1 percent). However, only in this period, the sign and magnitude of the residual were large enough (1.6 percent) to reverse this conclusion. Thus, although the 1874–1890 observation is located in a net convergence area, it is labeled as divergence (D) due to the effect of the residual term.

18.4 Taking stock: Toward a regionally inclusive industrial policy (RIIP)

In this section we take stock of the findings of the previous sections, summarize some key lessons, and discuss the potential role of a regionally inclusive industrial policy (RIIP) that aims to promote both industrial development and regional convergence. The key premise of a RIIP is that, at least in the short run, a standard industrial policy ends up favoring some industries over others and some regions over others. In the medium run and long run, however, a RIIP should facilitate the catch-up of lagging industries and regions. Thus, a RIIP is expected to ensure the sustainability and inclusivity of productivity-enhancing policies.

18.4.1 Lessons from the facts of industrial development and regional convergence

It is common to observe both large productivity differences across industries and large per-capita income differences across regions in developing countries. A growing body of literature has been pointing out that developing countries are facing a double challenge. On the one hand, the development of their industries in a much more globalized and competitive world economy, and on the other, the management of a regionally unbalanced growth process (Isaksen, 2001; Scott & Storper, 2005; Wei & Liefner, 2012). Thus, there is a need for a regionally inclusive industrial policy that should be able to manage both challenges at the same time.

The challenge of industrial development has two immediate tasks: (1) increasing productivity in current and potentially new (strategic) sectors; and (2) facilitating the smooth reallocation of workers from relatively low-productivity sectors to modern high-productivity sectors. Developing countries in Asia, Africa, and Latin America have faced this challenge with different results. On the one hand, countries in Asia appear to be successfully managing these two channels. Countries in Africa and Latin America, on the other hand, appear to be lagging behind mainly because of sectoral misallocation. That is, workers are moving from relatively low-productivity sectors to even lower productivity parts of the economy, which are typically related to the informal service sector (McMillan, et al., 2014). This problem of sectoral misallocation is both intertwined with and exacerbated by the premature deindustrialization tendency observed in developing countries (Rodrik, 2016).

The challenge of regional development has to do with the socioeconomic stability concerns associated with an uneven growth process in which some regions become rich and the rest remain poor. This initial disparity could be related to the discovery of natural resources or the implementation of a new technology that is highly complementary to the natural, physical, and human capital of a particular region. Thus, given these regional asymmetries in endowments and technologies, regional inequality could increase at low levels of development and undermine social and political stability (Ezcurra, 2018; Østby, 2008). To avoid regional polarization and potential conflicts, regional development polices should help lagging regions catch up as they develop their own endowments and capabilities for technology adoption (Barrios & Strobl, 2009). When analyzing the recent evidence on regional development, new data sources, based on satellite nighttime lights, reveal that regional divergence is much more prevalent in Africa than in any other continent.

18.4.2 Lessons from an industry-based model of regional convergence

Industrial and regional development are not independent processes, they continuously interact with each other (Scott & Storper, 2005). The model of Fukao and Paul (2018) described in Section 18.3 highlights some of these interactions and helps us identify the following lessons:

- The two sources of industrial development (within-sector growth and structural change growth) have their equivalent effects when studying regional convergence. That is, overall regional convergence can be decomposed into within-sector convergence and structural change convergence.
- Improvements in physical capital, human capital, and technology affect both industrial growth and regional convergence. The effect of within-sector growth on regional convergence depends on the initial spatial distribution of resources and technologies.
- Structural change could either improve or deteriorate the process of regional convergence.
- The effects of within-sector convergence and structural change convergence could have opposite signs. Thus, the net effect needs to be carefully evaluated.
- The Japanese industrialization experience illustrates both alternative forms of regional convergence. In the pre-war period, regional convergence was

mostly led by within-sector growth. In contrast, in the post-war period, it was mostly led by structural change growth.

- Industry-based models of regional convergence, such as the one developed by Fukao and Paul (2018), may prove useful as monitoring devices that track the multiple effects of industrial development on regional convergence.

18.4.3 Implementing a regionally inclusive industrial policy (RIIP)

The successful implementation of a RIIP largely depends on the strength and weaknesses of the institutional environment of a country (Acemoglu & Robinson, 2000; Laffont, 1996; Robinson, 2009). Specifically, a country needs to build up enough state capacity to solve coordination failures, both across industries and regions (Harrison & Rodriguez-Clare, 2010; Milio, 2007; Shapiro & Taylor, 1990). It also has to set up new vertical and horizontal policy linkages to exploit scale economies and spatial spillovers.

18.4.3.1 Building up state capacity to solve coordination problems

In their comprehensive review of industrial policy alternatives, Harrison and Rodriguez-Clare (2010) argue that modern industrial policy should be less focused on interventions that distort prices and more focused on interventions that promote the coordination among government, industry, and cluster-level organizations. The objective is to increase productivity in both existing and raising sectors through the supply of skilled workers, technology adoption and innovation, and investment in infrastructure. To achieve this goal, however, developing countries need to build up their state capacity at multiple levels of administration. Otherwise, any coordination and policy effort is likely to be eroded by rent seeking and corruption (Fukuyama, 2004). Lastly, a rigorous system of accountability must be established and followed by all the participating organizations (Whitfield & Buur, 2014).

18.4.3.2 Setting up vertical policy linkages to exploit scale economies

Although decentralization of political power from the central to local governments adds flexibility and independence to the design and implementation of public policy, an effective vertical coordination of tasks and responsibilities is still needed. Specially for large and multi-region industrial projects, vertical policy linkages are needed to effectively invest in large public infrastructure projects and exploit scale economies.

18.4.3.3 Setting up horizontal policy linkages to exploit spatial spillovers

A common finding in the spatial econometrics literature is that spatial dependence accelerates the rate of regional convergence through spillovers effects. In this context, to maximize the positive effect of spatial spillovers among regions, local governments need to further coordinate their policy efforts. Also, to accelerate the convergence speed, additional policy effort should focus on facilitating the mobility of workers across regions. Providing modern transportation infrastructure to integrate the production hubs of a country is a low-hanging fruit policy that has not yet been fully implemented in many developing countries.

Notes

1 Particularly relevant for this analysis the dataset of Timmer, De Vries, and De Vries (2015).
2 In this chapter the words "industry" and "sector" are used as synonyms.
3 To economize notation, the region index j is omitted without any loss of generality.
4 Equations (18.10) and (18.11) are particularly useful when the approximation error is small. Fukao and Paul (2018) show that this error becomes small when the Gini correlation coefficients are close to one. It also becomes small when the expected values of the main variables, $E\left(y^{t+1}\right)$, $E\left(y_{WS}^{t+1}\right)$, $E\left(y_{SC}^{t+1}\right)$, and $E\left(y^{t}\right)$, have similar magnitudes.
5 Although many studies in the growth empirical literature use the coefficient of variation (for example, Friedman, 1992) or the standard deviation (for example, Sala-i-Martin, 1996) to evaluate sigma convergence, Yitzhaki et al. (2003) argue that the Gini coefficient shares many properties of the variance and could also be used as an informative indicator of dispersion.
6 Consistent in within-sector divergence of the post-war period, Dominguez and Mendez (2019) document that since the early 1990s, there have been larger and increasing labor productivity differences across industries in Japan.

Appendix

Derivation of Equation (18.3)

Let us first restate the structural change equation as

$$\Phi(SC) = \sum_{i=A,M,S}(\Delta L_i)\left(y_i^t\right) + \sum_{i=A,M,S}(\Delta L_i)(\Delta y_i),$$

where, without loss of generality, the region index, j, has been omitted to simplify the presentation. Then, expand Equation (18.12) as

$$\Phi(SC) = \left(L_A^{t+1} - L_A^t\right)y_A^t + \left(L_M^{t+1} - L_M^t\right)y_M^t + \left(L_S^{t+1} - L_S^t\right)y_S^t$$

$$+\left(L_A^{t+1} - L_A^t\right)\left(y_A^{t+1} - y_A^t\right) + \left(L_M^{t+1} - L_M^t\right)\left(y_M^{t+1} - y_M^t\right) + \left(L_S^{t+1} - L_S^t\right)\left(y_S^{t+1} - y_S^t\right)$$

$$= \left(L_A^{t+1} - L_A^t\right)\left[y_A^t + \left(y_A^{t+1} - y_A^t\right)\right] + \left(L_M^{t+1} - L_M^t\right)\left[y_M^t + \left(y_M^{t+1} - y_M^t\right)\right]$$

$$+\left(L_S^{t+1}-L_S^t\right)\left[y_S^t+\left(y_S^{t+1}-y_S^t\right)\right]$$

$$=\left(L_A^{t+1}-L_A^t\right)y_A^{t+1}+\left(L_M^{t+1}-L_M^t\right)y_M^{t+1}+\left(L_S^{t+1}-L_S^t\right)y_S^{t+1}. \tag{18.13}$$

Next, define the employment share in agriculture as

$$L_A=1-L_M-L_S, \tag{18.14}$$

which implies that

$$\left(L_A^{t+1}-L_A^t\right)=1-L_M^{t+1}-L_S^{t+1}-\left(1-L_M^t-L_S^t\right)$$

$$=-\left(L_M^{t+1}-L_M^t\right)-\left(L_S^{t+1}-L_S^t\right). \tag{18.15}$$

Finally, substitute Equation (18.14) into Equation (18.15):

$$\Phi(SC)=-\left(L_M^{t+1}-L_M^t\right)y_A^{t+1}-\left(L_S^{t+1}-L_S^t\right)y_A^{t+1}+\left(L_M^{t+1}-L_M^t\right)y_M^{t+1}+\left(L_S^{t+1}-L_S^t\right)y_S^{t+1},$$

Thus, the structural change equation can be expressed as

$$\Phi(SC)=\left(L_S^{t+1}-L_S^t\right)\left(y_S^{t+1}-y_A^{t+1}\right)+\left(L_M^{t+1}-L_M^t\right)\left(y_M^{t+1}-y_A^{t+1}\right).$$

References

Acemoglu, D., & Robinson, J. A. (2000). Political losers as a barrier to economic development. *American Economic Review*, 90(2), 126–130.

Barrios, S., & Strobl, E. (2009). The dynamics of regional inequalities. *Regional Science and Urban Economics*, 39(5), 575–591.

Breinlich, H., Ottaviano, G. I., & Temple, J. R. (2014). Regional growth and regional decline. In P. Agion, & S. Durlaf (Eds.), *Handbook of economic growth*, vol. 2. Amsterdam: Elsevier.

Dominguez, A., & Mendez, C. (2019). Industrial productivity divergence and input-output network structures: Evidence from Japan, 1973–2012. *Economies*, 7(2), 1–14.

Ezcurra, R. (2018). Interregional inequality and civil conflict: Are spatial disparities a threat to stability and peace? *Defence and Peace Economics*, 30, 1–24.

Fabricant, S. (1942). *Employment in manufacturing, 1899–1939*. New York: NBER.

Friedman, M. (1992). Do old fallacies ever die? Journal of Economic Literature, 30(4), 2129–2132.

Fukao, K., & Paul, S. (2018). A framework to study the role of structural transformation in productivity growth and regional convergence. Working Paper No. 833. Asian Development Bank Institute.

Fukuyama, F. (2004). The imperative of state-building. *Journal of Democracy*, 15(2), 1–31.

Gollin, D. (2014). The Lewis model: A 60-year retrospective. *Journal of Economic Perspectives*, 28(3), 71–88.

Harrison, A., & Rodríguez-Clare, A. (2010). Trade, foreign investment, and industrial policy for developing countries. In D. Rodrik & M. Rosenzweig (Eds.), *Handbook of development economics*, vol. 5. Amsterdam: Elsevier.

Isaksen, A. (2001). Building regional innovation systems: Is endogenous industrial development possible in the global economy? *Canadian Journal of Regional Science*, 24(1), 101–120.

Kirkpatrick, C., & Barrientos, A. (2004). The Lewis model after 50 years. *Manchester School*, 72(6), 679–690.

Kuznets, S. (1955). Economic growth and income inequality. *American Economic Review*, 45(1), 1–28.

Laffont, J.-J. (1996). Industrial policy and politics. *International Journal of Industrial Organization*, 14(1), 1–27.

Lessmann, C. (2016). Regional inequality and internal conflict. *German Economic Review*, 17(2), 157–191.

Lessmann, C., & Seidel, A. (2017). Regional inequality, convergence, and its determinants: A view from outer space. *European Economic Review*, 92, 110–132.

Lewis, W. A. (1954). Economic development with unlimited supplies of labour. *Manchester School*, 22(2), 139–191.

McMillan, M., Rodrik, D., & Verduzco-Gallo, Í. (2014). Globalization, structural change, and productivity growth, with an update on Africa. World Development, 63, 11–32.

Milio, S. (2007). Can administrative capacity explain differences in regional performances? Evidence from Structural Funds implementation in southern Italy. *Regional Studies*, 41(4), 429–442.

Mitton, T. (2016). The wealth of subnations: Geography, institutions, and within-country development. *Journal of Development Economics*, 118, 88–111.

Østby, G. (2008). Polarization, horizontal inequalities and violent civil conflict. *Journal of Peace Research*, 45(2), 143–162.

Restuccia, D., & Rogerson, R. (2013). Misallocation and productivity. *Review of Economic Dynamics*, 1(16), 1–10.

Restuccia, D., & Rogerson, R. (2017). The causes and costs of misallocation. *Journal of Economic Perspectives*, 31(3), 151–174.

Robinson, J. A. (2009). Industrial policy and development: A political economy perspective. World Bank Working Paper, Annual World Bank Conference on Development Economics.

Rodrik, D. (2016). Premature deindustrialization. *Journal of Economic Growth*, 21(1), 1–33.

Sala-i-Martin, X. (1996). The classical approach to convergence analysis. *Economic Journal*, 106, 1019–1036.

Scott, A. J., & Storper, M. (2005). *Pathways to industrialization and regional development.* London: Routledge.

Shapiro, H., & Taylor, L. (1990). The state and industrial strategy. *World Development*, 18(6), 861–878.

Timmer, M., de Vries, G. J., & De Vries, K. (2015). Patterns of structural change in developing countries. In J. Weiss & M. Tribe (Eds.), *Routledge handbook of industry and development*. London: Routledge.

Vollrath, D. (2009). How important are dual economy effects for aggregate productivity? *Journal of Development Economics*, 88(2), 325–334.

Wei, Y. D., & Liefner, I. (2012). Globalization, industrial restructuring, and regional development in China. *Applied Geography*, 32(1), 102–105.

Whitfield, L., & Buur, L. (2014). The politics of industrial policy: Ruling elites and their alliances. *Third World Quarterly*, 35(1), 126–144.

Williamson, J. G. (1965). Regional inequality and the process of national development: A description of the patterns. *Economic Development and Cultural Change*, 13(4), 1–84.

Yitzhaki, S. et al. (2003). Gini's mean difference: A superior measure of variability for nonnormal distributions. *Metron*, 61(2), 285–316.

Name Index

Acemoglu, D. 38n10, 257, 272
Acs, Z. J. 164
Aggarwal, V. K. 27
Agosin, M. R. 17, 59
Aguiar, A. 240, 250
Ahn, S. 27
Aiginger, K. 38n5
Akamatsu, K. 161
Akkemik, K. A. 50
Albaladejo, M. 165
Albors, J. 165
Alcorta, L. 24
Altenburg, T. 14, 17
Alvarez, C. V. 13, 39n20
Amable, B. 39n13
Amaeshi, K. 209
Amann, J. 95, 97, 100, 104, 122, 128
Americo, B. Z. 27
Amin Guitierrez de Pineres, S. 17
Amit, R. 165
Anand, R. 7
Ancharaz, V. 183, 184
Anderson, K. 22
Andreoni, A. 20, 91n5
Armington, P. S. 249
Audretsch, D. B. 164

Bah, E.-h. M. 70
Balchin, N. 219
Baldwin, J. R. 148
Baldwin, R. 46, 55, 84
Banerjee, Abijit 38
Banerji, S. 232n13
Barrett, P.M. 228, 231n7
Barrientos, A. 257
Barrientos, S. 204
Barrios, S. 139, 271
Bartelme, D. 139
Baumann-Pauly, D. 228, 231n7
Bayo-Moriones, A. 151
Becker, S. O. 138, 140
Bernard, A. B. 138
Bilal, S. 203
Bleaney, M. 60
Blomstrom, M. 167
Bluestone, B. 95
Brady, D. 95
Braunerhjelm, P. 164
Bräutigam, D. 192
Breinlich, H. 260
Brenton, P. 135, 136
Buratti, N. 166
Busse, M. 185, 191
Buur, L. 272
Byiers, B. 203

Cadot, O. 135
Calabrese, N. 219
Caneque, F. C. 206
Cantner, P. 166
Carlsson, B. 164
Carlsson-Kanyama, A. 122
Carrico, C. 240
Caves, R. E. 139, 145, 158n1
Chang, H.-J. 6, 7, 20, 24, 26, 38n6, 50, 74, 91n5, 165
Chang, J.-M. 24
Charvet, E. 207
Chen, W. 191
Chen, Y. 184, 191, 192, 200n1
Chenery, H. 16, 70, 96–97, 106, 123n2, 123n3
Cheng, C. F. C. 100, 114, 124n8
Cheng, M. 190, 191
Chin, G. 186
Cho, Y. 135
Cimoli, M. 6
Clark, C. 63, 70

Colebourne, D. 151
Cook, S. 192
Correa, C. M. 27
Crepon, B. 138, 139, 147
Crespi, G. 7

Dadush, U. 17
Dasgupta, S. 63, 65, 98, 99, 102, 151
Davies, M. 166
Demetriades, P. 192
Denniston, R. 95
Desalegn, Hailemariam 216, 222
Dessai, S. 120
Devlin, R. 24, 39n20
de Vries, G. J. 47
de Vries, K. 47, 256, 273n1
Diao, X. 63
Dietzenbacher, E. 139, 146
Di Maio, M. 9, 26, 38n6
Dixon, P. B. 240
Dollar, D. 191
Dominguez, A. 273n6
Donou-Adonsou, F. 190
Dosi, G. 6
Dreher, A. 190
Duarte, M. 79, 81
Duguet, E. 139, 147
Dustmann, C. 39n10

Earley, K. 232n13
Edinger, H. 183, 184
Egger, P. H. 138, 140
Erdogan, C. 191
Evans, P. 24
Evenett, S. J. 27
Eyob, T. T. 24
Ezcurra, R. 271

Fabiani, S. 151
Fabricant, S. 264
Feenstra, R. 128
Felipe, J. 6, 8, 14, 17, 63
Fernández-Arias, E. 7
Ferrantino, M. J. 17
Ferraz, J. C. 7
Feyisa, B. D. 222
Fontana, R. 151
Fosfuri, A. 167
Fredriksson, T. 27
Friedman, M. 273n5
Fuchs, A. 190
Fukao, K. 257, 264, 267–269, 271, 272, 273n4
Fukuyama, F. 272

Gabriele, A. 7
Gallagher, K. P. 26
Gebremariam, F. M. 222
Gelan, A. 222, 228
Gereffi, G. 204
Ghani, E. 39n15, 99, 117
Ghosh, A. R. 60
Ghosh, S. 206, 208
Gibbs, M. 26
Gollin, D. 257
González, A. J. 122
Görg, H. 139
Gorodnichenko, Y. 139
Greenaway, D. 60
Greenwald, B. C. 13
Grimm, M. 135
Gronum, S. 165
Große-Puppendahl, S. 203, 205
Grossman, G. M. 121
Guadagno, F. 29
Guerrieri, P. 99
Guillén, M. F. 165
Günther, T. 24

Habiyaremye, A. 215
Hackenesch, C. 222, 223, 226
Hadjimanolis, A. 165
Haggard, S. 37
Hall, B. H. 27, 148
Halland, H. 186
Hallward-Driemeier, M. 8, 21
Halpern, L. 139
Hammond, A. L. 203, 206
Hanauer, L. 189
Hanel, P. 148
Haraguchi, N. 95, 97, 100, 104, 108, 114, 124n8, 128
Hardy, V. 228
Harrison, A. 272
Harrison, B. 95
Harrison, W. J. 251
Hart, S. L. 206
Harttgen, K. 17
Hauge, J. 228
Hausmann, R. 6–7, 13, 16, 59
Hayashi, F. 138
Herrendorf, B. 70, 71
Hertel, T. W. 240, 249, 250
Herzberg, B. 39n20
Herzer, D. 17, 59
Hidalgo, A. 165
Hidalgo, C. A. 7
Hirschman, A. O. 16
Hollenstein, H. 151

Honorati, M. 135
Hopenhayn, H. 138
Hummels, D. 240
Hwang, J. 6, 16, 59

Iacovone, L. 135
Ianchovichina, E. 240, 250
Ibrahim, I. 183, 191
Idemudia, U. 209
Inklaar, R. 128
Inomata, S. 240
Isaksen, A. 270
Isaksson, A.-S. 190, 191, 198
Itakura, K. 239, 240, 242, 244, 246, 248, 250–252, 254
Ito, T. 55

Jager, U. 206
Jakob, M. 121
Javorcik, B. S. 139, 145
Jensen, J. B. 138
Jerneck, A. 120
Jorgenson, D. W. 240
Jovanovic, B. 138

Kaldor, N. 16, 95
Kastelle, T. 165
Katz, R. S. 206
Khan, S. R. 26
Kirkpatrick, C. 257
Kirzner, I. M. 162
Klapper, L. 165
Kleinknecht, A. 148
Klepper, S. 138
Klien, R. J. T. 120
Klinger, B. 6, 7, 16, 59
Kobukura, K. 212
Komoda, F. 165
Konya, K. 207
Konzelmann, S. 91n5
Kotsadam, A. 190, 191, 198
Kragelund, P. 204
Kramer, M. R. 203, 230n2
Kramer, W. J. 206
Kremer, Michael 38
Krueger, A. B. 121
Krueger, A. O. 6, 39n10
Kuan, M. L. 20
Kupfer, D. 7
Kuznets, S. 70, 95, 121, 261

Laffont, J.-J. 257, 272
Lall, S. 13, 38n8, 39n11
Landry, G. D. 186, 200n4
Law, S. H. 192
Lederman, D. 17, 59, 136, 142
Lee, H. 240, 251
Lee, K. 27
Lera-López, F. 151
Lessmann, C. 260–263
Lewis, W. A. 95, 257
Li, B. G. 138
Liefner, I. 270
Lim, S. 190
Lin, J. Y. 6, 13, 14, 99, 100
Liu, A. 190
Llobet, G. 219, 222, 224
Lo, D. 8
Lööf, H. 149
Lu, J. 192
Lu, Y. 58
Lundstrom, S. 7

MacAllister, P. 232n13
MacDonald, G. M. 138
Mairesse, J. 139, 147–149
Maloney, W. F. 17, 59
Marques, F. S. 7
Masuyama, S. 26
Maswana, J. C. 166
Matsuyama, K. 95
McDougall, R. 240, 249, 250
McGowan, A. M. 135
McKenzie, D. 135
McMillan, M. 256, 257, 259, 271
McMillan, M. S. 16, 59, 63, 81
Mehta, A. 63
Meliciani, V. 99
Melitz, M. J. 138
Mendez, C. 256, 258, 260, 262, 264, 266, 268, 270, 272, 273n6, 274
Mihretu, M. 24, 219, 222, 224
Milio, S. 272
Minor, P. 240
Mishra, S. 6
Mitchell, B. 47, 65, 70
Mitton, T. 256
Moguillansky, G. 24
Mohnen, P. 147, 149
Monga, C. 6, 13, 99, 100
Morgan, A. 151
Morris, L. J. 189
Motta, M. 167
Mourao, P. 191, 197
Mueller-Hirth, N. 209
Muhlen, H. 191
Muraközy, B. 139

Murillo, F. 207
Muûls, M. 152

Narayanan, B. 240
Nasrullah, N. M. 208, 210
Natsuda, K. 27
Nayyar, G. 8, 21
Nesta, L. 151
Newfarmer, R. S. 80, 82
Newman, C. 38n7
Ngai, R. 79
Nicolas, F. 215, 222
Nowak-Lehmann, F. D. 17, 59

Oguzlu, T. 215
Ohno, I. 207, 211, 213, 226
Ohno, K. 17, 25, 39n20, 226
Olsson, L. 120
Oqubay, A. 218–219
Ortt, R. 148
Østby, G. 271
Ostry, J. 60
Otchia, C. S. 46, 50
Otsubo, S. 3, 23, 31–32
Ottaviano, G. I. 260
Oya, C. 222, 228
Oyamada, K. 240, 250

Pack, H. 13, 39n11
Paffhausen, A. L. 135
Page, J. 14, 22, 38n7, 80
Palma, J. G. 97
Parks, B. 190
Paul, S. 257, 264, 267–269, 271, 272, 273n4
Pearson, K. R. 251
Pelling, M. 120
Penco, L. 166
Peneder, M. 39n13
Peres, W. 38n6
Pesaran, M. H. 192
Pierce, J. R. 139
Pierola, M. D. 135
Pissarides, C. 79
Porter, E. M. 203, 230n2
Pouliotte, J. 120
Prahalad, C. K. 203, 206
Primi, A. 38n6
Pritchett, L. 104
Pyka, A. 166

Quesada, J. M. 165

Rahim, M. M. 208, 210
Rajan, J. 206, 208
Rauch, F. 135
Redding, S. J. 138
Restuccia, D. 79, 81, 258
Rhee, C. 63
Robinson, J. A. 257, 272
Robinson, S. 16
Rodrik, D. 6, 13–14, 16, 17, 24, 26, 37, 39n11, 39n13, 58, 59, 63–65, 67, 82, 97–99, 256, 259, 260, 266, 271
Rogerson, R. 70, 79, 258
Romer, P. M. 164
Romijn, H. 165
Ronde, T. 167
Rossi, A. 204

Saggi, K. 13, 39n11
Sala, D. 151
Sala-i-Martin, X. 273n5
Salazar-Xirinachs, J. M. 6
Sandrey, R. 183, 184
Sathe, V. 206
Sato, H. 55
Schaefer, F. 222, 228
Schipper, E. 120
Schipper, L. 120
Schivardi, F. 151
Schönberg, U. 39n10
Schott, P. K. 138, 139
Scott, A. J. 256, 270, 271
Seidel, A. 260–263
Shadlen, K. 26
Shapiro, H. 272
Shiga, H. 207
Shipman, A. 91n5
Signé, L. 190
Singh, A. 63, 65, 98, 99, 102
Sisombat, L. 39n20
Smeets, E. 100, 113, 124n8
Smit, B. 120
Solow, R. M. 164
Staritz, C. 219
Steckel, J. C. 121
Stein, E. 7
Stiebale, J. 152
Stiglitz, J. E. 6, 13, 82
Storper, M. 256, 270, 271
Strange, A. 190
Strobl, E. 139, 271
Strutt, A. 22

Sutton, J. 158n1
Sweeney, E. 165
Syrquin, M. 16, 70, 96–97, 106, 123n2, 123n3
Szirmai, A. 39n13, 99, 102, 117
Szogs, A. 165

Tang, B. 190
Tang, H. 191
Tang, K. 224, 225, 231n8
Tang, X. 191, 192, 214
Tarp, F. 80
Taylor, L. 96, 123n2, 272
Temin, P. 63, 65
Temple, J. R. 260
Thoburn, J. 27
Thomas, B. 151
Tierney, M. 190
Timmer, M. P. 47, 128, 130, 240, 256, 258, 260, 267, 273n1
Tiwari, P. 219, 223
Todo, Y. 152
Tran, J. T. 206
Treichel, V. 14
Trento, S. 151
Tugendendhat, H. 192
Tyson, J. E. 215

Ueda, T. 211

Valentinyi, Á. 70
van Beers, C. 148
Van Beveren, I. 140
Vandenbrink, D. 26
Vandenbussche, H. 140
Verburg, R. 148
Verdier, T. 38n10
Verduzco-Gallo, Í. 16, 59
Verreynne, M. L. 165
Verspagen, B. 99, 102, 117
Vollrath, D. 258

Wade, R. H. 24, 26, 27
Walmsley, T. 240, 250
Wan, M. 214
Wang, J. 58
Wang, J. Y. 167
Wang, Z. 138
Wangwe, S. 63
Wasmer, E. 39n10
Wei, Y. D. 270
Weil, P. 39n10
Weiss, J. 10, 12, 33
Westerhoff, L. 120
Whitfield, L. 219, 272
Williamson, J. G. 261
Woodruff, C. 135
Wu, M. 8

Xi Jinping 185

Yalcin, E. 151
Yitzhaki, S. 266, 273n5
Yue, C. S. 26

Zenawi, Meles 216, 219, 222
Zhu, L. 58

Subject Index

Note: Page numbers in *italics* and **bold denote figures and tables, respectively. Page numbers followed by "n" denote notes.**

3 Risers 54
6 Risers 55

Abiy 228, 230
absorptive capacity, of firms 166
Accountable Garment Sector Challenge Fund 209
actionable subsidies 26
advanced manufacturing and services GVCs 84–86, *85*
Africa 6, 14, 22, 36; Chinese-funded special economic zones (SEZs) 184; Chinese loans to 186; deficiencies in governance 13; dependence on natural resources 183; diversification in 184; economic development 163; industrialization drive 184, 185; industrialization intensity 50; industrialization opportunity from Asian countries' demand 22; industrial performance and potential 86; infant industries 189–190; and Japan 214; service sector in 80; special economic zones (SEZs) in 89–90; state-owned enterprises 186; structural change in 50, 72, *73*, 74; technology upgrading in 166; trade unions, on Chinese cheap imports 183; and Turkey 215; unemployment in 20; value-added manufacturing 184; *see also* China's interest in Africa; Sub-Saharan Africa (SSA)
African Development Bank Group 191
African firms: export survival of 156–158; high-growth entrepreneurship, promotion strategies for 135; low survival rate of 135; survival in international markets 136, *137*; survival mechanisms of 155–156; *see also* firm survival
African Lions 22, 39n18
African Union (AU) 13, 34, 215
aggregate labor productivity 257
Agreement on Subsidies and Countervailing Measures (SCM) 26, 29
Agreement on Trade-Related Aspects of Intellectual Property Rights (TRIPS) 26, 27, 29
Agreement on Trade-Related Investment Measures (TRIMS) 26–27, 29
agriculture sector 16, 17; in Africa 86; productivity growth rate 81, *82*; structural change 70–78, 101–102, 108; time series pattern 63
Akamatsu's theory of follower-country 161
Algeria: Chinese infrastructure projects in 188; Chinese workers in 189
Anadolu Agency 231n9
Angola: Chinese infrastructure projects in 188; Chinese loans to 186; Chinese workers in 189
anti-poor agenda 31
apparel and garment GVCs 229–230
approximation error 273n4
Arab Spring 38n3
Armington's assumption 249
ASEAN 9, 32, 250; *see also specific member countries*

ASEAN Economic Community (AEC) 34
Asia: flying geese patterns of development and industrialization in 74–78; newly industrializing economies (NIES) 9; special economic zones (SEZs) in 89; structural change within 71, *72*; *see also specific countries*
Asian financial crisis 31
Asian Tigers 4, 9, 21, 22
assisted technology transfer (ATT) 179–180
Association for Overseas Technical Cooperation for Sustainable Partnership (AOTS) 211, 226
asymmetric information, and industrial policies 13
Australia 250
automation 8, 46
autoregressive distributed lag (ARDL) model 192
Ayka 219, 226, 231n9

backward linkages 23, 117, 131, 156
Bangkok 34
Bangladesh: Bangladesh Economic Zones Authority (BEZA) 231n5; corporate social responsibility in 208; structural change 77; workplace tragedies 209
Base of the Pyramid (BOP) business 203, 205–206, 208
Basix East Asia Ltd. 175–176
Belt and Road initiative 185, 200n2, 215
beta-coefficients of unconditional convergence 58
Better Cotton Initiative 209
Big Three (Japan, Korea, Taiwan), structural change of 74, *75*; versus China and India 78, *78*; versus East Asia 74, *75*, 76; versus South Asia *77*, 77–78; versus Southeast Asia *76*, 76–77
bilateral donors 208, 209, 230
bilateral trade agreements 26
Brazil 20
Brexit 30
BSDC 208
Business and Sustainable Development Commission 208
Business and Technology Incubator Program, Tanzania 164
business environment, enabling and constraining factors of 168–173, *169*, *170*, *171*, *172*

capital accumulation 99, 108
capital-intensive industries 56, 109, 111, 114
carbon dioxide emission 121–122, *122*
cascading system, tariff protection 26
"catch-up" industrialization 4, 97
Center for Agricultural Mechanization and Rural Technology (CAMARTEC) 164
centralization of industries 114
Chile 20
China 4, 7–8, 13, 21–22, 100, 250; Belt and Road initiative 185, 200n2, 215; Equity Joint Venture Law 8; and Ethiopia 222–226; as factory of the world 3, 8; industrial growth 198–199, 200; industrialization in 23; integrated industrial policies 36–37; involvements 204; Made in China 2025 23; manufacturing jobs in 56; manufacturing sector 21, 50; Ministry of Commerce of People's Republic of China (MOFCOM) 214–215, 223; production system in 22; productivity growth 81; public and private partnership model 214–215; rapid development factor 8; role of state in 7; share of world manufacturing value-added 52; special economic zones (SEZs) in 58, 214–215; structural change 77, 78, *78*; value-added manufacturing 184, 193, 198–199
China Africa Research Institute (CARI) 186, 187–188, 189
China Development Bank 186
China's interest in Africa 183–184, 198–200, 215; and African industrialization drive 199; Chinese development finance, effect on trade union involvement 190; Chinese-funded special economic zones (SEZs) 184; Chinese migrants 192; Chinese official development assistance (ODA), impact of 190–191; Chinese Outward Direct Investment, impact of 191; Chinese workers 189, *189*;

contracts, impact on manufacturing and industry GDP 198, **199**, 200; and corruption 191, 195, 196, 198, 200; development space creation 204; direct investments 186, 187, *188*, 191, 192, 195, 197, *198*, 200; and economic cooperation of African countries 191; economic relations 185–189; exports 195, 196–197, **197**, 199; government effectiveness 195–196, 200; impact on economic growth 190, 191; industry GDP growth 195, 196–197; infrastructure contracts 187–189, *188*; institutional and governance framework 185, 193, 196, 200; institutional variables, description of **194–195**; literature review 189–192; loans to Africa 186, *187*; manufacturing GDP growth 195, 196–197; manufacturing industry 191–192; and political stability 195, 196; and regulatory quality 195, 196, 200; resource for infrastructure (RFI) 186; and rule of law 196, 200; technology transfer 192; trade 186–187, *187*
Chinese labor migrations into Africa 161
Chinese-owned SMEs, and Tanzanian SMEs 178
civil society organizations (CSOs) 209, 229
climate change mitigation 119–121
colonization 35
commercial or non-concessional loans 186
commodities GVCs 84–85
comparative advantage 7, 98, 111, 189, 190; of ASEAN countries 26; of Bangladesh 29–30; of China 21; and deindustrialization 104–105; exploitation of 99–100; of Laos 84
competition: and firm size 154; and product innovation 152
competition pressure, and ICT adoption 151
competitive advantage 6, 26
competitive grants 209
competitiveness: export market 32; and GVCs 32; and income level 112; international competitiveness 6; policy action on 8
computable general equilibrium (CGE) models 35, 253; with global value chains 248–250, 253–254; multi-region input-output (MRIO) tables 240; simulation 240, 251, 254
computer-based technologies 17
Confederation of Tanzanian Industries (CTI) 164
connectivity 14, 123
constant difference of elasticities (CDE) 249
constant elasticity of substitution (CES) function 249
consumption patterns 63
coordination and monitoring within government 24
coordination problems 272
corporate social responsibility (CSR): definition of 204; in value chain management 208–210, 229
corruption, and industrial policies 13, 36
Cotton made in Africa 209
credit constraints and firm export behavior 152
Crepon, Duguet, and Mairesse (CDM) structural model 139, 147–149, 156

Dar es Salaa 166, 170, 173, 174–175, 180
DBL Group 227
de facto industrial policy 25, 29
deficiencies in governance 13
deindustrialization 46–47, 63, 64, 65, 100, 259, *260*; in advanced economies, aggregate figures 100; in Central and South America 72; by geographical regions and sub-regions 67–68, *68*, *69*; in high-income group 96, 97; by income group 67, *67*; in Indonesia 31; in Pakistan 77; patterns of 96, *96*, 100–101, 105, 106; present state of 16–21; productivity and demand 80, 99; and productivity rate 82; and service sector 84; in Southeast Asia 71–72; time series test for 65–69, *66*, 79, 90; and unemployment 79; *see also* premature deindustrialization
demand 99, 101, 109, 122
Desalegn, Hailemariam 216, 222
Development Innovation Ventures (DIV) 207–208
development partnerships with the private sector 203, 229; Base of the Pyramid (BOP) business 205–206;

corporate social responsibility, in value chain management 208–210; Japanese partnership 210–214; PPPs for sustainable development 206–208
development patterns within manufacturing 27, 70, 95, 96–97, 100, 106–112
develoPPP.de program 207, 210
diagonal matrix 242, 244, 245, 246
Director-General for Policy Planning 240
Dire Dawa University 228
diversification 6–7, 14, 17, 48, 59, 60

East Asia: industrialization in 50; industrialization intensity 50; structural change in 8, 74, *75*, 76; *see also specific countries*
East Asia and Pacific (EAP): manufacturing exports index 52; per capita manufacturing value-added 48, 50
East Asian miracle 15, 25–26
East Asian Miracle: Economic Growth and Public Policy 5–6
East Asian model 26, 74
Eastern Seaboard Development, Thailand 211
economic agents 241, 248–249, 252, 253, 254
economic upgrading, aid to 204
economies of scale 99
education and training, importance of 163, 170–171
elasticities 111, *112*
electrical machinery industry 106, 111, 112
emerging economies and partnerships for industrial upgrading 229; China's public and private partnership model 214–215; Turkey involvement in Africa 215
employment: elasticity, in least developing countries 79; generation of 4, 5, 104–105, 106, 108–109, 114–116; global manufacturing 46, *47*; low-technology industries 105, *105*; mobilization of 119, *118*, *119*, *120*; relocation 56–59; in Tanzania 168; *see also* manufacturing employment; manufacturing value-added and employment
employment share 46–47, 63, 64, 258, 259, 266, 274
entrepreneurs, technical knowledge of 37
entrepreneurship 14, 164
environmental sustainability, and manufacturing 119–122, *121*, *122*
Ethiopia 216, 229, 230; Agricultural Development Led Industrialization (ADLI) 216; apparel and textile sector 228; and China 222–226; Chinese infrastructure projects in 188; Chinese migrants role in agri-food sector 192; Chinese workers in 189; Democratic Developmental State 216; development partnerships in apparel and textile GVCs 227–228; Eastern Industrial Zone 223–224; economic growth, sustained 217; endeavor to industrialize and recent FDI trends 216–219, *217*, *218*, **220–223**; external financial flows to 217, *218*; FDI inflows to 217, *218*, 219; garment GVCs 231n7; and Germany 228; Growth and Transformation Plans (GTP I and II) 216–217, 227; and India 228; industrialization, and development partnerships 219, 222–227, *225*; industrial parks and special economic zones in 205, 210–212, 214, 217–224, **220–223**, 227, 228; Industrial Parks Development Corporation (IPDC) 218; and Japan 216, 226; manufacturing-led growth 184; Partnership for Sustainable Textiles 227; policy initiatives 216, 217–218; productivity, Japanese influence on 211, 216–217, 226, 228, 229, 231–232n11; setbacks 228; and Turkey 226
Ethiopia Kaizen Institute (EKI) 226
Ethiopian Investment Commission (EIC) 217–218, 226
Ethiopian SEZs 89
Ethiopian Textile Industry Development Institute (ETIDI) 226, 228
Ethiopia Public Private Consultative Forum (EPPCF) 24
Europe and Central Asia (ECA) 48, 67
evidence-based policy making 9, 24, 37
exchange rate, real effective exchange rate (REER) 32

Eximbank 186
exporter status, determinants of **150**, 151–152
export-oriented industrialization, in Vietnam 89
export processing zones (EPZs) 8, 26, 86
exports: of commercial services 20; diversification toward manufacturing 17; and heterogeneity in global manufacturing 50–52; manufacturing exports index 50–52, 53; South Asia 50; structural diversification 48; Sub-Saharan Africa (SSA) 50–52; of value-added 245–246; *see also* export-oriented industrialization; export processing zones (EPZs)

fabricated metals industry 117
Factory Asia 21, 22
FDRE 216, 217
final demand 240–242, 244–246, 249–250, 252, 253, 254
finance access, and exporter status 152
financial crisis in 2008–2009 25
firm age, and exporting status 151
firm entry, and survival 156, **157**
firm size: and exporter status 151; and ICT adoption 151; and product innovation 152
firm survival 135; determinants of 158; export history of firms 136; GTAP data for social accounting matrices 140; impact of innovation on 154–155; profitability and productivity growth, factors of 135; role of policy in 158; sectoral linkages from input-output tables 138; structural equation model 136–138; and variables **145**; WBES data on firm exports and survival 140, **141**
firm survival, and innovation 135; determinants of innovation 152, **153**; and exporter status 151–152; ICT adoption, determinants of 149–152, **150**; innovation types 147; process innovations 138, 139, 143–144, **144**, 152, **154**; product innovations 138, 139, 143, **144**, 152, **154**; spillover effects of 145–146; technological innovation experience 136–138; value of innovation to firm growth 138–139
firm survival, and innovation propagation 138, 140–144, 146; backward linkages 138; economic linkages 138, 139; and export patterns 142–143, **143**; forward linkages 138; production costs channel 138; role of ICT adoption in 140; self-induced input effect 138; self-induced output effect 138; speed of diffusion of innovation 139; survivor and non-survivor, comparison of 142; technology diffusion 139; technology gap channel 139
flying geese model 74–78, 210
food processing industry 22
foreign contents, in Tanzanian SMEs 169
foreign direct investments (FDIs) 145, 161, 229; to Asian countries 62, 74; to China 8; by China to Africa 186, 187, *188*, 191, 192, 195, 197, *198*, 200
foreign-owned firms 36, 161, 167; and exporter status 152; and ICT adoption 151; and process innovation 154; and product innovation 152
forward propagation, and firm entry and survival 156
free trade 4
free trade area of the Asia-Pacific (FTAAP) 240
functionalism 6

G7, manufacturing value-added share of 52, 54
garment industry 9, 29
GDP: definition of 245; impact of Regional Comprehensive Economic Partnership (RCEP) on 252–253, 253; per worker 259
GDP value-added sectors 39n16
General Agreement on Tariffs and Trade (GATT) 26
General Agreement on Trade and Services (GATS) 26, 27
Generalized Method of Moments (GMM) model 192
Generalized System of Preferences (GSP) 9, 29
geographical regions, and GVC linkages 84, *85*, 86

Germany 209; develoPPP.de program 207, 210; and Ethiopia 228; Federal Ministry for Economic Development and Cooperation (BMZ) 207, 209, 227, 228; German Agency for International Cooperation (GIZ) 207, 227; Partnership for Sustainable Textiles 209–210
Ghana: Chinese manufacturing investments in 191–192; Chinese migrants role in agri-food sector 192; impact of Chinese cheap imports 183
Global Development Alliance (GDA) 207–208
global industrial landscape 54–55
globalization 5, *7*, 35, 64, 99
global labor mobility 161
global manufacturing 21–22, 90; changing state of 48–62; employment 46, *47*; Factory Asia 21, 22; global concentration of manufacturing production 52–56, 100; manufacturing employment relocation 56–59; manufacturing growth, heterogeneity in 48–52; manufacturing upgrading 59–60; output trends **49**; value-added 46; volatility 60–62; *see also* manufacturing
global trade, current trend 21, 81
Global Trade Analysis Project (GTAP) 136, 240
global value chains (GVCs) 46, 91, 203–204, 212, 229, 239; advanced manufacturing and services 84–86, *85*; backward participation in 246–248, 254; commodities GVCs 84–85; in computable general equilibrium (CGE) model 248–250, 253–254; corporate social responsibility in 208–210; forward participation in 246–248, 254; impact on manufacturing 84, *85*, 86; Innovative activities 84, *85*; limited manufacturing 84–86, *85*; and multi-region input-output (MRIO) tables 248; role in the US–China trade war 240; and service sector 84–86, *85*; and SMEs 31–32; social and environmental compliance in 204, 208, 210, 229; and trade in value-added 244–248, 253; vertical integration of firms within 155
globotics 46
governance, deficiencies in 13, 36
gross output 241–242, 244
growth-enhancing structural change 81
growth-reducing structural change 81, 257–258

Happiness Furniture 173–174
Hawassa Industrial Park (HIP) 218, 219, 224
Hennes and Mauritz (H&M) 219, 227
higher productivity 4, 7, 8, 14, 20, 32, 59
higher-value-added manufacturing 7, 8, 14, 21
high-income countries (HICs) 50, 52, 60, 97; global manufacturing value-added 90; and GVC linkages 84; manufacturing jobs in 56; manufacturing value-added trends over time 67; production process 108
high-skilled workers 56
high-technology goods 60, 86; export of 60; Sub-Saharan African share 86
high-technology sectors/industries 100, 104, 106, 109, 112, 113, 115, 117, 118; development potentials 112–113; and income levels 100; increase in 115; in low-income countries 106; OCED classification 128; service sector 117; value-added generation 109
high-value manufacturing 14, 17, 46
Hindustan Unilever 206
Hong Kong 74, 76
horizontal industrial policy 13
horizontal policy linkages 272–273

ICT adoption: in process innovation 152–154; in product innovation 152
IDE-JETRO 39n19, 240
import restrictions *see* Generalized System of Preferences (GSP); Multi-Fiber Arrangement (MFA)
inadequately educated workforce: in process innovation 154; in product innovation 152
inclusive development 14–16, 35
inclusive industrial development 4, 24, 32
inclusiveness 15, 30–33, 38, 77
income group: and GVC linkages 84, *85*; and manufacturing employment

relocation 56–57, *57*; and manufacturing labor productivity 82, *83*, 84; manufacturing value-added and decentralization 67, *67*; manufacturing value-added convergence 54–55, *55*; *see also* high-income countries (HICs); lower middle-income countries (LMICs); low-income countries (LICs); upper middle-income countries (UMICs)
income inequality 261, 264
income trajectories 97, 109, 119, 121
India 4, 8, 21, 250; as back office of the world 3, 21, 78, 91; Base of the Pyramid business in 206; and Ethiopia 228; National Institute of Fashion Technology (NIFT) 226, 228; service sector in 39n17; share of world manufacturing value-added 54; structural change 77, 78, *78*
Indonesia 20; premature deindustrialization 31; world manufacturing value-added share 54
Indonesia 4.0 20, 23
INDSTAT 104, 127, 128
industrial development: challenge of 270; cross-country patterns evaluation of 257; modern 256
industrial development and regional convergence 257, 264; industry-based model 265–266; Japanese experience, empirical evidence from 266–270; premature deindustrialization 258, *260*; regional income gaps and convergence 260–264; regionally inclusive industrial policy (RIIP) 270–271, 271–272; sectoral productivity gaps 257, *258*; simple model 264–265; structural change growth 257–258, *259*
industrial diversification 14
industrialization 256, 267; in Asia 74–78; impact of 30; intensity of 50–50; present state of 16–21; speed of 63; time series test for 65
industrial parks in East Asia, Japan's support to 205, 210–212, 214, 217–224, **220–223**, 227, 228
industrial policies: arguments and theoretical underpinnings for 13–14; country specificity 7, 14; debates, review of 5–8; definition of 165; definitions of 9–10, **10–12**; efficacy assessment 37–38; government-led interventions 99–100; modern/ new industrial policies, need for 24–25
industrial promotion 4, 13–14, 16–37
industrial promotion agencies 179
industrial revolution: fourth 99; third 99
industrial structure change *see* structural change
industrial upgrading 14; and Japanese PPPs 210–212
industries without smokestacks 46, 80, 81
industry-based models of regional convergence 272
inequalities 5, *7*, 16
infant industries 189–190
informal economy, employment share of 258
Information and Communication Technologies (ICT) 20, 30, 34, 168
infrastructure, Chines projects in Africa 186, 187–189, *188*
Initiative for Policy Dialogue (IPD) 6
innovation 4, 13, 14, 22–23, 30, 32, 33–34; *see also* firm survival, and innovation
innovation capacity 234
innovation patterns, sectoral differences in 100
innovative activities GVCs 84, *85*
input coefficient matrix 242, 244
input-output (IO) tables **129**, 130, 240, **241**, 253
institutions 4, 5, 8, 9–10, 13, 16, 24, 36
integrated industrial policies designing, dimensions of 33–34; China's presence 36–37; Regional Comprehensive Economic Partnerships (RCEPs) 34–35; service-tourism industry 35–36
Intellectual Property Rights (IPRs) 26, 27
inter-industry relationships 239, 240
intermediate input, trade in 239, 241–242, 244, 246, 247, 251, 252
International Financial Corporation (IFC) 205–206, 209
International Labour Organization (ILO), Decent Work Programme 209, 227, 231–232n11
International Monetary Fund (IMF) 230, 250
international tourism 35–36

international trade, disruption in 240
Internet of Things (IoT) 20
intersectoral productivity gaps 257
Itochu 226

Japan 4, 229, 250; and Africa 214; Business Supporting Survey (BSS) 212; development pattern 74, *75*; and Ethiopia 226; financial instruments diversification 211–212; Kaizen project 211, 216; manufacturing in 244; Ministry of Economy, Trade and Industry (METI) 213, 214, 226–227; Official Development Assistance (ODA) 210–211, 212, 213, 226; structural change 71; Trinity Model 210, 229
Japanese development partnership with the private sector: classification of 210; commercial interests and development outcomes 214; new form of PPP for SDGs 212–213; support for industrial parks and SEZs development 211–212; traditional PPPs for industrial upgrading 210–212
Japanese SMEs 213
Japan External Trade Organization (JETRO) 212, 213, 226
JICA 211–214, 212, 216, 226, 229, 231n4, 231n5, 231n6

Kagome 212–213
Kaizen method 211, 216, 226, 229
Kenya: Chinese infrastructure projects in 188; Chinese workers in 189; manufacturing-led growth 184
knowledge spillovers 164
knowledge transfer activity, for SMEs 163

labor force 63, 104; inclusive mobilization, and manufacturing 99, 103; labor-intensive industries 108; mobilization 111, 117; in SMEs 31
labor-intensive approach 107–108
labor-intensive industries 209
labor-intensive manufacturing 212
labor productivity: change in 264; regional convergence process of 267, 268, *268*; and value-added growth 112; see also manufacturing labor productivity
labor reallocation 264
labor-saving technology 64
Laos 31–32; Ministry of Industry and Commerce 16; National Socio-Economic Development Plans (NSEDP) 32
larger cities: ICT adoption in 151; process innovation in 154; product innovation in 152
latecomer economies 9, 14, 21–22, 25, 32, 36, 74, 79
late industrializers 54, 55, 70, 74, 90
Latin America 6, 13, 72, *73*
Latin America and the Caribbean (LAC) 52
least developing countries (LDCs), employment elasticity in 79
Leontief's inverse matrix 242
liberalization: of investment 31; of trade 32, 35
limited manufacturing GVCs 84–86, *85*
local SMEs, and GVCs *see* global value chains (GVCs), and SMEs
lower middle-income countries (LMICs) 50, 52; export activities 60; and GVC linkages 84; manufacturing jobs in 56, 108; manufacturing value-added share 54, 67
lower-value-added manufacturing sectors 8
low-income countries (LICs) 28, 50, 52, 97, 101; catching up behavior 55; employment opportunities 109; environmental sustainability 121; export activities 60; and GVC linkages 84; industrialization 122; low-technology industries 104–105; manufacturing value-added share 62, 67; production process 108–109; value-added generation 109
low product trap 14
low-technology industries 109–110, 116, 117, 128; employment mobilization 117; labor-intensive 107–108, 111, 122; in low-income countries 104; manufacturing value-added and employment *105*, 106, 109, 113–114; primary sectors 117
low-wage labor 112

Made in China 2025 23
manufacturing 46; accumulated value-added by income 110; development

patterns within 70, 95, 96–97, 100–101, 106, 113; and economic development 16–21; and employment 266; as engine of growth 16, 35, 95–103; growth, heterogeneity in 48–52; heterogeneity within 100; and inclusive labor-force mobilization 99; premature deindustrialization across 112–117; productivity growth rate 81, 82, *82*, *83*, 84; unconditional convergence in *58*, 58–59
manufacturing, and economic growth: effect, losing of 97, *98*; empirical studies 95–97; fragmentation across countries 98–100; heterogeneity within manufacturing 100–101; pro-poor growth 101–103, *102*, *103*; *see also* pro-poor growth, and manufacturing development
manufacturing development 95–103
manufacturing employment 47, 56–57, *57*, 59, 63, 108; accumulated employment by income100; changes in 46, 64, *64*, *66*, 67; economic development 117, *119*, *120*; employment-to-population by income 106, *108*; and GDP growth 17, *18*; versus manufacturing labor productivity *83*; and premature deindustrialization 78–79, *80*; relocation of 56–59; and SEZs 86, *88*, 89; *see also* employment
manufacturing exports 123n3; *see also* exports
manufacturing exports index 50–52, *53*
manufacturing growth volatility 60, 62
manufacturing-induced employment 117, 123
manufacturing labor productivity: versus manufacturing employment 56, *83*; sectoral growth rates 81–82, *82*; unconditional convergence *58*, 58–59; see also labor productivity
manufacturing production 46, 52–56, 99, 111, 114
manufacturing-related services 20, 21, 22, 31, 47, 56, 91
manufacturing upgrading 20, 59–60, 90
manufacturing value-added *47*, 48, *50*, 52, 54, *54*; China 52; convergence by income group 54–55, *55*; convergence by time period 55, *56*; East Asia and Pacific 48, 50; G7 52, 54; growth rate 54–55, *55*, 56, *56*; growth rate, since financial crisis 52; India 54; Indonesia 54; and SEZs 86, *87*, 89; South Korea 54; *see also* value-added
manufacturing value-added, income level: convergence 54–55, *55*; and decentralization 67, *67*; high-income countries (HICs) 67; low-income countries (LICs) 111; upper middle-income countries (UMICs) 67, 106; *see also* manufacturing value-added
manufacturing value-added and employment *64*, 64–65, 104–106, *105*; and income levels 17, *18*, *19*, 20; low-technology industries 104, *105*, 106, 107–109, 113–114
market failures 13–14, 24
Mauritius, impact of Chinese cheap imports 183
medium and high-tech manufacturing 59–61, *60*, *61*, 84
medium-technology industries/sectors and goods 106, 109, 117, 128; export of 60; Sub-Saharan African share 86; value-added generation 109
mega-regional trade agreement (MRTA) 35, 239, 253, 254; Regional Comprehensive Economic Partnership (RCEP) as 250–253
Micronesia 68; *see also* MIRAB model
Middle East and North Africa (MENA) 50
migration 35, 161, 179, 192
Millennium Development Goals (MDGs) 203, 229
MIRAB model 35
modern/new industrial policies, need for 24–25
Mombasa SEZs 231n5
Mongolia 76
Multi-Fiber Arrangement (MFA) 9, 29
multinational corporations (MNCs) 4, 25, 34, 208, 209, 229, 230; corporate social responsibilities 204, 208; expansion after financial crisis (2008) 203
multi-region input-output (MRIO) tables 240, 242, 243, 253; basic structure of 240–244; and global value chains 248; incorporation into computable general equilibrium (CGE) model 240

Myanmar: and Japan 211–212, 229–230, 231n5; structural transformation 76
Myanmar Japan Thilawa Development, Ltd (MJTD) 212, 231n5

National Estates & Designing Consultancy (NEDCO) 174–175
natural resource-based economies 16, 20, 48, 86
neoliberalism 6, 25
Nepal 77
newly industrializing economies (NIEs) 9
New Zealand 250
Nigeria: Chinese FDI and technology transfer in 192; Chinese infrastructure projects in 188; Chinese workers in 189; manufacturing-led growth 184
non-manufacturing value-added 46
non-profit organizations (NPOs) 208, 209, 229
non-tariff barriers 239, 251, 254
North America 48, 84

Official Development Assistance/Aid (ODA) 25, 203, 205, 210–211, 212, 213, 226
Oqubay, Arkebe 218–219
Organization for Economic Co-operation and Development (OECD) 6, 38n5, 128, 230n1, 240; Development Assistance Committee (DAC) countries 203, 204; inter-country input-output (ICIO) tables 241, 245, 253
outsourcing 84
Overseas Economic Cooperation Fund of Japan (OECF) 231n4
overseas investments 4; *see also* foreign direct investments (FDIs)

Pacific Island countries: MIRAB model *see* MIRAB model; SITEs model 35; TouRAB model 35
Pacific Small Island Developing States (SIDS), service-tourism industry in 35
Pakistan 77
Pareto efficiency 38–39n9
part of larger firm, and exporter status 152
patent rights 27
Philip-Van Heusen (PVH) 219, 224
place-based policy 58, 86
Poland 55
policy interventions, classification of **12**
policy space 6, 25–30
pooled mean group (PMG) 192
positive externalities 8
post-war period: industrialization in 267; regional convergence in 257, 269; structural change patterns in 266
poverty, reduction of 3–4, **4**, 5, 17, 34, 59, 79, 107, 111; *see also* pro-poor growth, and manufacturing development
poverty-growth-inequality triangle 5, *7*, 15
poverty triangle 5
preferential arrangements 29
preferential market access 239
premature deindustrialization 31, 46–47, 90, 97, 112–117, 258, *260*; and manufacturing employment 78–79, *80*; and structural change 70–74, *71*; three pillars of 98; *see also* deindustrialization
pre-war period: regional convergence in 257, 271; within-sector growth in 267, 269
private finance 203; *see also* development partnerships with the private sector
private sector 24–25
process innovation and firm survival *see* firm survival, and innovation
process innovators 143–144
product innovation and firm survival *see* firm survival, and innovation
product innovator 143
production 46, 99, 111, 114; global concentration of 52–56; processes fragmentation 203–204
productivity 48, 91; differences across sectors 257, *258*; and servicification 79–84; unconditional convergence 57–59
pro-poor growth, and manufacturing development 95, 101–103, *102*, *103*, 123; baseline case 106–109, *108*; development classification 109–111; employment mobilization 117–119, *118*, *119*; input factors substitutability 111–112; overview 104–106, *105*; premature deindustrialization 112–117; sustainability 119–122, *121*, *122*

pro-poorness 30–33
public bureaucracy 35
public policies 9
public-private partnerships (PPPs) 5, 24, 33, 204; definitions of 24; German PPPs 207, 210; Japanese PPPs 210–223; for sustainable development 206–208; in Thailand 25

quality certifications 168, 172
quality-cost-delivery (QCD) 212

Rana Plaza collapse (2013) 209
randomized controlled trials (RCTs) 38
Regional Comprehensive Economic Partnerships (RCEPs) 34–35, 239, 240, 253, 254; impact on GDP 252–253, 253; mega-regional trade agreement scenario of 250–253
regional convergence 256; industry-based models of 272; of labor productivity 267, 268, *268*; structural change and within-sector growth on 268, *269*; *see also* industrial development and regional convergence
regional development, challenge of 271
regional disparities 33, 34, 260, *261*, 267
regional divergence 256
regional inclusiveness 15, 30–33
regional income gaps 260, *260*; and convergence 260–264, *263*; spatial distribution of *262*
regional inequality: change in 266; reduction of 269
regionally inclusive industrial policy (RIIP) 256, 270; horizontal policy linkages, setting up 272–273; implementation of 272–273; industrial development and regional convergence 270–271; industry-based model of regional convergence 271–272; state capacity, building up 272; vertical policy linkages, setting up 272
regional productivity 264, 265–266
regional trade agreements (RTAs) 239
regression analysis 128–130
reindustrialization 48, 84
remittances 35
research and development 128
resource-backed loans 186
resource-based economies 16, 20, 48, 86
resource misallocation 258
returnee migrants 161, 179; enterprises owned by 161, 167; role in spreading technical knowledge 161
returnee-owned firms 36–37

scale economies, and vertical policy linkages 272
sectoral misallocation 271
sectoral productivity differences 264
self-induced input propagation 156
self-induced output propagation 156
Senegal, SDG business in 212–213, *213*
Senegal Sarl 212
service-related manufacturing 64, 78, 117
service sector 20, 27, 39n17, 71, 76, 118; in Africa 22, 86; changing landscape *81*; employment share in *19*, 80, *81*; importance of 79–81, 80, *81*; in India 39n17; in Indonesia 20; manufacturing labor productivity and employment in 82, *83*, *83*; productivity in 81; and technological innovation 79–80; value-added share in *19*, 80, *81*
service-tourism industry 35–36
servicification 79, 91; and deindustrialization 84; and GVCs 84; and manufacturing productivity differences 79–84, *81*; and reindustrialization 84; and special economic zones (SEZs) 86–90
shared value 207, 230–231n2
shift-share decomposition methodology 264
sigma convergence 266, 273n5
Singapore: Jurong Town Corporation 218; structural transformation 76
SITEs model 35
small and medium-sized enterprises (SMEs) 31, 161; and ICT adoption of 151; knowledge transfer activities 163; labor force in 31; spillovers 166; technical upgrading, aspiring factors 165; technological upgrading institutions/agencies 163; technology acquisition 165–166; *see also* global value chains (GVCs), and SMEs; Tanzanian SMEs
smart factory 99

smart manufacturing 23
Smile Curve approach, to GVCs 23
social accounting matrices (SAM) 145
social and environmental compliance, in GVCs 204, 208, 210, 229
sophisticated industries 6, 56
South Africa, manufacturing-led growth 184
South Asia: industrialization intensity 50; manufacturing exports index 50; structural change *77*, 77–78
Southeast Asia, structural change *76*, 76–77
Southern Africa 68
South Korea 13, 54, 250
spatial spillovers, horizontal policy linkages to exploit 272–273
special economic zones (SEZs) 10, 91; in Africa 89–90; in Asia 89; in China 58, 214–215; in Ethiopia 89, 223–224; Japanese ODA in partnership with the private sector 211–212; and manufacturing employment 86, *88*, 89; and manufacturing value-added 86, *87*, 89; in Myanmar 211–212, 231n5; and servicification 86–90; in Vietnam 89
Speshoz 174
spillover effects 16, 36, 48, 89, 99, 161
spillovers 166
Spring City Enterprises 177
Sri Lanka 77
state capacity, building up 272
strategic industries 26
structural change 8, 59, 90–91, 257–258, *259*; in African countries 50, 72, *73*, 74; in Asian countries 71, *72*; component 258, *259*; in developed countries 71, *71*; effect of 264–265; government interventions for promotion of 13; and growth 6–7; in Latin America 72, *73*; in manufacturing, sectoral 96; manufacturing development 119–122; patterns 266, *267*; and premature deindustrialization 70–74, *71*; productivity 265; regional convergence 267, **268**, *269*; regional productivity 264; toward service sector 80–81, *81*
structural change, of Big Three (Japan, Korea, Taiwan) 74, *75*; versus China and India 78, *78*; versus East Asia 74, *75*, 76; versus South Asia *77*, 77–78; versus Southeast Asia *76*, 76–77
Sub-Saharan Africa (SSA): economic development 163; industrialization intensity 50; manufacturing exports index 50–52; public-private partnership (PPP) in 24; *see also* Africa
Sub-Saharan Africa (SSA), firm survival 135; and innovation 149–155; innovation propagation of 146–149
subsidies 26–27
supply/value chains 22
sustainability, and manufacturing 119–122, *121*, *122*
sustainable development: of domestic industries 4; PPPs for 206–208
Swedfund 227
Swedish International Development Cooperation (SIDA) 208, 209, 219, 227
Switzerland 209

TAFSIO (Tanzanian Federation of Small Industries Organizations) 164
Taiwan 13
Tanzania 162; Business and Technology Incubator Program 164; Center for Agricultural Mechanization and Rural Technology (CAMARTEC) 164; Commission for Science and Technology (COSTECH) 164; Confederation of Tanzanian Industries (CTI) 164; economic growth 162, 163, 164–165; employment growth 168; entrepreneurship in 164–165; export industry 168; Global Competitiveness Index (GCI) 163; Industries Development Organization (SIDO) 163–164; innovation index 163, 168; knowledge enablers 163–164; labor productivity 168–169; Mennonite Economic Development Associates (MEDA) 163; National Income Generation Program (NIGP) 163; power supply in 170; Pride Tanzania 163; private-sector institutions 164; TAFSIO (Tanzanian Federation of Small Industries Organizations) 164; Technology Development and Transfer Centre of the University of Dar es Salaam 164; use of bank

financing by firms in 170; vocational training in 177, 178
Tanzania Engineering and Manufacturing Organization (TEMDO) 164
Tanzania Industrial Research Development Organization (TIRDO) 164
Tanzanian SMEs 180–181; assisted technology transfer (ATT) 179; bank financing, use of 170; Basix East Asia Ltd. 175–176; business obstacles 169, *169*; competition with Chinese-owned enterprises 178; customers as source of interaction 178; development policy 163; education and training plans 178; foreign origin inputs 169, *170*; foreign technology, use of 171, *172*; formal training 170–171, *171*; Happiness Furniture (case study) 173–174; inability to utilize publicly available technical details 179; incentives 173, 180, 181; industry-promoting agency 179; international aspect of technical information sharing 179; internationally recognized quality certifications 172, *172*; National Estates & Designing Consultancy (NEDCO) (case study) 174–175; need for financial improvement 181; power outages 170; skills/competence deficits 178–179; Speshoz (case study) 174; Spring City Enterprises 177; technical knowledge transfer by 163, 176, 179; technical knowledge upgrading 178; technology development for 163–164, 181; technology-diffusion parks 181; technology-enabling context and institutions for 162–166; technology upgrading 178–179; TTR Auto 176–177
tax incentives 13, 49
Tazreen tragedy (2012) 209
technological capacity 162
technological innovation 14, 23, 30, 79–80
technology, definition of 165
technology acquisition 165–166
Technology Development and Transfer Centre of the University of Dar es Salaam 164
technology-diffusion parks 181
technology-enabling environments 162–166
technology upgrading 37, 57, 162; associated institutions/agencies 163; Tanzanian SMEs 178–179
textile exports, quota system *see* Generalized System of Preferences (GSP); Multi-Fiber Arrangement (MFA)
Thailand 25; Eastern Seaboard Development 211; economic integration 34
Thailand 4.0 23
Than Long Industrial Parks, Vietnam 211
Thilawa SEZs 211–212, 231n5
time-dependent dynamics: for employment by income 113–116, *113*, *114*; for value-added by income *113*, 113–115, *115*
time series test 63; deindustrialization 65–69, *66*, *67*; indicator choice 63–65; of patterns of industrialization 65, *66*
Tokyo International Conference of African Development (TICAD 7) 214
TouRAB model 35
tourism 35–36
tradable services 14, 81
trade in value-added, and global value chains 244–248, 253
trade liberalization 32, 35
trade policies 26, 27, 50
traditional donors and private sector *see* development partnerships with the private sector
traditional industrial policies, in East Asia 23
traditional manufacturing-led growth strategy 21
training agencies 163
Transatlantic Trade and Investment Partnership (TTIP) 239
Trans-Pacific Partnership (TPP) 239, 240
Trinity Model 210, 229
Trouble in the Making? The Future of Manufacturing-Led Development 8, 21
TTR Auto 176–177
Turkey: and Africa 215; and Ethiopia 226; Justice and Development Party (Adaletve Kalkınma Partisi, AKP) 215

Turkish Confederation of Businessmen and Industrialists (TUSKON) 215
Turkish International Cooperation and Development Agency (TIKA) 215

unconditional convergence, in manufacturing labor productivity *58*, 58–59
United Kingdom, Department for International Development (DFID) 209
United Nations, Business Call to Action (BCtA) 208
United Nations Conference on Trade and Development (UNCTAD) 79, 86, 211, 215
United Nations Development Programme (UNDP) 208
United Nations Economic Commission for Africa (UNECA) 10, 20, 26, 27, 39n21
United Nations Global Compact 206, 231n3
United Nations Industrial Development Organization (UNIDO) 16, 22, 24, 39n13, 99, 109, 121, 227
United Nations Millennium Development Goals (MDGs) 3–4, **4**
United Nations Sustainable Development Goals (SDGs) 3, 4–4, *5*, 203, 204, 207, *207*, 212, 229
United States, 1992 Hawkins Bill 208
United States Agency for International Development (USAID): and development partnerships 206, 208, 209; Global Development Alliance (GDA) 207–208
unskilled labor 21, 32
upper middle-income countries (UMICs) 50, 52, 60, 109, 112; environmental sustainability 122; and GVC linkages 84; manufacturing jobs in 56, 106, 108; manufacturing value-added share 67, 106
upstream-downstream linkages 31

value-added 242, 244; accumulated value-added by income110; Chinese manufacturing 184, 193, 198–199; global manufacturing 46; higher-value-added manufacturing 7, 8, 14, 21; by income for selected manufacturing industry 63, 64, 106, *107*, *108*; inputs 249; and labor productivity 112; lower-value-added manufacturing 8; non-manufacturing value-added 46; service sector's share *19*, 80, *81*; time-dependent dynamics, by income *113*, 113–115, *115*; trade in 244–248, 253; *see also* manufacturing value-added
vertical policy linkages 272
Vietnam (Viet Nam) 253–254; decomposition of the export volume to Japan 251–252, *252*; exports of value-added *246*; exports of value-added from 245–246; input-output (IO) table 240–244; participation in global value chains 246–248, *247*, *248*; SEZs in 89; Than Long Industrial Parks 211; trade in value-added and global value chains 244–248

wage differences 261, 264
Western donors 209, 210–211, 229
within-sector growth, on regional convergence 257, 258, *259*, 267, 268, 269, *269*
within-sector productivity 264, 265
World Bank 6, 16, 21, 184, 186, 190, 193, 210–211, 227, 230, 231n10, 239; classification of countries based on income 50; *Trouble in the Making? The Future of Manufacturing-Led Development* 8
World Bank Enterprise Surveys (WBES) 136
World Bank Group 135
World Development Indicators (WDI) 47, 62, 67, 70, 79, 184, 193
World Development Report 239
World Governance Indicators (WGI) 192
World Trade Organization (WTO) 39n22, 239; developing world's industrial policy space under 25–30; dispute settlements 27–28; policy options under **28–29**

Xi Jinping 185

Zenawi, Meles 216, 219, 222

For Product Safety Concerns and Information please contact our EU representative GPSR@taylorandfrancis.com
Taylor & Francis Verlag GmbH, Kaufingerstraße 24, 80331 München, Germany

www.ingramcontent.com/pod-product-compliance
Lightning Source LLC
LaVergne TN
LVHW052249200926
848481LV00002B/317

9780367611767